INDUSTRIAL RELATIONS RESEARCH
ASSOCIATION SERIES

U. S. Industrial Relations 1950-1980: A Critical Assessment

AUTHORS

RICHARD N. BLOCK

JAMES W. DRISCOLL

PETER FEUILLE

FRED K. FOULKES

RICHARD B. FREEMAN

ROBERT B. MCKERSIE

JAMES L. MEDOFF

D. QUINN MILLS

DANIEL J. B. MITCHELL

THEODORE J. ST. ANTOINE

JACK STIEBER

ANDREW THOMSON

PHYLLIS A. WALLACE

HOYT N. WHEELER

EDITORIAL BOARD

i

First Edition

Library of Congress Catalog Card Number 81-84473

Price $15.00

INDUSTRIAL RELATIONS RESEARCH ASSOCIATION SERIES

PROCEEDINGS OF THE ANNUAL MEETING (Spring Publication)

PROCEEDINGS OF THE SPRING MEETING (Fall Publication)

Annual Research Volume (Fall Publication)
  (MEMBERSHIP DIRECTORY every sixth year in lieu of research volume)

IRRA NEWSLETTER (Quarterly)

INDUSTRIAL RELATIONS RESEARCH ASSOCIATION
7226 Social Science Building, University of Wisconsin
Madison, WI 53706 U.S.A. Telephone 608/262-2762

Pantagraph Printing, 217 W. Jefferson, Bloomington, IL 61701

CONTENTS

Preface

This collection of articles has been assembled on the premise that the three decades between 1950 and 1980 represented a very important period of reckoning for the U.S. system of industrial relations. There has always been a penchant on the part of scholars in this field to think in terms of time periods that mark an era: for example, the 1920s, the decade of company unionism and the human relations movement; the 1930s, the rise of industrial unionism; and the 1940s, initially the consolidation of collective bargaining under the aegis of the War Labor Board and subsequently the stabilization of collective bargaining during the postwar years. And that brings us to the time period under scrutiny, the 30-year period that began as the system of industrial relations hit its stride with the establishment of key principles and procedures during the late 1940s (such as managements' rights, grievance systems, and long-term contracts) and a period that ended as the decade of the Eighties began.

Only time will tell whether this time period that might be referred to as the Golden Age of Collective Bargaining really came to an end around 1980. Certainly, a number of signs became evident during the 1970s that suggested that the system had reached a turning point, albeit very gradually and incrementally. This is not the place to enumerate the long lost of well-known attributes that characterize the current industrial relations system such as declining union membership, growth of government regulations, and the shift in union leadership with the departure of the "giants" who established many key unions.

It is interesting to speculate whether the trends that are bringing industrial relations to some new departure have been most manifest throughout the full period (e.g., during the 1950s) or only during the decades of the Sixties and Seventies. Whether we are thinking about the passage of civil rights and occupational safety and health statutes, the emergence of aggressive strategies to remain nonunion by employers, or the explosive growth of quality-of-work programs, most of these critical events that have shaped (and are continuing to shape) the system of industrial relations emerged during the past 20 years. I will leave it to readers of this volume to decide for themselves (in the light of the papers) whether the relevant time demarcation is indeed 1950–1980 or whether we are examining a system that has experienced severe shocks and pressures for change during the latter half of this 30-year period.

Perhaps at this point it would be useful to compare this volume with others that have taken stock of the industrial relations system in the United States. Dunlop's classic book, *Industrial Relations Systems*, appeared over 20 years ago, while the comprehensive documentation of collective bargaining as it operated in practice by Slichter, Healy, and Livernash, *The Impact of Collective Bargaining on Management*, appeared a few years later in 1960. Thus, in this respect alone (the passage of 20 years), it is appropriate to bring forth a volume that attempts to assess the nature of the industrial relations system and the practice of collective bargaining as it has been carried on in the United States, largely in the private sector. This latter point is important since no rendering of developments during the past 30 years in the field of industrial relations could overlook the rapid development of collective bargaining in the public sector. However, this development has been analyzed in many forums and quarters (and some people feel to the detriment of proper attention to the private sector) and the course of collective bargaining in the public sector is still unfolding—consequently, our focus in this volume is primarily on the private sector in the United States.

This volume attempts to be different from other annual IRRA volumes. It is not a summary of research (such a volume is scheduled for publication next year, following a traditional periodic assessment by IRRA of research in the industrial relations field). Nor is this collection an analysis of collective bargaining on an industry-by-industry basis—such a "cut" of the subject matter has occupied a prominent place in the scholarship of the field, starting with the classic study sponsored by the Twentieth Century Fund entitled *How Collective Bargaining Works* and most recently represented by the volume edited by the late Gerald Somers entitled *Collective Bargaining: Contemporary American Experience.*

v

Now to state more affirmatively what this book attempts to do: The book as a whole is designed to present a comprehensive picture of modern U.S. industrial relations, its strengths and weaknesses, and suggestions for improvements in the system. Some of the chapters use categories and dimensions that are well known and have been used ever since this subject area established itself as a field of study and practice—for example, management performance, labor law, industrial conflict, and the economics of collective bargaining. Other chapters deal with important new developments such as the nonunion employer, and the social issues of collective bargaining (especially equal employment opportunity, OSHA, and quality of work). In order to avoid too much insularity, we have asked Andrew Thomson of the University of Glasgow to present a view from abroad.

The authors of the papers range over a wide spectrum: from economists to behavioral scientists, from senior members of the field to newly arrived members, from theorists to more applied researchers, and from all "belts" in the country.

In many respects this volume represents a "period piece" and, given the importance that this interval will occupy in the historical annals of the U.S. industrial relations system, we hope that this volume substantially increases our understanding.

ROBERT B. MCKERSIE
Massachusetts Institute of Technology

CHAPTER 1

Collective Bargaining and the Economy

DANIEL J. B. MITCHELL

University of California, Los Angeles

The economic impact of collective bargaining is potentially a huge topic. Many possible impacts might be considered, including some which are often considered to be beyond the scope of conventional economics. This chapter explores only some of the areas in which collective bargaining might be expected to have an influence, with an emphasis on macroeconomic concerns. It explores the impact of bargaining on wages, on wage determination and inflation, and on anti-inflation policy including guidelines and controls. Also put forward are alternative analyses of the bargaining process including the significance and incidence of strikes.

A study of the economic effects of collective bargaining must necessarily concentrate on the past two or three decades. Prior to that period, data become scarce and the character of collective bargaining changes. In the pre-1930s period, unionization and bargaining generally covered a small fraction of the labor force so that its overall economic effects were probably negligible. During the 1930s and 1940s, a period of rapid growth, the union movement was in a state of such flux that its properties were hard to determine. In contrast, by the mid-1950s, greater stability characterized the union movement and the collective bargaining system, a "maturity" noted by contemporary authors.[1]

To the disappointment of some, and to the delight of others, the union movement stopped expanding as a proportion of the labor force after the mid-1950s and the overall unionization rate began to decline. Union leaders turned more toward day-to-day bargaining relationships and the working out of a modus vivendi with already organized employers. Such devices as multiyear agree-

---

[1] See Richard A. Lester, *As Unions Mature: An Analysis of the Evolution of American Unionism* (Princeton, NJ: Princeton University Press, 1958).

1

ments, escalator clauses, and elaborate fringe packages became commonplace. But major new industrial conquests—at least in the private sector—were rare. In the public sector, the major area where unionization and bargaining did expand significantly after the 1950s, the "industrial model" has been generally adopted. Completely new styles of public employer-union relations have not developed.[2] Of course, the ongoing properties of unions and bargaining after the Korean War should not be confused with the economist's idealized notion of a "steady state." Changes have occurred, but they have been gradual and adaptive. Some of the developments expected by observers in the 1950s have not been borne out. Strike activity did not wither; after a decline in the early 1960s, it accelerated. Management did not simply accept unionization as a given; by the late 1970s unions complained bitterly of management antagonism and "class warfare."[3]

Economists' perceptions of unions and their impacts are naturally shaped by the classical economic model. Within that model, labor is viewed as an intermediate good (or more recently as an investment asset) which is traded at market price. In effect the supply/demand diagram is modified by substituting the words "wage" for "price" on the Y-axis and "hours" for "quantity" on the X-axis. To the extent that unions are considered in labor-market analysis, the economist tends to draw on the theory of the firm.

Unions are often seen as a labor-market variant of the "monopoly" firm. Just as monopolistic pricing is seen as inefficient, because it causes the price to rise relative to marginal cost, so the union's wage raising impact is seen to have a similarly distorting effect. As Henry Simons, a leading spokesman for the Chicago School in the 1930s and 1940s put it, "unionism . . . rests basically on rejection of free pricing in labor markets," a charge which to Simons was the essence of the case against "syndicalism."[4] The empirical evidence to be discussed in this chapter suggests that the mechanical application of elementary price theory to union be-

---

[2] Tim Bornstein, "Legacies of Local Government Collective Bargaining in the 1970s," *Labor Law Journal* 31 (March 1980), pp. 165–73.

[3] See the statement by Lane Kirkland in *Daily Labor Report*, May 30, 1978, pp. D1–D2.

[4] Henry C. Simons, "Some Reflections on Syndicalism," reprinted in Henry C. Simons, *Economic Policy for a Free Society* (Chicago: University of Chicago Press, 1948), p. 149.

havior can be misleading. But with modification, a useful economic analysis of the union impact on the economy can be made.

The nonunion lay public often views union activities with suspicion. There is general agreement in public-opinion polls that the right to organize should be protected. But, on the other hand, aggressive behavior on the part of unions (such as strikes) is often viewed with disfavor.[5] Some of this ambiguity can be accounted for by the association between unionization and lower-status jobs and the limited progress in unionization of white-collar workers.[6] Part is due simply to the prevailing American value system which favors individualism and free enterprise in principle, even though some readers might question their implementation in practice. Thus, it is not unusual for economic ills to be blamed on unions and collective bargaining despite the fact that union workers are a distinct minority of the workforce.

I. Key Economic Impacts

It will be argued below that unions and collective bargaining appreciably change the character of wage setting. Union wages can easily be shown to be higher than nonunion wages as a general rule. A more difficult question is causality. The wage gap could be the product of other influences which happen to be associated with unionization. Such other influences might include occupational, skill, and demographic differences between union and nonunion workers or differences in industrial characteristics (establishment size, capital intensity of production) between the union and nonunion sectors. Or, as some economists have argued recently, higher-wage workers might have a higher propensity to unionize, thus creating a statistical optical illusion.

A view on union impacts on wage differentials is an essential ingredient to research on the determination of wage *change*. If it is believed, for example, that unions have only a negligible impact on wage differentials, that is, that they don't raise wages, then it is difficult to entertain theories that suggest that unions have much influence on wage change or inflation. At most, transitory lags in

---

[5] See Hazel Gaudet Erskine, "The Polls: Attitudes Toward Organized Labor," *Public Opinion Quarterly* 26 (Summer 1962), pp. 283–84. Subsequent polls reveal the same tendencies.

[6] See C. Wright Mills, *White Collar: The American Middle Classes* (New York: Oxford University Press, 1951), Ch. 14, for a classic study of the resistance to, and suspicion of, unions by white-collar workers.

wage response might be expected due to multiyear labor-management agreements. On the other hand, if it is believed that unions do create union/nonunion wage differentials, then it is worthwhile investigating whether unions create appreciable differences in wage-change responsiveness to business-cycle and other influences. Since wage-change and price-change determination are interconnected, it is further possible to consider questions of the union influence on inflation and on traditional anti-inflation policy. Views on union wage-change practices are also relevant to nontraditional anti-inflation policies such as controls and guidelines. Thus, the question on union/nonunion wage differentials is very much a starting point for other important concerns.

In the sections that follow, the issue of whether unions create wage differentials relative to the nonunion sector will first be discussed. Rather than keep the reader in suspense, the conclusion will be that significant and sizable wage differentials are created. Given that conclusion, the question of what consequences are implied by those differentials will be explored. It will be suggested that the relative wage effects are unlikely to be translated into substantial relative price effects. Their most probable influence is an increase in employer resistance to new organization and a tendency for production to shift to nonunion sources of supply.

Second, evidence will be presented that wage-change determination outcomes in the union sector differ from those of the nonunion sector. Union wage change is less sensitive to real business conditions, a characteristic that has implications for macroeconomic policy. The union sector is also characterized by multiyear contracts and, in many cases, by escalator clauses. Implications of these special features for macroeconomic policy in the context of a simple macro model will be explored. Also to be considered are implications of union wage-change determination for the occasional government forays into wage-price controls and guidelines. Finally, a linkage to the economic impact of strikes will be suggested, along with a revision of traditional economic analysis of strike frequency.

II. Relative Wages

Do Union Workers Earn More?

There is one question on union/nonunion wage differentials

which can be readily answered. If it is simply asked whether union workers on average earn more than nonunion workers, the answer is emphatically "yes." Table 1 presents a series of tabulations drawn from the Current Population Survey. In 1966, the Census

TABLE 1

Union/Nonunion Earnings Differentials
by Occupation, Sex, and Race

	Private Sector	Total Economy	
	1966[a]	1970[a]	1977[b]
All workers	1.20	1.16	1.19
Males	1.06	1.00	1.07
Nonwhite	1.52	1.31	1.30
Females	1.12	1.08	1.29
Nonwhite	1.52	1.19	1.34
White-collar	n.a.	1.04	1.06
Blue-collar	n.a.	1.30	1.37
Service	n.a.	1.52	1.58

Source: U.S. Bureau of Labor Statistics, Earnings and Other Characteristics of Organized Workers, May 1977, Rep. 556 (Washington: U.S. Government Printing Office, 1979), Table 11; U.S. Bureau of Labor Statistics, Selected Earnings and Demographic Characteristics of Union Members 1970, Rep. 417 (Washington: U.S. Government Printing Office, 1972), Table 6; U.S. Bureau of the Census, Labor Union Membership in 1966, Series P-20, No. 216 (Washington: U.S. Government Printing Office, 1971), Table 9.

[a] Figures refer to median annual earnings for year-round full-time wage and salary workers by union membership.

[b] Figures refer to mean usual weekly earnings in May of full-time wage and salary workers for labor organization representation.

Bureau published a report showing that private full-time wage and salary workers who were union members had a median annual earnings about 20 percent more than full-time nonunion workers.[7] Differentials were especially marked for nonwhites and more pronounced for females than for males. A similar study, covering both public and private sector workers in 1970 provided additional support for these generalizations, although the union/nonunion differentials reported tended to be lower. A study covering mean usual weekly earnings in May 1977 reported wider differentials

[7] See Table 1 for references to these studies and other related studies cited below. Note that the male and female union/nonunion differentials shown in Table 1 are less than the gross (both sex) union/nonunion wage differential. This seeming anomaly is caused by the higher proportion of males in the union sector relative to the nonunion sector. As indicated later in the text, since males on average earn more than females, the gross differential between all union and all nonunion workers would tend to be positive even if the within-sex differentials were zero.

than in 1970. Unfortunately, changes in definition and coverage between the three surveys make judgment about trends difficult from these data. Both the 1970 and 1977 studies show relatively large earnings premiums for blue-collar and service workers and small premiums for white-collar workers.

The figures from the Current Population Survey omit such fringe benefits as employer contributions to pension plans. However, union workers typically have more fringe compensation than nonunion workers and have a greater proportion of their compensation in fringe benefit form. In 1974, for example, the Bureau of Labor Statistics reported that straight-time earnings of nonoffice workers in union establishments were 49 percent higher than those received in nonunion establishments. But on a total compensation basis, the premium was 67 percent.[8]

Unions typically ask for more in bargaining than management initially offers. There is some limited evidence that the outcome usually comes closer to the initial management offer than to the initial union demand.[9] Nevertheless, the process will give the appearance of a union wage-raising effect. But without knowledge of what the wage outcome would have been under nonunion circumstances, the appearances of collective bargaining are not conclusive evidence of causality.

As Table 2 shows, the presence of unionization is associated with various factors which might have an influence on earnings levels. The table is based on a sample of 93 industries which have been divided into two sectors: those with above- and below-average ratios of union employment to total employment. More heavily unionized industries can be seen to have lower proportions of female employees in their total workforces than lightly unionized industries. They also tend to have lower quit rates, larger establishment sizes, and more capital-intensive methods of production (measured by depreciation per employee). And, of course, earnings levels are generally higher.[10]

---

[8] U.S. Bureau of Labor Statistics, *Employee Compensation in the Private Nonfarm Economy, 1974*, Bull. 1963 (Washington: U.S. Government Printing Office, 1977), p. 33.

[9] Roger L. Bowlby and William R. Schriver, "Bluffing and the 'Split-the-Difference' Theory of Wage Bargaining," *Industrial and Labor Relations Review* 31 (January 1978), pp. 161–71.

[10] The two sectors had similar proportions of nonwhite employees and exhibited similar median education levels. See reference on Table 2 for details.

TABLE 2

Correlates of Unionization: 93 Selected Industries

Mean Industry Characteristic	Industries with Above-Average Unionization Rates[a]	Industries with Below-Average Unionization Rates[a]
Proportion of female workers, 1976	22%	32%
Quit rate, 1976[b]	0.9%	1.9%
Workers per establishment, 1974	326	65
Depreciation per employee, 1973[c]	$2310	$1533
Average hourly earnings, 1976	$6.15	$4.83

Source: Daniel J. B. Mitchell, Unions, Wages, and Inflation (Washington: Brookings Institution, 1980), Tables 3-1, 3-5, and Appendix A.

[a] Unionization rates were calculated by dividing estimated workers covered by union agreements known to the Bureau of Labor Statistics in Summer 1977 by payroll employment in 1976.

[b] Data available for only 52 industries.

[c] Data available for only 92 industries.

Female workers typically earn significantly less than males. While it would be inappropriate to explore the reasons for the sex differential in this chapter, it is evident that the lower proportion of females in the highly unionized sector could contribute to the sectoral earnings gap. Women are also more prone to be found in occupations and industries with shorter job tenures. Hence, their presence might be associated with higher quit rates, as Table 2 suggests. Quit rates can be viewed as a measure of employee quality, with "better" employees showing longer attachment to the employer. If so, the lower quit rate in the union sector could be a proxy for higher employee quality. Union agreements often contain seniority clauses dealing with layoff order, promotion opportunities, and other job-related matters. Such clauses reinforce and formalize employer-employee attachments, especially for long-service employees.

In theory, establishment size per se should not affect wage differentials. However, it has been argued that larger establishments require workers with greater ability for self-supervision.[11] Thus, establishment size may be a proxy for a type of employee quality. Similarly, the capital intensity of production does not have a theoretical linkage to wages. But physical-capital intensity may

[11] Richard Lester, "Pay Differentials by Size of Establishment," Industrial Relations 7 (October 1967), pp. 64-65; Stanley H. Masters, "An Interindustry Analysis of Wages and Plant Size," Review of Economics and Statistics 51 (August 1969), p. 341.

be a proxy for human-capital intensity. Since all these characteristics may have a bearing on wage differentials, some means for
standardizing for their effects is needed.

Do Unions Cause Wage Differentials?

The usual approach to sorting out the union influence on wages
from other possible influences has been some type of multiple-
regression analysis with a measure of labor compensation as the
dependent variable, an explanatory variable indicating the presence of unionization, and other explanatory variables representing
other potential influences, such as those reported on Table 2. There
are many problems inherent in this approach. As pointed out in
the oft-cited study of this technique by H. G. Lewis in 1963, union
wage impacts may affect both union and nonunion workers.[12] Nonunion wages might be pulled up toward union levels if nonunion
employers feel threatened by organization or if nonunion employees are substituted for union workers. On the other hand, some
nonunion workers may be complementary to union workers and
suffer a demand decline if demand for union workers decreases
due to the wage impact. And workers from the union sector may
be displaced by lessening employer demand into the nonunion sector, increasing supply and depressing nonunion wages.

Although there are definite statistical problems, given the assumption that unionization is basically an exogenous influence, the
weight of existing studies points to substantial union-caused wage
premiums.[13] There is evidence, indeed, that these premiums have

[12] H. G. Lewis, *Unionism and Relative Wages in the United States: An
Empirical Inquiry* (Chicago: University of Chicago Press, 1963), Ch. 2.

[13] The literature is reviewed in Daniel J. B. Mitchell, *Unions, Wages, and
Inflation* (Washington: Brookings Institution, 1980), Ch. 3. Lewis, in *Unionism
and Relative Wages*, put the premium at 10–15 percent. However, Lewis him-
self was apparently impressed by later studies which indicated larger differ-
entials. See Albert Rees, "H. Gregg Lewis and the Development of Analytical
Labor Economics," *Journal of Political Economy* 84 (August 1976) II, p. S5.
For a sampling of estimates since the late 1960s, see Frank P. Stafford, "Con-
centration and Labor Earnings: A Comment," *American Economic Review* 58
(March 1968), pp. 174–81; Sherwin Rosen, "Unionism and the Occupational
Wage Structure in the United States," *International Economic Review* 11
(June 1970), pp. 269–86; Sherwin Rosen, "On the Interindustry Structure of
Wage and Hours Structure," *Journal of Political Economy* 77 (March/April
1969), pp. 249–73; Michael J. Boskin, "Unionism and Relative Real Wages,"
American Economic Review 62 (June 1972), p. 467; Adrian W. Throop,
"The Union-Nonunion Wage Differential and Cost-Push Inflation," *American
Economic Review* 58 (March 1968), pp. 79–99; William R. Bailey and Albert
E. Schwenk, "Wage Differences Among Manufacturing Establishments."

enlarged since the Lewis study, and that the trend to wider union/nonunion differentials has characterized much of the post-Korean War period. Figure 1 provides a breakdown of industry earnings

FIGURE 1

Annual Rates of Earnings Increase in
Heavily and Lightly-Unionized Industries

 = Heavily-Unionized Industries

 = Lightly-Unionized Industries

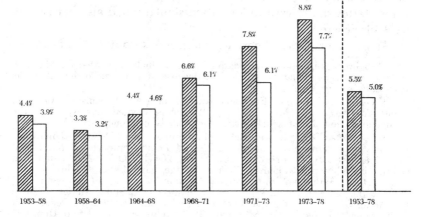

Source: See fn. 14.

trends according to the heavily unionized and lightly unionized categories used on Table 2. Over the entire period 1953–1978, the annual rate of hourly earnings increase in the heavily unionized sector exceeded that of the lightly unionized sector by about 0.5

Monthly Labor Review 94 (May 1971), pp. 16–19; Stephen E. Baldwin and Robert S. Daski, "Occupational Pay Differences Among Metropolitan Areas," Monthly Labor Review 99 (May 1976), pp. 29–35; Paul M. Ryscavage, "Measuring Union-Nonunion Earnings Differences," Monthly Labor Review 97 (December 1974), pp. 3–9.

percentage points per year.[14] This is a small discrepancy in a one-year period, but over a period of 25 years its continuous effect is substantial. Average union/nonunion pay differentials of 20–30 percent for production and nonsupervisory workers seem a reasonable estimate for the late 1970s.

It has been argued by some researchers that the assumption of union exogeneity is incorrect and that the observed correlations, even after standardization for influences other than unions, may simply be the result of a preference of high-wage workers for union "services."[15] This line of approach has produced several interesting, but conflicting, studies.[16] However, its basic premise is ultimately unconvincing. The pattern of unionization in the U.S. was largely determined in the 1930s and 1940s. Although wage variations across individuals may cause changes in tastes for unionization, it is doubtful that these tastes can be actualized in a substantial way. An auto worker whose "tastes" run against unionization had better find another industry of employment; a bank clerk whose tastes run toward unionization similarly had also better seek work elsewhere.[17]

Apart from these theoretical objections to the "high-wages-

[14] Figure 1 is based on an update of data originally tabulated for Mitchell, *Unions, Wages, and Inflation,* Table 2-4. Because of a change in the SIC code, 1978 data are for June.

[15] George E. Johnson, "Economic Analysis of Trade Unionism," *American Economic Review* 65 (May 1975), p. 25. Johnson noted, however, that the endogenous view "is *not* widely shared by other labor economists" (his italics).

[16] See Peter Schmidt and Robert P. Strauss, "The Effect of Unions on Earnings and Earnings on Unions: A Mixed Logit Approach," *International Economic Review* 17 (February 1976), pp. 204–12; Orley Ashenfelter and George E. Johnson, "Unionism, Relative Wages, and Labor Quality in U.S. Manufacturing Industries," *International Economic Review* 13 (October 1972), pp. 488–508; Harlan David Pratt, "A Simultaneous Equations Model of Wage Determination Under Collective Bargaining," doctoral dissertation, Department of Economics, University of Michigan, 1976; John M. Abowd and Henry S. Farber, "An Analysis of Relative Wages and Union Membership: Econometric Evidence Based on Panel Data," unpublished paper presented at the December 1977 meetings of the Econometric Society, New York; Lung-Fei Lee, "Unionism and Wage Rates: A Simultaneous Equations Model with Qualitative and Limited Dependent Variables," *International Economic Review* 19 (June 1978), pp. 415–33; Peter Schmidt, "Estimation of a Simultaneous Equations Model with Jointly Dependent Continuous and Qualitative Variables: The Union-Earnings Question Revisited," *International Economic Review* 19 (June 1978), pp. 453–65.

[17] The question of "tastes" toward unionization can be investigated directly by attitude surveys. Such an approach does not confuse desires with outcomes. A dissertation by Ronald L. Seeber is currently under way at the University of Illinois which uses attitudinal data.

cause-unions" view, there is anecdotal evidence that is hard to explain without recourse to union-caused wage differentials. Nonunion employers typically try to maintain their status; they don't behave as if a decision of their workers to join unions was as irrelevant to costs as a decision to join the Elks. In recent years, it appears that an industry of experts and consultants in maintaining nonunion status has developed. At the same time, employers have vigorously opposed changes in labor law which were perceived to enhance the ability of unions to organize. In short, it appears that union wage differentials are significant enough to provide many employers with a strong incentive to avoid unionization and to spend resources in this pursuit.

THE UNION/NONUNION WAGE DIFFERENTIAL AND BARGAINING THEORY

The existence of a union/nonunion wage premium does no violence to standard economic models of union behavior. If unions can impose (or credibly threaten to impose) strike costs on unionized employers, then these employers should be willing to pay a wage premium to avoid these costs. However, the apparent widening of union/nonunion differentials over a quarter of a century suggests that a simple "monopoly" view of union behavior is misleading. Under the monopoly view, unions are seen as variants of monopolistic firms which generate an initial price impact when created (relative to competitive circumstances), but thereafter adjust prices at a rate no different than would prevail under competition.[18]

Under the union-as-a-firm approach, the union leadership is seen as facing a wage-employment trade-off stemming from the downward-sloping demand curve for labor. The union selects the optimum point on the trade-off curve, based on a utility function of some kind, presumably representing membership views. This approach, unfortunately, has several pitfalls. First, it assumes that members "perceive" the wage-employment trade-off. Second, it

---

[18] This is essentially the argument put forward by Milton Friedman to demonstrate that unions do not cause inflation. Only if their monopoly power increases, he argues, will there be a temporary wage-raising effect. That is, the union effect is a one-shot influence. See Milton Friedman, "What Price Guideposts?" in *Guidelines, Informal Controls, and the Market Place*, eds. George P. Shultz and Robert Z. Aliber (Chicago: University of Chicago Press, 1966), p. 21, especially fn. 3.

ignores the bargaining process through which wage outcomes are determined.

The downward slope of the demand for labor comes from two sources: the downward slope of the demand curve for the employer's product and the availability of substitution possibilities. There is evidence, however, that unions tend to face inelastic demand curves.[19] An important element of the product-market effect is the ratio of labor costs, especially when substitution possibilities are limited as is usually the case in the short run.[20] In most industries, this ratio falls into the 20–40 percent range, so that a 10 percent *relative* wage increase would translate into a 2–4 percent relative price increase, assuming a mechanical cost pass-through into prices and no substitution to factors other than union labor.[21] As Arthur Ross pointed out many years ago, the employment effect of such a cost increase is likely to be lost in the noise of other factors influencing product and labor demand such as the ups and downs of the business cycle and "exogenous" technical change.[22]

As noted, the labor demand curve might present a substantial wage-employment trade-off due to substitution possibilities. To the extent that these possibilities are effectuated by employers, however, they will be viewed as discrete events by union members. A new labor-displacing machine is installed. Work previously done by union members is subcontracted elsewhere. The employer shifts production to nonunion plants, or begins buying imported components. Unions and union members will certainly "perceive" these developments, but they may not attribute them to any particular wage increase and they are likely to try to deal with them on a case-by-case basis. For example, a demand for job-protecting work-rules or an anti-subcontracting clause may be put forward. Those

---

[19] R. B. Freeman and J. L. Medoff. "Substitution Between Production Labor and Other Inputs in Unionized and Non-Unionized Manufacturing," unpublished discussion paper 581, Institute of Economic Research, Harvard University, October 1977.

[20] The "importance of being unimportant" is one of the four Marshallian rules for determining the elasticity of labor demand. As Hicks showed, ease of technical substitution can override this condition. See J. R. Hicks, *The Theory of Wages,* 2d ed. (New York: St. Martin's Press, 1963), pp. 241–46.

[21] Further discussion of relative price effects will follow in the text surrounding Table 5 below.

[22] Arthur M. Ross, *Trade Union Wage Policy* (Berkeley: University of California Press, 1948), pp. 80–93.

who advocate economic models in which the union dictates the wage, subject to the demand for labor, must explain why such dictatorial unions cannot "set" employment levels as well.[23] Presumably, if dictatorial unions—unions which can obtain any concession from an employer subject only to the ultimate constraint of putting the employer(s) totally out of business—perceive a negative employment impact, they would not behave passively toward it as the simple trade-off model supposes.

It is possible to draw up models in which insensitivity to employment opportunities is a rational union response. For example, if layoffs are determined by reverse seniority, and if the union political apparatus is dominated by senior workers, then concern for layoffs would clearly be reduced at any point in time. But such models may lead to improbable predictions. For example, if wage demands will cause a reduction of employment of less than 50 percent, a majority of the union membership (those with median or higher seniority) should favor them. Unless the membership is forward looking, and assuming the union dictates the terms, each negotiation would produce an employment reduction of just under 50 percent. Observers of the industrial relations scene will not find such sequences to be commonplace.

This observation points to the second drawback of the wage-employment trade-off approach: its neglect of the management

---

[23] Originally, such models developed in the 1940s as analytical concepts. See Daniel J. B. Mitchell, "Union Wage Policies: The Ross-Dunlop Debate Reopened," *Industrial Relations* 11 (February 1972), pp. 46–61. More recently, the prospect of estimating econometric models of union behavior has attracted renewed interest. The problem arises in interpreting the results of models as resulting exclusively from union wage goals. Goals cannot be measured directly, not even from records of bargaining demands when these are available. What can be measured is outcomes, which are the product of labor-management interaction, and not just of union goals. For examples of recent studies which attribute outcomes to union goals, see Henry S. Farber, "The United Mine Workers and the Demand for Coal," in *Research in Labor Economics*, Vol. 2, ed. Ronald G. Ehrenberg (Greenwich, CT: JAI Press, 1978), pp. 1–74; J. N. Dertouzos and J. H. Pencavel, "Wage and Employment Determination under Trade Unionism: The International Typographical Union," unpublished paper January 1980 presented at UCLA Labor Economics Workshop, April 8, 1980. Union goals are probably more closely reflected in outcomes when the mix of benefits rather than the total hourly compensation package is considered. (Compensation mix was a major element in the Farber study.) For example, the tendency of unions to tilt the compensation package toward fringes valued by older workers (such as pensions) probably reflects the internal union political process and the preferences of the inframarginal employee. Even in the case of compensation mix, however, some degree of employer preference is likely to be represented.

role in collective bargaining.[24] Few unions are faced with passive employers who readily accept any union proposal. The very language of industrial relations is often misleading. When references are made to "union wages," what is really meant is "wages which have been determined through a union-management interaction as opposed to wages determined unilaterally by the employer." Similarly, "union contract" is a short-hand expression for a "union-management contract." An increase in wage costs above the level the employer would unilaterally determine tends to cut into profits. Hence, it gives rise to management resistance, usually in the form of willingness to "take" a strike. Since strikes are costly to both sides—not just the employer—employer resistance is a critical element of collective bargaining; indeed, it is the reason that the process is one of bargaining rather than just dictating.

Management resistance transforms the internal calculus in the union. All members of the bargaining unit, not just those whose jobs might be hypothetically threatened by a given wage level, will have costs imposed on them in the event of a strike. The senior union member may actually be more concerned about strike costs (due to family responsibilities and immobility) than the younger, more junior member, whose job is theoretically more threatened by the wage-employment trade-off. Certainly, it is not unusual to find instances in which young workers have been more militant than their elders. This observation is directly in conflict with simple models which emphasize the trade-off.

With management resistance, the need for perception of, or information about, the wage-employment trade-off is obviated.[25] The further the union attempts to push up wages (climb the demand curve), the more strongly will management resist. Thus, the bargaining process has a natural stopping point, even if the union ignores the trade-off or is unaware of it. Employer resistance is a crude proxy for the elasticity of the labor demand curve in many cases. The potential costs of conflict dictate the positions of both sides and dwarf the short-run considerations relating to minor movements along the wage-employment trade-off.

---

[24] This point is acknowledged by Farber in a paper related to the one cited in the previous footnote. See Henry S. Farber, "Individual Preferences and Union Wage Determination: The Case of the United Mine Workers," *Journal of Political Economy* 86 (October 1978), p. 926.

[25] Mitchell, "Union Wage Policies," pp. 51–52.

Over the long haul, however, it is not clear that employer resistance will serve to stabilize employment opportunities. Presumably, employers may find ways of responding to increased labor costs in the long run that are not available in the short run. Or possibly market demands for the products of union workers might be diminished relatively to what they would otherwise have been as costs pass into prices. In either case, if the erosion is gradual enough, it is unlikely to be perceived by unions as a consequence of their wage policies, particularly since employment and membership may be expanding in absolute terms.

THE UNION/NONUNION WAGE DIFFERENTIAL AND THE DECLINE IN UNIONIZATION

There is evidence of a gradual slippage in the proportion of workers unionized since the mid-1950s, especially in the private sector. National unions reported membership of 20.2 million to the Bureau of Labor Statistics (BLS) in 1978, 23.6 percent of nonagricultural payroll employment. In contrast, this ratio varied between 31 and 35 percent from the mid-1940s to the mid-1950s.[26]

Unfortunately, the BLS membership data are ill suited to determine the causes of the decline. Although membership data are broken down by industry (generally at the two-digit SIC level in recent years), the figures include unemployed and retired members and members in other countries (mainly Canada). Thus, it is difficult to relate industry membership trends to employment developments. Other data sources are available, but these also have drawbacks.

Table 3, for example, uses 1966 unionization ratios in ten sectors of the private economy to project union membership totals in May 1977. The data are drawn from the Current Population Survey and are based on membership reported by respondents rather than on union membership claims. Estimates for 1977 are biased upwards relative to the 1966 figures, since the earlier survey referred only to membership in labor "unions" while the later survey re-

---

[26] The figures exclude membership in associations which did not consider themselves to be unions and certain local unions. See U.S. Bureau of Labor Statistics, "Labor Union and Employee Association Membership—1978," press release USDL: 79–605, September 3, 1979; U.S. Bureau of Labor Statistics, *Handbook of Labor Statistics 1978*, Bull. 2000 (Washington, U.S. Government Printing Office, 1979), Table 150.

TABLE 3

Union Membership Trends, 1966–1977

Industry	Total Employment (000s) May 1977 (1)	Labor Union Membership as Percent of Employment 1966[a] (2)	Actual Labor Organization Membership May 1977 (3)	Projected Labor Membership May 1977 (1) · (2) = (4)	Difference (3) − (4) = (5)
Durable manufacturing	11,831	41.3	4,612	4,886	− 274
Nondurable manufacturing	8,332	32.1	2,547	2,675	− 128
Transportation	3,055	56.3	1,529	1,720	− 191
Communications & utilities	2,402	41.8	1,067	1,004	+ 63
Wholesale trade	3,477	13.6	408	473	− 65
Retail trade	13,122	12.3	1,366	1,614	− 248
Personal services	2,977	7.0	233	208	+ 25
Mining	729	35.9	256	262	− 6
Construction	4,494	41.4	1,606	1,861	− 255
All other private[b]	17,154	4.8	1,530	823	+707
Total[c]	67,573	23.9	15,154	15,526	− 372[d]
Percent of total employment	100.0	—	22.4	23.0	.6

Source: U.S. Bureau of Labor Statistics, Earnings and Other Characteristics of Organized Workers, May 1977, Rep 556 (Washington: U.S. Government Printing Office, 1979), Tables 5, 8, 18; U.S. Bureau of the Census, Labor Union Membership in 1966, Series P-20, No. 216 (Washington: U.S. Government Printing Office, 1971), Table 8.

[a] Based on private sector only.
[b] Excludes government.
[c] Excludes public administration and those government workers excluded under the "all other private" category.
[d] Tends to understate differences since the 1977 survey included labor organization membership, not just union membership.

ferred to membership in labor "organizations."[27] Nevertheless, the overall unionization ratio reported on Table 3 fell from 23.9 percent of private employment in 1966 to 22.4 percent in 1977. Unfortunately, problems of data availability prevent substantial disaggregation of the figures. Nevertheless, an estimate of hypothetical union membership in 1977, assuming unions had maintained their 1966 unionization ratios in each sector, can be made. Of the 1.5 percentage point drop in the overall unionization ratio (from 23.9 percent to 22.4 percent) about 0.9 percentage points can be "explained by" changes in employment composition between industries. The remaining 0.6 percentage points, about 37 percent after taking account of rounding, cannot be so explained.

The one major sector of gain on Table 3 is the miscellaneous group entitled "all other private." Sadly, this sector is a mixture containing services other than personal services—finance, insurance, and real estate, and agriculture. More detail is not available. The gain may reflect well-publicized union advances in this period in health care, private educational institutions, and farming. It is also in this sector that union employment gains may have been exaggerated by the use of "organization" rather than "union" in the 1977 survey.

Obviously, alternative data sources would produce somewhat different results. It has been suggested that the growth of supervisory workers relative to other occupations has played a role in the decline of the overall unionization rate.[28] Table 4, based on data from BLS area wage surveys, indicates that the decline is pervasive, by industry sector, occupational class, and region. The table compares the unionization rate from surveys conducted in 1960–1961 with surveys conducted in 1974–1976. In every industry and region, the unionization rate for urban plant workers and office workers shows a decline.[29]

Moreover, evidence other than membership data suggests a similar story. The union win rate in NLRB elections has been de-

---

[27] The 1977 survey also has data on nonmembers covered by union agreements. Nonmembers were excluded from Table 3 to make the figures more comparable to the 1966 survey.

[28] Lane Kirkland, "Labor's Outlook—Building on Strength," *The Federationist* 87 (March 1980), pp. 1–8, especially p. 2.

[29] A total of 42 region-industry-occupation groups were available from the original source (see Table 4). Only 10 groups show no decline. Of these, four reported gains in the unionization rate; the others were unchanged.

TABLE 4

Labor-Management Agreement Coverage Rate
All Metropolitan Areas[a]

	Plant Workers			Office Workers		
	1960–61	1965–66	1974–76	1960–61	1965–66	1974–76
Manufacturing	79%	76%	71%	12%	13%	10%
Nonmanufacturing	61	57	48	20	17	14
Transportation, communication, and utilities	95	94	91	65	63	61
Wholesale trade	56	56	53	9	8	5
Retail trade	39	37	30	17	15	10
Finance, insurance, and real estate	—	—	—	3	1	2
Selected services	56	53	41	11	11	7
Northeast	77	73	66	19	16	13
South	48	46	39	14	14	10
North Central	80	79	75	16	15	13
West	80	72	59	18	17	16
All industries and regions	73	69	61	17	16	13

Source: U.S. Bureau of Labor Statistics, Handbook of Labor Statistics 1978, Bull. 2000 (Washington: U.S. Government Printing Office, 1979), pp. 546–47.

[a] Percentage of workers employed in establishments in which a contract or contracts covered a majority of workers. Based on area wage surveys.

clining, even in the manufacturing "heartland" of unionization, suggesting more effective employer resistance.[30] Decertification elections, while still affecting only small numbers of workers, have mushroomed since the mid-1950s.[31] Union spokesmen complained bitterly of increased employer hostility and sophisticated antiunion campaigns. The possibility that the widening of the union/non-union wage differential has contributed to this climate cannot be dismissed.

[30] In fiscal 1954, the union win rate was 66 percent in total and in manufacturing representation elections. By fiscal 1978 these figures had fallen to 46 percent total and 43 in manufacturing. Source: National Labor Relations Board, Annual Report, 1954 and 1978 editions.

[31] See John C. Anderson, Charles A. O'Reilly III, and Gloria Busman, "Union Decertification in the U.S.: 1947–1977," Industrial Relations 19 (Winter 1980), pp. 100–107.

Focusing only on the decline in the unionization rate may understate the impact of the wage differential. Rather than why the unionization rate declined, the question could just as easily be why did it not keep rising. In the late 1950s and early 1960s, many observers believed that the unionization rate would rise, despite adverse shifts in labor force composition.[32] Even taking account of such shifts, many production workers in the traditional sectors of unionization remain nonunion. In May 1977, labor organizations represented 48 percent of the blue-collar workers in manufacturing. Thus, about half of the most likely potential target group in this sector remained unorganized.[33]

The discussion above has focused primarily on employer resistance as a reaction to the extra costs employers perceive when operating under a union contract. Simply looking at the differential may overstate the actual costs, since higher union wage rates may allow employers to hire better quality (more productive) workers.[34] However, the assertion that the productivity differential completely offsets the added wage costs is hard to accept, given the observed fact of employer resistance to organizing campaigns. Classical economic theory suggests that a union-imposed wage differential will lead to an increase in the marginal productivity of labor. But the substitution involved is not costless to the employer, although the ability to make substitutions does help the employer in dealing with the higher wage.[35]

THE UNION/NONUNION WAGE DIFFERENTIAL AND THE PATTERN OF DEMAND

It seems unlikely that union wage differentials have themselves had a substantial impact on patterns of final product demand. Even if union wage changes are passed along into prices, the im-

---

[32] Irving Bernstein, "The Growth of American Unions, 1945–1960," *Labor History* 2 (Spring 1961), pp. 131–57.

[33] U.S. Bureau of Labor Statistics, *Earnings and Other Characteristics of Organized Workers, May 1977*, Rep. 556 (Washington: U.S. Government Printing Office, 1979), p. 25.

[34] Steven G. Allen, *Unionized Construction Workers are More Productive* (Washington: Center to Protect Workers' Rights, 1979); Charles Brown and James Medoff, "Trade Unions in the Production Process," *Journal of Political Economy* 86 (June 1978), pp. 355–78.

[35] In the case of a Cobb-Douglas production function, the marginal and average products of labor are proportionate. Thus measured productivity (which is apt to be the average product) will move with the marginal product.

pact on *relative* prices is likely to be quite small. Table 5 presents a simulation of a substantial jump in the union/nonunion wage differential on the relative prices of 30 industrial sectors composing the private economy. It should be stressed that the table presents simulation results, not estimates of actual effects. The goal is simply to demonstrate the comparative insensitivity of relative prices to changes in union wages.

Suppose all union wages were suddenly to rise by 30 percent while nonunion wages remained constant. Suppose further that this union-induced cost increase were passed into prices on a dollar-for-dollar basis. As a first approximation, it might be assumed that prices in each industry will rise more or less according to whether or not labor is a big component of total input costs and whether union labor is a big component of total labor costs. A further assumption might be that industry prices will reflect a weighted average of union and nonunion sector costs. (An equivalent assumption is that unions raise the wages of all workers—union and nonunion—by a maximum of 30 percent in a manner proportionate to the percent of compensation in the union sector). Since industry input costs for goods and services purchased from other industries will also rise due to the general union wage increase, these indirect costs must be added to the calculation. Through input-output analysis, an adjustment for indirect costs can be made. This calculation is shown on Table 5, column (1). In terms of consumption effects, the main impact on the mix of goods consumed will arise from relative prices changes. Relative prices can be calculated by computing the ratio of the new prices charged to a price index composed of all prices weighted by final sales.[36] As column (2) of Table 5 shows, the relative price effect

---

[36] The computations of Table 5 were made as follows: First, the business sector of the 1972 input-output table (the "A" matrix) was condensed to the 30 industries shown plus government enterprises. The total coefficients were then calculated using the standard matrix-inversion technique. Second, the union proportion of labor compensation in each industry was calculated. It was assumed that full-time workers work twice as many hours as part-time workers in the union and nonunion sector. This permitted a calculation of union versus nonunion hours. Then, using data on unadjusted union/nonunion differentials in usual weekly earnings, an estimate of the proportion of total payroll in the union sector of each industry could be calculated. It was assumed that this proportion also applied to total compensation. In turn, data on compensation and value added by industry were used to calculate the proportion of value added represented by union compensation. Column (1) of Table 5 is essentially the matrix-multiplication product of the vector

is quite mild, never exceeding 4 percent in any industrial sector. Obviously, other assumptions about wage or price behavior would produce different results. But the general point, that is, the limited sensitivity of relative prices to relative union wage effects, is demonstrated.

To the extent that unions have affected the distribution of employment, it is likely that the impact has come mainly from impacts on the *way* goods are produced and on sources of supply (including imports) rather than *what* is supplied. From 1953 to 1978, the proportion of real GNP originating in manufacturing, mining, construction, transportation, communications, and utilities decreased very slightly; it fell from 40.9 percent to 39.7 percent. However, full-time-equivalent employment in these sectors—all centers of private-sector unionization—fell from 45.6 percent to 35.6 percent of total domestic employment.[37] Thus, differential productivity growth rather than industry mix changes seems to have been the dominant explanation of the declining proportion of employment in the union sector. It is here that the evidence that unionization is accompanied by higher productivity may be most relevant.[38] There is a tradition in the industrial relations literature going back to the Webbs which associates union wage pressures with the adoption of more highly productive techniques.[39] If so, it would not be surprising to find that the most

---

$v[1 + (c \cdot r \cdot .3)]$ and the matrix $(I - A)^{-1}$, where v is the vector of value added per dollar of input in each industry, c is the vector of the compensation per dollar of value added in each industry, and r is the vector of union compensation per dollar of total compensation in each industry. The following data sources were used: The A matrix and the v coefficients were drawn from U.S. Bureau of Economic Analysis, *Updated Input-Output Table of the U.S. Economy: 1972,* staff paper BEA SP 79-032, April 1979 (available from the National Technical Information Service). The r coefficients were estimated from data appearing in U.S. Bureau of Labor Statistics, *Earnings and Other Characteristics of Organized Workers May 1977,* Rep. 556 (Washington: U.S. Government Printing Office, 1979), Tables 11 and 18, and other miscellaneous sources. The c coefficients were taken from Philip M. Ritz, Eugene P. Roberts, and Paula C. Young, "Dollar-Value Tables for the 1972 Input-Output Study," *Survey of Current Business* 59 (April 1979), pp. 51–72.

[37] Source: U.S. Bureau of Economic Analysis, *The National Income and Product Accounts of the United States, 1929–74* (Washington: U.S. Government Printing Office, 1977), Tables 6.2 and 6.8; and *Survey of Current Business* 59 (July 1979), pp. 52, 55. Note that GNP originating is essentially a value-added rather than a gross output measure.

[38] See fn. 34 for references.

[39] Sidney and Beatrice Webb, *Industrial Democracy,* 2d ed. (New York: Longmans, Green and Co., 1920), p. 43.

TABLE 5

Impact on Relative Prices in 30 Private-Sector Industries of a
Hypothetical 30% Widening in the Union/Nonunion Compensation
Differential[a]   (Prewidening Index = 100)

Industry	Impact of a 30% Increase in Union Compensation with No Change in Nonunion Compensation (1)	Relative Price Shift Created by 30% Widening of the Union/Nonunion Compensation Differential[b] (2)
1 Agriculture	102	97
2 Mining	104	99
3 Construction	109	103
4 Ordinance	109	104
5 Food products	105	99
6 Tobacco products	102	97
7 Textiles	104	99
8 Apparel	106	100
9 Lumber products	104	99
10 Furniture	106	101
11 Paper products	107	102
12 Printing	106	101
13 Chemicals	105	100
14 Petroleum products	104	99
15 Rubber products	106	101
16 Leather products	106	101
17 Stone, clay, glass	108	102
18 Primary metals	109	104
19 Finished metals	108	103
20 Machinery	107	101
21 Electrical equipment	107	102
22 Transportation equipment	109	104
23 Instruments	105	99
24 Miscellaneous mfg.	105	100
25 Transportation	109	104
26 Communications	107	102
27 Utilities	106	100
28 Trade	103	98
29 Finance, ins., real estate	102	97
30 Services	105	100
All 30 industries	105[c]	100

Source: See fn. 36 for source and computation techniques.

[a] Estimates calculated using the 1972 input-output table with industry classifications condensed to the 30 industries shown plus government enterprises, imports, and certain miscellaneous classifications. Price increases are calculated on the assumption that increases in labor costs are passed into prices on a dollar-for-dollar basis.

[b] Column (1) divided by the "all 30 industries" index at the bottom of column (1).

[c] Mean index weighted by final demand in each industry.

heavily organized sectors would seek ways to reduce labor costs
and to economize on union labor.

Economists will not be surprised by the proposition that rising union/nonunion pay differentials could slow, halt, and even reverse the upward trend in the unionization rate which developed in the 1930s and 1940s. There is a tendency to look for an equilibrium in such a situation, however, when in fact none may develop. Some studies have found evidence that a rise in union pay relative to nonunion pay will tend to put downward pressure on union pay.[40] Presumably, this pressure would eventually bring the rise in the union/nonunion differential to a halt. However, the evidence for a strong linkage—one which would *definitely* halt such a rise—is at best ambiguous.[41] It is conceivable, moreover, that if the union pay advantage continues to widen, pressures by employers and markets to rid themselves of unionization could be overwhelmed by the growing incentive for nonunion workers to organize and seek the higher union pay levels. During the 1970s, union workers' pay rates proved to be better protected from inflation than those in the nonunion sector. If the 1980s prove to be a period of continued economic uncertainty and duress, it may be possible for organizers to capitalize on union escalator clauses and bargaining records. The rapid union growth which began in the 1930s, was—after all—initially a product of economic deterioration. But no such trend in organizing is yet apparent.

III. Collective Bargaining and Inflation

Is collective bargaining "inflationary"? Some economists have asserted that wage-push theories of inflation are fallacious and that inflation has other causes. The division of views on this question is by no means delineated along a conservative-liberal spectrum. To Milton Friedman, for example, "inflation is always and everywhere a monetary phenomenon," that is, the result of improper monetary policy.[42] Bargaining has nothing to do with it. Friedman has long been willing to concede that union wages may be char-

---

[40] See George E. Johnson, "The Determination of Wages in the Union and the Non-union Sectors," *British Journal of Industrial Relations* 15 (July 1977), pp. 211–25; and Robert J. Flanagan, "Wage Interdependence in Unionized Labor Markets," *Brookings Papers on Economic Activity* (3:1976), pp. 635–73.

[41] Daniel J. B. Mitchell, "Union-Nonunion Wage Spillovers: A Note," *British Journal of Industrial Relations* 8 (November 1980), pp. 372–76.

[42] Milton Friedman, *An Economist's Protest: Columns in Political Economy* (Glen Ridge, NJ: Thomas Horton and Co., 1972), p. 29.

acterized by a certain "rigidity" and even that collective bargaining "makes for a steady upward pressure on the wage rate." But he has seen this as a transitory problem which will eventually produce a "moderate amount of unemployment" sufficient to limit the wage pressure.[43] Others have been less sanguine about the union impact on inflation and have suggested that upward wage pressure would lead to what Haberler termed "chronic creeping inflation."[44] And still others, such as F. A. Hayek, have feared that union wage pressures, when combined with full-employment monetary policies, would lead to escalating inflation.[45]

In the late 1940s, economists who worried about wage-push inflation stemming from the union sector sometimes suggested government wage policy as a solution.[46] By the 1950s, the language describing the process had changed. There was a tendency to speak more generally of "markup inflation," "wage-price spirals," and "administered inflation," language which has persisted. And there was also a tendency to look at price determination, along with wage determination, as a source of inflation.[47]

Perhaps more significantly, federal government policy—under both Democrats and Republicans—at times has reflected a belief that direct intervention in wage and price decisions (and especially in wage decisions) was required to restrain inflation. This view can be seen in the Kennedy-Johnson guideposts, the Nixon controls, and the Carter guidelines. In all of these efforts, absolute numerical norms were established for wage increases, norms which

[43] Milton Friedman, "Some Comments on the Significance of Labor Unions for Economic Policy," in *The Impact of the Union*, ed. David McCord Wright (Freeport, NY: Books for Libraries Press, 1969 [1951]), pp. 226–27.

[44] Gottfried Haberler, "Wages Policy and Inflation," in *The Public Stake in Union Power*, ed. Philip D. Bradley (Charlottesville: University of Virginia Press, 1959), p. 80.

[45] F. A. Hayek, "Unions, Inflation, and Profits," in *The Public Stake in Union Power*, ed. Philip D. Bradley.

[46] Sumner H. Slichter, *The American Economy: Its Problems and Prospects* (New York: Alfred A. Knopf, 1948), p. 43; Charles E. Lindblom, *Unions and Capitalism* (New Haven, CT: Yale University Press, 1949), Ch. XVIII.

[47] As examples, see Gardner Ackley, "A Third Approach to the Analysis and Control of Inflation," reprinted in *Inflation: Demand-Pull or Cost-Push?* ed. Richard Perlman (Boston: D. C. Heath and Co., 1965), pp. 39–63; Gardner C. Means, "Simultaneous Inflation and Unemployment: A Challenge to Theory and Policy," in *The Roots of Inflation: The International Crisis*, eds. Gardner C. Means et al. (New York: Burt Franklin & Co., 1975), pp. 1–31.

were central elements of the programs.[48] It is reasonable to suppose, therefore, that the concern of those establishing these programs was more on the wage side than on the price side. And since direct-intervention programs seem inevitably to focus on the larger, more visible units of wage determination, it is also reasonable to assume that concerns about the collective bargaining sector were at the forefront of official thinking.

Before it is possible to discuss whether unions and collective bargaining are "inflationary," the term itself must be defined. One possible definition of "inflationary" is an influence that causes inflation, that is, an influence which by itself can transform a noninflationary situation into an inflationary one. An alternative definition, however, could be an influence which hinders the restraint of inflation by orthodox policies. In the latter case, the initial cause of inflation is not an issue. What matters is whether the influence (in this instance, collective bargaining) tends to perpetuate inflation, *once* it is under way.

There is little support among economists for the proposition that collective bargaining has been an initiating cause of any of the major inflations since World War II, that is, since unions became a significant influence on wage determination. In particular, the era of inflation which began in the mid-1960s is generally viewed as having been initiated by traditional demand pressures emanating from monetary and fiscal policies surrounding the Vietnam War buildup and the Great Society social programs. If anything, as Figure 1 has already shown, union wages tended to lag in their response to rising prices and aggregate demand during 1964–1968. While there may well be something to Haberler's "chronic creep" notion, the inflation of the late 1960s and of the 1970s was more than just a creep. Thus, even if it is believed that unions put a low-level floor on the rate of inflation, the floor was not approached except briefly during the early stages of the Nixon controls program.

Evidence that unions and bargaining were the root cause of inflation is sorely lacking. This conclusion suggests that the alternative definition of "inflationary," that is, a tendency to perpetuate on-going inflation, needs a further look. Before an analysis of this

---

[48] The Kennedy/Johnson norm was 3.2 percent, the Nixon norm was 5.5 percent, and the Carter norm began as 7 percent and was subsequently raised to a range of 7.5 to 9.5 percent.

possibility can be made, however, certain characteristics of union wage-change determination need to be explored.

MAJOR CHARACTERISTICS OF UNION WAGE-CHANGE DETERMINATION

Wage agreements in the union sector differ from nonunion practices in that they are formalized (written and legally binding) and often multiyear. The one-year agreement in the "major" union sector (agreements covering 1,000 or more workers) has become a comparative rarity. Three years is the common duration for these larger settlements; according to the BLS, 71 percent of the major private-sector agreements surveyed in 1976 had durations varying between 25 and 36 months. Although comparable data for contracts covering fewer than 1,000 workers are spotty, it appears that the duration pattern is roughly similar.[49] The practice of negotiating formal multiyear agreements differentiates the union and nonunion sector. While practices which mimic union contracts are certainly not unknown in the nonunion sector, nonunion wage decisions are more likely to be annual in character and are more easily altered in mid-course. Thus, union wage changes will be more likely than nonunion to reflect influences and pressures which developed in the past.

Because collective bargaining contracts tend to "lock in" wage decisions for comparatively long periods, contingencies are often built into the agreements. The major contingency provision is the escalator clause, which gears wage changes to changes in the consumer price index, and the use of such clauses is quite widespread. Forty-four percent of the contracts covering 60 percent of the workers in the BLS survey had such clauses. Not surprisingly, the use of escalators was highly correlated with contract duration. Escalators are found mainly in longer-term agreements. And they are concentrated in contracts covering large numbers of workers.[50]

---

[49] See U.S. Bureau of Labor Statistics, *Characteristics of Major Collective Bargaining Agreements, July 1, 1976,* Bull. 2013 (Washington: U.S. Government Printing Office, 1979), p. 40. The Bureau of National Affairs, Inc., conducts a survey of contracts of all sizes. In 1979 it found that 1-year contracts constituted 3 percent of those surveyed, 2-year contracts constituted 32 percent, and 3-year contracts constituted 62 percent. See *Daily Labor Report,* January 11, 1980, p. B-19

[50] The major union sector, consisting of agreements covering 1,000 or more workers, accounts for roughly half of the number of workers represented by labor organizations in the private sector. In November 1978, 5.6 million

Escalator clauses are extremely rare for nonunion workers.[51] This does not mean that price inflation considerations do not enter nonunion wage decisions, either through cost-of-living changes or increases in the marginal revenue product of labor. However, escalator clauses do mean that wage adjustments in the indexed component of the union sector will react very quickly to price changes. Thus, the institutional phenomenon of escalator clauses may decrease the lag between price changes and wage changes. In effect, union wage changes are subject to two, somewhat contradictory, influences. The existence of long-term agreements suggests that at any moment in time, a component of the wage package is a product of past influences. But for escalated contracts, another component is sensitive to recent price movements.[52]

Union wage changes tend to be less sensitive than nonunion to labor-market conditions. It appears, indeed, that the observed sensitivity of aggregate wage measures to indicators of labor-market tightness or looseness (or business-cycle ups and downs), such as the unemployment rate, comes mainly from the nonunion sector.[53] Table 6 illustrates this tendency. Annual regressions explaining changes in hourly earnings were run for the period 1954–1976 (or 1959–1976 if earlier data were not available) for the 93 industries previously used to compose Table 2. Independent variables were the inverse of the unemployment rate and the rate of change of the consumer price index lagged one year. Those industries with above-average sensitivity to unemployment, that is, coefficients of the unemployment variable greater than the mean,

workers in the major union sector were reported to be covered by escalators, but only 1.1 million workers under "non-major" agreements were so covered. See Beth A. Levin, "Scheduled Wage Increases and Escalator Provisions in 1979." *Monthly Labor Review* 102 (January 1979), pp. 23, 25.

[51] Levin, "Scheduled Wage Increases," p. 25.

[52] This does not mean that escalator clauses provide complete protection against inflation. During 1968–1977, escalators on average triggered a 0.57 percentage point increase for each 1 percent increase in the consumer price index. See Victor J. Sheifer, "Cost-of-Living Adjustment: Keeping Up with Inflation?" *Monthly Labor Review* 102 (June 1979), p. 15. In 1975, 46 percent of those covered by escalators under major union agreements had quarterly escalator adjustments, 11 percent had semi-annual, and 38 percent annual reviews. See Robert H. Ferguson, *Cost-of-Living Adjustments in Union-Management Agreements*, Bull. 65 (Ithaca: New York State School of Industrial and Labor Relations, 1976), p. 22.

[53] Daniel J. B. Mitchell, "Union Wage Determination: Policy Implications and Outlook," *Brookings Papers on Economic Activity* (3:1978), pp. 537–591.

were separated from those with below-average sensitivity.[54] Typically, industries with below-average unionization rates were more sensitive to labor-market conditions and those with high unionization rates were less sensitive.

One interpretation of this finding is that the lower sensitivity is merely the result of union use of long-term contracts. Even if unemployment were an important influence in union wage-change decisions, at any moment in time a large fraction of the union workforce is simply living under old agreements which cannot respond to current labor-market conditions. This factor alone would produce short-run insensitivity.

However, there may be more to the story. As Table 6 shows, the industries with below-average sensitivity to unemployment are also those with relatively fewer females, lower quit rates, larger establishment sizes, higher capitalization, and higher earnings. All of these characteristics fit neatly into the newer theories of "obligational" or "career" labor markets in which employer and employee are linked in long-term relationships, even in the nonunion sector.[55] Under these theories, turnover costs produce wage behavior which departs from the textbook "auction" model. To employers, new hires involve screening, hiring, and specific training costs. Quits inflict these costs on the employer since departing employees must be replaced. From the employer perspective, there is incentive to enter long-term "understandings" with workers which have quasi-contractual properties. Wage decisions are laid out over horizons which extend across the business cycle, even if they are formally

---

[54] Forty-two of the 93 industries had coefficients above the mean. The mean was 11.96. Thus, for the mean industry an increase in the unemployment rate from 6 to 7 percent would result in a slowdown of the rate of wage increase of about 0.3 percentage points as an immediate response.

[55] See Arthur M. Okun, *Prices and Quantities: A Macroeconomic Analysis* (Washington: Brookings Institution, 1981), especially Chs. 2 and 3. After Okun's untimely death in early 1980, his Brookings colleagues edited the book to completion. The book is an elaboration of previous work appearing in Arthur M. Okun, "Inflation: Its Mechanics and Welfare Costs," *Brookings Papers on Economic Activity* (2:1975), p. 351–90. Another reference is Michael L. Wachter and Oliver E. Williamson, "Obligational Markets and the Mechanics of Inflation," *Bell Journal of Economics* 9 (August 1978), pp. 549-71. These discussions had their antecedents in earlier literature on the costs of labor turnover and descriptive studies of the internal labor market. See Walter Y. Oi, "Labor as a Quasi-Fixed Factor," *Journal of Political Economy* 90 (December 1962), pp. 538–55; Peter B. Doeringer and Michael J. Piore, *Internal Labor Markets and Manpower Analysis* (Lexington, MA: D. C. Heath and Co., 1971).

made annually. Wage premiums and fringe benefits are offered to valued employees to tie them to the employer. Wage structures become relatively inflexible and demand fluctuations are accommodated by variations in hours, employment, layoffs, and unfilled vacancies.

TABLE 6

Industry Characteristics Related to Wage-Change
Sensitivity to Unemployment Rate: 93 Selected Industries

Mean Industry Characteristic[a]	Above-Average Sensitivity to Unemployment Rate[b]	Below-Average Sensitivity to Unemployment Rate[b]
Unionization rate	23.9%	38.3%
Proportion of female workers, 1976	36.8%	21.5%
Quit rate, 1976	2.3%	1.0%
Workers per establishment, 1974	64	241
Depreciation per employee, 1973	$908	$2,587
Average hourly earnings	$4.65	$5.86

Source: Data collected by author. For details on data sources, see reference cited in source note, Table 2.

[a] See fns. b and c, Table 2.

[b] Sensitivity to unemployment is measured by the coefficient of the inverted unemployment rate in annual regressions explaining change in hourly earnings during 1954–1976 (or 1959–1976 where earlier data were not available). Independent variables were the inverted unemployment rate and percent change in the consumer price index lagged one year. Above-average (below-average) sensitivity refers to a coefficient greater than (less than) the mean. See fn. a, Table 2.

As noted, the industries which exhibit the lower wage-change sensitivity to unemployment also tended to have characteristics which suggest strong employer-employee linkages. Female workforces typically have weaker employer attachments than heavily male workforces, despite the ongoing trend toward higher female participation in the workforce.[56] Moreover, observed quit rates

---

[56] Although differences in participation rates have narrowed, the female participation rate was still well below the male rate in 1979 (51.1 percent versus 78.4 percent) and still exhibited a marked drop at the outset of childbearing years. Women constituted 68.1 percent of the part-time civilian labor force (those voluntarily working part time or seeking part-time work), but only 37.7 of the full-time labor force (those working full time, involuntarily employed part time, or seeking full-time work). Forty percent of unemployed women aged 20 and over reported themselves to be reentrants to the labor force and 16.3 percent reported being job-leavers as opposed to 19.3 percent and 14.1 percent, respectively, for males. For data, see Employment and Earnings 27 (January 1980), pp. 158–59, 165, 168. Among nonagricultural wage and salary earners in January 1978, women reported a median tenure on their current job of 2.6 years compared with 3.7 years for men. See Edward S. Sekscenski, "Job Tenure Declines as Work Force Changes," Monthly Labor Review 102 (December 1979), pp. 48–50.

are a direct measure of attachment. In the discussion of Table 2, it was noted that larger establishment sizes and capital-per-worker ratios may suggest higher human capitalization which may involve more specific training. The wage differential between the less sensitive industries and the more sensitive may reflect premiums to reduce turnover as well as general skill, unionization, etc.

Implications for Traditional Anti-Inflation Policy

The traditional policy response to "excessive" inflation is demand restraint. Demand restraint, through such devices as a reduction in the rate of growth in the money supply, has empirically been associated with slowdowns or drops in real economic activity, a painful process which raises unemployment. That is, demand restraint has never been successful in producing only a reduction in the rate of inflation without adverse real consequences. The "soft landings" that government officials are prone to promise on the eve of such exercises have not been achieved.

Some economists have argued that if the authorities were more "determined" to restrain inflation, and were willing to declare and demonstrate their determination to a doubting public, demand restraint would be a more effective tool than it has been.[57] Others place less emphasis on the notion of credibility. However, it seems clear that the adverse real consequences of demand restraint do act as a check on the authorities. Thus, characteristics of the labor market which impede the effectiveness of demand-restraint policy in influencing inflation make it likely that efforts at deflation will be less successful and/or more painful in terms of lost real output and unemployment.

What are the impacts of the special characteristics of union wage-change determination on traditional demand-restraint policy? That is, how do characteristics such as insensitivity to labor-market conditions, long-term contracts, and escalator clauses influence the anti-inflation effectiveness of, say, changes in the rate of growth of the money supply? Obviously, the answers will depend on the precise model of the economy one has in mind. But, there are a number of common assumptions about the workings of the economy that are likely to be included in any model.

---

[57] For example, see William Fellner, "The Credibility Effect and Rational Expectations: Implications of the Gramlich Study," *Brookings Papers on Economic Activity* (1:1979), pp. 167–78.

Economists view control of the money supply as a key element of orthodox anti-inflation policy. The public's demand for money is viewed as determined by the price level, the amount of real economic activity, and the rate of interest that can be earned on other financial assets. A change in the growth of the supply of money by the Federal Reserve, relative to the demand for money, sets in motion changes in prices, real economic activity, and interest rates, in order to restore a balance between demand and supply. If the growth of the money supply is constricted for anti-inflation reasons, the monetary authorities hope that the major impact of the restriction will be on price inflation. Indeed, the "effectiveness" of monetary policy—a concept used below—can be defined as the percentage point reduction in the inflation rate associated with a given degree of monetary restriction. But if the effectiveness of monetary policy in influencing inflation is reduced, the impact of a monetary constriction will fall mainly on real output.

A key question, therefore, is whether union wage determination causes a reduction in monetary effectiveness by changing the character of wage determination. If monetary policy is highly effective, then an adjustment to a lower rate of inflation can be accomplished with little pain. But if monetary policy is relatively ineffective, the Federal Reserve is constrained to squeeze more forcefully to reduce the inflation by a given amount. The tighter squeezing means more depressed economic conditions, that is, a larger rise in unemployment and unused capacity.

Statistical studies of aggregate wage determination have generally found today's rate of wage change to be linked to past rates of wage and/or price change and some measure of real economic conditions such as the unemployment rate. Of course, those union workers who have escalator clauses will also have their wage change determined by current (or quite recent) changes in prices. It is through these relationships that the union impact on anti-inflation policy enters the economic system.

Unions appear to weaken the linkage between real economic conditions and the rate of change of wages. Put another way, when unemployment rises, the rate of increase of wages in the nonunion sector slows appreciably (although not dramatically). In the union sector, however, this effect is attenuated. The attenuation influence is shown on Figure 2 as Impact (A). It occurs for reasons already discussed including the prevalance of long-term union contracts and the "career" labor market relationships associated with the union sector. In Appendix A, a formal model including the impacts summarized on Figure 2 is presented. The model suggests that Impact (A) weakens the effectiveness of monetary policy in dealing with inflation. Essentially, if economic slack does not produce much reaction in the rate of wage inflation, then the effect of slack on price inflation will also be attenuated. If anti-inflation monetary policy works through the creation of economic slack, then its influence on price inflation is diminished.

FIGURE 2

The Varied Union Impacts on the Anti-Inflation
Effectiveness of Monetary Policy

Union Impacts	Influence on Effectiveness of Monetary Policy	Implications for Inflation Restraint
(A) Attenuation of influence of labor-market conditions on wage change	Reduces effectiveness	If inflation has occurred in past, difficulty in slowing inflation through demand restraint is increased.
(B) Linkage of wage change to past price and wage inflation through long-term contracts.	No change	If inflation has been high in the past, it will tend to be high in the present.
(C) Linkage of wage change to current price inflation through introduction of escalator clauses	Increases effectiveness	Difficulty in slowing inflation through demand restraint is reduced. Exogenous price shocks will be more quickly reflected in wage and price inflation.

The use of long-term contracts in the union sector elevates the importance of past inflation in the determination of today's rate of wage change. This influence—Impact (B) of Figure 2—contributes to inflation momentum. Past inflation in wages and prices is reflected in current wage determination, which in turn is reflected in current price inflation. By itself, this linkage to the past does not reduce monetary policy effectiveness; a given amount of monetary constriction might still be capable of reducing the underlying inflation rate by a specified amount. But if inflation has been high in the past, the underlying rate—even after the reduction—will be that much higher today. That is, if inflation has been high in the past, a linkage between the past and the present ensures that there will be more inflation to reduce today. A monetary exercise that reduces the inflation rate by one percentage point will seem much more dramatic if the inflation rate that is reduced is initially 5 percent than if it is 15 percent.

Although Impacts (A) and (B) of unions on monetary policy effectiveness are negative, the widespread use of escalator clauses in the union sector can have the opposite effect. Escalator clauses tie wage change to current (or slightly lagged) rates of price inflation, Impact (C) on Figure 2. As long as there is *some* inflation responsiveness to economic slack in the economy, escalator clauses will amplify that effect. Consider the following sequence: A monetary restriction is imposed, which increases unemployment. The higher unemployment rate reduces wage inflation in the nonunion sector, an impact which is reflected by a slowing of price inflation. Union escalator clauses cause union wage changes to slow down in response to the price deceleration. This wage impact is again reflected in prices and again picked up through escalators and reflected in wages. And the process repeats.

Escalator clauses are not always good news, however. In the event of an upward external price shock, such as a large OPEC price increase, escalator clauses will quickly step up the rate of wage increase, thus spreading the initial shock. However, this impact is symmetric; a downward price shock, such as might be associated with bumper harvests in the world agricultural markets, will also be quickly diffused by escalator clauses.

It is evident from this review that the question of whether unions make it more or less difficult to halt ongoing inflation cannot be answered generally. The question can only be answered in the context of economic circumstances, a particular view (model) of the wage and price determination system, and a specific policy toward aggregate demand. In the analysis presented above, unions will tend to make achievement of a low inflation rate more difficult if past inflation has been high and if external price shocks are currently being felt. Under these circumstances, demand restraint will have only a small impact on inflation (Impact (A)), non-escalated long-term contracts will tend to perpetuate past inflation

(Impact (B)), and external price shocks will quickly become part of the price-wage spiral via escalator clauses (Impact (C)). Under other circumstances, however, union escalator practices could reinforce the impact of monetary restraint in reducing inflation.

The union impacts on monetary policy effectiveness can work in reverse. In the mid 1960s, for example, when demand policy became more stimulative, the presence of the union sector probably retarded the acceleration of inflation. Demand pressures reduced unemployment and economic slack. While the nonunion sector reacted quickly with an acceleration in wage increases, the union sector did not. The decline in unemployment had little initial impact on wage change in the union sector. Long-term union contracts tended to carry the momentum of *low* inflation from the early 1960s into the future. Those union contracts with escalator clauses did amplify the acceleration of price inflation caused by increased demand. But in many cases, negotiators in the union sector had discontinued the use of escalators in the early 1960s, thus reducing the significance of the escalator effect.

Three provisos need to be added to the analysis. As previously noted, union wage change should not be viewed as a world apart from nonunion wage change. Rather, there is a spectrum of practices running from casual labor markets through career labor markets to formalized contractual unionized labor markets. There are areas of nonunion wage determination that tend to be "unionesque" and areas of union wage change determination that are "nonunionesque." The influences summarized on Figure 2 will be the same whether they come from the union or the nonunion sector. But since the properties discussed are associated with formality (explicit contracts and written escalator formulas), they have been discussed in this chapter as union impacts. In any case, wage developments in the nonunion sector, because of its sheer size in the U.S., will tend to dominate aggregate wage-change indexes. Hence, there is a definite limit on the ability of bargainers in the union sector to alter aggregate wage-change determination.

The second proviso is that the discussion has deliberately avoided an exploration of price-change determination. If there are elements of pricing which carry past inflation into the present (say, firms which set prices in advance based on expectations of rising costs extrapolated from past experience), the influence would be much like that of Impact (B) in the labor market. If some influence reduces the responsiveness of price markups to product-market conditions (say, the presence of average cost pricers who tend to raise prices as demand falls because of the impact of fixed costs on unit costs), the impact will be much like that of Impact (A) in the labor market. And, of course, the influence of costs on prices has an escalator-like effect because price changes tend to reflect other price changes and—through input-output connections—ultimately reflect themselves. Such an effect is similar to Impact (C). The focus in this chapter on wage-change and inflation does not mean that aspects of price-change determination are irrelevant to inflation control and to the effectiveness of demand policy.

Proviso number three is that there may well be other aspects of union wage-change determination that have been neglected. There is, for example, a considerable literature on wage imitation, pattern bargaining, wage-wage inflation, and the like. The link between past and present wage inflation could be interpreted as such a wage-imitation phenomenon. To the extent that wage change in the union sector is influenced by the nonunion sector, Impact (A) might be reduced. But, to the extent that the union sector influences the nonunion sector, Impact (A) could be increased. There is considerable controversy, however, in the literature on the implications of wage-wage imitation and it seems best to withhold judgment on its impact based the limited evidence presently available.[58]

IMPLICATIONS FOR NONTRADITIONAL ANTI-INFLATION POLICY

Industrialized countries, including the U.S., have been experimenting with "incomes policies," wage-price controls, and guidelines of various types since the end of World War II. Since the early 1960s, both Democratic and Republican administrations have dabbled with alternative forms of direct intervention into wage and price setting. Models such as the one presented above can provide a rationale for such efforts under certain circumstances.

In a situation in which inflation has been "excessive" for a long period of time and/or when external price developments, for ex-

---

[58] For discussion of the question of wage-wage imitation, see Mitchell, *Unions, Wages, and Inflation*, Ch. 5.

ample, OPEC price increases, are unfavorable, aspects of wage determination may hinder efforts at reducing inflation to an acceptable target level. Past inflation tends to be passed into the present, exogenous price increases tend to become quickly embedded in the wage-price mechanism, and the main effect of demand restraint is to lower real output and employment. Direct intervention in the labor market, in effect to make it act as if it were more like a classical market where a whisper of excess supply quickly reduces the price, could enhance the effectiveness of monetary policy. Viewed in this way, direct intervention is primarily a transition mechanism which helps to reduce the pain of deflation.[59]

When restrictive monetary or fiscal policies are followed, the resulting economic slack is supposed to act as a "signal" to wage and price setters to moderate their behavior. In the textbooks, the reason wage and price setters follow the signal is generally framed in terms of a classical response to excess supply. However, the reason for following the signal is less important than the following itself. If the signal is followed—for any reason—then demand restraint is effective in reducing inflation and will be relatively painless. If the signal is not followed, demand restraint will be ineffective and the pain will be severe.

Suppose demand restraint is imposed in an effort to reduce inflation, but the signal is largely ignored. Under such circumstances, the use of direct intervention can be viewed as an effort to persuade, coerce, or force wage and price setters to act *as if* they regarded the signal as important. At one extreme, mandatory controls may be imposed, which simply order wage and price setters to respond to the signal. At the other, a "voluntary" guideline is announced—usually with a great deal of hoopla—designed to convince wage and price setters that a new, less inflationary era is at hand. If they believe it, that is, if their inflationary expectations are altered, the beliefs will tend to be self-fulfilling.

Efforts at direct intervention in wage and price setting often end up with a special focus on union wage determination. This is partially because the union sector presents the potential for dramatic confrontations with the government, that is, large-scale

---

[59] This point is developed more fully in Daniel J. B. Mitchell, "Direct Intervention in Wage and Price Decisions," in *Economic Perspectives*, Vol. 2 ed. Maurice B. Ballabon (New York: Harwood Academic Publishers, forthcoming).

strikes in support of wage demands beyond the allowable limits. It is also because the union sector contains large groups of workers which tend to be highly visible. (Roughly half of the private union sector is covered by agreements involving 1,000 or more workers). And it is because the authorities are concerned about union Impacts (A) and (B), the attenuation of response to the signal and the tendency to reinforce inflation momentum. On the other hand, since Impact (C)—the use of escalators—could reinforce the impact of the signal, it is not surprising that recent intervention efforts have adopted rules which favor the use of such clauses.[60]

The difficulty with direct intervention in wage and price setting is more one of technique than rationale. What are the appropriate rules in the labor market to deal with myriad complexities of wage determination? Merit plans, fringe benefits, productivity bargaining, spot labor shortages, and incentive systems all require treatment in the rules of the program. Apart from these technical issues, there is the delicate question of maintaining "credibility" for programs and in obtaining at least tacit support of organized labor. In the product market, where the linkages between buyer and seller are generally looser than in the labor market, the rules for pricing can easily result in shortages and distortions which try public patience.

Even the remedies for some of these difficulties tend to founder on practical application rather than theory. During the 1970s, various proposals for tax-based incomes policies (TIPs) were advanced.[61] Under these proposals the tax system would be used to

---

[60] Under Phase II of the Nixon Administration's wage controls, wage adjustments resulting from escalators could be "time-weighted," a procedure that reduced the calculation of the percentage wage increase. Thus, it was easier to comply with the wage standard if a component of the wage increase came from an escalator than if it was simply negotiated in advance. See Arnold R. Weber and Daniel J. B. Mitchell, *The Pay Board's Progress: Wage Controls in Phase II* (Washington: Brookings Institution, 1978), pp. 56–57. Under the Carter guidelines program, which required approval for negotiated contracts at the time of negotiation rather than as wage adjustments occurred, escalators were "costed" at assumed rates of inflation below the prevailing rates. This rule reduced the calculated rate of wage increase relative to the actual rate, thus making compliance with the guidelines easier. See U.S. General Accounting Office, *The Voluntary Pay and Price Standards Have Had No Discernible Effect on Inflation* (Washington: U.S. Government Printing Office, 1980), pp. 90–92.

[61] Discussion of the TIP idea can be found in Arthur M. Okun and George L. Perry, eds., *Curing Chronic Inflation* (Washington: Brookings Institution, 1978).

reward "good" behavior or penalize "bad" behavior of wage and/or price setters. The principle behind the proposal is a simple one; if wage and price setters have financial incentives to comply with whatever guidelines are in effect, obtaining compliance will be easier.

Originally, the Carter Administration wage-price guidelines program was to have a variant of a labor-market TIP, known as real wage insurance. Under this proposal, workers in units which complied with the then-prevailing 7 percent wage standard would have been eligible for tax rebates if prices rose by more than 7 percent. Thus, workers' real wages were to have been protected from unanticipated inflation, at least for the period that the proposal was in effect.

A major criticism of TIP plans has been their complexity. Even when confined only to wages, a TIP plan requires writing into the Internal Revenue Code all the intracacies of compensation determination. The same issues that pose problems for guidelines and controls rules—merit plans, fringe benefits, etc.—must be dealt with in a TIP plan. Moreover, there is little room for exceptions and flexibility, since the rules must be auditable by tax officials. The Carter Administration's real wage insurance plan, because it was less flexible than the guidelines, had rules which diverged from the program it was intended to reinforce. Moreover, the plan's payout was to be contingent on the rate of inflation. In the event of external price pressures, government expenditures would have been boosted. These complications led Congress—which must approve changes in the tax code—to reject the real wage insurance proposal shortly after it had been submitted.[62]

In short, no one has yet devised an ideal strategy for obtaining labor cooperation with programs of direct intervention. Novel ideas such as real wage insurance have not developed to the point of practical application. Labor cooperation seems to be forthcoming mainly during efforts to phase out controls and guidelines. Phase III of the Nixon controls program—which was intended as a step toward decontrol—in 1973 attracted labor participation on an ad-

---

[62] For a discussion of the development of the real wage insurance plan, see Robert J. Flanagan, "Real Wage Insurance as a Compliance Incentive," *Eastern Economic Journal* 5 (October 1979), pp. 367–77. For a more skeptical look at the plan, see Daniel J. B. Mitchell, "The Rise and Fall of Real Wage Insurance," *Industrial Relations* 19 (Winter 1980), pp. 64–73.

visory committee. The second year of the Carter guidelines program included a social compact with organized labor involving
labor participation on a Pay Advisory Committee. That committee
recommended a substantial loosening of the wage standards,
recommendations which were generally adopted.

Despite the ambiguous record of direct intervention programs,
and the difficulty of obtaining labor support, the intractability of
ongoing inflation remains a major economic problem. Periodic
episodes of direct intervention are likely to occur in the future.
Exploration of unorthodox approaches to inflation control is bound
to continue.

IV. Wage Determination and the Economic Impact of the Strike

When large-scale work stoppages occur, newspapers often report estimates of the "costs" of the stoppage to the workers, firms,
and communities involved. For reasons well known to industrial
relations specialists, simple tabulations of wages not paid or sales
not made during a dispute are likely to overstate the costs. Workers
may work overtime before or after a strike to make up for lost production, firms may sell out of inventory, sales may be diverted to
nonstruck suppliers, etc. Academics generally take a skeptical
view of alarmist estimates of strike impacts, even of disputes
which attract governmental concern because of their seemingly
large potential for disruption.[63] And the well-known fact that
strikes account for only a very small proportion of total working
time in the U.S. economy—about 0.2 percent for the period 1970–
1979—is often cited as evidence that the public has an overblown
notion of the economic impact of the strike.

If economic impact means disruption, the small fraction of
worktime lost is a sufficient indicator that the impact is small indeed. On the other hand, the strike is the ultimate sanction of the
union against the employer. It is ultimately the cause of the wage
differentials the union is able to achieve, as well as other concessions from the employer. While it can be argued that the union
may provide certain benefits to the employer in the form of grievance handling and communications, it is doubtful that in the

---

[63] For example, see John A. Ackerman, "The Impact of the Coal Strike
of 1977–1978," *Industrial and Labor Relations Review* 32 (January 1979),
pp. 175–88.

absence of the strike threat and legal sanctions most private employers would perceive a need to maintain a relationship with a union.

Although a strike imposes costs on the employer, it also imposes costs on striking workers and their union. Despite this fact—which provides an incentive to both sides to come to an accommodation without a strike—the empirical potential for a strike is surprisingly large. The small proportion of worktime lost to disputes is misleading for three reasons. First, most worktime is in the nonunion sector where strikes are extremely rare.[64] Second, the strike data include stoppages arising during the life of the contract which tend to be short and which, in any case, do not involve contract negotiations. Third, even a comparatively long strike subtracts a relatively small amount of worktime lost from the affected employer. A one-month strike, for example, subtracts only one-twelfth of potential annual hours.

A more meaningful statistic is the probability that a strike will occur in the course of a contract renegotiation. Unfortunately, complete data on contract expirations are not available. In a study of major contract expirations in manufacturing during 1954–1975, Kaufman found that about 13 percent led to a strike and that about 19 percent of workers covered by such contracts became involved in strikes.[65] This suggests that strike propensities rise with the number of workers covered by the agreement, perhaps a reflection of "pattern bargaining" in which larger units do the battling and smaller units avoid the costs of an impasse by following along. It appears that in the period 1970–1977, private-industry strike propensities averaged about one in five on a contract basis and almost 30 percent on a worker basis in the major union sector.[66]

---

[64] In 1977, for example, 1.1 percent of the work stoppages reported to the Bureau of Labor Statistics involved no union. See U.S. Bureau of Labor Statistics, *Analysis of Work Stoppages 1977*, Bull. 2032 (Washington: U.S. Government Printing Office, 1979), p. 14.

[65] Bruce E. Kaufman, "The Propensity to Strike in American Manufacturing," in *Proceedings* of the Industrial Relations Research Association, December 28–30, 1977, p. 423.

[66] These estimates were made from annual data on work stoppages (and numbers of workers involved) stemming from renegotiations and contract reopenings in situations involving 1,000 or more workers from estimates of contract expirations and reopenings (and numbers of workers involved) for agreements covering 1,000 or more workers. The stoppage data appear in U.S. Bureau of Labor Statistics, *Analysis of Work Stoppages*, various issues. Expiration and reopening data appear in the December or January issues of

Since the threat of a strike is very real, both parties have an incentive to avoid the potential costs by reducing the frequency of negotiations. Thus, the strike threat not only lies behind the improved wages and benefits unions are able to win; it also lies behind the tendency to negotiate long-duration agreements. In turn, these agreements reinforce the long-term horizons which are already latent in the union sector and contribute to the observed insensitivity of the wage to labor-market conditions.

Not only do such contracts limit the number of situations in which responsiveness is possible in a given year; they also ensure that at any point in time the parties to a negotiation will take the long view and will tend to ignore short-run business-cycle influences. Thus, it takes dire circumstances (imminent bankruptcy, massive unemployment, etc.) to provoke much response. On the other hand, long-term contracts are associated with escalator clauses which, under some circumstances, may increase wage responsiveness to demand-restraint policies. In short, the differences between union and nonunion wage-change determination are intimately involved with the strike threat. The main economic impact of the strike is not production disruption, but the reinforcement of these differences in the labor market.

V. Strikes and Recent Economic Theory

The empirical strike record has posed an interesting dilemma for economic theory. Strikes are costly to both labor and management. If both could predict what the wage outcome of a strike would be, they would be better off accepting that outcome in the first place and avoiding strike costs. Since the future cannot be known with certainty, however, the parties can only guess at the eventual outcome. Hence, strikes have sometimes been viewed as simple "mistakes" by the parties, that is, inconsistent guesses.[67]

When strikes are viewed as simple mistakes, other theoretical consequences follow. In principle, strikes should not be correlated

---

the *Monthly Labor Review*. Unfortunately, the latter series excludes government while the former series includes the government sector. Hence, the calculated propensities will be somewhat overstated.

[67] This view is often associated with the early exposition by Hicks of a theory of strikes. Hicks did suggest, however, that unions might strike periodically simply to remind employers of their potential to impose such costs. See J. R. Hicks, *The Theory of Wages* (New York: St. Martin's Press, 1963), pp. 140–47.

with observed economic variables. For example, if the level of unemployment were observed to decrease labor militancy, thus causing a decline in the incidence of strikes, both parties would become aware of this relationship. Once this awareness developed, both parties would adjust their estimates of eventual wage outcomes to changes in the unemployment rate. Management would find it worthwhile to bargain harder during periods of high unemployment, given its perception that union militancy would decrease. Strikes would soon come to be uncorrelated with the unemployment rate.[68]

Despite this theoretical prediction, strikes are well known to be correlated with business-cycle and other variables.[69] Thus it appears that a modification of strike theory must be developed. Once it is recognized that union and management are locked into a long-term relationship, the elements of such a modification begin to emerge. The simple "mistake" theory of strikes views each negotiation as an isolated event. Its conclusion—that strikes should not be predictable—results from the erroneous assumption that both parties seek to minimize conflict costs in each negotiation taken separately. Given their long-term relationship, it is more reasonable to suppose that the parties would seek to minimize conflict costs over the indefinite horizon of current *and* future negotiations. These two goals would be the same if what happened in today's negotiation had no bearing on what happens in tomorrow's. But, what happens today will condition the outcome in the future so that the negotiations are not independent.

If, for example, the union in today's negotiation proves to be unexpectedly conciliatory, if it backs down from what management thought were strongly felt positions, management may reduce its estimate of the union's strike threat in the future. During the next negotiation, management may press its case more strongly, to de-

---

[68] Economists will recognize the relationship between the simple mistake theory of strikes and the theory of rational expectations.

[69] For some examples of explorations of economic variables which seem to explain strike incidence, see Albert Rees, "Industrial Conflict and Business Fluctuations," *Journal of Political Economy* 60 (October 1952), pp. 371–82; and Orley Ashenfelter and George E. Johnson, "Bargaining Theory, Trade Unions, and Industrial Strike Activity," *American Economic Review* 59 (March 1969), pp. 35–49. A review of this literature and additional empirical results can be found in Michael Shalev, "Trade Unionism and Economic Analysis: The Case of Industrial Conflict," *Journal of Labor Research* 1 (Spring 1980), pp. 133–73.

termine if the union has truly weakened. Or, if management were unexpectedly conciliatory today, the union might put forward more militant demands in the future to test whether management resistance had actually decreased. Similarly, if labor or management demonstrates unexpectedly high aggressiveness in today's negotiation (greater willingness to strike or take a strike), the other party might be more cautious in future negotiations.

In a long-term relationship, the parties must constantly watch each other's behavior for signs of a change in relative bargaining strength. Any behavior which suggests that a re-evaluation of bargaining strength would be appropriate is likely to result in a period of experimentation in which both sides test each other's resistance points. Such a period of testing and uncertainty increases the probability of a mistake and a costly strike. If the parties wish to minimize strike costs over the long term, their best strategy may be to establish a modus vivendi and to behave consistently from negotiation to negotiation.

Consistent behavior, however, may lead to strike predictability in line with empirical observation. Suppose that a particular union had established in past negotiations that it was very concerned about keeping up with inflation, that is, that it would strongly resist accepting wage proposals that did not maintain worker purchasing power. Suppose that the management side had established in previous negotiations that it was very concerned about profitability and would strongly resist high wage demands during periods of low profits. If a negotiation happened to fall during a period of high inflation and low profits, the chance of a strike would be quite high. But both would have a strong incentive to "stick to their guns" to avoid creating future uncertainty about their long-term bargaining goals and positions. A skilled mediator might be able to suggest a formula whereby concessions made by either or both sides would clearly be labeled as temporary. Absent such a formula, a strike which both parties had anticipated might nevertheless ensue.

The application of theories of long-term relationships and implicit contracts to strikes is just one example of the possible development of these theories in the 1980s. They promise to bring new insights into many aspects of labor-management relationships. It is ironic that exciting new advances in the economic analysis of the collective bargaining process are being made in a period in which the unionized proportion of the workforce has shown a steady decline.

VI. Conclusions

Unions have significant economic impacts. They do create wage differentials between union and nonunion workers, possibly contributing at the margin of the relative decline of the overall unionization rate. And they do change the structure of wage-change determination, primarily by reducing the sensitivity of wage change to labor-market tightness and looseness, and—in the case of escalated contracts—by increasing sensitivity to recent price changes. Under some circumstances, these characteristics of union wage change can hinder anti-inflation efforts using traditional demand restraint. Under other circumstances, they may have the opposite effect. It is in those situations where demand restraint policy is frustrated in influencing wage movements that direct government intervention into wage determination is often suggested.

The economic impact of the strike is sometimes viewed as exclusively a question of measuring the consequences of production disruption during work stoppages. But as is well known to industrial relations specialists, when weighed against total economywide output, the production effect is generally quite small. A more important economic consequence of strikes (both actual and potential) is that they induce the parties to reduce strike costs by adopting long-term contracts. Such contracts reinforce the latent insensitivity of wage change to labor-market conditions and they encourage the use of escalator clauses. These features, in turn, have implications for anti-inflation policy.

The impact of unions depicted here is not a total revision of economic structure. In the U.S. case, the heavy majority status of the nonunion workforce must be recognized. And in the union sector, management plays an important role in wage decisions. On the other hand, unions cannot be simply incorporated into a simple demand/supply framework and neglected. They are not simply variants of monopoly firms which "mark up" wages of their members but otherwise have no dynamic consequences.

Appendix A

In the text surrounding Figure 2, reference was made to a simple short-run model for analyzing three union impacts on the effectiveness of monetary policy. This outlines the model. Consider the following four-equation system representing a money market, a labor market, a wage-change determination process, and a goods market.

$$(1) \quad M_s = M_d = A(P, Y, r) \qquad \text{Money market}$$
$$(2) \quad L = B(W/P) \qquad \text{Labor market}$$
$$(3) \quad \%W = C(\%P, \%P_{-1}, \%W_{-1}, L) \qquad \text{Wage-change process}$$
$$(4) \quad Y = D(M_s/P, r) \qquad \text{Goods market}$$

The symbols used are defined as follows: M_s = money supply controlled by the central bank and considered an exogenous variable; M_d = money demanded by the public; P = price level; $\%P$ = percent change in the price level during the current period; $\%P_{-1}$ = percent change in the price level during the previous period; Y = real income = real product; r = rate of interest; W = wage rate; $\%W$ = percent change in the wage rate during the current period; $\%W_{-1}$ = percent change in the wage rate during the previous period; and L = level of employment.

In the money market, the demand for money (which must be equated with supply) is positively related to P and Y and negatively related to r. Note that the money equation is compatible with a quantity theory view, with velocity dependent on r. The real wage (W/P) is negatively related to the demand for labor in the labor market. All arguments in the wage-change function are positively related to $\%W$. The real money supply (M_s/P) is positively related to the demand for output, while the interest rate is negatively related to output demand. These assumptions are in line with conventional models.

To close the model, a fifth equation relating real output to labor input is needed. In the short run, the aggregate production function reduces to a positive relationship between real output and labor input, $Y = E(L)$. The following identities are also useful: $W = (1 + .01\%W)W_{-1}$, $P = (1 + .01\%P)P_{-1}$, and $M_s = (1 + .01\%M_s)M_s$, where W_{-1}, P_{-1}, and M_{s-1} are last period's wage level, price level, and money supply, and $\%M_s$ is the percent in the money supply. The substitution of these equations into the original system of four and the linearization of the results produces the following modified system:

(1') $\quad \%M_s = A'\,(\%P,\,L,\,r) = c_1 + a_{11}\,\%P + a_{12}\,L - a_{13}\,r$
(2') $\quad L = B'(\%W,\%P) = c_2 - a_{24}\,\%W + a_{21}\,\%P$
(3') $\quad \%W = C'(\%P,\,\%W_{-1},\,\%P_{-1},\,L) = c_3 + e\%W_{-1} + f\%P_{-1}$
$\qquad + a_{31}\,\%P + a_{32}\,L$
(4') $\quad L = D'(\%M,\%P,\,r) = c_4 + g\%M_s - a_{41}\,\%P - a_{43}\,r$

This system can be solved since it consists of four equations and four unknowns $(\%P,\,L,\,r,\,\%W)$. The exogenous variables are $\%M_s$ (under central bank control) and $\%W_{-1}$ and $\%P_{-1}$, both "givens" because they occurred in the past. Note that all parameters except the constants are assumed to be positive.

Since the main point of the model is to isolate the impact of union wage-change determination on the anti-inflation effectiveness of demand policy (in this case money-supply growth policy), the concept of effectiveness needs to be defined. The effectiveness of monetary policy (E) in influencing the rate of inflation is defined as $\triangle\%P/\triangle\%M_s$, i.e., the change in the inflation rate associated with a change in the rate of money supply growth. Thus, the larger the value of E, the more effective will monetary restraint be in reducing the rate of inflation.

Using equation system (1')–(4'), the impacts of the various coefficients on E were computed. Thus, to explore the effect of increasing the linkage of wage change to past wage and price inflation (Impact (B) of Figure 2) on E, the impact of an increase in coefficients e and f on E was calculated. An increase in e and f turns out to have no effect on E. Since unions bring with them escalated contracts (Impact (C)), their presence increases coefficient a_{31}. The effect of this increase on E was calculated and found to be positive. If unions reduce the sensitivity of wage change to the level of employment (Impact (A)), then a_{32} should decrease. The effect of that decrease on E is negative.

In general, in an inflationary environment an increase in E is a Good Thing since it means that monetary policy will quickly bring inflation under control. Similarly, a decrease in E is a Bad Thing since it suggests that monetary policy will have only a small influence on inflation. These findings are summarized on Figure 2.

CHAPTER 2

The Impact of Collective Bargaining: Illusion or Reality?*

RICHARD B. FREEMAN
JAMES L. MEDOFF
Harvard University and
National Bureau of Economic Research

In recent years there has been an outpouring of empirical studies on the impact of collective bargaining on the economy. While many of these analyses focus on the traditional question of wage determination under unionism, considerable effort has also been devoted to estimating the effect of the institution on other market outcomes. As a result of this work we have a large body of new evidence regarding differences between union and nonunion workers and union and nonunion enterprises along many dimensions.

Can the observed union/nonunion differences be explained primarily in terms of preunion characteristics of firms or individuals? Is it that all union/nonunion differences arise only because of the "union wage effect" and are observed only when one or more price-theoretic responses to this effect are being ignored? Or can it be that unions have important effects on the performance of our economic system through routes ignored in standard price theory?

There are a number of different positions on whether union effects are real or illusory. One belief is that the apparent union/

* While many individuals were most helpful in the preparation of this chapter, we are particularly appreciative of the comments and suggestions offered by K. Abraham, S. Allen, C. Brown, G. Cain, G. Chamberlain, J. Fay, T. Kochan, R. McKersie, K. McLoughlin, and M. Podgursky. We are also most grateful for the helpful feedback from participants at seminars at Boston University, the University of Chicago, the University of Connecticut, Harvard, North Carolina State University at Raleigh, Princeton, and the University of South Carolina. In addition, we wish to thank G. Bialecki and C. Frazier for their very able assistance. Our research is supported by a National Science Foundation grant (DAR-7828104) to the National Bureau of Economic Research.

nonunion differences are illusory because of the way trade unions were superimposed on various groupings of establishments or individuals. A second view is that unions have real effects on economic performance, but that all of these effects operate through price-theoretic routes; any effects which appear to be inexplicable in terms of standard price theory are taken as illusory. Finally, there is the perception that unions influence outcomes through institutional channels and, in so doing, have important real nonwage effects on our economy.

The preunion characteristics belief that apparent union/nonunion differences are illusory seems to be held primarily by those who see the world as close enough to satisfying the conditions of perfect competition that, in the short run, unions are more of an epiphenomenon than a substantive force. While it is unlikely that anyone really believes that every apparent union effect is an apparition, the preunion characteristics view lies behind many attempts to explain away particular results suggesting that unions have meaningful economic impacts.

Those whose vision of what unions do comes from standard price theory tend to focus on what we have elsewhere called the "monopoly face" of unionism and believe that every real effect of unions works through price-theoretic channels.[1] Thus, these individuals tend to limit their focus to the size and ramifications of "the union wage effect," treating any estimated union effect which cannot be rationalized in terms of a price-theoretic response to the wage effect as illusory, that is, as reflecting the poor quality of the experiment at hand.

Those in the industrial relations tradition believe that unionism influences outcomes primarily through what are often labelled "institutional channels" (the "collective voice/institutional response face" in our just-cited work). While this group accepts the existence of important real price-theoretic union effects, it believes in the reality of non-price-theoretic effects as well. In fact, a primary concern of researchers with an industrial relations world view is with the nonwage effects of collective bargaining.

This chapter examines the arguments and empirical evidence concerning whether union/nonunion differences represent illusion or reality, defined in accordance with either the price-theoretic or

---

[1] See Freeman and Medoff (1979, 1982).

institutional views. In it we seek to determine the extent to which the union/nonunion differences found in myriad market outcomes are: (1) illusory, explicable in terms of the innately different characteristics of union and nonunion workers or firms; (2) real, working through price-theoretic routes of impact; and (3) real, working through institutional routes of impact.

While we recognize that to some extent we have set up artificial polar cases, and that no sensible researcher would be expected to rely solely on any one of the views for explaining all union/nonunion differences, we believe that the differences noted permeate much of the recent literature on unionism and that the "ideal types" provide a fruitful guide to understanding efforts to determine what unions in fact do.

The chapter is divided into four sections. Section I summarizes the recent empirical findings about union/nonunion differences on which the interpretative debate focuses. The second section lays out the theoretical and econometric explanations of the observed union/nonunion differences that have been put forth by the various camps in illusion/reality debates. Section III provides a summary of the results of new studies which can be used to assess whether the effects set out in Section I are best interpreted as illusory, real for price-theoretic reasons, or real for reasons that can be called "institutional." The final section presents a brief summary of our findings.

By way of anticipation, we reach two main conclusions. First, unions and collective bargaining have substantial real effects on diverse economic outcomes; union/nonunion differences appear to reflect much more than the poor quality of our econometric "experiments." Second, many of the real union effects are the result of institutional factors, which many economists have neglected in recent years; the price-theoretic view of reality seems to be much too narrow.

I. The Evidence In Question

It is important at the outset to lay out the union/nonunion differences about which illusion/reality interpretative questions have arisen. Accordingly, this section briefly summarizes the results of recent research concerning the impact of unionism on certain key aspects of the labor exchange. As a guide to the discussion,

TABLE 1

Recent Evidence on Union/Nonunion Differences Based on Cross-Sectional Data

Variable	Finding	Partial Listing of Relevant References
Compensation		
Wage rates	All else (measurable) the same, union/ nonunion hourly wage differential is between 10% and 20%.	Ashenfelter (1976), Freeman & Medoff (forthcoming a), Lewis (1980), Mellow (1981a), Oaxaca (1975), Welch (1980).
Fringes[a]	All else the same, union/nonunion hourly fringe differential is between 20% and 30%. The fringe share of compensation is higher at a given level of compensation.	Duncan (1976), Freeman (1981), Goldstein & Pauly (1976), Leigh (1979), Solnick (1978), Viscusi (1980).
Wage dispersion	Wage inequality is much lower among union members than among comparable nonmembers and total wage dispersion appears to be lowered by unionism.	Freeman (1980c), Hyclak (1979, 1980), Plotnick (1981).
Wage structure	Wage differentials between workers who are different in terms of race, age, service, skill level, and education appear to be lower under collective bargaining.	Ashenfelter (1976), Bloch & Kuskin (1978), Johnson & Youmans (1971), Kiefer & Smith (1977), Leigh (1978), Pfeffer & Ross (1980), Schoeplein (1977), Shapiro (1978).
Cyclical responsiveness of wage rates[a]	Union wages are less responsive to labor market conditions than nonunion wages.	Ashenfelter (1976), Hamermesh (1972), Johnson (1981), Lewis (1963), Medoff (1979), Mitchell (1980a, 1980b), Pierson (1968), Raisian (1979).
Determinants of compensation differential	Other things equal, the union compensation advantage is higher the greater the percent of a market's workers who are organized. The effects of market concentration on wage differentials is unclear. The differentials appear to be very large in some regulated markets. They appear to decline as firm size increases.	Dalton & Ford (1977), Donsimoni (1978), Ehrenberg (1979), Freeman & Medoff (forthcoming a), Hayden (1977), Hendricks (1975), Kahn (1978), Kochan (1980), Lee (1978), Mellow (1981b), Weiss (1966).
Internal & External Mobility		
Promotions	Seniority independent of productivity is rewarded substantially more in promotion decisions among union members than among otherwise comparable nonunion employees.	Halasz (1980), Medoff & Abraham (1980b, 1981b), Yanker (1980).

TABLE 1 (*Continued*)

Variable	Finding	Partial Listing of Relevant References
Internal & External Mobility (Continued)		
Quits[a]	The quit rate is much lower for unionized workers than for similar workers who are nonunion.	Blau & Kahn (1981), Block (1978a), Farber (OLS Results 1979), Freeman (1976, 1980a, 1980b), Kahn (1977), Leigh (1979).
Temporary layoffs[a]	There is much more cyclical labor adjustment through temporary layoffs in unionized manufacturing firms than in otherwise comparable firms that are nonunion.	Blau & Kahn (1981), Medoff (1979).
Terminations[a]	Terminations are more likely to be on a last-in-first-out basis among union employees, ceteris paribus.	Blau & Kahn (1981), Medoff & Abraham (1981a, 1981b).
Work Rules and Environment Rules[a]	There are important differences in the prevalence and nature of various rules in union and nonunion settings, such as those stipulating the role of company service and the way grievances are to be handled. Union work places appear to be run more by rules, with more rigidity in the scheduling of hours and less worker flexibility.	Freeman (1980a), Kochan & Bloch (1977), Kochan & Helfman (1979), Medoff & Abraham (1981b).
Management practices	Management in unionized cement firms appears to be more professional (less paternalistic or authoritarian), more standards oriented, and more in touch with work performance than management in similar nonunion firms.	Clark (1980a).
Management flexibility[a]	Management in unionized manufacturing firms appears less able to substitute nonproduction worker hours for production worker hours, but seems no less able to substitute capital for production labor than similarly situated nonunion management.	Freeman & Medoff (forthcoming b).
Worker Assessment of Jobs		
Satisfaction with job overall[a]	The stated level of overall job satisfaction is lower, but the wage gain required to induce a job change is higher for union members than for otherwise comparable employees who are not members.	Borjas (1979), Freeman (1976, 1978a), Kochan & Helfman (1979), Mandelbaum (1980).

Table 1 gives the central findings of these studies categorized by the following substantive issues: compensation; internal and external mobility; work rules and environment; and inputs, productivity, and profits. The reader will notice that our set of issues is not exhaustive. We have, in particular, neglected such important

TABLE 1 (*Continued*)

Variable	Finding	Partial Listing of Relevant References
Evaluation of rules and conditions[a]	Unionized workers state that they are more satisfied with their wages and fringes, less satisfied with their supervision, and less satisfied with their working conditions than nonunion workers. The extent to which stated job security grows with tenure is substantially greater under unionism. While the probability of viewing promotions as fair declines with service among nonunion employees, it increases among union members.	Duncan & Stafford (1980), Kochan & Helfman (1979), Viscusi (1980).
Inputs, Productivity, & Profits		
Prefirm quality of workforce	Other things equal, workers in unionized firms tend to have more "human capital."	Allen (1979), Brown & Medoff (1978), Farber (1979), Frantz (1976), Kahn (1979), Kalachek & Raines (1980).
Capital intensity[a]	Unionized firms in manufacturing, construction, and underground bituminous coal appear to have higher capital-labor ratios than similar nonunion enterprises.	Allen (1979), Brown & Medoff (1978), Clark (1980b), Connerton, Freeman & Medoff (1979), Frantz (1976).
Productivity[b]	In manufacturing and construction and in the underground bituminous coal industry in nonturbulent times, unionized enterprises appear to have greater productivity than those that are nonunion, all else equal. In underground coal, productivity appeared to be lower under unionism in the turbulent years around 1975.	Allen (1979), Brown & Medoff (1978), Clark (1980a), Connerton, Freeman & Medoff; (1979), Frantz (1976).
Profitability	While profit per unit of sales appears to be the same in similar union and nonunion manufacturing firms, the rate of profit per unit of capital appears to be lower under unionism.	Brown & Medoff (1978), Clark (1980a), Frantz (1976), Freeman & Medoff (forthcoming b).

[a]Wages or total compensation was held constant in generating this finding.

[b]Variables reflecting price-theoretic responses were held constant as well as possible in generating this finding.

topics as the internal operation of unions, strikes, and the survival of the organization itself, in part because these subjects do not lend themselves to the union/nonunion comparisons which motivate the research in the table. In addition, we concentrate exclusively on the private sector. While, as noted, we have no pretense that our set of issues is all-encompassing and while our listing of relevant references is undoubtedly incomplete, we believe that the table provides a reasonably accurate picture of the empirical results in question.

COMPENSATION

The first and probably still the most widely studied issue is the differential between union and nonunion wages. The early literature on this differential was summarized in Lewis's influential 1963 book, *Unionism and Relative Wages in the United States.* Since the publication of Lewis's book, a number of new sources of individual-level data (such as the May Current Population Survey) which permit estimation of the wage effect have become available. With micro-data of this kind, it is possible to compare the wages of union and nonunion workers with similar demographic characteristics who are also in the same detailed industry and/or occupation. As Johnson (1975) has reviewed some of this work, our summary will be brief. The post-Lewis micro-data estimates (derived with Ordinary Least Squares (OLS)) have generally found wage differentials noticeably above the 10 to 15 percent range given in Lewis's book. However, the analyses that have looked within more detailed cells, especially those with industry as a dimension, have tended to yield estimated differentials near the top end of the 10 to 15 percent range. This makes very good sense given that the studies summarized by Lewis normally examined a very narrowly defined group of workers. A comparison of the union wage effect by groups suggests larger impacts for blue-collar as opposed to white-collar workers, for younger as opposed to older employees, and for the less as opposed to the more educated. In addition, substantial differences have been noted in the size of the differential by industry.

Another form of data which has been used in recent studies pertains to individual establishments. These data (from surveys such as the Employer Expenditures for Employee Compensation

Survey (EEC)) permit the estimation of wage effects for production or nonproduction workers among firms of the same size within the same 3-digit Standard Industrial Classification (SIC) industry. Estimates using these data are quantitatively closer to those of Lewis, yielding union/nonunion differences of 10 percent or so. All told, with rare exception, recent studies confirm the existence of a sizable union/nonunion wage differential.

While a tremendous amount of effort was devoted in the past to studying union/nonunion differentials in wage rates, very little attention was devoted to analyzing union/nonunion differentials in fringe benefits. With the passage of time, this allocation of resources has become less defensible since the share of total compensation associated with voluntary fringes has been growing rapidly. In contrast to Rice's 1966 cross-industry analysis, which found no union effect on fringes, the recent studies cited in Table 1 have demonstrated that the "union fringe effect" is bigger, in percentage terms, than the "union wage effect." Data from the 1968, 1970, and 1972 EEC indicate, for example, that holding constant the characteristics in employees' establishments, blue-collar workers covered by collective bargaining received fringe benefits that were about 28 to 36 percent higher than those of blue-collar workers who were not covered (compared to a union wage advantage of 8 to 15 percent). For workers receiving the same total compensation per hour, the fringe share of labor cost was markedly higher in the union setting (Freeman (1981)). Looking at separate fringes, the largest union/nonunion percentage differentials on a per hour basis are for pensions, life, accident and health insurance, and vacation pay.

One key question to ask about the union/nonunion wage differentials is, "How do they vary across settings?" Recent empirical work on this subject has been based on the notion that union wage gains will be high where the elasticity of demand for labor, and hence the cost of increased relative wages in terms of lost members, is low. The evidence that, at least in the manufacturing and construction sectors of our economy, union wages but not nonunion wages grow with the fraction organized in the relevant product market is consistent with this claim; this is because a high percentage organized is likely to be associated with a low demand elasticity for union products and thus a low demand elasticity for union members. Other work has concentrated on the effect of market regulation on the union wage effect. Ehrenberg (1979) presents evidence consistent with the claim that union wages are raised by the regulation of public utilities. Hayden (1977) argues that the sizable impact of unionism on trucker wages (40 percent or so) is attributable both to ICC regulation of the sector and to the National Master Freight Agreement, which created industry-wide bargaining.

Since their inception, unions in our country have been concerned with the structure as well as the level of wage rates. The practice which most exemplifies unions' efforts on this front is the long-standing policy of pushing for "standard rates"; that is, uniform rates for comparable workers across establishments and for given occupational classes within establishments. Estimates presented in Freeman (1980c) show that, for blue-collar workers, wage inequality is substantially lower among union members than among similar nonmembers. Consistent with this, estimates of separate wage equations for union and nonunion workers have found that virtually all standard wage-determining variables are associated with smaller earnings differentials under unionism. Moreover, union wage policies appear to contribute to the equalization of wages by decreasing the differential between covered blue-collar workers and noncovered white-collar workers. If we add the apparent decrease in inequality due to wage standardization and the apparent decrease due to reduction in the white-collar/blue-collar differential to the apparent increase due to the greater wages ot blue-collar union workers, we find that the apparent net effect of unionism is to reduce total wage inequality. Evidence on inequality of net earnings across standard metropolitan statistical areas (SMSAs) and states and over time also shows a negative relationship between unionism and dispersion in pay. In short, it appears that the structure of wages in the United States has been compressed by the wage policies of organized labor.

Finally, with respect to wage adjustments under varying economic conditions, recent analyses of cyclical variation in wage rates have confirmed the earlier finding of Lewis that the union/nonunion wage differential has tended to be greater during economic downturns, which suggests that the reduction in (the growth of) real wage rates in response to a reduction in product demand is smaller under trade unions. Interestingly, the work of Johnson (1981) and Mitchell (1980b) and an analysis of Current Wage Developments establishment-level data suggest that the union wage effect grew substantially during the 1970s to a point where it is roughly comparable to its level in the 1930s.

INTERNAL AND EXTERNAL MOBILITY

The new work on trade unions has, as noted earlier, expanded the set of outcomes under study. One of the most important topics receiving attention has been the impact of unionization on the internal and external mobility of employees.

To evaluate the effects of unionism on firms' employment policies (the awarding of promotions, the ordering of layoffs, etc.), it is necessary to have knowledge of what is actually happening inside both union and nonunion firms. Survey evidence collected by and discussed in Medoff and Abraham (1980b, 1981a, 1981b) and recent case studies have provided relevant information concerning the role of seniority independent of performance in firms' promotion and termination decisions. With respect to promotions, the survey data reveal that whereas 68 percent of private-sector unionized employees outside of agriculture and construction work in settings where senior employees are favored substantially when promotion decisions are made, only 40 percent of the nonunion workforce is employed in such settings. When the analysis is restricted to hourly employees, the estimates of concern are 68 percent for union members and 53 percent for the nonunion labor force. Regressions with the survey data which include controls for firm size, industrial sector, and geographic region yield differences similar to those just given. Moreover, case studies of a number of U.S. firms tell the same story: company service counts more in promotion decisions in union settings.

One of the essential tenets of the collective voice/institutional response model is that among workers receiving the same pay, unions reduce employee turnover and associated costs by offering "voice" as an alternative to "exit." Recent evidence using newly available information on the job changes of thousands of individuals and on industry-level turnover rates shows that with diverse factors (including wages) held constant, unionized workers do have substantially lower quit rates than nonunion workers who are comparable in other respects. The reduction in quits and the accompanying increase in tenure appear to be as substantial for blacks as for whites and greater for older than for younger workers.

With less ability to reduce (the growth of) real wage rates and with lower quit rates, unionized firms can be expected to make greater use of other adjustment mechanisms, such as average hour reductions and layoffs. Both establishment-level and individual-level data sets demonstrate that temporary layoffs and recalls are a more important form of labor adjustment in unionized manufacturing firms than in otherwise comparable firms that are nonunion. Moreover, temporary layoffs tend to be used instead of average hour reductions to a greater extent under unionism. Hence, it appears that the layoff/recall syndrome which has received much recent attention is, for the most part, a unionized manufacturing (in particular, durables) phenomenon.

In union settings, length of service appears to be a much more important determinant of the order of both temporary and permanent layoffs than in comparable nonunion settings. Evidence from the seniority survey just cited reveals that, among those who had witnessed workforce reductions, rules protecting senior workers against being permanently laid off before their junior co-workers are more prevalent and stronger under trade unions. For hourly employees, 95 percent of the responses pertaining to groups covered by collective bargaining indicated that seniority in and of itself receives substantial weight in termination decisions, compared to 70 percent of the responses pertaining to noncovered groups. As for "strength," 68 percent of the survey responses pertaining to unionized hourly employees stated that a senior worker would *never* be involuntarily terminated before a junior worker, whereas only 28 percent of the responses pertaining to nonunion hourly employees stated that this is so. These survey results could not be explained in terms of company characteristics and are consistent with the findings of Blau and Kahn (1981) who used individual-level data.

Work Rules and Environment

Other personnel practices and procedures also appear to be affected by the presence of unionism. In Clark's (1980a, 1980b)

study of six cement firms which were recently unionized, management practices appear to have changed significantly with the coming of a union, in directions which can be labelled "productivity
oriented." These observations gain credence from the fact that
they are similar to those of Sumner Slichter, James Healy, and
E. Robert Livernash, who conducted myriad case studies concerning the relationship between unionism and management behavior
for their classic 1960 opus, *The Impact of Collective Bargaining
on Management*. It should be noted that, with evidence of the
type which has been collected, it is difficult to infer whether managers were moved from non-cost-minimizing behavior to cost-
minimizing behavior or whether the type of behavior which is
cost-minimizing is different in union and in nonunion environments.

It would seem reasonable, given what is believed about the
objective function of the typical union, to find less management
flexibility in unionized establishments than in otherwise comparable establishments that are nonunion. Consistent with this view,
evidence drawn primarily from the *1972 Census of Manufactures*
and the EEC show that within U.S. manufacturing the ease of
substitution for production labor, particularly substitution of nonproduction for production labor, is lower under trade unionism.
However, it should be mentioned that the limited evidence does
not indicate that unionism is associated with a lower elasticity of
substitution between labor and capital and thus with whatever
technological change is embodied in new capital.

WORKERS' ASSESSMENT OF JOBS

Several recent studies examining the impact of unionism on the
stated job satisfaction of workers have found union workers expressing less satisfaction, or in some instances no more satisfaction,
with their jobs than similar nonunion workers, even when compensation is *not* held constant. At the same time, however, union
members are also more likely to state that they are "unwilling to
change jobs under any circumstance" or "would never consider
moving to a new job" than are their "more satisfied" nonunion
counterparts, even when the wage is fixed. One interpretation of
these results is that the collective voice of unionism provides workers with a channel for expressing their preferences to management

and that this increases their willingness to complain about undesirable conditions.

Evidence has also been accumulated concerning workers' stated satisfaction with particular aspects of their jobs. Some of the findings most relevant to the discussion at hand are: (1) union members are much more likely to state that they are happy with their wages and fringes than are otherwise comparable nonunion employees; (2) there appears to be a strong tendency for unionized workers to state they are less happy with their supervisors and have worse relations with them; (3) there is a tendency for unionized workers to report their physical work conditions as less desirable than those reported by nonunion workers; (4) the extent to which stated job security grows with tenure is substantially greater under unionism; and (5) while the probability of viewing promotions as fair is negatively related to seniority in nonunion settings, it is positively related to seniority under unionism.

INPUTS, PRODUCTIVITY, AND PROFITS

When unions raise wages or otherwise alter labor costs, enterprises can be expected to change factor inputs and modes of organization in such ways as to raise the marginal revenue product of labor up to the point where it equals the new marginal cost of labor. Two of the most important ways in which firms could potentially do this are to hire "higher quality" workers and to increase their capital/labor ratios. Evidence has been offered showing that blue-collar union workers do in fact have somewhat more "human capital" than similar nonunion workers. With May CPS data for 1973–1975, blue-collar union members are found to be three to four years older than otherwise comparable nonunion blue-collar workers, and to have slightly more education. Separate wage equations for males and females, which differentiate workers by schooling, age, and region, lead to the conclusion that unionized production labor has about 6 percent more "human capital" within 2-digit manufacturing industries (Brown and Medoff (1978)). It should be noted, however, that an index of labor quality based on weights from wage regressions is at best only a crude approximation to an index based on "true" productivity weights, as is implied by evidence that a substantial fraction of seniority/earnings differentials cannot be explained by seniority/productivity differentials (Medoff (1977) and Medoff and Abraham (1980a, 1981a)). Moreover, it should be recognized that indices of the sort being discussed ignore potentially very important, but not measured, worker characteristics.

There have been a number of recent studies which have attempted to isolate "as well as is possible with existing data" the effect of trade unionism on the productivity of otherwise comparable workers utilizing the same amount of capital. The Brown and Medoff (1978) study, based on 1972 state-by-industry data for U.S. manufacturing, found that unionized enterprises had 24 percent higher productivity than otherwise comparable nonunion establishments within the same 2-digit SIC industries. Studies of particular manufacturing industries—wooden household furniture and cement—have also found a positive productivity differential. Allen reports sizable differences in construction, using a value output measure. His result is supported by the findings of Mandelstamm (1965), who avoided the potential problems of measuring output in dollar terms by having union and nonunion contractors cost out an identical project.

That unionism can be associated with lower as well as higher productivity has been documented for the U.S. underground bituminous coal sector, where unionized mines were estimated to be 25 percent more productive than comparable nonunion mines in 1965, but 20 percent less productive a decade later. One potential explanation for the observed change in union/nonunion productivity differentials is that the "quality" of industrial relations in that sector appeared to change over time.

Some effort has been devoted to explaining the routes underlying the apparent union impact on productivity. One relevant finding is that roughly 25 percent of the union/nonunion productivity differential in the manufacturing sector can be explained by the union/nonunion differential in quit rates. Other evidence suggests that a significant piece of the union productivity effect can be explained by the union/nonunion differential in the quality of management practices.

The association of unionism and profitability has been examined only recently, in part because, like labor quality and capital, profits are an extremely difficult variable to measure. What the available evidence does suggest is that while the gross profit margin (profit as a percentage of the value of output) is no different in unionized firms than in similar nonunion firms, the rate of return on capital is lower in unionized settings. Thus, it appears that productivity under unionism is not sufficiently greater than productivity in nonunion settings to offset the higher compensation plus the higher capital intensity, which would be necessary if profits per unit of capital were to be left unaffected.

II. Conceptual Explanations of the Estimated Differences

Consider the union/nonunion differences in economic outcomes presented in Table 1. How can each finding be explained? Which conceptualization of markets and unions is most consistent with the observed differences? How can alternative theoretical perspectives be analyzed empirically?

In this section we examine the arguments underlying the three potential explanations of union/nonunion differences set out at the beginning of the paper: (1) the "preunion characteristics" explanation under which union differences are "pure illusion," explicable by the unique characteristics of organized workers or firms; (2) the "price-theoretic" explanation, under which unions increase the relative compensation of their members through their monopoly power, eliciting in turn certain price-theoretic responses which explain all other differences; (3) the "institutional response" explanation, under which unions have, along with their price-theoretic effects, important nonwage effects.

THE PREUNION-CHARACTERISTICS EXPLANATION

In many discussions of estimated associations between unionization and other variables, we have heard that observed union/nonunion differences only reflect the preunion characteristics of workers or firms. As the column headed "Potential Explanation" in Table 2 indicates, the preunion characteristics under discussion are workforce quality, the preference structures of workers, firm quality, and the production functions of firms. As the table's second column portrays, these preunion characteristics have been offered as explanations of virtually every union/nonunion difference shown in Table 1. While not a necessary condition for the view, those who offer the preunion characteristics explanation of union/nonunion differences generally assume that there are no excess

TABLE 2

Theoretical Explanations of Observed Union/Nonunion Differences

Potential Explanation	Offered, for Example, to Explain Observed or Hypothesized Differences in:
Preunion Characteristics	
Quality of workforce	Wages rates; fringes; wage dispersion; quit rates; productivity.
Workers' tastes	Fringes; cyclical responsiveness of wage rates; role of seniority in promotions and terminations and other rules; quit rates; temporary layoffs; physical working conditions; job satisfaction.
Quality of firms	Wage rates; fringes; quit rates; certain rules; management practices; management flexibility; productivity; profitability.
Firms' technologies	Physical working conditions; productivity.
Price-Theoretic Responses	
Substitution between workers of different quality	Cross-market union compensation differentials; productivity; profitability.
Substitution between capital (or other non-labor inputs) and labor	Cross-market union compensation differentials; productivity; profitability.
Substitution between compensation and non-compensation quality of jobs	Wage rates; fringes; cyclical responsiveness of wage rates; temporary layoffs; rules; physical working conditions.
Postunion sorting	Postunion quality of workforce; postunion workers' tastes (and, thus, the differences listed above under preunion quality of workforce and preunion workers' tastes).
Survival of firms	Postunion quality of firms; postunion firms' technologies (and, thus, the differences listed above under preunion quality of firms and preunion firms' technologies).
Institutional Responses	
New means for preference revelation and aggregation	Fringes; wage dispersion; cyclical responsiveness of wage rates; quit rates; role of seniority in promotions and terminations and other rules; temporary layoffs; physical working conditions; job satisfaction; management practices; productivity; profitability.
More channels for complaints, suggestions, and other relevant information	Quits; job satisfaction; productivity; profitability.
Increased pressure for cost-minimizing behavior	Productivity; profitability.

profits or quasi-rents in the economy and, hence, that systematic differences in wages or other cost-affecting factors among competing establishments in the same product market cannot exist. If they did, the enterprise with higher (lower) costs would be driven out of business (dominate the market). Since observed differences cannot reflect cost differences, they must be offset by counterbalancing forces in the form of differences in (observed or unobserved) worker or enterprise characteristics. Under this view, the commonly observed union wage advantage would be attributed to unobserved aspects of labor or firm quality or unobserved differences in work conditions, which require compensating differentials of the classic type; if union workers are paid more, then their pay "advantage" solely reflects compensation for more human capital or less desirable nonwage dimensions of the job.

The grouping of several union/nonunion differences in Column 2 in Table 2 reveals the following logical problem with using the preunion characteristics argument to explain the entire set: in several instances the analysis leads to contradictory statements about the direction of the differences prior to unionization. For example, one way of explaining lower quit rates at unionized firms is to posit that union workers quit less than nonunion workers at given wages because they are not as potentially productive in the outside market as otherwise comparable nonunion employees. However, this runs counter to the preunion characteristics explanation of higher union wages and productivity, that unionized workers are innately better. Similarly, if, with wages fixed, unionized workers quit less, a logical deduction might be that, for whatever reason, unions happen to be located at better plants. However, this runs counter to the compensating differential explanation of the union/nonunion wage differential, that unionized workplaces are worse than those that are nonunion. Because preunion characteristics arguments are usually invoked to explain observed differences in outcomes one at a time, these logical problems have not received adequate consideration among adherents of the preunion characteristics view of the set of observed union/nonunion differences.

The preunion characteristics analysis runs into a second logical problem with respect to the mechanism by which unionized workers or firms can be expected to have any particular set of preunion characteristics. Put most strongly, if unions have *no* real effects on economic variables, there is no reason to expect them to locate or survive among workers or firms with any given characteristic. This suggests that, by itself, an explanation of *all* observed union/non-union differences in terms of differences in preunion character-istics of workers or firms is exceedingly tenuous; it relies on *post hoc ergo propter hoc* arguments about the locus of unionism. It could be that unions happen to organize high-wage workers or firms, low-quit employees, high-productivity firms, workplaces with bad conditions, and so on, without having any real economic ef-fects. However, there is, as far as we know, no mechanism that would produce such a locus of organization under the null hy-pothesis that unions have no real effect on any of the specified variables.

Finally, there are two questions which must be asked of those who hold the preunion characteristics view of *all* observed union/nonunion differences: "If all union effects are illusory, why do workers join unions?" and "Why do employers oppose them (in many cases with vigor)?"

THE PRICE-THEORETIC (MONOPOLY FACE) EXPLANATION

In the monopoly model of unionism, unions are assumed to raise wages above competitive levels in the organized sector. This creates higher costs of production in organized firms. How can these firms survive?

One possible answer to this question is that unions organize the entire relevant product market so that unionized firms face no nonunion competition. If production costs are higher for all estab-lishments in a sector, the sector's output and employment will be lower than in the absence of unionism, but the sector will survive.

Another possible explanation is based on the assertions that product markets are not perfectly competitive and/or that firms in a given industry have different cost structures (for reasons un-associated with unionism), which permit companies to make excess profits and/or quasi-rents. In this world, even if labor costs per effective labor unit rose as a result of unionism, firms could remain in business. As long as the increased unit labor costs came at the expense of excess profits and/or quasi-rents, but not at the expense of normal profits, the enterprises would not go out of business.

Thus, this view stresses the idea that unions are likely to survive where we find limited entry possibilities for firms, where entry takes time, and/or where some enterprises have cost advantages over their competitors.[2]

The price-theoretic arguments just given imply that unions are likely to be located where their gains induce small price-theoretic responses in the form of either factor or product market substitution; that is, where the demand elasticity for labor is relatively low. It is likely, in turn, that the comparisons of union/nonunion differences overstate, to some extent at least, the potential impact of unionism on currently unorganized labor, inasmuch as the set of price-theoretic responses relevant to today's unorganized are likely to be larger than the responses relevant to those who became unionized in the past.

While the monopoly model of unionism sees union/nonunion differences which are explicable in price-theoretic terms as real, there is one variant of the model under which the differences border on being labelled "illusory." This variant relies heavily on the "postunion sorting" of workers with different innate abilities and tastes. It grants the possibility that unions can cause wages to rise, but then adds that these increases will be met by essentially costless offsetting responses in labor quality or work conditions. For the labor-quality response to accomplish the offset, the elasticity of substitution between different groups of workers must be infinite over the period of concern. If so, an initial union wage effect, defined in terms of an average labor unit working at a workplace with average noncompensation characteristics, will lead firms to substitute higher quality for lower quality labor until the entire initial wage effect is eliminated, and thus will bring about a sorting of workers in terms of their quality. For the work-conditions response to effect the offset, the firm must be able costlessly to let workplace quality deteriorate. If so, the firm would let work conditions worsen until the entire wage advantage has been "paid for" by poorer nonwage job characteristics. In this world, when the dust settles, the only real observed differences between union and otherwise comparable nonunion firms will be a difference in

---

[2] A related possibility is that unions organize enough new firms in a competitive industry to offset the demise of existing firms whose costs were raised by unionism. In this scenario, the relevant capital market condition is that firms earn a normal *expected* rate of return over their lifetimes.

the uncorrected (for differences in labor quality and the quality of work conditions) wage differential, a difference in workforce quality, a difference in the quality of work conditions, and a difference in any ratio defined in terms of non-quality-corrected labor units.[3]

Analogous responses by employers can also turn apparent union nonwage effects into a mere sorting of workers by tastes. Consider, for example, what might happen if unions were to raise fringes relative to wages in an establishment. Workers with strong preferences for fringes, who might be expected to seek those fringes in their current firms, would seek employment in the union sector. Unionized firms would attract fringe lovers, and would devote a larger share of each compensation dollar to fringe benefits than would other firms, even though the aggregate expenditures on fringes might be unchanged in the economy.

In short, in this framework unions can have real immediate effects, but these effects are posited to erode away through essentially costless adjustments so that any differences observed over a longer run might properly be called "illusory."

THE INSTITUTIONAL-RESPONSE EXPLANATION

Economists in the industrial relations tradition view the observed union/nonunion differences from yet another perspective: in terms of "institutional responses" to union-induced changes.

The institutional-response explanation differs from those considered earlier in that it is based on the premise that, for a variety of reasons, the economy differs from the Pareto optimal world in which only standard price-theoretic responses are possible. Several reasons are often cited for such divergence between the real world and the economic model. First, while many firms (individuals) seek to maximize profits (utility), they do not achieve the optimum in the relevant period. Second, there are important public goods and externalities which are found, among other places, where people work. Third, there are important barriers to exit and entry in external and internal labor markets and other markets of less immediate concern. Fourth, there is imperfect information in internal and external labor markets and in other markets as

---

[3] We ignore the case of an infinite elasticity of substitution between labor and other factors, since this would imply that we would not observe unionized workforces to compare with those which are nonunion.

well. Fifth, firms making excess profits and quasi-rents are found in many industries. Sixth, some firms (individuals) may be satisfied with less than an optimum, as emphasized by Simon (1955) in his model of "satisficing" behavior. In various related guises this view of the world has been the basis of a number of views about the labor exchange, such as: the internal labor market view (Doeringer and Piore (1971)), the X-efficiency view (Leibenstein (1966)), the idiosyncratic exchange view (Williamson, Wachter, and Harris (1975)), and the collective voice/institutional response view. What is most important about these views is that they suggest that understanding the effects of trade unions requires analyses of, among other things, the internal operation of firms, relevant organizational issues, the provision of various public goods at workplaces, and the quality and quantity of information flows.

The belief that labor in internal and external labor markets is, at least to some extent, immobile is very important to the institutional response view. In a world where there is not perfect exit and entry in labor markets and workers cannot express fully their preferences by "voting with their feet," there are opportunities for unions to influence economic behavior through means not generally recognized in standard price-theoretic analyses and possibly to increase efficiency and social welfare as well.

In light of the discussion of labor immobility, it should be noted that a union can increase both the rate of compensation and the number of its members if it organizes firms with monopsony power. While monopsony is usually presented as an extremely rare event in the labor economic texts—"Today we have very few one company towns"—the tendency for workers to be tied to the same firm for many years (for whatever reasons) is consistent with the belief that elements of monopsony are omnipresent. The point is that as long as firms face upward sloping labor supply curves, which is quite likely given the costs to employees of switching jobs (embodied in unvested pensions, rights accruing with seniority, etc.) and to employers of finding and training new employees, the firm can act like a monopsonist (equating marginal revenue product with the marginal, as opposed to the average, cost of labor). This creates a situation in which unionism can increase employment and social welfare by raising wages (see Viscusi (1980)).

THE PRICE-THEORETIC/INSTITUTIONAL DEBATE
OVER WHAT IS REAL

Most researchers try to control for the potential price-theoretic routes of union impact in estimating union/nonunion differences in nonwage variables. Hence, as indicated by the notes to Table 1, many of the union/nonunion differences under discussion cannot be explained in terms of measurable price-theoretic variables. For instance, the substantial union/nonunion differential in quit probabilities exists even when individuals' wages and fringes are held constant. Or to choose another example, the union/nonunion productivity differentials discussed above were estimated with models which controlled for labor quality and capital intensity.

Analysts in the industrial relations tradition interpret the existence of significant union effects, above and beyond measured price-theoretic routes, as real—reflecting the nature of the economy's basic institutions. These individuals believe that the key task for research on trade unions involves gaining a better understanding of the origins, operations, and interactions of the institutions, since the non-price-theoretic actions of firms and unions matter greatly in determining economic performance.

Devotees of the standard price-theoretic model perceive the union/nonunion differences quite differently; they see these differences as illusory—the result of the poor quality of the empirical experiments which can be conducted. In their eyes, nonwage union/nonunion differences are only observed because the relevant price-theoretic routes have not been captured.

In sum, there is a clear and very important split among those who believe that unions have some important real impacts: one group says that only the wage matters; the other says that while the wage matters, it most certainly is not all that matters.

FROM THE CONCEPTUAL TO THE ECONOMETRIC

Each of the conceptual views just discussed has implications for how one would approach observed union/nonunion differences econometrically. The preunion characteristics perspective would push us toward searching for observed or unobserved differences which existed between individuals or firms before they were unionized. Alternatively, the price-theoretic view would lead us toward searching for important price-theoretic stimuli or responses which had not been captured by our models or with our data and which could be causing the estimated union/nonunion differences. Finally, the institutional response framework would encourage us to seek important institutional factors with the potential to explain estimated union impacts not explicable in terms of measurable price-theoretic variables. This section provides a general nontechnical summary of the potential econometric issues which arise in empirical work on unions and the ways the issues are approached.

At the outset, it is important to recognize that the econometric problems of concern occur because the observed union/nonunion differences do not come from the "ideal" experiment needed to estimate the effects of unions (at this point in time) on economic outcomes. This experiment would involve unionizing a randomly chosen nonunion individual or firm, while holding all else of relevance in the world fixed, and observing the resultant changes.

Unfortunately, most of the statistical "experiments" we conduct depart from the ideal for two reasons. First, we cannot hold all the relevant factors perfectly fixed when we compare unionized individuals or firms to themselves when they are nonunion. Second, it is unlikely that individuals or firms with similar measured characteristics became unionized on a random basis.

POTENTIAL ECONOMETRIC EXPLANATIONS AND ASSESSMENTS OF THEIR VALIDITY

> The real reason you have obtained those union/nonunion differences is that you have omitted (mismeasured, not observed) a key variable which is correlated with unionization, and that variable is . . . .

> But you have the wrong causality. It is not that unionism causes . . .; it is that . . . causes unionism.

> It seems obvious that your results are due to selectivity; there is an unobserved factor out there which affects whether or not workers are unionized and the market outcome of concern.

> —Frequently heard assertions at
> seminars throughout the country.

There are three key econometric problems that can arise in doing empirical work on the impact of unionism (or any factor) on economic outcomes: omitted, mismeasured, or unobserved variable bias; simultaneous equations bias; and sample selection bias. Each of these potential reasons why estimated union/nonunion differences might be spurious arises because of the aforementioned lack of an ideal experiment.

These potential problems have been appealed to in attempts to explain the observed union/nonunion differentials depicted in Table 1. Those whose priors come from the preunion characteristics view have used the three potential forms of bias to argue that the observed differentials in Table 1 are illusions. Those whose priors are based on the price-theoretic view have used the biases to offer econometric explanations of union/nonunion differentials observed *after* measurable price-theoretic effects have been netted out. In contrast, those in the institutional response camp tend to believe that the observed relationships between unionism and other variables are real and merit further investigation concerning their existence and locus across specified institutional settings.

There are various methods for dealing with each of the potential bias problems which arise in analyses of cross-sectional data. Heuristically, these methods can be divided into three broad categories: (1) Approaches which probe the cross-sectional results through various forms of "sensitivity" analysis designed to see how the results might be "driven" by the poor quality of the relevant experiment. In this category we include such techniques as: expanding the list of controls, using the omitted variable bias formula, imposing coefficients on mismeasured variables, and using the variance/covariance matrix of coefficients to examine the sensitivity of results to alleged experimental problems. Given outside information on, for example, the relationship between the omitted variable and included variables or on the degree of measurement error in the variables of concern or on the likely magnitude of selected coefficients, estimates can be made of the likely impact of omitted, mismeasured, or unobserved variables. By making particularly strong assumptions or picking particularly large (or small) values of the relevant correlation coefficients, one can "stack the deck" against the estimated union effect and thus get a good notion of its strength. (2) Techniques which seek to treat the alleged experimental problem through complex systems of equations in which both the relevant variables and/or the exact functional forms and distributions for the equations are used to identify the "true" union impact. Such techniques can be used to deal with unobserved or mismeasured variables, but are most commonly used to treat the simultaneous equations and sample selection problems. The methodology is to postulate a "true" model which enables one to deal with the alleged experimental problem and to solve the resultant equations to obtain the coefficient of concern. (3) Approaches which seek to obtain new and better quality data designed specifically to deal with particular experimental problems, especially measurement error and omitted variables.

A very different approach to the three types of problems described is to apply a different experimental design to the problem of estimating union effects by examining longitudinal (before/after) rather than cross-sectional data. Longitudinal information provides what is perhaps the most direct way of dealing with the essential cross-sectional data problem—that we are comparing *different* people or firms rather than conducting the ideal experiment described earlier. If one obtains longitudinal data in which omitted, mismeasured, or unobserved variables are constant over time, one can obtain estimates of union effects purged of biases due to these problems. Similarly, by enabling us to compare outcome variables before and after unionization, such data provide the proper recursive structure for dealing with both the "union causes" versus "causes unionism" question and the problem of cross-sectional selectivity bias.

It is important to recognize, however, that longitudinal studies are themselves subject to potential experimental problems not unlike those which can arise in research based on cross-sectional data. One potential difficulty is that when persons change jobs, other relevant variables are also likely to change, such as occupation or industry or tasks at work, which may be omitted, mismeasured, or unobserved in the analysis. Another potential problem is that classical measurement error bias may become more severe because the systematic parts of variables are differenced away. Third, since only a limited number of persons are likely to change union status in a given period of time, longitudinal studies may be prone to a sample selection problem not unlike that in cross-sectional studies.

Longitudinal calculations reveal the effects of changing union status on the position of workers who change: if those persons differ in some fundamental way from other workers, the results may not generalize to the entire population. Whether the selectivity of union and nonunion changers is an important phenomenon and, if so, in what way it affects results are unclear a priori.[4]

Recognizing the problems of longitudinal analyses does not, of course, vitiate the fact that before/after data provide a distinct and real set of potential experiments which can go a long way toward dealing with the potential difficulties with cross-sectional work discussed above. By following the same individual or firm over time as he/she or it changes status from nonunion to union or vice verse, one is able to control in a more natural way for all missing or unobserved variables which do not change over time. The longitudinal data are an invaluable complementary form of information to the more widely used cross-sectional data.

III. Illusion or Reality? Econometric Probes

Much recent work on unionism has used the econometric techniques alluded to earlier to probe the union/nonunion differentials summarized in Table 1. What have been the results of these efforts to obtain better estimates of the "true" union effect on economic outcomes? To what extent are the Table 1 differences "moved" by sensitivity probes which use new data or information to evaluate the effect of omitted, mismeasured, or unobserved variables in a specified study? How sensitive are the empirical results to probes which rely on extensive cross-sectional modeling in which unionization is taken as endogenous, for reasons of either

---

[4] Several arguments can be advanced regarding the possible problems involved in inferring union effects for the population from what happens to a sample of changers. To see the first, consider wages. To the extent that voluntary job changing is viewed as an investment in mobility, there is likely to be a tendency for both union and nonunion job changers to experience the same absolute wage gains, as both would change only if they could earn the appropriate return. This would bias comparisons of the differences in the wage growth of union-to-nonunion and nonunion-to-union changes toward zero. One would most likely get better estimates by looking solely at changers who left their firm involuntarily for reasons unrelated to their individual actions (e.g., those whose firms went out of business). Another point is that observed wage changes of the union-status changers depend on where the changers fell in the relevant wage distribution. If union or nonunion changers came disproportionately from either end of the distribution of concern, the estimated wage changes would not reflect the overall mean differential.

simultaneity or selectivity? What are the results of panel or longitudinal studies designed to deal with the potential "experimental"
problems with cross-sectional studies? In short, what does the evidence say about possible ways of answering, and about possible
answers to, the frequently heard seminar assertions regarding the
potential problems with the cross-sectional analyses of the impact
of collective bargaining?

In this section we review the relevant econometric studies
which address these important questions. Our review yields the
following two key conclusions. First, the econometric probes do
not invalidate the findings summarized in Table 1 by attributing
all or the vast bulk of observed differences to the inadequacies of
the experimental comparisons. Studies which probe the sensitivity
of cross-sectional findings to omitted, mismeasured, or unobserved
variables show that while these experimental problems appear to
bias union coefficients somewhat, they are far from the sole explanation of the ordinary least squares regression results. Studies
which use longitudinal data to deal with the problems of unobserved factors, simultaneity, or sample selectivity tend to yield
lower estimates of union effects than do OLS studies using cross-
sectional information, but they also fail to eliminate the bulk of
estimated impacts. Studies which seek additional data regarding
the potential causality of union effects through surveys of firms
also tend to find real union impacts on behavior.

Second, studies which use systems of equations with cross-
sectional data to "correct for" potential simultaneous equations
and sample selection bias provide very little insight into whether
the Table 1 union/nonunion differences are real or illusory. The
models employed rely on "restrictions" or "exclusions" which are
far from convincing. Moreover, the results show great instability
in the face of seemingly small changes in the model or the sample
analyzed. In some cases these techniques yield union effects much
below those obtained with OLS; in others they yield effects much
above those from OLS; in yet others the systems of equations
give about the same results as does OLS. In a surprisingly large
number of cases, these techniques yield results so implausible on
a priori grounds as to be dismissed out of hand. While this instability and implausibility does not demonstrate that the OLS union/
nonunion differences are unbiased, it does indicate that the system

of equations methodology does not offer a reliable and useful way of improving on these estimates.

We consider next the evidence regarding these two conclusions. We review first the results of efforts to probe cross-sectional findings with sensitivity analysis, better data designed to deal with omitted variables, and systems techniques. Then we review the growing body of evidence which uses longitudinal experiments to check on the cross-sectional findings.

PROBING THE CROSS-SECTIONAL EVIDENCE

Table 3 summarizes some recent efforts to assess the validity of cross-sectional findings using one or more of the methods discussed in the preceding section. For each study the table shows: the type of bias being focused on, the econometric technique employed, the variable analyzed, the data used, the key empirical results, and the appropriate references. While our listing is undoubtedly incomplete, we believe it is broadly representative of the pattern of results in extant work. Because of the initial concentration of quantitative analyses on wages, the table is top heavy with the results of econometric probes into the union wage effect.

The first and undoubtedly the most widely used technique for dealing with data inadequacies is to test the sensitivity of results to the inclusion of detailed industry or occupation controls in the data set under study. Addition of such controls in some sense leads to finer experiments by focusing on union effects within more detailed groupings. Alternatively, to the extent that missing or mismeasured variables differ across the relevant sectors, inclusion of a large number of variables can be justified by pointing out that they help control for those variables. Even when one might argue that exclusion of detailed controls is theoretically "correct," it is useful to know whether these variables "matter." In many studies attempts are made to obtain information on the posited missing variables at an industry level and to add those variables in place of the dummy controls. This provides a means of evaluating what industry dummies in fact stand for, but offers a weaker test of the extent to which results stand up to addition of numerous covariance controls.

In most cases in which additional controls are added to analyses, either by deriving and using industry-level information or

TABLE 3

Evidence of Econometric Probes into Union/Nonunion Differences using Cross-Sectional Data[a]

Issue, Technique	Variable, Data Set, Sample	Result	Reference
Omitted, Mismeasured, or Unobserved Variable Bias			
Enter additional dummy variable(s), or other variables to obtain finer comparisons	*Wages; quits; layoffs; dispersion; productivity; etc.*	Addition of various dummies for 2- and where possible 3-digit Census or SIC industry or for occupation can reduce but not eliminate estimated union/nonunion differential; similar results from	Diverse studies.
	Diverse	adding average characteristics	
	Diverse	using industry figures and from adding variables capturing workplace characteristics.	
Set coefficient on mismeasured variable at predetermined level.	*Productivity* Census of Manufactures; CPS	Union coefficient is reduced substantially by forcing estimated coefficient of capital/labor variable to equal an upper bound of capital's share of value added in Census of Manufactures	Brown & Medoff (1978).
	All workers in manufacturing industries	data set, but still implies that unionized establishments are moderately more productive (by a lower bound of 6%).	
Use omitted variable formula to discern likely bias	*Quits* CPS; PSID; NLS Older Men; NLS Young Men;	Correcting for omitted fringe benefits variable and mis-measured alternate earnings variable can most likely reduce large union coefficient	Freeman (1980b).
	All Workers	by no more than $\frac{1}{4}$.	

TABLE 3—Continued.

Issue, Technique	Variable, Data Set, Sample	Result	Reference
	Productivity Cement company data Production workers	Capturing true labor quality is unlikely to greatly reduce the union productivity effect in cement.	Clark (1980a, 1980b).
Collect new data	*Productivity* Cement company data Underground bituminous coal mine data Production workers	Physical output data for cement plants and coal mines obtained to deal with problems of distinguishing output variation from price variation indicate that the fact that the earlier union productivity studies used a value measure cannot explain the estimated positive union effect; in addition, these data point to the importance of the quality of labor-management relations as a mediating factor in the union-productivity relationship.	Clark (1980a, 1980b), Connerton, Freeman, & Medoff (1979).
	Role of Seniority per se Surveys of companies All workers	Union/nonunion differences in the relationships between seniority and both terminations and promotions cannot be explained in terms of an unobserved union/nonunion differential in the relationship between seniority and contribution to firm.	Medoff & Abraham (1980b, 1981a).

TABLE 3—Continued.

Issue, Technique	Variable, Data Set, Sample	Result	Reference
Construct unobserved variable model	*Fringes* EEC Production workers	Magnitude of union coefficient is sensitive to precise model for unobserved establishment characteristics, but qualitative conclusion that unions are associated with higher fringe benefits is not.	Freeman (1981).
Simultaneous Equations Bias			
Replace a union variable with a predicted union variable	*Wages* E&E; Census All workers	Union/nonunion wage differential declines for 49 manufacturing industries from 37% with OLS to 27% in a 2–SLS model.	Pencavel (1970).
	Wages E&E; Census All workers	Union/nonunion wage differential declines for 2-digit SIC manufacturing industries from 46% OLS to 19% or 4% in 2–SLS models and to −9% in a 3–SLS model.	Ashenfelter & Johnson (1972).
	Wages; quits E&E; Census Production workers	Both wage and quit differentials grow substantially (in absolute value) with data for 3-digit SIC manufacturing industries, when 2–SLS replaces OLS; the wage differential rises from 50% to 80%.	Kahn (1977).
	Wages SEO All workers	Wage differential reduced from 11% to 6% by fitting a system of equations in which the estimated union coefficient is unbiased by assumption.[b]	Schmidt & Strauss (1976). Olsen (1978). Schmidt (1978).

TABLE 3—*Continued.*

Issue, Technique	Variable, Data Set, Sample	Result	Reference
	Wages; quits NLS Young Men All workers	Wage differential rises with selectivity correction from 32% to 51%; differential in quit probability switches from significant negative (−.487) to near significant positive (.878).	Farber (1979).
	Wages NLS Young Men All workers	With selectivity adjustment, union differential rises from 22/38% to 28/58.9% for young and middle-aged black employees and from 25/13% to 37/46% for young and middle-aged white employees.	Leigh (1980b).
	Wages CPS detailed occupation data Hospital workers	Results vary with data set and model, with estimated differentials moving, in many cases quite substantially, in both directions (presented in Table 4).	Cain et al., (1980); McLaughlin (1980); Podgursky (1980).
	Wages PSID; Michigan Time Use Survey All workers	Differential increases from 19% to 24% with union made endogenous on work conditions.	Duncan & Stafford (1980)
Sample Selection Bias Add an inverse Mills ratio term to outcome equation or estimate a system which explicitly recognizes correlation between selection and outcome equation	*Wages* NLS Older Men All workers	Coefficients in separate union and nonunion equations are only moderately affected by addition of inverse Mills ratio; estimated union/nonunion differential rises moderately.	Duncan & Leigh (1980).
	Wages SEO Operatives	Sizable wage differential declines slightly (from 17% to 16%) with selectivity correction.	Lee (1978).

TABLE 3—*Continued.*

Issue, Technique	Variable, Data Set, Sample	Result	Reference
	Wages PSID All workers	Estimated union wage differential rises significantly to 40% from its OLS value of 13% in one calculation and modestly in another (from 6% to 9%).	Neumann (1977).
	Wages CPS detailed occupation data Hospital workers	Results vary with data set and model with estimated differentials moving, in many cases quite substantially, in both directions to large positive or large (in absolute value) negative (see Table 5 for specific results).	Cain et al., (1980); McLaughlin (1980); Podgursky (1980).
	Wages CPS detailed occupation data Health care employees	Sizable increases in wage differential for nurses aides (to 89%); moderate increases for health aides and technical workers; decline to –6% for nurses.	Feldman, Lee, and Hoffbeck (1980).
	Wages Survey of Hospital Directors of Nursing Nurses	Union coefficient in wage equation goes from insignificant positive (OLS) to insignificant negative (2–SLS).	Sloan & Elnicki (1979).
	Turnover Hospital survey data Health care workers	Percentage reduction in turnover associated with unionism is large (50%) even when 2–SLS is used to correct for selectivity.	Becker (1978).

[a]The following abbreviations are used throughout this table and the remainder of this chapter for data sources: CPS represents the Current Population Survey, E&E represents *Employment and Earnings*, EEC represents the Expenditure for Employee Compensation survey, NLS represents the National Longitudinal Survey, PSID represents the Panel Study of Income Dynamics survey, and SEO represents the Survey of Economic Opportunity, and for statistical techniques: OLS represents ordinary least squares, 2–SLS represents two-stage least squares, and 3–SLS represents three-stage least squares.

[b]This result is reported in the Schmidt response to Olsen's piece, which pointed out a flaw in the original Schmidt & Strauss model.

by relying on of numerous industry or occupation dummy variables, the greater refinement of the comparison set reduces the
estimated impact of unionism. But this occurs only up to the point
of, say, major or 2-digit industry or occupation controls. Additional controls appear to have only a modest effect on the estimates. Consider, for example, the effect of adding industry controls
to the equations estimating the effect of unionism on the usual
hourly pay of private, male wage and salary workers using 1976
May CPS data. With a standard log-linear hourly earnings functional form which includes race, years of education, age minus
years of education minus six and its square, three region dummies, and a blue-collar dummy variable, the effect of adding industry controls on the estimated coefficient of the union membership dummy (member $= 1$) is shown below.

Industry Controls	Estimated Union Member Coefficient in May 1976 CPS (Standard Error)
None	.29
	(.01)
Major Census (20)	.21
	(.01)
2-digit Census (45)	.19
	(.01)
3-digit Census (200)	.18
	(.01)

As is common in such sensitivity probes, the reductions (in absolute value) in union coefficients approach zero very quickly as the
number of industry dummies grows, and the estimated union/
nonunion difference of concern does not vanish.

Addition of other variables designed to reflect union/nonunion comparisons by holding fixed workplace conditions likely to
cause compensating differentials yields similar results: union/
nonunion wage differentials diminish but do not disappear. The
most sizable reduction, obtained by Duncan and Stafford (1980),
showed that addition of variables relating to the nature and intensity of work to a ln (wage) equation reduced a union coefficient estimate of .29 to .19. Other studies by Brown (1980)
and Leigh (1981), however, show no such relation between
union/nonunion differentials and characteristics of workplaces.

There have been a limited number of studies which have sought to evaluate the effect of measurement error or omitted variables on estimated union/nonunion differentials. In their study of productivity, Brown and Medoff (1978) probed the extent to which the coefficient on unionism could be explained by classical measurement error in the capital/labor ratio by exploiting the fact that with the Cobb-Douglas production function, under profit maximization, the coefficient of this ratio should equal capital's share of value added. Because the OLS estimate of the coefficient was below capital's share and because unionization and capital/labor ratio are positively correlated, they found that mismeasurement of the capital intensity variable may have substantially biased upward the estimated impact of unionism on productivity. However, even when the coefficient of the capital/labor variable was forced to equal an upper-bound estimate of capital's share, there remained a nonnegligible positive union productivity effect. In a study of quits, Freeman (1980a, 1980b) used the omitted variable bias formula to assess the sensitivity of the apparent union effect on quits to the omission of fringe benefits from the analysis and to measurement error in alternative wages. The formula was applied using information from other data sets in conjunction with strong assumptions designed to yield lower-bound estimates of the union effect. The lower-bound estimates showed a significant and large effect about half as large as the initial OLS impact. In another study, dealing with omitted variables, Clark (1980a, 1980b) examined the likely effect of omitted labor quality on the union/ nonunion productivity differential. Using a formula describing how labor quality enters the production process, and exogenous information on possible quality changes during the period since his sample of cement plants had gone from nonunion to union, he concluded that only a small piece of the differential he had originally estimated could be explained by this uncaptured workforce dimension.

There have been some recent efforts to generate new data sets to deal with omitted or mismeasured variable problems. To determine whether union effects on value added or value of shipments might be due to union effects on prices rather than physical units of output, Connerton, Freeman, and Medoff gathered data on tons of coal, while Clark gathered data on tons of cement. The coal study found sizable positive union productivity effects when industrial relations in the sector were good but negative effects in years of poor industrial relations. The cement study found positive union effects on physical output per worker in that industry. To determine whether union/nonunion differentials in the extent to which seniority reduces the probability of termination and increases the chance of promotion could be explained by an unobserved union/nonunion differential in the relationships between company service and current contribution, Medoff and Abraham (1981b) asked a large sample of companies to compare the termination and promotion probabilities of senior and junior employees whose performance was equal. Based on the responses to this survey, it was concluded that the greater importance attached to seniority per se under unionism could not be explained in terms of an uncaptured differential in the way performance and seniority were related.

Finally, the recently developed "unobservables" models (see Chamberlain (1977)) were used by Freeman (1981) to assess the possibility that part of the estimated union impact on fringes was due to an omitted firm characteristic. The analysis showed that the extent to which the OLS differential could be attributed to unobserved firm differences depended greatly on the way the model was constructed. When it was assumed that there was no within-firm spillover from blue-collar unionization to white-collar fringes, the original fringe differential was reduced substantially by the firm-effects correction. However, when a within-firm spillover was allowed, which seems to be the more reasonable assumption, the original differential was not lowered by the correction. Hence, any conclusion concerning the impact of unobserved firm effects on the union/nonunion fringe differential depends crucially on one's a priori logic concerning the "true" unobservable model to be used.

SIMULTANEOUS EQUATIONS

Several analysts have sought to explore the causality of observed union effects using simultaneous equations models in which unionism is endogenous, that is, determined by the equations in the system. In the outcome equation(s) the actual union variable is replaced by a predicted variable. Identification of the system is obtained either by exclusion of one (or more) variables from the outcome equation, but not from the unionism equation, or on the basis of the functional forms and distributions assumed for the relevant equations.

The first analyses using the simultaneous equations technique focused on industry aggregates. Both Ashenfelter and Johnson (1972) and Pencavel (1970) showed that, depending on the particular model employed, a large positive OLS union/nonunion wage differential in U.S. manufacturing was substantially reduced; Ashenfelter and Johnson estimated a differential of 46 percent with a single equation (OLS) model, a differential of 19 percent with one two-stage model, a differential of 4 percent with another two-stage model, and a differential of −8 percent with a three-stage model. The more recent work on manufacturing by Kahn (1977), who used 3-digit SIC data, whereas the previous researchers used 2-digit data, but followed the same general procedure, generated quite different results: substantial *increases* (in absolute value) in both the union wage and quit effects upon correcting for the endogeneity of unionism. Kahn's estimated wage differential rose from 50 to 80 percent when he changed his technique from OLS to two-stage least squares and his estimated quit effect also rose noticeably. Hence, seemingly small changes in the models employed and in the degree of data aggregation have yielded very different results with systems designed to correct for potential simultaneous equations bias in analyses of aggregate cross-sectional data.

A widely divergent pattern of results has also been obtained when roughly similar simultaneous equations models have been estimated with similar bodies of individual-level data. Schmidt (1978) estimated a model with a union member status equation and a wage equation and reported a decline in the effect of unionism from 10 percent to 4 percent with SEO data (his two-equation model was not, however, needed to obtain unbiased estimates, since it assumed away the correlation that gives rise to the bias problem). On the other hand, Duncan and Stafford (1980) showed an increase in the estimated coefficient of unionism when unionism was made endogenous in their model which focused on work conditions, as did Leigh (1980a). Applying a simultaneous equations model with both a wage and a quit equation to the young men NLS data, Farber (1979) obtained an increase in the union wage effect while at the same time switching the sign on the standard quit effect from negative to positive, the opposite of Kahn's quit result. Farber found his results somewhat puzzling. Overall, in the regressions cited in Table 3 (including those from Cain et al. presented in detail in Table 4), there is an alarming amount and pattern of instability when actual unionism is replaced by predicted unionism; in somewhat more than half the cases, the estimated union coefficient rises, counter to expectation, often to rather large values, while in many cases in which the coefficient declines it becomes negative.

While most authors have not discussed the sensitivity of their findings to minor changes in specification, the statements of those who have indicated that the instability discussed above is not a purely cross-researcher phenomenon, since a given individual working with a given data set appears likely to find that slight changes in specification lead to large changes in results. For example, Duncan and Stafford (1980, p. 367) wrote that "the estimated union coefficient [is] sensitive to the exogenous variables omitted from the [wage] equation." Similarly, Mitchell (1980, p. 204) stated: "In general simultaneous-equation estimates require assumptions concerning which variables are exogenous and which serve to identify particular equations. Experiments by this author suggest that changing assumptions can produce wide variations in results ranging from negative union wage effects to ridiculously large positive effects."

Perhaps the most far-reaching work on the stability of models which replace a union variable by a predicted value, in the context of a model in which unionism is taken as endogenous, has been done at the University of Wisconsin by Cain et al. (1980), McLaughlin (1980), and Podgursky (1980). Their findings for the wage differential, summarized in Table 4, show that the same simultaneous equations model, estimated with data for comparable employee groups, yields results which swing back and forth over a highly implausible range (from —84 percent to 95 percent).[5]

---

[5] Specifically, counting the number of cases in Tables 3 and 4 in which actual unionism was replaced by predicted unionism shows 8 instances in which union coefficients declined from OLS levels, 4 to negative values, and 12 in which the coefficient rose compared to OLS values, 5 of which reached levels in excess of 40 percent.

TABLE 4

Results of "Wisconsin" Regressions with CPS Data in which Unionism is Treated as a Predicted Endogenous Variable or in which there is a Sample Selection Term.

Reference, Sample	OLS Union Effect	Union Effect with Predicted Unionism	Union Effect with Inverse Mills Ratio
Cain et al. (1980)[b] Hospital employees		Percentage Wage Differential[a] (level of significance)	
Private, nonprofessional workers	6 (.10)	64 (.06)	31 (.05)
Private, registered nurses	−15 (>.10)	16 (>.10)	− 6 (>.10)
Government, nonprofessional workers	− 3 (.07)	95 (.06)	16 (>.10)
Private, technicians	−20 (.10)	31 (>.10)	4 (>.10)
Government, registered nurses	3 (>.10)	−24 (>.10)	1 (>.10)
Private, licensed practical nurses	16 (>.10)	13 (>.10)	28 (>.10)
Government, technicians	−10 (>.10)	−84 (>.10)	−72 (>.10)
Government, licensed practical nurses	20 (>.10)	55 (.07)	21 (>.10)
McLaughlin (1980)[c] Hospital employees		Percentage Wage Differential[a] (t-statistic)	
Private, nonprofessional workers	6 (1.74)	36 (1.69)	22 (1.30)
Private, registered nurses	3 (.66)	16 (.46)	6 (.22)
Government, nonprofessional workers	4 (1.41)	5 (.07)	− 22 (.51)
Government, registered nurses	0 (.00)	−57 (1.37)	−27 (.77)
Podgursky (1980)[d] Private-sector production workers	10 (3.0)	−72 (4.3)	−63 (4.0)

[a]These differentials give the estimated percentage amount by which the wages of union members exceed those of otherwise comparable nonunion employees. Although the data were transformed where necessary to yield differentials, the original t-statistic or level of significance (depending on what the author presented) is given.

[b]The data set used to derive these estimates is a pooled file of 1973–1976 May CPS micro-data. The dependent variable for each occupational group in the particular government/nongovernment sector was the real hourly wage rates of individual hospital workers. Regressors in the OLS Union Effect model included a zero-one union status

The Podgursky results, which show the union/nonunion wage differential swinging from a positive 10 percent with OLS to a most certainly absurd negative 72 percent using a two-stage least squares procedure, are particularly striking as they relate to one of the groups most frequently studied in the literature.

We conclude that the highly sensitive results obtained with both aggregate industry and individual-level data sets when unionism is "predicted" raise serious questions about the usefulness of the simultaneous equation methodology for analyses of what unions really do. The technique appears to be trying to squeeze out of the data more than the data contain; it does not, in our view, provide a reliable way of addressing the illusion/reality question.

SAMPLE SELECTION

The recently popular technique for dealing with potential sample selection bias—adding an inverse Mills ratio term to outcome regressions, which corrects for the potential bias under certain assumptions (see Heckman 1976)—has been used in a number of analyses of the union/nonunion wage differential. In the first such piece, Lee (1978), making assumptions about the functional form and distribution of the relevant equations to identify his wage equation, reduced slightly the OLS wage differential for operatives (from 17 to 16 percent) with data from the SEO. Leigh (1980b), fitting models very similar to those used by Lee, analyzed NLS data for both older and younger men. He found

---

dummy variable as well as a vector of personal characteristics, region of country, size of SMSA, year, and sub-occupation group. In the Union-Effect-with-Predicted-Unionism model, predicted union status (provided by a probit computation) replaced the zero-one union status variable. In the Union-Effect-with-Inverse-Mills-Ratio model, the hazard ratio was added as a regressor to the OLS Union Effect model. Interactions of the union status dummy variable with variables for race, year, and full time/part time status were included in each model. The significance level refers to the combined effect of the set of union and union-interaction variables.

[c]The data set used and the variables included in the models are essentially the same as in note b above, except that part-time workers were excluded. The only important difference in the specification is that interaction terms were not included as additional regressors in the McLaughlin regressions. In fact, the McLaughlin results are virtually identical to the Cain et al. specifications without the interaction terms.

[d]The data set used was the March 1971 CPS. The dependent variable in these regressions is the log of annual earnings of full-time, full-year, nonfarm, private-sector production workers. In addition to a zero-one union status dummy variable and a percent-of-industry unionized variable, regressors included a vector of personal characteristics, region of country, size of SMSA, industry, and industrial concentration.

that wage differentials were increased, rather than decreased, by the selectivity adjustment in both samples. In several cases they were increased by extremely large amounts; in three of six sets he presented, the selectivity-adjusted percentages were at least three times as large as the OLS estimates. Another very substantial increase in estimated wage differentials was obtained by Neumann (1977); with PSID data for 1974 his adjusted estimate was 40 percent while his OLS estimate was 13 percent. However, when Neumann used average data for 1968–1974, the difference was much smaller: 9 percent versus 6 percent. Overall, the results from adding sample selectivity "correction" terms to wage regressions appear to be as unstable and divergent as those obtained with simultaneous equations "corrections." Studies that differ only slightly in specification, data, or group covered show wide differences in the impact of the "corrections" on OLS results.[6]

Work focusing on the wage differential in a given sector, hospitals, also does not yield stable or seemingly plausible results. Becker (1978) and Sloan and Elnicki (1979) found that selectivity adjustments reduced estimated union coefficients, whereas the results in Table 4 from Cain et al. (1980) and McLaughlin (1980) for various groups in this sector show as many increases as decreases in the union coefficient upon addition of the inverse Mills ratio to regressions using the same survey data and model. In yet another study, Feldman, Lee, and Hoffman (1980) obtained increases in the union wage effect for several occupations in the health sector, but obtained decreases in the union wage effect for nurses when they corrected for selectivity.

Podgursky's (1980) work with the CPS files provides yet additional evidence which calls into question the usefulness of the inverse Mills ratio technique for analyses of union/nonunion differentials. In this work on private-sector production workers, an initial positive OLS differential of 10 percent (significant at the .01 level) becomes a highly dubious negative 63 percent (again significant at the .01 level) when an inverse Mills ratio term is added to a wage equation.

What is one to make of the aberrant results obtained with the

---

[6] Specifically, counting the number of cases in Tables 3 and 4 in which a selectivity correction term was introduced shows 10 instances in which union coefficients declined from OLS levels, 6 to negative values, and 11 in which the coefficients rose compared to OLS values, 2 of which reached levels in excess of 40 percent.

simultaneous equations (predicted unionism) technique and with the inverse Mills ratio technique for examining whether observed union/nonunion differences are real or illusory? We believe that the empirical results just presented strongly suggest that there is little to be learned from using either of the two techniques for analyzing the impact of unionism. The techniques can yield useful results only to the extent that we *really* know what affects union status but not wages and that we *really* know the functional forms and distributions of the relevant equations. The actual exclusion criteria and functional form/distribution restrictions used for identification in the systems model make it clear that we simply lack the requisite knowledge. For example, in one model the four-firm concentration ratio is included in the unionization equation but is excluded from the wage equation. In many others, the variables in both equations are the same, but enter in a linear way in the union status equation but both linearly and through a nonlinear term in the outcome equation. While the problems addressed by the techniques may be real, the econometric solutions offered can do little to solve them with extant cross-sectional data. Econometric manipulations of these data do not appear to be a good substitute for better data, for experiments more suitable to answering the problems of concern, or for genuine institutional or theoretical knowledge about the interactions between unions, employers, and workers.

LONGITUDINAL DATA

The results of some recent studies of union effects that exploit the before/after nature of longitudinal data sets to obtain estimates of the effect of unionism on the same person or firm are summarized in Table 5. As before, there are more results on wage rates than on other outcomes of concern. The wage studies, which ask "How does the wage of a worker change when he/she goes from union to nonunion status or vice versa?" yield estimates of union wage effects which, while lower than those obtained in comparable cross-sectional analyses, are of sizable and significant magnitude, supporting the claim that unionism does indeed raise the wages of individuals. In contrast to the attempts to deal with the problem of causality and selectivity with systems of equations, in no case does a longitudinal analysis result "blow up."

TABLE 5

Evidence of Econometric Probes into Union/Nonunion Differences
Using Longitudinal Data

Variable, Data Set, Sample	Result	Reference
Wages NLS Young Men All workers	Changes in wages from going union to nonunion (UN) as opposed to remaining union (UU) and of going nonunion to union (NU) as opposed to remaining nonunion (NN) are about six-tenths as large as the comparable cross-sectional differentials.	Chamberlain (1980)
Productivity Cement company data Production workers	NU change is roughly the same as the comparable cross-sectional differential.	Clark (1980a, 1980b)
Wages, Work Conditions PSID; Michigan Time Use Survey All workers	Change in wages: UN 7%; NU 55%; UU 33%; NN 40%. Estimated UN change in "choice of work" is positive while NU change is negative. Estimated UN changes in "freedom to increase work hours" is near zero while NU change is negative and substantially so in absolute value.	Duncan & Stafford (1980)
Quits PSID All workers	Quit differential in longitudinal study is roughly the same as in comparable cross-sectional studies.	Freeman (1978b)
Wages, Work Conditions NLS Young Men All workers	Changes in wages: UN 45%; NU 118%; UU 71%; NN 81%. Estimated UN change in "progress at work" is positive while NU change is negative. Estimated UN change in "job pressures" is negative while NU change is positive. Estimated UN change in "job pace" is positive while NU change is zero.	Leigh (1980a)
Wages May CPS All workers	Wage differential of about 8% in longitudinal analysis compared to 19% in cross-sectional analysis.	Mellow (1979)
Wages PSID; NLS Men	UN and NU changes are about two-thirds as large as the comparable cross-sectional differential.	Mincer (1980)

The magnitude of the difference between longitudinal and cross-sectional estimates of union wage effects varies somewhat by study. Chamberlain found that the effect of unionism estimated with the longitudinal data in the young men NLS was about six-tenths as large as the effect estimated with cross-sectional data. Mincer, using both PSID and NLS data for male workers, found the longitudinal effect roughly two-thirds as large as the cross-sectional effect. Mellow's analysis of the May-May matched CPS tapes, by contrast, obtained a longitudinal effect that was about 40 percent of that estimated in CPS cross-sectional regressions. One possible explanation of the greater difference between the CPS results and other results is that in the CPS, unlike in the other relevant surveys, workers do not typically respond for themselves, raising the possibility of greater measurement error in the union variable using the CPS than using the other surveys. As noted earlier, classical measurement error can be expected to become a more serious problem in longitudinal than in cross-sectional data. Finally, with respect to wages, Duncan and Stafford and Leigh have presented figures on the change in wages for workers who switch union status and those who remain union or nonunion. These figures, given in Table 5, provide several interesting comparisons which illuminate the nature of the longitudinal experiment. From them one can compare the wage changes of workers who were nonunion in the first period and became union members in the second period to the wage changes of workers who were nonunion in both periods or to the changes of those who began as members but left their unions or to the changes of workers who were unionized in both periods. A similar set of comparisons can also be made for workers who began as union members but left their union. Each comparison provides an answer to a different question concerning the impact of unionism on wage rates. For present purposes, it suffices to note that in all relevant comparisons, the results in Table 5 show a substantial wage impact of a magnitude somewhat smaller than, but consistent with, the Table 1 findings.

Longitudinal data have also been used to study the union effect on quits, productivity, and work conditions. With respect to quits and productivity, the results confirm the cross-sectional findings. Longitudinal analysis of quit behavior in a pooled PSID sample yields estimated coefficients on the union variable roughly equal to those obtained in cross-sectional analyses, indicating that the lower quits of union workers cannot be explained by an unobservable variable labeled "innate propensity to quit." With regard to productivity, Clark (1980a) found only a modest diminution in his estimated effect of unionism on productivity in the cement industry when he went to a before/after sample.[7] With respect to work conditions, the results are somewhat less clear. Duncan and Stafford (1980) found a decline (increase) in the quality of certain work conditions when workers joined (left) unions in the PSID whereas Leigh (1980a) found no such effects in the NLS.

Overall, the longitudinal analyses suggest that much of the cross-sectional union/nonunion differentials presented in Table 1 are real rather than illusory. Since, as noted earlier, it is likely that there are some potential problems with analyses which estimate union impacts by focusing on marginal as opposed to average workers, we endorse neither the longitudinal nor the cross-sectional results as *the* answer. However, the fact that they regularly point in the same direction is reassuring.

IV. Conclusions

This paper has reviewed a significant body of evidence regarding the impact of trade unionism on economic performance and sought to evaluate antithetical views regarding whether estimated differences between union and nonunion workers and firms represent: illusions created by poor experiments, real effects explicable solely in price-theoretic terms, or real effects which reflect the nonwage-related dimensions of trade unions. The review has yielded conclusions on both the substantive questions at hand and the methodologies which have been used to address their validity.

With respect to the illusion/reality debate, the preponderance of evidence indicates that union effects on a wide variety of eco-

---

[7] Brown and Medoff gathered data by 2-digit industry for 1929 and 1953 to use with data on unionization in these two years found in Lewis (1963, pp. 289–90) in an effort to capture productivity before and after unionization. They regressed the change in ln (value added/labor) on the change in ln (capital/labor) and the change in fraction unionized. With only 20 observations they could not estimate the union productivity effect with any precision. The estimated coefficient on the change in fraction-unionized variable ranged from negative to positive depending on the data used and the assumptions made.

nomic variables estimated with cross-sectional data are real. Diverse econometric probes into these findings and examination of longitudinal as well as cross-sectional data have supported the reality of the union impact on economic performance. While magnitudes of coefficients have been altered by the probes, in almost no case has the evidence been explained away as due solely to the poor quality of the relevant econometric experiments. Moreover, since the effects of unions on nonwage outcomes generally come from models which hold fixed the levels of wages and variables affected by wages, the evidence supports the view that unions do much more than simply raise wages as an economic monopolist. While, in this study, we have not examined interpretations of these nonwage effects, the effects represent an empirical foundation for the institutional view of unionism described in Section I.

With respect to methods for evaluating the quality of standard cross-sectional experiments, some techniques appear more useful than others. In particular, we have found that sensitivity analyses of single-equation results and longitudinal experiments provide valuable checks on cross-sectional findings while multiple-equations approaches produce results which are much too unstable to help resolve the questions of concern.

Our conclusions seem to have three messages for future research on trade unionism. First, the operating assumption that trade unions have important and real wage and nonwage effects is strongly supported by the extant evidence. Second, the search for a valid answer to the question of what unions do should involve more than just manipulating existing data with sophisticated techniques; it should have at its heart the collection of new evidence concerning the functions and operations of trade unions and their interactions with firms and employees. Third, the illusion/reality question should be asked not only of empirical results on the impact of collective bargaining, but also of the efforts used to probe these findings.

References

Allen, Steven G. "Unionized Construction Workers Are More Productive." (Mimeograph 1979)
Ashenfelter, Orley. "Union Relative Wage Effects: New Evidence and a Survey of Their Implications for Wage Inflation." (Mimeograph 1976)

Ashenfelter, Orley, and George E. Johnson. "Unionism, Relative Wages, and Labor Quality in U.S. Manufacturing Industries." *International Economic Review* 13 (October 1972), pp. 488–507.

Becker, Brian. "Hospital Unionism and Employment Stability." *Industrial Relations* 17 (February 1978), pp. 96–101.

Blau, Francine D., and Lawrence M. Kahn. "The Exit-Voice Tradeoff in the Labor Market: Some Additional Evidence." (Mimeograph 1981)

Bloch, Farrell E., and Mark S. Kuskin. "Wage Determination in the Union and Nonunion Sectors." *Industrial and Labor Relations Review* 31 (January 1978), pp. 183–92.

Block, Richard N. "The Impact of Seniority Provisions on the Manufacturing Quit Rate." *Industrial and Labor Relations Review* 31 (July 1978), pp. 474–81.

Borjas, George J. "Job Satisfaction, Wages, and Unions." *Journal of Human Resources* 14 (Winter 1979), pp. 21–40.

Brown, Charles. "Equalizing Differences in the Labor Market." *Quarterly Journal of Economics* 94 (February 1980), pp. 113–34.

Brown, Charles, and James Medoff. "Trade Unions in the Production Process." *Journal of Political Economy* 86 (June 1978), pp. 355–78.

Cain, Glen G., Brian E. Becker, Catherine G. McLaughlin, and Albert E. Schwank. "The Effect of Unions on Wages in Hospitals." (Mimeograph 1980)

Chamberlain, Gary. "Are Brothers As Good As Twins?" In *Kinometrics: The Determinants of Socio-Economic Success Within and Between Families*, ed. Paul Taubman. Amsterdam: North Holland, 1977. Pp. 287–98.

———. "Multivariate Regression Models for Panel Data." (Mimeograph 1981)

Clark, Kim B. "The Impact of Unionization on Productivity: A Case Study." *Industrial and Labor Relations Review* 33 (July 1980a), pp. 451–69.

———. "Unionization and Productivity: Micro-Econometric Evidence." *Quarterly Journal of Economics* 95 (December 1980b), pp. 613–39.

Connerton, M., Richard B. Freeman, and James L. Medoff. "Productivity and Industrial Relations: The Case of U.S. Bituminous Coal," (Mimeograph 1979)

Dalton, James A., and E. J. Ford, Jr. "Concentration and Labor Earnings in Manufacturing and Utilities." *Industrial and Labor Relations Review* 31 (October 1977), pp. 45–60.

Doeringer, Peter B., and Michael J. Piore. *Internal Labor Markets and Manpower Analysis.* Lexington, MA: D. C. Heath, 1971.

Donsimoni, Marie-Paule Joseph. "An Analysis of Trade Union Power: Structure and Conduct of the American Labor Movement." PhD thesis, Harvard University, 1978.

Duncan, Greg J. "Earnings Functions and Nonpecuniary Benefits." *Journal of Human Resources* 11 (Fall 1976), pp. 462–83.

Duncan, Gregory M., and Duane E. Leigh. "Wage Determination in the Union and Nonunion Sectors: A Sample Selectivity Approach." *Industrial and Labor Relations Review* 34 (October 1980), pp. 24–34.

Duncan, Greg J., and Frank P. Stafford. "Do Union Members Receive Compensating Wage Differentials?" *American Economic Review* 70 (June 1980), pp. 355–71.

Ehrenberg, Ronald G. *The Regulatory Process and Labor Earnings.* New York: Academic Press, 1979.

Farber, Henry S. "Unionism, Labor Turnover, and Wages of Young Men." (Mimeograph 1979)

Feldman, Roger, Lung-Fei Lee, and Richard Hoffbeck. "Hospital Employees' Wages and Labor Union Organization." (Mimeograph 1980)

Frantz, John. "The Impact of Trade Unions on Productivity in the Wood Household Furniture Industry." Senior Honors Thesis, Harvard College, 1976.

Freeman, Richard B. "Individual Mobility and Union Voice in the Labor Market." *American Economic Review* 66 (May 1976), pp. 361–68.
————. "Job Satisfaction as an Economic Variable." *American Economic Review* 68 (May 1978a), pp. 135–41.
————. "A Fixed Effect Logit Model of the Impact of Unionism on Quits." (Mimeograph 1978b)
————. "The Effect of Unionism on Worker Attachment to Firms." *Journal of Labor Research* 1 (Spring 1980a), pp. 29–61.
————. "The Exit-Voice Tradeoff in the Labor Market: Unionism, Job Tenure, Quits, and Separations." *Quarterly Journal of Economics* 94 (June 1980b), pp. 643–73.
————. "Unionism and the Dispersion of Wages." *Industrial and Labor Relations Review* 34 (October 1980c), pp. 3–23.
————. "The Effect of Trade Unionism on Fringe Benefits." *Industrial and Labor Relations Review* 34 (July 1981), pp. 489–509.
Freeman, Richard B., and James L. Medoff. "The Two Faces of Unionism." *The Public Interest* 57 (Fall 1979), pp. 69–93.
————. "The Percent Organized Wage Relationship for Union and Nonunion Workers." *Review of Economic and Statistics* (forthcoming a).
————. "Substitution Between Production Labor and Other Factors in Unionized and Nonunionized Manufacturing." *Review of Economics and Statistics* (forthcoming b).
————. *What Do Unions Do?* New York: Basic Books, 1982.
Goldstein, Gerald, and Mark Pauly. "Group Health Insurance as a Local Public Good." In *The Role of Health Insurance in the Health Services Sector,* ed. R. Rosett. New York: National Bureau of Economic Research, 1976. Pp. 73–110.
Halasz, Peter. "What Lies Behind the Slope of the Age-Earnings Profile." Senior Honors Thesis, Harvard College, 1980.
Hamermesh, Daniel. "Market Power and Wage Inflation." *Southern Economic Journal* 39 (October 1972), pp. 204–12.
Hayden, James F. "Collective Bargaining and Cartelization: An Analysis of Teamster Power in the Regulated Trucking Industry." Senior Honors Thesis, Harvard College, 1977.
Heckman, James D. "The Common Structure of Statistical Models of Truncation, Sample Selection, and Limited Dependent Variables and a Simple Estimator for Such Models." *Annals of Economic and Social Measurement* 5 (1976), pp. 475–92.
Hendricks, Wallace. "Labor Market Structure and Union Wage Levels." *Economic Inquiry* 13 (September 1975), pp. 401–16.
————. "Conglomerate Mergers and Collective Bargaining." *Industrial Relations* 15 (February 1976), pp. 75–87.
Hyclak, Thomas. "The Effect of Unions on Earnings Inequality in Local Labor Markets." *Industrial and Labor Relations Review* 33 (October 1979), pp. 77–84.
————. "Unions and Income Inequality: Some Cross-State Evidence." *Industrial Relations* 19 (Spring 1980), pp. 212–215.
Johnson, George E. "Economic Analysis of Trade Unionism." *American Economic Review* 65 (May 1975), pp. 23–28.
————. "Changes Over Time in the Union/Nonunion Wage Differential in the United States." (Mimeograph 1981)
Johnson, George E., and Kenneth Youmans. "Union Relative Wage Effects by Age and Education." *Industrial and Labor Relations Review* 24 (January 1971), pp. 171–79.
Kahn, Lawrence M. "Union Impact: A Reduced Form Approach." *Review of Economics and Statistics* 59 (November 1977), pp. 503–507.
————. "The Effect of Unions on the Earnings of Nonunion Workers." *Industrial and Labor Relations Review* (January 1978), pp. 205–16.

―――. "Unionism and Relative Wages: Direct and Indirect Effects." *Industrial and Labor Relations Review* 32 (July 1979), pp. 520–32.
Kalachek, Edward, and Fredric Raines. "Trade Unions and Hiring Standards." *Journal of Labor Research* 1 (Spring 1980), pp. 63–75.
Kiefer, Nicholas, and Sharon Smith. "Union Impact and Wage Discrimination by Region." *Journal of Human Resources* 12 (Fall 1977), pp. 521–34.
Kochan, Thomas A. *Collective Bargaining and Industrial Relations.* Homewood, IL: Richard D. Irwin, 1980.
Kochan, Thomas A., and Richard N. Block. "An Interindustry Analysis of Bargaining Outcomes: Preliminary Evidence from Two-Digit Industries." *Quarterly Journal of Economics* 91 (August 1977), pp. 431–52.
Kochan, Thomas E., and David E. Helfman. "The Effects of Collective Bargaining on Economic and Behavioral Job Outcomes." In *Research in Labor Economics,* Vol. IV. Greenwich, CT: JAI Press, 1981.
Lee, Lung-Fei. "Unionism and Wage Rates: A Simultaneous Equations Model with Qualitative and Limited Dependent Variables." *International Economic Review* 19 (June 1978), pp. 415–33.
Leibenstein, Harvey. "Allocative Efficiency vs. 'X-Efficiency.'" *American Economic Review* 56 (June 1966), pp. 392–415.
Leigh, Duane E. "Racial Discrimination and Labor Unions: Evidence from the NLS Sample of Middle-Aged Men." *Journal of Human Resources* 13 (Fall 1978), pp. 568–77.
―――. "Unions and Nonwage Racial Discrimination." *Industrial and Labor Relations Review* 32 (July 1979), pp. 439–50.
―――. "Do Union Members Receive Compensating Wage Differentials?" (Mimeograph 1980a)
―――. "Racial Differentials in Union Relative Wage Effects: A Simultaneous Equations Approach." *Journal of Labor Research* 1 (Spring 1980b), pp. 95–114.
Lewis, H. Gregg. *Unionism and Relative Wages in the United States.* Chicago: University of Chicago Press, 1963.
―――. "Interpreting Unionism Coefficients in Wage Equations." (Mimeograph 1980)
Mandelbaum, David. "Responses to Job Satisfaction Questions as Insights into Why Men Change Employers." Senior Honors Thesis, Harvard College, 1980.
Mandelstamm, Allan B. "The Effects of Unions on Efficiency in the Residential Construction Industry: A Case Study." *Industrial and Labor Relations Review* 18 (July 1965), pp. 503–521.
McLaughlin, Catherine G. "The Impact of Unions on Hospital Wages." PhD Thesis, University of Wisconsin-Madison, 1980.
Medoff, James L. "The Earnings Function: A Glimpse Inside the Black Box." (Mimeograph 1977)
―――. "Layoffs and Alternatives Under Trade Unionism in U.S. Manufacturing." *American Economic Review* 69 (June 1979), pp. 380–95.
Medoff, James L., and Katharine G. Abraham. "Experience, Performance, and Earnings." *Quarterly Journal of Economics* 95 (December 1980a), pp. 703–36.
―――. "Years of Service and Probability of Promotion." (Mimeograph 1980b)
―――. "Involuntary Termination Under Explicit and Implicit Employment Contracts." (Mimeograph 1981a)
―――. "The Role of Seniority at U.S. Work Places: A Report on Some New Evidence." (Mimeograph 1981b)
―――. "Are Those Paid More Really More Productive? The Case of Experience." *Journal of Human Resources* (Spring 1981c), pp. 186–216.
Mellow, Wesley. "Unionism and Wages: A Longitudinal Analysis." *Review of Economics and Statistics* 63 (February 1981a), pp. 43–52.
―――. "Employer Size and Wages." (Mimeograph 1981b)

Mincer, Jacob. "The Economics of Wage Floors." (Mimeograph 1980)
Mitchell, Daniel J. B. "Some Empirical Observations of Relevance to the
    Analysis of Union Wage Determination." *Journal of Labor Research* 1
    (Fall 1980a), pp. 193–215.
———. *Unions, Wages, and Inflation.* Washington: The Brookings Institu-
    tion, 1980b.
Moore, William J., and John Raisian. "Cyclical Sensitivity of Union/Nonunion
    Relative Wage Effects." *Journal of Labor Research* 1 (Spring 1980),
    pp. 115–132.
Neumann, George. "Union Wage Differentials and the Decision to Join
    Unions." (Mimeograph 1977)
Oaxaca, Ronald L. "Estimation of Union/Nonunion Wage Differentials Within
    Occupational/Regional Subgroups." *Journal of Human Resources* 10 (Fall
    1975), pp. 529–36.
Olsen, Randall J. "Comment on 'The Effect of Unions on Earnings and Earn-
    ings on Unions: A Mixed Logit Approach.'" *International Economic Re-
    view* 19 (February 1978), pp. 259–61.
Pencavel, John. *An Analysis of the Quit Rate in American Manufacturing In-
    dustry.* Princeton, NJ: Industrial Relations Section, Princeton University,
    1970.
Pfeffer, Jeffrey, and Jerry Ross. "Union-Nonunion Effects on Wage and Status
    Attainment." *Industrial Relations* 19 (Spring 1980), pp. 140–151.
Pierson, Gail. "The Effect of Union Strengths on the U.S. 'Phillips Curve.'"
    American Economic Review 58 (June 1968), pp. 456–67.
Plotnick, Robert. "Trends in Male Earnings Inequality." (Mimeograph 1980)
Podgursky, Michael John. "Trade Unions and Income Inequality." PhD Thesis,
    University of Wisconsin-Madison, 1980.
Raisian, John. "Cyclic Patterns in Weeks and Wages." *Economic Inquiry* 17
    (October 1979), pp. 475–95.
Rice, Robert G. "Skill, Earnings and the Growth of Wage Supplements."
    American Economic Review 56 (May 1966), pp. 583–93.
Schmidt, Peter. "Estimation of a Simultaneous Equations Model with Jointly
    Dependent Continuous and Qualitative Variables: The Union-Earnings
    Question Revisited." *International Economic Review* 19 (June 1978),
    pp. 453-65.
Schmidt, Peter, and Robert P. Strauss. "The Effect of Unions on Earnings and
    Earnings on Unions: A Mixed Logit Approach." *International Economic
    Review* 17 (February 1976), pp. 204–12.
Schoeplein, Robert N. "Secular Changes in the Skill Differential in Manufac-
    turing, 1952–1973." *Industrial and Labor Relations Review* 30 (April
    1977), pp. 314–24.
Shapiro, David. "Relative Wage Effects of Unions in the Public and Private
    Sectors." *Industrial and Labor Relations Review* 31 (January 1978),
    pp. 193–204.
Simon, Herbert. "A Behavioral Model of Rational Choice." *Quarterly Journal
    of Economics* 69 (February 1955), pp. 99–118.
Slichter, Sumner, James Healy, and E. Robert Livernash. *The Impact of Col-
    lective Bargaining on Management.* Washington: The Brookings Institu-
    tion, 1960.
Sloan, Frank, and Richard A. Elnicki. "Determinants of Professional Nurses'
    Wages." In *Research in Health Economics,* Vol. 1. Greenwich CT: JAI
    Press, 1979. Pp. 217–54.
Solnick, L. M. "Unionism and Fringe Benefit Expenditures." *Industrial Re-
    lations* 17 (February 1978), pp. 102–107.
Viscusi, W. Kip. "Wealth Effects and Earnings Premiums for Job Hazards."
    Review of Economics and Statistics 60 (August 1978), pp. 408–16.

————. "Unions, Labor Market Structure, and the Welfare Implications of the Quality of Work." *Journal of Labor Research* 1 (Spring 1980), pp. 175–92.

Weiss, Leonard. "Concentration and Labor Earnings." *American Economic Review* 56 (March 1966), pp. 96–117.

Welch, Stephen W. "Union-Nonunion Construction Wage Differentials." *Industrial Relations* 19 (Spring 1980), pp. 152–62.

Williamson, O. E., M. L. Wachter, and J. E. Harris. "Understanding the Employment Relation: The Analysis of Idiosyncratic Exchange." *Bell Journal of Economics* 6 (Spring 1975), pp. 250–78.

Yanker, Robert H. "Productivity Versus Seniority: What Is the Determining Factor in Regard to Wages and Promotion?" Senior Honors Thesis, Harvard College, 1980.

CHAPTER 3

Management Performance

D. QUINN MILLS
Harvard University

The purpose of this chapter is to make an overall assessment of management's performance in industrial relations without summarizing or recapitulating other chapters in this volume. This is not an easy task, for it constrains this chapter in somewhat peculiar ways. Specifically, considerable attention is devoted to those aspects of management performance not treated at length elsewhere. In particular, because of the content of these other chapters, the philosophy and objectives of managers in industrial relations receive as much discussion as the results that managers have achieved.

Herbert Heneman has defined industrial relations as having "a central concern with the employment relationship." And Gerald Somers described the "essence of industrial relations" as "the complex interconnection between the need for cooperation and the inevitable conflict of individuals."[1]

These definitions do not limit the term industrial relations to union-management relations. Instead, they appear to cover situations in which employees are not represented by unions as well as those situations in which there is representation. I have chosen, therefore, not to limit this discussion to unionized companies, but to consider management performance generally, and I will use the terms "industrial relations" and "employee relations" interchangeably.

These observations make it reasonably clear what industrial relations is to encompass, but do not prescribe how the performance of management is to be evaluated.

---

[1] Herbert G. Heneman, Jr., "Toward a General Conceptual Scheme of Industrial Relations," and Gerald G. Somers, "Foreword," in *Essays in Industrial Relations Theory*, ed. Gerald G. Somers (Ames: Iowa State University Press, 1969), pp. 4 and x, respectively.

Corporate Objectives in Industrial Relations

What of the industrial relations performance of American business? There are several perspectives from which management performance may be evaluated. For example, the social and economic consequences of managerial performance may be studied, as is done in the last sections of this chapter. But it is tempting to start with a narrower perspective, asking what has been the quality of the industrial relations performance of American business as measured against its own objectives. Unfortunately, evaluation against a standard of corporate objectives is virtually impossible to perform in the aggregate.

Firms are not alike. Each has its own history, traditions, reputation, and style. Also, firms have different objectives. While all private business firms may be said to seek to maximize profit, this tells us much less than it seems to about managerial behavior. Some firms pursue profit maximization in the short term, others in the long term. For some, growth is a primary objective, taking precedence over short-term profitability. Recent economic research shows that the degree of market share a firm possesses is an important determinant of relative profitability.[2] Because of this, some firms continually trade off profitability against hoped-for increases in market share. Similarly, firms differ in their policies and objectives with respect to compensation. Some try to minimize compensation in the short run; others try to keep compensation abreast of competitors. Still other firms have a high-wage policy, hoping to obtain and keep especially gifted employees.

Because of this variety of objectives, it is very hazardous to attempt to evaluate management performance in industrial relations in the aggregate. There are few objectives which may be framed on an overall basis. Furthermore, each firm finds itself in particular circumstances at different times. Top management may interpret what those circumstances require in various ways, and so impose different short-term objectives for the firm's industrial relations. Line managers, personnel and industrial relations managers must attempt to take actions consistent with the objectives set by top management.

---

[2] Richard E. Caves and Michael E. Porter, "Interfirm Profitability Differences: Comment," *Quarterly Journal of Economic* 91 (November 1977), pp. 667–75.

Thus, while avoiding work stoppages might be expected to be an objective of a firm's industrial relations policies, in many instances a firm prefers to take a strike instead of agreeing to union demands. Furthermore, while it is generally an objective of firms to keep labor costs under control, the necessity to hire and retain employees in a tight labor market may cause cost considerations to be secondary. In the end, the performance of managers in the industrial relations area can only be evaluated against the specific needs of a corporation at a point in time. All overall objectives are tempered by the balance of power between companies, unions, and employees, and by the reality of economic forces.

The Conference Board has attempted to identify the basis on which labor relations staffs are evaluated in corporations. Among unionized companies, 20 percent reported that they did not evaluate the labor relations function and another 60 percent reported that any evaluation was informal. Among nonunion companies, 42 percent did not evaluate labor relations, and 45 percent did so only informally. Despite this, when pressed in the survey, unionized companies listed the effect of negotiations on labor costs, the size of a settlement compared to those at other companies in the industry, employee attitudes and morale, cooperative relations with the union, and new union organizing as factors considered in evaluating labor relations performance.[3]

It is useful to simplify this list to one of three overall objectives for industrial relations in the firm under ordinary circumstances: (1) to limit labor costs to a level that is commensurate or lower than that of competitors; (2) to hire and retain staff and maintain a level of morale which encourages high employee productivity; and (3) to preserve nonunion status for as many employees as possible.

Industrial Relations Performance

COMPENSATION, PRODUCTIVITY, AND LABOR COSTS

Compensation in recent years has been much affected by price increases. Inflation has accelerated dramatically in the American economy in recent decades. During the 1950s consumer prices rose approximately one-third, during the 1960s they rose approximately

[3] Audrey Freedman, *Managing Labor Relations* (New York: The Conference Board, 1979), Rep. No. 765, pp. 72–73.

one-half, and during the 1970s prices doubled. This has been a significant factor influencing compensation developments, and one which has created a major challenge for management.

In general, management has attempted to balance certain objectives against each other with respect to compensation. First, management has attempted to keep compensation increases in general lagging behind price changes, but it is only in recent years that this policy has been effectively pursued. Prior to 1974, increases in compensation per hour exceeded those in the consumer price index in every year (1947–1974). But in 1974, and in 1979 and 1980, double-digit price inflation was not accompanied by double-digit wage inflation. For example, in the two years 1979–1980, taken together, the consumer price index rose 24 percent, while compensation per hour worked rose only 19 percent. In support of this policy, which managers and many government officials describe as tending to lessen inflation, business has on balance opposed adjusting wages mechanically to a price index. Many unions have supported indexation, however, and by 1980 a majority of collective bargaining agreements which cover more than 5,000 employees have provisions indexing wages in at least some degree to price increases.

Managers have generally refused to extend indexing to nonunion employees, but have periodically adjusted wages to keep a desired relationship between the pay of union and nonunion employees. The Carter Administration's wage-price guideposts for 1978–1979 permitted substantially higher increases for workers (virtually all unionized) covered by cost-of-living escalators. Thereafter, the business community lobbied successfully to modify the guideposts to permit so-called "catch-up" pay increases for employees not covered by escalator clauses (under a "tandem" regulation).

In an international context, U.S. hourly compensation in manufacturing has risen much more slowly than it has for our trading partners (where foreign compensation is measured on a U.S. dollar basis). From 1960 to 1978, for example, hourly compensation tripled in the U.S., rose twenty times in Japan, seven times in France, and twelve in West Germany.[4]

---

[4] *Economic Report of the President, 1980* (Washington: U.S. Government Printing Office, 1980).

Productivity performance has been declining in the American economy on what appears to be a long-term basis (see Table 1). The decline in labor productivity has attracted considerable public comment and also has spawned many economic analyses in recent months.

TABLE 1

Annual Rate of Growth
Real Gross National Product Per Hour—Percent

1947–1953	4.20
1953–1968	2.61
1968–1973	1.41
1973–1978	0.80

Source: Data except for period 1973–1978 from Michael D. McCarthy, "The U.S. Productivity Growth Recession: History and Prospects for the Future," *The Journal of Finance* 33 (June 1978), p. 977; data for the 1973–1978 period from the *Economic Report of the President,* 1979 (Washington: U.S. Government Printing Office, 1979).

The American worker is, on average, still more productive than workers in the countries that are our major trading partners, but the gap has been closing. For example, in 1960 Germany produced only 56 percent as much real output per employee as did the U.S. In 1977 the figure was 85 percent. In 1960 Japan produced only 27 percent as much real output per employee as the U.S.; by 1977 the figure was 69 percent.[5] As the 1970s ended, the gap was rapidly closing. Between 1972 and 1978, for example, while output per hour worked rose one-third in France, Japan, and Germany, it rose only 12 percent in the United States.[6]

Labor, government, and management have each been blamed for the decline. But the decline in the rate of productivity advance is only one of a series of developments in the American economy which marks a break from the past, and which should be reviewed here briefly. Managers are certainly at least partly responsible for the decisions that have led to these developments—both good and bad.

Underlying the decline in the rate of productivity growth has been falling real investment per worker. Table 2 shows this decline from 1956 until recently.

[5] Council on Wage & Price Stability, Executive Office of the President, *Report on Productivity* (Washington: July 1979).

[6] U.S. Bureau of Labor Statistics, *Manufacturing Productivity Rates,* issued July 9, 1979.

TABLE 2

Annual Percentage Changes in the Stock of
Fixed Capital to the Hours of Labor

1956–1966	2.7
1966–1975	1.7
1975	−0.2
1976	−0.2
1977	1.1

Source: Michael D. McCarthy, "The U.S. Productivity Growth Recession," The Journal of Finance 33 (June 1978), p. 980.

Manufacturing growth has been slower than that of the U.S. economy as a whole. Nonetheless, American manufacturing firms have added jobs in the 1970s while European and Japanese firms have reduced them. Table 3 shows employment changes in manufacturing from 1972 to 1978 for several countries. American firms have added workers to obtain the level of output increases achieved abroad, with the result that labor productivity growth in the United States is much slower. In this sense, the additional employment created in manufacturing by our companies has been a mixed blessing.

TABLE 3

Percentage Change in Employment, 1972–1978
All Manufacturing Industries

United States	6.5
United Kingdom	− 1.1
France	− 2.2
Japan	− 4.7
Germany	−12.0

Source: U.S. Bureau of Labor Statistics, Manufacturing Productivity Rates, issued July 9, 1979.

Unit labor costs are the result of adjusting compensation increases for changes in productivity. On an aggregate basis it makes little sense to compare labor costs within the domestic economy among industries since that tells us about the performance of managers in particular industries, but not about the performance of managers as a whole. We can, however, compare the performance of American managers and those abroad. This comparison can be made in two ways. First, increases in labor costs can be compared in each country's own currency. Second, increases can be compared in the currency of the United States for all countries. The latter comparison is affected by changes in the value of the dollar.

From 1960 to 1977 unit labor costs in manufacturing rose less in the U.S. (in own-currency terms) than in any other major western industrialized nation. From 1970 to 1977, only Germany's record was better, and then by only one-tenth of a percentage point. By the end of this period, and into 1979–1980, however, American labor cost increases accelerated while those in Germany and Japan declined.

In terms of U.S. currency, the advantage of the U.S. in unit labor costs was magnified in the 1960s and 1970s, due to the large devaluation of the dollar, especially against the mark and the yen.[7] By the late 1970s, many companies were acknowledging that among major industrialized countries, American labor costs were quite attractive. (Compared to labor costs in some nondurable manufacturing in South Asia and Latin America, however, American costs are very substantial.)

In general, American management and the economy itself have kept U.S. labor costs in a reasonably favorable position with respect to labor costs in other western industrialized nations, despite weakening productivity growth and substantial domestic inflation.

MORALE AND JOB SATISFACTION

Beginning in the mid-1960s, there has been an avalanche of surveys and publicity about the attitudes of workers toward their jobs. Employees are said to have lost the work ethic,[8] to be dissatisfied with their jobs, and to be resentful of and rebelling against management direction at the workplace. Accompanying these attitude shifts have been major changes in the demographic composition of the workforce. Younger persons, minority group members, and women came to be a large proportion of those employed during the 1960s and 1970s. How well did management respond to these developments?

The answer is mixed. Probably job dissatisfaction was never as

---

[7] Keith Daly and Arthur Neel, "Productivity and Unit Labor Costs in 11 Industrial Countries," *Monthly Labor Review* 101 (November 1978), pp. 11–17; and Bureau of Labor Statistics, *Manufacturing Productivity Rates*, issued July 9, 1979.

[8] R. A. Buchholz, "The Work Ethic Reconsidered," *Industrial and Labor Relations Review* 31 (July 1978), pp. 450–59.

prevalent as much of the publicity suggested,[9] but it has nevertheless been taken seriously by many managers. Employee resistance to direction and discipline has altered the employee relations climate in most plants, but not, I think, very greatly. However, there have been major changes in the climate in some facilities. In a few plants I have visited there is open conflict between workers and supervisors, and in other plants supervisors have relinquished virtually all control. Resistance to direction and a seeming lack of commitment to work have convinced many American managers that however well today's workers perform, they (the workers) do less work than workers did a generation ago.

Managers in many firms have grappled with the problems of employee job satisfaction and work attitude in a variety of ways. Many firms have introduced training for supervisors, stressing sensitivity to the new attitudes and practices of employees. The foreman's job, for example, has been redefined in some companies from that of direction to one of support for employees.[10] This transition is not being made without difficulty, however. Foremen have been reported to be generally dissatisfied with their changing and uncertain status. An Opinion Research Survey indicated that the percentage of first-level supervisors who felt confident about getting prompt and direct information from their supervisors had decreased from 60 percent in 1952 to 41 percent in 1970.[11] It is at the level of the first-line supervisor that the pressures generated by a changing workforce and changing business have met in the last decade. There has been no general breakdown of relationships between employees and supervisors, and nothing of the nature of the widespread unrest which gripped France and Italy in the late 1960s. Nonetheless, these problems continue to trouble management in the United States and to affect production volume, costs, and quality.

Many companies have been content to wait things out, hoping

[9] Institute for Social Research, University of Michigan, "Quality of Employment Survey," published in *Daily Labor Report*, No. 243, December 18, 1978.

[10] James M. Black, *The Basics of Supervisory Management: Mastering the Art of Effective Supervision* (New York: McGraw-Hill, 1975); also Keith Davis, *Human Behavior at Work* (New York: McGraw-Hill, 1977).

[11] Thomas H. Patten, Jr., *Manpower Planning and the Development of Human Resources* (New York: Wiley-Interscience, 1971), p. 7; see also Paul Pigors and Charles A. Myers, *Personnel Administration* (New York: McGraw-Hill, 1977), Ch. 7.

that in the 1980s an aging workforce will accept discipline and return to the work ethic. But some companies have been more innovative. They have worked unilaterally or in conjunction with unions to attempt to alter the nature of work itself by making it more attractive and challenging.[12] This effort constitutes a major alternative to the Taylorist school of thought which has long dominated American managerial thinking and which espouses a limited role for workers.

It would be too much to characterize these efforts as of great extent at this time, and some observers argue that there are inherent limitations to these experiments. The sources of skepticism are two—first, that the efforts will not work, and second, that they divert managerial interest and attention from improving the present system to what will probably be futile efforts to restructure it completely. To the critics there seems to be a Pollyanna-ish character to the entire effort.[13]

It is too early to make a final assessment of the impact of these programs, but at least two factors should qualify any skepticism. First, some major companies and some union officials seem committed to continuing efforts in the belief that they will pay off. Second, these efforts indicate a healthy direction of concern about the attitudes and experience of workers.

UNIONIZATION

American management has been remarkably successful in its attempts to limit union organization. The sources of management's commitment to thwarting union efforts to organize employees are explored in a later section, and data regarding union membership and union success in elections conducted by the National Labor Relations Board are cited elsewhere in this volume.[14] Here I will only review the record briefly. Since the mid-1950s, union membership has declined as a proportion of the overall workforce, and the decline has been most rapid in the private sector. The 1960s saw an upsurge of union organization of public employees which public management was largely unable or unwilling to forestall,

---

[12] Richard E. Walton, "Work Innovations in the United States," *Harvard Business Review* 57 (July-August 1979), pp. 88–98.

[13] Ivar Berg et al., *Managers and Work Reform* (New York: Free Press, 1978).

[14] See p. 129.

but no such upsurge has occurred in the private sector. Instead, there has been a steady erosion of union representation.

What brought this about? There are many factors and their relative importance is subject to considerable debate. But most important, I believe, are the following:

1. Relatively prosperous times have enabled many employers to provide substantial wages and benefits to employees and to avoid conflict with employees over the amount of compensation and benefits.

2. Employers have made very effective use of their influence with employees in persuading them not to undertake union activity.

3. The law (since amendments to the National Labor Relations Act in 1947 and 1959) has denied unions the use of important economic weapons in organizing campaigns.

4. Employers have been largely successful in the litigation which occurs in the union organization process.

5. Employers have shifted facilities and employees to largely nonunionized regions of the country.

6. Employers have successfully defeated efforts by the unions to strengthen their legal position. In particular, the employers persuaded President Ford to veto the "situs picketing" or "equal treatment" bill in 1975 and prevailed in the Senate by filibuster against the labor law reform bill in 1978.

Whether these measures, or others that may be developed, will be equally successful in thwarting union organizing efforts in the changing economic, political, and social environment of the 1980s remains to be seen.

Industrial Relations Philosophy

It is hazardous to write about the philosophy or attitudes of American management for several reasons. First, not all managers share the same attitudes. Second, there are few, if any, careful studies of the topic, in part because attitudes can be quite difficult to measure accurately. As a result, one has to depend to a large degree on impressions gained in personal experience. In that regard I have been fortunate in that I have had occasion in teaching over the past 15 years to encounter literally hundreds of corporation executives and to discuss these matters of attitude with them.

I am also fortunate in having as a guide Douglass Brown's and Charles Myers's excellent review of management's industrial relations philosophy which was published by the IRRA almost 25 year ago.

The underlying industrial relations philosophy of American management, particularly in the large firms, has its origins in the development of large manufacturing firms in the 1920s and 1930s. Harold Livesay, a business historian, has recently summarized the basic approach of Alfred P. Sloan at General Motors, as follows:

> Sloan believed that high salaries, bonuses, [and] the chance to multiply one's individual efforts through the corporation's financial and mechanical leverage preserved individualism for executives. In the case of workers, steady wages and increased leisure time more than compensated for the loss of independence and craftsman's pride.[15]

High salaries and bonuses were to be the devices by which executives were encouraged to give the same entrepreneurial effort to General Motors as they would have given to their own firms, if they had been working for themselves. Workers, in contrast, were expected to serve in narrowly defined jobs, designed for efficiency and low cost in production. Wages and other benefits could be reasonably liberal compared to other job opportunities available to workers because of the high productivity of mass production.

At General Motors Sloan pioneered in decentralizing operational responsibility of management, while centralizing financial controls. Decentralized management has become a major feature of American management practice, the implications and refinements of which are still being explored today. Similarly, Sloan's philosophy of employee relations at managerial and nonmanagerial levels continues to be refined today. The distinction as to what is expected of managers and workers which is embedded in Sloan's vision continues to this day. (Some companies, however, are now vigorously experimenting with reducing the distinction. In part, this experimentation derives from a managerial belief noted by Brown and Myers: "a pervasive belief in the existence of a positive correlation between the degree of 'morale,' 'job satisfaction,' or

---

[15] Harold C. Livesay, *American Made: Men Who Shaped the American Economy* (Boston: Little, Brown, 1979), p. 229.

'loyalty' on the one hand, and the productive efficiency of the enterprise on the other." [16] This belief has not materially changed since Brown and Myers wrote in 1956.)

An important corollary of management's overall philosophy involves attitudes toward trade unions. In 1956 Brown and Myers contrasted management's positions of the 1920s and early 1930s with those of the mid-1950s and noted some significant changes. Among the more important changes were:

- "an increased willingness on the part of management to admit that the interests of management and employees are not in all instances identical" (though Brown and Myers noted that this didn't necessarily "go very far");
- "the prospect of coexistence . . . with a union is less frightening and less repugnant"; and
- "not . . . opposition to unions as such, but more efforts to contain the union on substantive matters." [17]

By 1980, these conclusions seem less certain. If there is an increased willingness to admit a divergence of interest between employees and managers, it doesn't appear to have had consequences for managements' industrial relations behavior. Where they can, managers ordinarily oppose union representation for workers, and nonunion companies rarely involve neutrals in resolving possible conflict between managers and employees.

Where unions are established, companies often do seek a modus vivendi, but where unions are not established, managerial opposition appears to have intensified in the last two decades.

Before exploring further current management attitudes toward unions, there are several factors which Brown and Myers identified as having influenced the change in attitudes of management from the 1920s to the 1950s. How have those factors changed since 1955? First, Brown and Myers identified growing labor shortages. But since the Vietnam War buildup of the late 1960s, there have not been substantial labor shortages in our economy. In the 1970s,

[16] Douglass V. Brown and Charles A. Myers, "The Changing Industrial Relations Philosophy of American Management," *Proceedings* of the Ninth Annual Meeting, Industrial Research Association (Madison, WI: IRRA, 1956), p. 89.

[17] *Ibid.*, pp. 89, 92, and 94, respectively.

the official unemployment rate has averaged 6.2 percent in the United States.

Second, Brown and Myers spoke of the increasing government intervention in labor-management relations in the 1930s and 1940s. There have been only limited increases in government intervention in the labor-management relations process in the 1960s and 1970s. Increasing government regulation of substantive matters such as health, safety, and pensions has been of a different kind from that of the earlier period.

Third, Brown and Myers spoke of the increased strength of unions in the 1930s and 1940s. The opposite has more nearly been the case in the 1960s and 1970s, at least in the private sector. Writing in 1979, Heath Larry, then president of the National Association of Manufacturers, raised the question, "labor power: myth or reality?" It is myth, he answered. And he suggested that the American labor movement is founded in three myths—that the American working class wants union affiliation, that unions have significant political clout, and that the labor movement is a friend of the poor. Not so, Larry claimed.[18]

From the perspective of American managers, there is only a superficial contradiction between Larry's argument that union power is very much a myth and the findings of opinion surveys that business persons find unions too powerful in America today.[19] The surveys show strong opposition to the degree of union strength that exists today, while Larry's speech notes the belief among business executives that the unions may be increasingly vulnerable to challenges from management.

Fourth, Brown and Myers spoke of the increasing size of business organizations, which permitted more staff to be assigned to labor relations. This trend has continued.

Finally, Brown and Myers noted an increased separation of management and ownership in corporations, which represented a reduction in the role of family-based control of business. This is a trend that has probably continued, on a reduced scale, since the 1950s. Brown and Myers apparently viewed increased managerial staff and separation of corporate control from ownership as repre-

---

[18] R. Heath Larry, "Labor Power: Myth or Reality," *MSU Business Topics* 26 (Winter 1979), pp. 20–24.

[19] Chamber of Commerce of the United States, *Washington Report*, September 1979.

senting a professionalization of management. Increased professionalism would yield less emotional reactions by executives to union
challenges, they suggested. Since the 1950s, executives may have
reacted less emotionally to unions, but they seem to be not any
less determined in their opposition to increased union organizing.

On balance, a slack labor movement, stabilized (or declining)
union strength, and increasing confidence of management in its
own ability to manage employee (not union) relations have served
to lessen employer acceptance of unions since the mid-1950s.

By 1980, what I believe to be the prevailing attitudes of American managers toward trade unions can be summarized as follows:
Unions exist as a reflection of management failures. Unions are
able to organize only where an employer is insensitive to the needs
and desires of the workforce. Where managers are insensitive, the
workers will vote for a union, and the managers deserve it. Where
managers are alert and sensitive, employees will not want a third
party (that is a union) in the relationship between the company
and the employees. Furthermore, where managers are sensitive,
employees have no need for a union. (Interestingly, many union
officials privately support this view, saying that in a well-managed
company with good pay and benefits, the employees have no
need of a union. Other union officials do not agree, arguing that
no company is as well and fairly managed as the above argument
suggests. Further, there is a view held by some that all workers
should belong to unions, regardless of the quality of their employment in the absence of a union, in order to have their interests
represented at the workplace and in the political activity of
American society.)

Executives generally agree that unions complicate managers'
lives. Unions are believed to impose inefficient work practices, to
extract pay increases beyond productivity improvements which
contribute to inflation and undermine the competitive position of
a company, and to constitute a major factor opposing corporate
interests in the legislative and judicial arenas.

There are managers who would not subscribe to the above list
of views. Some executives who deal with unions that represent
their employees have a different view based on personal experience. Some executives who do not deal with unions have an open
mind on the subject. But broadly, among the majority of American

managers who are in nonunionized enterprises, and to a large degree in enterprises which do deal with unions, the above attitudes are strongly held, and are repeated continually.

What are the merits of the views listed above? Slichter, Livernash, and Healy conducted such an inquiry into the effect of collective bargaining on management in the 1950s,[20] and in the 1970s Clark investigated the impact of unions on productivity in the cement industry.[21] These studies suggest that an unqualified condemnation of unions as impeding industrial efficiency is not merited. Nonetheless, it is, in my view, the most widely held doctrine in American management. Also, it is permissible, I believe, to treat attitudes, however well or poorly founded, as a factor in determining industrial relations. According to Livernash, "Leadership attitudes and behavior may be a reflection of underlying conditions . . . but . . . frequently may be regarded as an independent variable."[22]

And John Dunlop commented on the basis of a study of five major industrial nations, "The attitudes of employers toward workers, unions and employer associations . . . have been influential in shaping industrial relations."[23]

A further extension of the attitude described above is common to businesspersons who think of themselves as realistic. Unions were necessary, they concede, because of management failure during the 1930s and 1940s. But, they argue, that time is now past. Government regulation of employment practices with respect to health, safety, pension benefits, and possible racial or sex discrimination, combined with a more enlightened management, have made unions obsolete as protectors of workers' interests.

In part, this attitude reflects a tacit presumption that it would

[20] Sumner H. Slichter, James J. Healy, and E. Robert Livernash, *The Impact of Collective Bargaining on Management* (Washington: Brookings Institution, 1960).

[21] Kim B. Clark, "Impact of Unionization on Productivity," *Industrial and Labor Relations Review* 33 (July 1980). See also David Lewin, "The Impact of Unionism on American Business," *Columbia Journal of World Business* 13 (Winter 1978), pp. 89–103.

[22] E. Robert Livernash, "Note on the Analytical Framework of the Labor Policy Association Seminar on the Dynamics of Power in Employee Relations" (Washington: Labor Policy Association, 1979), p. 7.

[23] John T. Dunlop, "Introduction," in *Labor in the Twentieth Century*, eds. John T. Dunlop and Walter Galenson (New York: Academic Press, 1978), p. 5.

be possible to have in America an industrial society largely without trade unions. This presumption has been challenged. John Dunlop, for example, suggests that if American business launches "a concerted attack on . . . unions," then American society faces a choice between a moderate and a radical trade unionism rather than a choice between unions or no unions at all.[24] And John Schmidman has argued that if one recognizes the inevitability of internal dissent and conflict, there are definite advantages for trade unions and employers in dealing with each other. An employer dealing with organized employees can hope to avoid being subjected to the tactics of unorganized guerilla bands.[25] American companies sometimes give indications that they are aware of the possible disadvantages of an unstructured, nonunion environment. Spokespersons for General Motors, in particular, have commented that at stake in GM's relationship with the UAW is the predictability and orderliness of employee relations in the plant.

For some particular companies, and on the level of society as a whole, Dunlop and Schmidman are probably correct. But most companies in the United States operate nonunion in whole or in part and have the possibility at least of operating entirely nonunion. Believing unions to be inefficient and to be testimony to management's failure, and hoping to become free of them, most American companies now pursue a policy of what they have come to term "union avoidance."

Union Avoidance

Much of American management is very explicit about its desire to avoid dealing with unions. A study of management objectives in the labor relations area indicated that for companies with some union representation, fully one-third placed keeping as much of the company nonunion as possible ahead of achieving the most favorable bargain as the more important role of the labor relations function in the company.[26] For nonunion companies, the objective

---

[24] John T. Dunlop, 'The Future of the American Labor Movement," in *The Third Century: America as a Post-Industrial Society,* ed. S. M. Lipset (Stanford, CA: Hoover Institution Press, 1979), p. 191. I called attention to this point in D. Quinn Mills, "Flawed Victory in Labor Law Reform," *Harvard Business Review* 57 (May-June 1979), pp. 92–102.

[25] John Schmidman, *Unions in Post-Industrial Society* (University Park: Pennsylvania State University Press, 1979), pp. 138–39.

[26] Freedman, p. 5.

of remaining nonunion is indisputably the highest priority objective in the employee relations area.

In organization campaigns companies ordinarily assert both a right and an obligation to actively oppose unionization by expressing management's opposition to unions and by campaigning among the workers against the union. Today, most elections held by the National Labor Relations Board apparently involve active opposition by the employer to union representation.

As a result, union organization has again become an issue in collective bargaining. In 1976 the UAW obtained a so-called "neutrality pledge" from the major auto companies. Under the pledge, the companies agreed to assume a posture of neutrality in a union-organizing campaign conducted by the UAW. In 1979 the Rubber Workers got a similar pledge from several smaller rubber companies, but not from the largest, Goodyear. Also in 1979, the International Union of Electrical Workers failed to get a neutrality pledge from General Electric. In 1979, however, the UAW obtained further concessions from General Motors that appear to constitute almost a prerecognition of the UAW as bargaining representative in certain new GM plants.

Union avoidance does not only take the form of active campaigning in NLRB-conducted elections. The evidence presented in the labor law reform debates in 1977 and 1978 indicate that, at least as determined by the NLRB and court review, some companies transgress the law in their zeal to remain nonunion. Companies ordinarily resort to attorneys and litigation in conjunction with organizing attempts, and unions do also. Finally, a growing number of consultants and consulting firms now exist to assist managements in avoiding unions.

In the end, what may be most surprising to an observer of American management is the degree to which opposition to unions seems to be a matter of general doctrine rather than of analysis of the specific situation involved. If there are, as is sometimes argued, benefits of being unionized in some instances, American managers do not seem to investigate them. Rarely does one find an investigation by a company measuring the potential benefits versus the costs of recognizing a union. Where potential costs of unionized versus nonunionized operations are compared, the estimates seem to be based more on assumptions than on careful surveys.[27] Thorough analyses of options open to management are ordinarily performed for other management decisions, and some companies perform them in industrial relations also. But in the prevailing attitude in most of the business community, it appears to be an act of disloyalty to ask whether a third party (that is, a union) might not in some instances be on balance in a corporation's interest in dealing with its employees.

Modern Personnel Practice

The theory of personnel administration now accepted in most large American firms involves three principal elements. First, the firm maintains a comprehensive set of policies, including those for compensation, hiring, promotions, employee complaints, discipline, etc. To the extent possible, these policies are kept both consistent with each other and up-to-date. Second, the firm seeks to establish an employee relations climate of confidence, trust, and openness. This is sought in both the union and nonunion environment. A recent study of managerial practices with respect to labor relations noted that "management is particularly interested in its communication with individuals, not choosing to leave this territory to the unions."[28] Third, certain basic organizational structures in the company are required; these will be discussed in a later section.[29]

Fred Foulkes's chapter elsewhere in this volume addresses the personnel practices of large nonunion firms, and I do not wish to replicate his discussion here. However, it should be pointed out that many of the practices of nonunion firms have been adapted from those pioneered in unionized firms. Conversely, in recent years unionized firms have begun to borrow from developments in the nonunion sector. In the 1940s and 1950s most of the flow of development of personnel practices was from union to nonunion firms. By the 1970s, the flow was moving in both directions.

The major developments in personnel practices may be described as follows: Unionized firms ordinarily serve as pacesetters in compensation, with large nonunion firms adjusting pay

---

[27] Livernash, p. 8.
[28] Freedman, p. 62.
[29] Freedman, p. 7.

to comparable levels.[30] Unionized firms have also set the pace in establishing new benefits and in increasing their significance. But nonunion firms have pioneered in attaching compensation to the individual's performance (so-called "merit pay," often differing from both piecework and incentives) and in providing a choice of benefits for employees.

Some nonunion firms have made much greater efforts to provide employees with security against layoffs caused by business downturns than have unionized firms.[31] In part, this is because unions have preferred layoffs by seniority (with the worker then receiving unemployment benefits provided by the corporation and/or the government) to work-sharing arrangements.[32]

Also, nonunion firms have made major efforts to monitor employee attitudes, to exchange information, and to respond to employee complaints. Most major companies now have various sorts of employee communications programs. In nonunion companies, these programs serve as a form of grievance procedure.[33] The Bank of America, for example, has recently described its six major supportive programs for employees.[34] In general, personnel executives in most firms, union and nonunion alike, believe that well-managed programs of communication with employees can head off discontent and can create an atmosphere of identification of employee aspirations with those of the corporation.[35]

Corporate Organization in Industrial Relations

Managers of various responsibilities are involved in industrial relations. Line managers direct the workforce. Staff managers have specialized responsibilities for personnel and labor relations func-

---

[30] Bruce R. Ellig, "Salary Surveys," *The Personnel Administrator* 22 (October 1977), pp. 41–48.

[31] "How IBM Avoids Layoffs Through Retraining," *Business Week*, November 10, 1975, pp. 110–12; also "How IBM Stays Nonunion," *Industrial Week*, November 26, 1979, p. 84 ff.

[32] James L. Medoff, "Layoffs and Alternatives Under Trade Unions in U.S. Manufacturing," *American Economic Review* 69 (June 1979), pp. 393–94.

[33] The Conference Board, *Nonunion Complaint Systems: A Corporate Appraisal* (New York: The Board, 1980), Rep. No. 770.

[34] A. W. Clausen, "Listening and Responding to Employees' Concerns," *Harvard Business Review* 58 (January-February 1980), pp. 101–14.

[35] Roger M. D'Aprix, *The Believable Corporation* (New York: ANACOM, 1977).

tions such as compensation, hiring, affirmative action, and collective bargaining, to name a few. General managers have overall responsibility for setting policies, coordinating line and staff, and for the results.

General managers in different companies structure the line and staff relationships differently. In some companies corporate staff is kept to a small size, providing primarily advice and overall policy direction. Organization of large corporations by semi-autonomous divisions under central controls is now pervasive in American business.[36] Line managers in the divisions have industrial relations and personnel staff reporting to them. In other companies, staff at the divisional or plant level have a dual reporting responsibility—partly to plant or divisional line management, and partly to corporate staff. Much of what appears in the literature on personnel as an appeal for more "power" for the personnel function is an argument for reporting by plant and division staff directly to corporate staff rather than to plant or division top managers.

Companies also organize the various personnel and labor relations functions differently. Some combine all functions. Others separate labor relations from personnel. General Motors, for example, has corporate vice presidents for both labor relations and personnel. General Electric, however, includes all such functions under a single corporate vice president for employee relations. Nor is the industrial relations–personnel function always at a corporate vice presidential level. Some companies have only directors of personnel or labor relations. The labels "personnel," "labor relations," "employee relations," and "industrial relations," when used in corporate organization by different firms, do not always have the same meaning. The detailed list of personnel and labor relations functions may be distributed differently in different companies between personnel and labor relations, for example.

The Conference Board in 1965 reported that a survey of 249 large companies showed the head of the corporate personnel office as reporting to the chairman or president of the firm in 65 percent of the companies queried.[37] In 1979 The Conference Board re-

---

[36] Richard F. Vancil, *Decentralization: Managerial Ambiguity by Design* (Homewood, IL: Dow Jones-Irwin, 1979), p. 3.

[37] National Industrial Conference Board, *Personnel Administration: Changing Scope and Organization* (New York: The Board, 1965), Studies in Personnel Policy No. 203, p. 16.

ported that, of firms responding and having the particular level in the company, labor relations staff was present at the cited levels of the organization as follows: corporate, 92 percent; division, 59 percent; and plant, 68 percent.[38]

According to a 1977 survey of major manufacturing companies, 39 percent of personnel services and 47 percent of industrial relations services were performed at the corporate rather than at the divisional or plant levels of management.[39]

These statistics suggest that specialists in personnel and labor relations have in the last several decades[40] established themselves particularly strongly at the corporate level of American firms where they have substantial access to senior management. But these achievements for the staff specialists have not resolved problems that occur in the interaction of line and staff managers throughout American corporations.

Central to the organizational requirements for employee relations in business today is a balance of line and staff responsibility. In the traditional formulation of line and staff, line managers were to make employee relations decisions, while staff managers were to provide advice and to administer certain central functions.[41] This formulation is largely unchanged, but in recent decades there have been some shifts in emphasis. Staff officers are now encouraged in some companies to raise issues to high managerial levels where there is a conflict between line and staff managers over matters of significance. But this additional check by staff officers on line managers is very much limited in many companies because staff officers report to senior line managers whose decisions they are, therefore, often unwilling to challenge. The degree to which staff employee relations managers are encouraged to challenge line decisions, and are protected when they do so, may be used as a test in various companies of the degree of top management commitment to a comprehensive employee relations policy.

Another slightly different formulation of the line-staff relation-

---

[38] Freedman, p. 27.

[39] Vancil, p. 244.

[40] Gerald E. Kohler and Alton C. Johnson, *The Development of Personnel Administration* (Madison: Graduate School of Business, University of Wisconsin, 1971), Monograph No. 3.

[41] Charles A. Myers and John L. Trumbull, "Line and Staff in Industrial Relations," *Harvard Business Review* 34 (July-August 1956), pp. 113–24.

ship that is evolving in American industry has been advanced by O. M. Sherman of Goodyear. "The personnel or industrial relations manager . . . ," he notes, "is concerned only with the behavior of groups of employees. Decisions with respect to individuals are for the most part the responsibility of line managers." [42]

Large numbers of staff specialists have grown up in American business to perform personnel and employee relations functions. By 1979, unionized companies reported a ratio of one staff manager per 200 to 400 union-represented employees.[43] This ratio is surprisingly close to the ratio of one officer to 300 members reported for American trade unions in 1962.[44] Thus, for unionized American firms, there have developed substantial staffs specializing in industrial relations matters on both the union and management sides.

In corporations, staff executives in labor relations have tended to spend their careers in the function. By 1979, according to The Conference Board, "fully four out of five top labor relations executives have spent their whole corporate life in the industrial relations or personnel function." [45] The large number of employee relations staff, and the longevity of managers in this specialty, suggest that a high degree of professionalism has been achieved by management.

A survey taken in the fall of 1979 of chief executives of large businesses found that personnel matters were getting substantially more time from chief executive officers, and that the relative pay status of top personnel officers (for example, vice presidents of personnel or labor relations) had risen in comparison to top executives in other functions (including finance, legal, administration, and manufacturing).[46] This increasing attention from chief corporate officers is a mixed blessing, however. In a number of companies, executives from other functions, who have been without employee relations training, have been suddenly placed in charge of the employee relations function, apparently because of

---

[42] Sherman, paraphrased by Livernash, p. 2.

[43] Freedman, p. 29.

[44] Seymour M. Lipset, "Trade Unions and Social Structure: II," *Industrial Relations* 2 (February 1962), p. 93.

[45] Freedman, p. 29.

[46] Information Science, Inc., Montvale, NJ, as reported in *The Wall Street Journal*, October 16, 1979, p. 1.

dissatisfaction by top corporate officers with the performance of the personnel staff. Also, writers about personnel lament that the personnel function too often possesses too little support in business organizations to accomplish what ought to be done.[47] These circumstances are evidence that even as employee relations has become more professionalized, certain strains have continued in the corporate world about the performance of the function and its status in the corporation.

Finally, the late 1970s have seen the beginnings of what may become a further major round of innovation in corporate organization. The divisional structure of large-scale business was pioneered in the 1920s and has come to be the dominant form in the United States.[48] But in the 1960s there began to be discussions of an alternative form—the matrix organization. Within the last five years a formal matrix organization has been adopted by several important companies,[49] and there are those who believe the formal matrix system will become more common in American business. The development of matrix organization is creating confusion among such concepts as staff, line, and function.

Most descriptions of matrix organization stress the shared responsibility between functional and business or product managers. In matrix organization, the functional manager[50] has control of resources, while the business manager has control of product decisions (that is, the product manager determines what is to be done while the functional manager determines how it is to be done). The functional manager has a cost responsibility. The business manager has the profit-loss responsibility. To many commentators on matrix organization, this division of responsibility suggests that staff (or functional managers) have received a degree of line responsibility. The distinction between line and staff is said to be blurred or lost.

But the direct responsibility of the personnel and labor relations staffs has been largely unchanged by this reorganization. Man-

[47] Fred K. Foulkes, "The Expanding Role of the Personnel Function," *Harvard Business Review* 53 (March-April 1975), pp. 71–84.

[48] Allen R. Janger, *Corporate Organization Structures: Manufacturing* (New York: The Conference Board, 1973), Rep. No. 598, p. 8.

[49] Allen R. Janger, *Matrix Organization of Complex Business* (New York: The Conference Board, 1980), Research Rep. No. 763.

[50] *Ibid.*, p. 40.

agers in such functions as marketing, sales, technical development, and finance have received elements of line responsibility, but not the personnel managers. Instead, "line" responsibility for personnel matters becomes lodged in functional managers (that is, in marketing, research, and financial executives as well as in business managers). The virtually exclusively staff role of personnel seems untouched by the move toward matrix organization.

The Quality of Union-Management Relations

There are only a few barometers of the quality of union-management relations in American industry. The record of time lost due to strikes indicates the degree of open conflict. In the United States time lost due to strikes has been moderate in recent years. A second barometer is labor costs. It is an old saying in management circles that industrial peace can be purchased at the cost of the firm's solvency. Here the record is mixed. Labor costs have risen rapidly in the United States in recent years, but not noticeably more than those abroad. A last barometer involves grievance rates in various plants and companies. Livernash and Peach made a careful study of the significance of different frequencies of grievances in different plants and concluded that aggressive union leadership and ineffective managerial decision-making created an unfavorable climate in which high grievance rates occurred.[51] Unfortunately, we have no aggregate statistics on grievance rates.

Companies have the option of seeking the type of bargaining relationship they wish, although the relationship that actually emerges is, of course, equally at the option of the union. Using Selekman's classification,[52] one can conclude that few companies now seek a conflict relationship with a union. In some well-publicized instances, companies which in the past sought aggressively to contain union strength in collective bargaining have now sought, usually successfully, to find a more accommodative relationship. In part this has been attributed to increased professionalization on both sides in negotiations.[53] But it surely reflects as well a policy

---

[51] E. Robert Livernash and David A. Peach, *Grievance and Resolution: A Study in Basic Steel* (Cambridge, MA: Harvard University Press, 1974).

[52] Benjamin M. Selekman, "Varieties of Labor Relations," *Harvard Business Review* 27 (March 1949), p. 125.

[53] James Kuhn, "Electrical Products," in *Collective Bargaining: Contemporary American Experience*, ed. Gerald G. Somers (Madison, WI: IRRA, 1980), pp. 261–62.

decision on management's side to seek a different type of relationship.[54] One large company which has made such a shift in policy described three basic changes that were required: to advise the union of the company's position well in advance of negotiations; to reduce points of conflict with the union, such as moving or selling facilities; and to make management personnel aware of emerging issues quickly, so that action could be taken by the company when circumstances require it.

There are, of course, some very rough areas in union-management relations. Grievance strikes have been frequent in coal and in electrical manufacturing, to mention only two industries. Also, there have been lengthy nation-wide strikes during negotiations in coal and petroleum refining in recent years, and major localized strikes in retail food, construction, and other industries. Despite the Experimental Negotiations Agreement, the basic steel industry endured a lengthy strike in the iron ore range in 1977. Public-sector bargaining has seen important strikes also—in New Orleans, Cleveland, and Chicago, for example. In 1979–1980, International Harvester and the UAW experienced a lengthy strike.

Yet despite these difficulties and others that are not cited here, union-management relations on balance have improved in numerous ways and conflict has subsided. Statistics show that the percentage of time lost due to work stoppages has not increased dramatically. This is, I think, a remarkable record considering the substantial difficulties which the economy has been experiencing. To a degree, management attributes this record to the changing attitudes of unions, but some of the credit is also management's.

Where union-management relations have persisted for years, union officials seem to many managers to have developed a better understanding of the requirements of a business. Furthermore, the cost of industrial relations turmoil has risen for employees, who now "have a great deal more to lose" in strikes, according to George Meany, because of higher living standards and larger debt burdens.[55] But not all the attitude change has been on the union side. Managers seem to be more aware of the political aspects of a trade union leader's position, and more willing to accommodate

---

[54] Philips Madison, "Developing Healthy Management Attitudes for Dealing with a Union," *Personnel* 54 (September-October 1977), pp. 68–71.

[55] George Meany, *The New York Times*, May 21, 1972.

the peculiar needs of persons who seek to be elected and thereafter reelected to office.

In some instances corporations have actively sought to establish programs to improve the quality of the relationship with a union at the plant level. The experiments under way in the automotive industry which are referred to as "quality of working life" projects have as a major element the effort to improve union-management relations in the plants. According to reports from some companies and unions, grievance rates have dropped dramatically in some instances where these programs exist. Ordinarily, these projects have been created at management's instigation.[56] (Other projects of the same name in nonunion companies sometimes have had as a purpose keeping a facility unorganized.)

The question of union organization which is so prominent a concern of both management and unions casts a shadow on the quality of relationships even where a union is already established. Many companies now make it a practice to operate both union and nonunion. In manufacturing, some companies utilize a two-source supply system, in which the corporation has both union and nonunion plants.[57] Other companies own subsidiaries that are nonunion. Erosion of union representation, at least partly as a result of corporate policy, is encountered in industry after industry, including coal, construction, rubber, trucking, and electrical products.[58]

Further, the doctrine of nonunionism has proceeded so far in American management that in most major American firms the corporate officer responsible for relationships with unions is also responsible for the company's union avoidance program. The Conference Board's study of the management of labor relations in major industrial companies found that corporate vice presidents in the labor relations function were responsible for overall labor relations policy, involving dealing with unions that represent any of the company's employees and responsibility for avoiding further unionization.[59]

---

[56] Robert H. Guest, "Quality of Work Life—Learning from Tarrytown," *Harvard Business Review* 57 (July-August 1979), pp. 76–87.

[57] *The AFL-CIO Federationist* 85 (February 1978), p. 20.

[58] William H. Miernyk, "Coal"; D. Q. Mills, "Construction"; Harold M. Levinson, "Trucking"; and James Kuhn, "Electrical Products, in *Collective Bargaining: Contemporary American Experience.*

[59] Freedman, p. 12.

Most discussion of the factors which contribute to a successful labor relations climate mention that certainty of existence for both partners is a prerequisite of harmonious relations. Trust among individuals across the bargaining table is another supposed prerequisite of harmonious relations. Yet in industry after industry, companies threaten union survival.

It is remarkable, I think, that this situation has not embittered collective bargaining more than it has. It appears that, by and large, management has been successful in its attempt to compartmentalize these matters, so that conflict over union organization does not spill over to any great degree into collective bargaining or other aspects of union-management relations.

Impact of Business on the American Economy

Business is such a large part of the American economy that some of the questions that Freeman and Medoff ask, in their chapter, about the impact of unions on the economy seem unanswerable when applied to business. The more narrow questions can be sensibly asked, however. For example, we may ask, what is the impact of business on the efficiency of the economy, and on equality in the economy, two standards that Freeman and Medoff use to evaluate union performance.[60]

There are, of course, all kinds of businesses. If one thinks primarily of large, multifacility corporations, then the impact of such firms on the economy is different from that of smaller companies. Attention will be directed here primarily at large firms.

Does Business Contribute to Economic Efficiency?

Neo-classical economic theory tells us to look for economic efficiency in a large number of small firms supplying homogeneous products in the marketplace (so-called price-takers). In such a system, in equilibrium, consumer prices are minimized and profit rates fall toward zero. But most large American firms neither operate this way nor wish to. Instead, companies search for market imperfections which can become the source of substantial profits. Such advantageous positions in the market can be developed through patents on new products or processes, by product identifi-

---

[60] Richard B. Freeman and James L. Medoff, "The Two Faces of Unionism," *The Public Interest* 57 (Fall 1979), pp. 69–93.

cation through advertising, by eliminating competition through mergers or acquisitions, by controlling natural resources through ownership or leases, and by exploiting such barriers to entry of other firms as large initial capital investments. Many American business-persons are adept at utilizing these means to develop large and profitable companies. To the extent that companies seek to develop protected market positions, they cannot be said to contribute to economic efficiency. However, even large companies create a more competitive environment when they enter product markets previously dominated by only a few other sellers.

Some observers take a very different view of the conditions which promote economic efficiency. Instead of identifying efficiency with small, competitive firms, they equate it with large-scale, low-cost production. To them, an efficient marketplace is one dominated by one or two large cost-effective firms.[61] Antitrust laws and other legal paraphernalia for preserving a competitive economy are viewed as hindering enhanced economic efficiency.

This is not the place to engage in a lengthy evaluation of these contrasting views. However, it is possible to make two less than global observations about the evolution of American business and its impact on economic efficiency. First, most firms attempt to minimize production costs in the search for higher profitability. The larger firms often seem the most sophisticated in cost-minimization.[62] In this search for cost-minimization, business does contribute to efficiency in our economy. Whether or not the gains of cost-cutting are realized by consumers depends, of course, on the structure of the marketplace.

Second, American business has in recent decades contributed to a more concentrated economy by the growth and consolidation of firms. In 1950 the 200 largest industrial corporations controlled 48 percent of all manufacturing assets. By 1978 the figure was approximately 60 percent.[63] Apparently, the structure of the economy is becoming less competitive. There were, however, some

---

[61] Bruce Henderson, *On Corporate Strategy* (Boston: Boston Consulting Group, 1979) (published by Abt Books, Cambridge, MA).

[62] See, for example, John Z. DeLorean's account of cost-cutting at Chevrolet in the early 1970s, in J. Patrick Wright, *On a Clear Day You Can See General Motors* (Grosse Pointe, MI: Wright Enterprises, 1979), pp. 120–26.

[63] Willard Mueller, former chief economist of the Federal Trade Commission, quoted in *Time*, May 21, 1978, p. 63.

offsetting influences. Concern for the financial health of large corporations and new technological developments have caused many large firms to diversify into a larger number of product markets. This process increases competition in many product markets and thereby lessens the degree of economic concentration in the economy.

According to a study by Richard P. Rumelt, in 1949 nearly 70 percent of the 500 largest industrial firms were in either a single or a dominant business. By 1969 only 35 percent could be so described. In fact, in 1969 65 percent of the largest industrial companies had diversified into a group of related or unrelated businesses.[64]

A more recent study suggests that large firms primarily seek entry into new and growing markets. As a result, "above-normal rates of return [that is, profitability] could persist in [mature] markets for many years." [65] But, over time, these new products emerge as a larger and larger part of the economy, so that larger and larger firms compete with each other in a growing number of markets. Whether or not this evolution adds to, or subtracts from, the efficiency of the American economy is, I think, uncertain.

DOES BUSINESS CONTRIBUTE TO EQUALITY?

It is not difficult to support an argument that business stands as a barrier to increased equality in American life, but such an argument tends to be dominated by a short-term perspective. At any given time, proposals are being discussed in public forums or are pending in the Congress and the state legislatures which would have the effect of lessening inequalities of income, wealth, education, and social status through reforms or various transfer programs. Business ordinarily does not support these initiatives. Where it does give public support to initiatives to lessen inequality, as in reducing racial and sex discrimination, for example, it is often faulted for adjusting its own procedures too slowly or adjusting them not at all.[66]

---

[64] Richard P. Rumelt, *Strategy, Structure and Economic Performance* (Boston: Division of Research, Graduate School of Business Administration, Harvard University, 1974), pp. 50–51.

[65] E. Ralph Biggadike, *Corporate Diversification: Entry, Strategy and Performance* (Cambridge, MA: Harvard University Press, 1979), p. 206.

[66] Nancy S. Barrett, "Women in the Job Market," in *The Subtle Revolution: Women at Work*, ed. Ralph E. Smith (Washington: The Urban Institute, 1979), pp. 31–62.

But in a longer-term perspective, business as a whole is a major engine of social change, much of it in the direction of increasing equality. Business has largely created the mass-consumption society and the high living standards for many people which accompany it. The search for markets has led some businesses to pioneer in the production of previously luxury items for the average person, and to provide credit for purchases of durable goods. Business investment creates jobs and future production. Business efforts to rationalize production and control costs help to keep American firms competitive with firms abroad. It is argued continually that business has done either too little or too much of the things mentioned above. For example, credit creation allows people to improve their living standards by increasing consumption, so that perhaps there should be more. But it also places an increasing burden of debt on the American family, so that perhaps there is too much. However, despite the concerns of each moment, over the long term business contributes to a rising living standard.

Also, business creates employment. In the twentieth century, manufacturing has absorbed millions of persons displaced from declining employment in the agricultural sector of our economy. More recently, as manufacturing employment has stabilized, services have created millions of additional jobs. Blacks and women have been drawn into the labor force to fill many of these jobs. These are substantial contributions by business to enhanced social and economic equality.

CHAPTER 4

Large Nonunionized Employers*

FRED K. FOULKES
Boston University

Introduction

Organized labor's share of the labor force has declined significantly in the past 30 years. While union membership as a percentage of employees in nonagricultural establishments increased from 12 percent in 1930 to 35 percent in 1945, between 1955 and 1978 it declined from approximately one-third to 24 percent. If employee association membership is included, the figure is about 27 percent. The only growth the labor movement has seen in recent years has been in the public sector. There also has been a dramatic decline in the percentage of elections that organized labor wins. Union victories in National Labor Relations Board (NLRB) elections have decreased from more than 65 percent in 1955 to about 45 percent in 1979, the lowest in the NLRB's 44-year history. While the union victory rate is dropping in both right-to-work states and non-right-to-work states, it is dropping faster in the latter states where unions won half the elections five years ago.

In addition to faring poorly in organizing new workers, organized labor is losing heavily in decertification elections. In 1979's 777 decertification elections, employees voted the union out in 75 percent of the cases, a 10-year high and the second highest percentage in 30 years. The figure for bargaining units of fewer than 49 employees is approximately 79 percent. In discussing the role of collective bargaining in the broader array of labor policies such as ERISA, EEO, OSHA, incomes policy, and public-sector

* I am indebted to Professors Thomas A. Kochan, E. Robert Livernash, Robert B. McKersie, and Jack Stieber for very helpful comments on an earlier draft of this chapter.

dispute resolution procedures, Thomas A. Kochan of MIT wrote in the introductory chapter of his recent book:

> . . . "free collective bargaining" is now being subjected to a more severe test in both the private and public sectors. Collective bargaining is no longer viewed as the most preferred mechanism for setting conditions of employment in all contexts, on all issues, or for all workers and employers. Instead, the costs and benefits of the bargaining process and its results are being weighed against the costs and benefits of alternatives.[1]

Kochan stresses that society no longer uses labor policy only to get the parties to the bargaining table and to regulate the process, then letting the parties alone to set the substantive terms of employment. Other challenges to the current usefulness of collective bargaining come from both employees and employers. Some employees also believe that unions today are either corrupt, racist, sexist, or simply generally ineffective organizations. These issues present additional challenges for labor organizations.

There can also be little doubt about the declining influence of organized labor on the legislative and political fronts as well. In 1978 the Carter Administration and organized labor unsuccessfully supported a series of changes in the nation's labor laws designed to facilitate union organizing efforts. In 1980 the AFL-CIO endorsed President Carter. According to Alexander E. Barkan, head of the AFL-CIO's Committee on Political Education, the Carter endorsement ". . . was the best labor effort we ever fielded and to lose it so badly is hard to take."[2] The defections of union members from the Carter camp show not only problems with organized labor's alliance with the Democratic Party but also, apparently, how out of touch the leaders of labor have become from the rank and file.

With these statistics to confront and with a very different mood in the country, it is not surprising that the AFL-CIO is encouraging steps to coordinate and improve union organizing and that it is entering into discussions regarding union mergers as well as

---

[1] Thomas A. Kochan. *Collective Bargaining and Industrial Relations* (Homewood, IL: Richard D. Irwin, Inc., 1980), p. 22.

[2] Phillip Shabecoff, "Voter Shifts and Conservatives' Gains Worry Labor," *The New York Times*, November 9, 1980.

alliances with various women's groups. Attempts to expand female membership and continued reliance on the political and legislative processes are understandable. Increased concern on the part of union leaders about the investment practices of pension funds as well as about management consultants who assist companies wishing to remain nonunion is also not unexpected. The movement of industry from the North to the South and the shift from manufacturing to services further exacerbates labor's efforts. It would appear that the union movement is now a mature product that is losing its market share.

But the battle between organized labor and management is not new. The National Labor Relations Board, now more than 40 years old, has heard many cases and written much case law with respect to unfair labor practices. Yet the workload increases each year. Management in the United States, unlike employers in many other industrialized nations, has always resisted the growth of unions.

There are many environmental factors and company characteristics that retard the growth of collective bargaining. From a company's view, some are fortuitous or serendipitous; others are carefully managed. In 1955, John T. Dunlop developed a list of seven factors which he believed would retard union growth and a list of four which would make union organization of the workplace less difficult.[3] At the time Dunlop thought that the labor movement, which then constituted approximately one-third of the nonagricultural workforce, would be doing well if it were able to hold its own. His prediction, unlike those of some others, has stood the test of time remarkably well. In 1980 I developed a list of environmental factors and company characteristics that seemed to me to be important with respect to company efforts to remain nonunion.[4] While some of my factors are the same as or very similar to Dunlop's, there are some significant differences. But the purpose of this chapter is neither to debate the future of the United States labor movement nor to contrast the U.S. experience with that of other industrialized countries. These data and trends

[3] See John T. Dunlop, "The American Industrial Relations System in 1975," in *U.S. Industrial Relations: The Next Twenty Years*, ed. Jack Stieber (East Lansing, MI: Michigan State University Press, 1958), pp. 27–54.

[4] See Fred K. Foulkes, *Personnel Policies in Large Nonunion Companies* (Englewood Cliffs, NJ: Prentice-Hall, Inc., 1980).

are dealt with more specifically in other chapters in this volume. Most nonunion employers are found among medium- and smaller-sized companies. As D. Quinn Mills points out, there are many different types of nonunion employers. "Some are very small companies; some are very large. They operate in many different industries and regions of the country. They follow many different kinds of labor policies."[5] He suggests that there is a continuum of nonunionized employers, with the "low-standards employer" at one end and the "better-standards nonunionized employer" at the other. It should be pointed out that this chapter is about the key personnel policies and practices of a group of large "better-standards" employers; it is not about employer-employee relations in the medium-sized and small nonunion companies.

In this chapter I will share with the reader the major findings of an exploratory field study that analyzed the key personnel policies and practices of a select group of large, entirely or predominantly nonunion companies in the United States. The findings make it possible to construct a model of the values, policies, and climates that characterize the sort of large corporation that will remain nonunion. In addition to providing a better understanding and some explanations of the policies and practices of an important group of previously unstudied companies, the model suggests the beginning of a theory of the effective management of human resources that will help managements develop more effective employee relations approaches in nonunion as well as unionized companies. The model has obvious relevance not only to management, but to union leaders, public officials, and students of personnel and labor relations—or, to use the popular jargon, students of human resources management.

Line managers as well as personnel managers need to understand not only what these companies do, but also why and how they do it. Union leaders need to understand what happens in some large nonunion corporations, for their assumptions about what goes on and why are frequently incorrect. Public officials, too, need to understand the unorganized sector better, for their legislative and regulatory approaches frequently apply well only in the unionized sector. Students need to understand work prac-

[5] D. Quinn Mills, *Labor-Management Relations* (New York: McGraw-Hill Book Co., 1978), p. 48.

tices and the nature of the nonunion world in large companies from a practical point of view. And field work is needed to supplement, if not substitute for, abstract theories, computer models, statistical techniques, and mathematical elegance, for many of the assumptions made about large nonunion companies need to be tested by observation.

There is in the United States a small but impressive group of large companies which are essentially or entirely nonunion. One study found that approximately 5 percent of the *Fortune 500* companies are entirely nonunion.[6] A much larger group of companies are predominantly nonunion: that is to say, in these companies a majority of the production and maintenance workers are unorganized. The study I wish to summarize, which is described more fully in my recent book, included field work with 26 such companies. The model derived from the study helps explain the statistics presented earlier, and it also shows both the direct and indirect impact of the institution of collective bargaining on the nonunion company.

The companies chosen—either entirely or predominantly nonunion—were, for the most part, engaged in manufacturing. Most were on the *Fortune 500* list. They ranged, in terms of number of employees, from approximately 2,200 to 300,000, with almost half having more than 25,000 employees. In terms of production and maintenance employees in the United States, however, the range was from approximately 2,000 to about 20,000. Most of the companies, moreover, enjoyed leadership positions in their respective fields; their names are household words.

The case study–interview approach was used in this exploratory field study, and interviews were conducted with key line managers, including chairmen and presidents; operating executives and lower level management people, including supervisors; and key members of corporate personnel, including the head and staff members of personnel departments. In addition, management consultants, trade association executives, business professors, union leaders, community leaders, and people employed by other companies also were interviewed to provide additional perspectives

---

[6] Michael R. Bruce and David W. Hunt, "Communications in Non-Union Companies," Master's thesis, Sloan School of Management, Massachusetts Institute of Technology, May 1976, Ch. 1.

on the companies studied. In total, more than 500 individuals were interviewed for this study; approximately 100 of the interviews were with first- and second-line managers.

The model to be presented is depicted schematically in Figure 1. As will be noted, the "bottom line" is the climate of the company—the so-called organizational climate—which, it is asserted, results from a combination of certain values and goals of top management and company performance with respect to several substantive policy areas.

The substantive policy areas, to be elaborated upon subsequently, are: (1) effective management of environmental factors; (2) effective management of company characteristics; (3) handling of sensitive employees and work; (4) employment security; (5) promotion from within; (6) influential personnel departments; (7) satisfactory compensation programs; (8) effective communication programs, feedback mechanisms, and complaint procedures; and (9) careful selection, development, and evaluation of managers.

Top Management Philosophy, Values, and Goals
Regarding People and Unions

In some companies, at least historically, there developed a well articulated set of values or philosophy with regard to employees and how they were to be treated. The philosophy now usually is in writing and generally was first articulated by the company founder. The nonunion status of these companies, at least initially in some instances, seems not to be a goal, but a result of the successful implementation of that philosophy. Inherent in top management's thinking, however, is the view that if the company does its job well, the employees—or at least a large majority of them—will believe that a union is unnecessary. The nonunion status of these companies, then, is an essential by-product.

Typical is the philosophy of the founder of one of the companies in the sample. The founder's son, later a chairman of the company, said that his father's philosophy was essentially a simple one:

> What I think is the most important is our respect for the individual. This is a simple concept, but in [our company] it occupies a major portion of management time. We devote more effort to it than to anything else.

Figure 1

Top Management's Stated Beliefs in the Worth of the Individual,
Equity, Leadership By Example and other Attitudes, Values,
Philosophies and Goals Concerning Employees

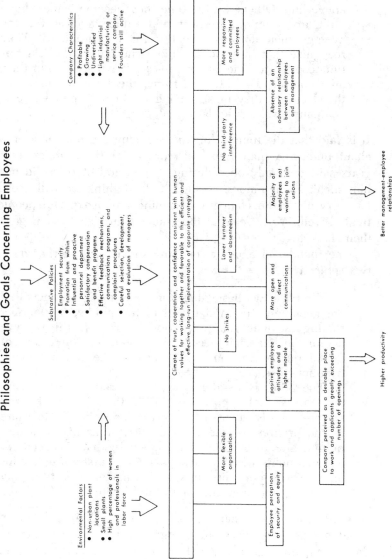

This belief was bone-deep in my father. Some people who start out in modest circumstances have a certain contempt for the average man when they are able to rise above him. Others, by the time they become leaders have built up a unique respect and understanding for the average man and a sympathy for his problems. They recognize that in a modern industrial nation the less fortunate often are victims of forces not wholly within their own control. This attitude forms the basis for many of the decisions they make having to do with people. [Our company] was in the latter category.

It is said that the founder of this company did not think or worry about unions. A man who had worked for the founder for three years said that only once during that period of time did he hear him speak about unions, saying: "I don't think we will ever have to worry about our company becoming unionized. Our people are treated well. We have what the unions want. That is our goal. Let them look to us."

The founder of another company spoke early of the company's twin objectives:

We have two basic aims. One is to make products that are genuinely new and useful to the public, products of the highest quality and at reasonable cost. In this way we assure the financial success of the company and each of us has the satisfaction of helping to make a creative contribution to society.

The other is to give everyone working for the company a personal opportunity within the company for full exercise of his talents—to express his opinions, to share in the progress of the company as far as his capacities permit, and to earn enough money so that the need for earning more will not always be the first thing on his mind. The opportunity, in short, to make his work a fully rewarding and important part of his life.

Other companies have clear-cut and well-articulated union-avoidance goals, policies, and programs. The top managements of these companies generally believe that being competitive means being nonunion. These views are usually particularly evident in the predominantly nonunion company—one wishing to contain the extent of unionization by keeping all new facilities nonunion.

Typical of the approach of such companies is the statement in one company's employee handbook. It states clearly and unequivocally the company's position with respect to unions:

> [The company's] personnel programs are designed to assist [workers] in satisfying their personal objectives in their work readily and without the need or cost of a labor union. [The company] does not say that unionism is either "bad" or "good." There are instances where employees have been helped by unions; but, on the other hand, there are many instances where unions have hurt employees. [Our company's] position is that unionism . . . would not help [our workers] in terms of pay and benefits or job challenge and satisfaction, and that unionism definitely would cost [our workers]—perhaps a great deal.
>
> During your employment with [us], you may be approached by a union organizer or another [company employee] trying to get you to sign a union card. You should be aware that no one can force you to sign such a card. If this does occur, we encourage you to, as a large majority of [our workers] all over the United States have done, reject the union's attempt to organize.

In another such company, which was originally family oriented but is now managed by "professionals," an internal memorandum on raises and benefits, written by the company's personnel vice president, states the nonunion policy well:

> It is [our] policy to take all lawful steps necessary or desirable to operate on a nonunion basis. In effect, we have an implied, unwritten contract with our employees which says . . . that we will voluntarily take those steps which are necessary to ensure that . . . they will receive compensation and benefits which in their totality are competitive with the unionized companies in our field in this area.

Fundamental to an assessment of the nonunion status of any company is an understanding of the objectives of top management with respect to employee relations. What is equally important, of course, is the way in which the values and goals of top management are expressed or made manifest in these organizations. How policies are developed and become effective must be understood. Both the importance and the difficulty of the diffusion and institutionalization processes cannot be overestimated. Nor can the importance of consistency and fit with business objectives be overemphasized.

Effective Management of Environmental Factors

In addition to top management's strong commitment to effective employee relations, several environmental factors clearly contribute to the nonunion status of the companies in the sample, as well as to the effectiveness of their personnel policies and programs. The existence of at least some of these factors appears to increase significantly the probability of developing and maintaining an organizational climate where unions are felt to be unnecessary. While some companies have benefited from some environmental factors that they had little to do with, others seem to have managed the conditions of their environments to their advantage.

The great majority of the management representatives in the sample believe that geographic location is a key factor determining the quality of a company's employee relations. With varying degrees of sophistication, several companies carefully scrutinize the labor climates of prospective sites for new plants. It is a common practice to avoid locating near large unionized companies; the proximity of an organized firm is believed to increase the risk of a union drive. Some companies shy away from urban locations, preferring rural or suburban settings where there may be strong antiunion community sentiments.

It should be observed, however, that not all of the companies studied had rejected what might be considered high-risk areas. (Only three of them, for example, had a significant workforce in the southern states.) One director of labor relations argued that there can even be advantages to operating in a highly industrialized, heavily unionized, urban area:

> A community of unionization sometimes is a plus for a company wanting to operate nonunion, for there will be a number of people who are down on unions as a result of the experience. It can be dangerous to build a plant in a cornfield. The risk is that sometimes another

company with poor personnel policies will come in. It will be nonunion and pay low wages. Then, if it becomes unionized and the first negotiation results in big increases, it can be an indirect message to your own employees.

Those nonunion companies in the sample that operated in cities where organized labor was strong attributed their success in staying nonunion to the nature and administration of their personnel policies. In the words of one manager, they "work hard" at staying nonunion.

Not only do some of the companies deliberately choose rural or suburban plant sites, but they frequently limit the size of their plants in order to keep employee relations on a personal, responsive basis. In the judgment of many managers, small plants are not only less vulnerable to organizational drives, but easier to staff with capable managers. Among the companies studied, the "ideal" size varied from 200 to 1,200 employees. Those with larger plants argue that in *very* small units, the high ratio of management staff to employees can reach inefficient levels. A facility also has to be large enough to justify the expenses of good supervision. Furthermore, from an employee relations point of view, tiny plants may actually be more vulnerable to organization: in the event of a union drive, the probability of a union's winning 51 percent of fewer than 100 votes in a representation election may be greater than if the unit has more than 100 employees.

In addition to location and plant size, a third environmental factor that appears to contribute to the likelihood of remaining nonunion is the proportion of women and professional employees in the workforce. More than one manager expressed the opinion that women are "antiunion," although many believe that this attitude is changing. At almost half of the companies studied, 50 percent or more of the production workers were female. Professional workers, too, are viewed as less likely than blue-collar workers to organize. To the extent that a company's business does not include much heavy industrial or assembly-line work, that company may attract an employee who has traditionally avoided unions.

Effective Management of Company Characteristics

Just as environmental characteristics may help a company remain nonunion, various company characteristics can also improve the working climate of a company and facilitate the implementation of proactive personnel policies. Healthy levels of profitability and growth are perhaps most important. The companies studied were generally profitable—some extremely so. Many were high technology, growth businesses, having dominant market positions and being leaders in their industry. Growth helps them implement promotion-from-within, an employment security policy, and profit-sharing. Although managers often argue that these attractive personnel policies contribute to their company's economic health, the policies might be reassessed if a reversal occurred in the profitability trend.

Second, highly diversified conglomerates probably have less opportunity to implement the kinds of personnel policies I shall describe in the following sections. The highly centralized, tightly controlled personnel departments that are typical of many of the relatively undiversified businesses studied seem to be best suited for carrying out comprehensive, consistent, and uniform personnel programs. In the companies studied, corporate personnel exercised a great deal of influence over local operations: wage increases, responses to grievances, and the content of training programs at individual plants were frequently subject to corporate approval. This sort of control is more common in an undiversified enterprise than in a conglomerate.

Certain industries may also provide less propitious environments than others for the successful implementation of positive personnel policies. Heavy manufacturing, for instance, has a large proportion of production and maintenance workers who cannot be shifted to alternate work when the market temporarily shrinks. To achieve "employment security," a large automobile manufacturer would have to designate everyone with several years of seniority temporary employees. The U.S. auto industry would appear to be simply too cyclical for an employment security program to be manageable; the companies would not know what to do with surplus workers when they are not building cars.

Finally, a company is probably more likely to succeed in putting a positive employee relations program into effect when ownership and management are either identical or closely associated with one another. Two of the companies in the sample were privately owned, with members of the founding family still active in management. In several of the public companies, a significant percentage of the stock was owned by one or more families, members of which were still active in top management. This is another way of illustrating that management must sincerely endorse the ideas of founders and owners for these ideals to be realized. As stated earlier, of crucial importance are the attitudes, values, and goals of top management.

It should be emphasized that no company in the sample enjoyed all of the positive environmental and company characteristics identified here. These factors are not necessarily a sine qua non for achieving the desired working climate and, in fact, some can even get in the way. The rapid growth and expansion of some companies, for example, while providing many promotional opportunities, can also create communications problems and cramped quarters that lead to unrest.

Handling of Sensitive Employees and Work

Although not actually part of the companies' substantive personnel programs, the manner in which these firms handled so-called "sensitive" employees contributed to their success in remaining nonunion. Sensitive work is defined as labor frequently done by unionized personnel. Some companies made it a practice to subcontract sensitive work. One company, for example, subcontracted its printing jobs, whereas many of its competitors did their own printing. In other cases, sensitive work was done on the company's premises by unionized employees of a subcontractor. When sensitive jobs *are* assigned to regular employees of a nonunion company, management pays special attention to the working conditions and wages of these workers and takes steps to listen to their concerns and to ensure that their wages and benefits are comparable to or better than those earned by unionized personnel.

Employment Security

In addition to top management's attitudes and certain important environmental factors and company characteristics, there are six substantive policies that seem to be key components of the successful effort to remain nonunion. The most important of these policies may be employment security. Many companies take steps to minimize the fears that employees have that they may lose their jobs due to lack of work.

Nearly all of the companies studied listed job security as one of their major personnel goals, and many provided this security through a full-employment policy—the practice of avoiding layoffs at almost any cost. Nine of the companies in the sample had never once had a layoff; six of the nine had never even reduced their hours. Even those companies that had laid off employees had devoted an unusual amount of thought and resources to the process.

A variety of techniques may be used to attain full or nearly full employment. To begin with, some companies maintain a lean permanent workforce, and when the workload expands to greater than normal levels, such firms rely on overtime, temporary employees, and subcontractors to relieve the pressure. For example, when one company launched a new product, it hired temporary workers for a specific period (90 days) to meet the increased need for labor. Some of these temporary workers were integrated into the permanent staff, as the workload permitted. In this way the company sheltered its permanent employees from temporary booms and busts in its need for labor. In essence, the practice transferred unemployment from the permanent labor force to part-time and temporary workers.

The practice of hiring subcontractors is another method of dealing with periods of increased or uncertain workloads. In these cases, the company's full-employment practice becomes the subcontractor's unemployment problem, since such contracts are curtailed or eliminated during slow periods.

The least radical methods that companies employ to weather a production slump are adoption of a hiring freeze and reliance on attrition to reduce the number of employees. In addition, a company may make it attractive for employees to take time off. One company, whose business was seasonal, offered an extra week to employees who took their vacations in the winter. Others permitted vacation banking and encouraged early retirement by offering generous financial incentives. One company offered two- to four-week leaves of absence during slack periods, a policy that was effective because the company employed a high percentage of women who took advantage of the offer to work around their homes.

Several more radical methods of avoiding layoffs are closely related to a company's business strategy. For example, some companies have built large warehouses so that during periods of idleness, the time is devoted to building up inventories. Another practice is to move work to idle plants, which one manager explained in the following words:

> We have a major buffer that is reserved for extreme and prolonged cases of demand dip, one that is available only to sizable companies that have diversified products. Even in times of general business recession, a company like ours has one or more products, usually new ones, for which the demand is expanding. What we have done on occasion is to move some of the manufacturing of those high-demand products to a plant whose regular products are in temporary trouble. Such a transfer, of course, is expensive and can seldom be justified purely on a cost basis. But we consider it imperative on a people basis. Having hired a workforce for a particular plant, the company is obligated to provide work for that force.

Building inventory, retraining workers, and moving workers to busy plants or moving work from busy to less busy plants are all costly methods of ensuring employment security.

Work-sharing, whereby tasks are redistributed at the same time that hours and sometimes pay are temporarily reduced, is another solution to a decline in demand. During the 1970 recession, for example, one company chose to cut everyone's pay by 10 percent (and reduce the workweek) for a six-month period rather than to lay off any employees. The pay cut applied to all employees, from the chairman of the board to the assembly-line worker. Work-sharing is used judiciously, however. None of the companies in the sample reduced schedules as much as one-third, and the reductions lasted for relatively short periods of time. If work-sharing were not strictly limited, workers might prefer the combined security of unemployment compensation and supplemental unemployment benefits that exists in some cyclical industries that are unionized.

If layoffs do become necessary, the companies studied believed that it is essential to adopt an equitable layoff system. Those that had layoffs relied fundamentally, if not exclusively, on the principle of seniority in deciding which employees to let go. Furthermore, special efforts were made to communicate openly to the workers the business conditions that necessitated the layoffs. In addition, the companies adopted programs to make re-employment easier. Job placement services and generous severance pay are two examples of how those nonunion companies tried to cushion the impact of layoffs.

There is no doubt that commitment to employment security contributes to workers' sense of well-being. Layoffs at competing, unionized companies are very visible to employees whose own managements are trying vigorously to maintain stable employment. Greater loyalty to the organization, less resistance to technological change, and better employee relations certainly are advantages that contribute to higher levels of productivity. On the other hand, the expense of an employment security program in terms of the planning necessary to implement it cannot be ignored. Although those companies that take extraordinary measures to provide their permanent employees with job security boast of the flexibility they gain from their nonunion status, one freedom that they have denied themselves is the ability to lay off workers as a response to changed business conditions. Although they may reassign and even transfer employees, the costs associated with such practices are substantial. Also essential to such approaches, of course, is the integration of manpower planning with business planning.

Promotion from Within

The policy of promoting from within, especially when accompanied by career counseling, training, and educational opportunities, was another fundamental principle among the nonunion companies studied. Indeed, many of the top-level executives interviewed started as hourly workers. Several of the companies made a practice of teaching existing employees new skills rather than hiring specialists from outside. The path from blue-collar, assembly-line work to an office or laboratory position was a common route for employees at many of these companies.

Sixty-five percent of the firms in the sample had institutionalized the principle of promotion from within by posting job openings. The rules of a job-posting system can vary in the following ways:

1. Range of job levels included. Some companies post many exempt positions as well as nonexempt jobs.
2. Size of the unit involved. In most cases studied, posting was very broad—either company-wide or regional.
3. Nature and number of exceptions. Some companies designate certain situations when in-line promotion may override the posting requirement.
4. Treatment of lateral moves. Some companies permit employees to take advantage of job posting in order to make lateral moves; others do not.
5. Length of time jobs are posted, length of service required before employees can apply for posted jobs, and limits on the number of posted jobs an employee can turn down.

The major advantage of job posting as perceived by those nonunion companies that practice the system is the benefit to individual career development and, hence, to employee morale. This translates into reduced turnover and, perhaps, lower hiring costs. Proponents also argue that the posting process keeps supervisors "honest," insofar as it reduces favoritism and fosters impartial promotions. Furthermore, widely publicized job openings are likely to uncover hidden talent, and they have the advantages of generating knowledge about the company's areas of growth and state of economic health, giving employees not selected helpful feedback so that they might be successful sometime in the future. Finally, its advocates believe that job posting helps realize affirmative action goals.

The major disadvantage of job posting cited is that it is time-consuming and, therefore, expensive. Critics also believe that, in practice, job posting is often undermined by preselection. Especially for high-level jobs, "favorites" and specifically groomed personnel are likely to be selected in preference to unfamiliar candidates. This can lead to disappointment and a decline in morale. Supervisors, too, may resent job posting if it robs them of good workers, or if the personnel department swamps them with unqualified candidates to interview, or if it takes too much time to fill vacancies.

In the opinion of its critics, job posting also frequently leads to the use of seniority as the primary criterion in making promotion decisions. Indeed, in the nonunion companies studied, much weight was given to seniority, in some cases even more than the typical union contract requires. Although at only two companies were senior qualified employees *always* given preference, in practice many seemed to rely heavily on seniority because it is easy to defend when justifying a decision to an unsuccessful applicant. This is, of course, especially the case for some lower level jobs.

Those companies that have rejected job posting prefer either management-initiated promotions or an employee-application system. The former method may vary from a sophisticated program of communicating employees' job skills and career goals to managers, to an informal ad hoc process. Both the management-initiated and the employee-application methods are defended on the grounds that they result in less weight for seniority as the primary standard for promotion and that they eliminate or reduce the many problems usually associated with a job-posting system.

Regardless of how it was implemented, all of the companies defended the practice of promotion from within. Yet it appears that such a policy may become more and more difficult to follow in the future because of the increasing importance of specialized knowledge, advanced education, and equal employment opportunity requirements. Will the company that relies on promotion from within as its exclusive source of talent remain competitive? To be viable, promotion from within requires high entry-level standards and sound management-development programs. Furthermore, changing government regulations have the potential for creating hostility between management and employees. An employee who is not promoted because of perceived discrimination prohibited by statute is free to take the charge to a government agency for review. In any case, companies today must do a better job than ever before of documenting and defending their promotion decisions.

Influential Personnel Departments

Among the companies studied, the heads of personnel frequently were included among the top-ranking members of management. More than half of the personnel vice presidents, for example, reported directly to the president. If they did not, their boss frequently was the former personnel head. The vice president of personnel may be involved in planning, pricing, sales campaigns, facilities use, and other business strategy along with the heads of finance, marketing, and manufacturing. At four of the companies, personnel vice presidents serve on their company's board of directors. In other cases, they frequently were members of the executive or management committees.

The unusually strong influence of personnel in many of these nonunion companies often originated with the founder or his successors, who established effective employee relations as a priority. One occasionally hears of legendary personnel "czars" who were close to the founder and reportedly exercised power ruthlessly. Personnel's power then, and to some extent now, derived from the fear of unionization. Today, government regulations and environmental considerations are also enlarging personnel's role.[7]

Another important reason for the influence of personnel departments at the companies studied was the common system of reward and punishment for line managers. When a department manager is accountable for the results of an attitude survey or the number of open-door complaints filed, he becomes receptive to the expert advice of the personnel department. Because effectiveness in employee relations is usually a measure of managerial competence at those companies, the influence of the personnel departments can be strong.

The organizational structure of many of the companies enhanced the authority of personnel as well as assuring that line and staff roles in the employee relations area were clearly defined. Personnel generally is highly centralized and exercises a great deal of power over division and plant officers in setting local policy. Typically, local personnel officers report on a "dotted line" basis to the corporate personnel director and on a "solid line" basis to their line managers, although in three of the companies studied employee relations officers at the plant level reported directly to

---

[7] See, for example, Allen R. Janger, *The Personnel Function: Changing Objectives and Organization* (New York: National Industrial Conference Board, 1977); Stewart C. Sheppard and Donald C. Carroll, eds., *Working in the Twenty-First Century* (New York: John Wiley & Sons, Inc., 1980); and *The Eighties: An Employee Relations Forecast* (New York: Organization Resources Counselors, Inc., February 1980).

corporate personnel rather than to their line managers. The "dotted lines," however, usually are very strong, for career advancement is typically through the personnel organization.

The personnel department, in general, performed three major functions at the companies studied: it assisted in the development and implementation of company-wide personnel policy, advised and counseled employees and line managers, and reviewed and monitored administration of personnel policy. In all of these areas, the strength of the department was visible. Personnel was typically involved in all hiring, sometimes even up to the rank of executive vice president. The authority to veto or otherwise influence all discharge and promotion decisions is common. Training and developing managers as well as employees of humbler ranks are also usually among personnel's responsibilities.

Perhaps it is accurate to compare the personnel departments in the companies studied to those found in Japanese corporations. In a paper entitled "Toward Convergence of Japanese and American Management Practices," Yoshi Tsurumi writes:

> Traditionally, in any Japanese firm, the personnel department is very close to the president who is, in turn, expected to maintain a personal interest in individual employees. The personnel department (and the personnel manager) is indeed a power center within the Japanese firm. Therefore, there is very little chance that the initiative and authority of the personnel department might be undermined or over-ridden by other departments.[8]

This quotation captures the essence of my findings.

Satisfactory Compensation Programs

The companies in the sample strove to insure that their pay and benefit policies were, and were perceived as, fair and equitable. The result, in my view, is that it is extremely unlikely that any of the companies studied will be vulnerable to a unionization drive on the basis of either pay or benefits. It was the stated policy of all of the companies to compensate employees at average or above-average levels for the industry and plant location. The

---
[8] Yoshi Tsurumi, *Multinational Management: Business Strategy and Government Policy* (Cambridge, MA: Ballinger Publishing Co., 1977), p. 213.

companies studied paid well by both industry and community standards.

In addition to paying as liberally or more liberally than their unionized competitors, the compensation plans at the companies studied had several other features in common. First, management usually set wages for production and maintenance workers according to local labor markets rather than adopting a national standard as is sometimes the basis of union wage scales. Second, the companies closely monitored union settlements in order to maintain equal or superior compensation. Third, these companies communicated their pay and benefit policies well, and in many cases had been doing so since before the passage of ERISA (1974).

There were two major types of wage plans among the companies in the study: merit pay and general wage increases. The entirely nonunion companies preferred merit pay and maintained that the ability to reward according to performance was a significant advantage of their nonunion status. As an incentive, they argue, merit pay encourages greater work effort than the system of single rates with the across-the-board increases that are typical of union contracts.

Critics of merit pay, who include personnel officials of the partially unionized companies in the study, believe that employees dislike the system. The absence of objective measures of performance, the fallibility of the supervisors who judge merit, and the difficulty of distinguishing one worker's performance from that of the next in many machine-paced processes all make merit pay for production and maintenance workers almost impossible to administer, they argue. Furthermore, inflation can totally disable a merit-pay system when companies struggle to determine and explain to employees what percentage of an increase is due to inflation and what percentage is the reward for merit.

In practice, it seems that wage increases based on merit are nearly as automatic as general increases. Some companies in fact use merit pay in combination with yearly or semiannual general increases. Others have adopted a "step" system of raises in which the earlier increases are automatic and the later ones supposedly are based on performance. Even where merit pay is neither supplemented by general increases nor partially automatic, however, many supervisors who administer it prefer to give similar increases to all their employees. Merit raises tend to be closely related to seniority because it is much easier to justify pay differences based on experience and seniority rather than on performance. The only real advantage of the merit pay system to most companies appears to be greater freedom to withhold increases in cases where performance is clearly inadequate, and the opportunity it affords to meet and talk with employees on an individual basis.

Many of the companies studied, in addition to offering merit pay programs, paid salaries rather than hourly wages: approximately half did not have any "hourly employees" at all. Bestowing the status of salary on blue-collar workers represents an attempt to remove the "we-they" distinction between management and labor, or between office and plant personnel. The allowances for illness, tardiness, or personal business impart respect and responsibility to the employees. The absence of a time clock imparts psychological status, these companies believe. Salary plans also serve to distinguish a company favorably from other firms in its industry or community.

Just as the nonunion companies studied paid a great deal of attention to their wage scales, they attempted to be leaders, or at least competitive, in the benefits they offered. Designing benefit packages from surveys of their competitors' practices and analysis of their own employees' needs, many of the companies had a history of being the first in their industry with an innovative profit-sharing, medical, or other benefit plan. Those companies that could not afford to be leaders in terms of the number of dollars they spent devoted much effort to making themselves appear competitive by designing unique or unusual benefit packages whose actual cost might be far less than that of traditional offerings.

Two principles were generally manifest in the benefit policies of the companies studied: a commitment to leadership and equality, and a desire to communicate benefit provisions effectively. Regarding equality, employees of all ranks were eligible for the same programs, just as executives and production workers often shared the same cafeteria and other company facilities. These companies also energetically publicized their benefit policies through periodic publications, audio-visual presentations, and even contests.

The amount of money the companies spent at the time of the study ranged from 18 to 52 percent of payroll. However, because they calculated costs in different ways, the list of nonunion companies studied was submitted to the Economic Analysis and Study Section of the U.S. Chamber of Commerce, which has developed a uniform system for comparing benefits. The Chamber reported that the average employee benefits for 1973 of the 11 manufacturing companies in the sample was 39.5 percent of pay, 180.5 cents per payroll hour, and $3,821 annually, compared to the manufacturing industry average of 32 percent of pay, 146.2 cents per hour, and $3,111 annually.[9]

The companies studied also offered a variety of other financial plans. Traditional pension plans, which used a formula that combined earnings and years of service to determine the level of retirement income, were often supplemented at the entirely nonunion companies by deferred profit-sharing plans, under which the money the employee received was related to the company's profitability. In addition, half of the companies offered some type of cash bonus program, tied either to company profitability or to employees' earnings. Finally, 24 of the 26 companies offered investment programs—either savings programs under which the company typically matched 50 percent of the employee's contribution, or opportunities to purchase the company's stock, usually at a discount. Such plans are designed to make employees identify with and feel more a part of the enterprise.

Effective Communications and Feedback Mechanisms, Complaint Procedures

The managements of the companies studied frequently argued that the most important single factor in keeping a company nonunion was effective communications. They had devised a number of communications programs that, on the one hand, disseminated information about the company to its workforce and, on the other, elicited employees' attitudes about the company's treatment of its personnel. These communications programs gave employees the opportunity to voice complaints, offer opinions, and make sugges-

---

[9] This comparison may be misleading for the following reasons: (1) the industry averages are not weighted by size or corporation; (2) levels of pay are not taken into consideration; (3) cost does not necessarily reflect quality of benefits, since some companies may be able to provide them more efficiently than others; and (4) cost does not necessarily reflect the value of benefits to the employee.

tions, while allowing management to uncover problems and respond constructively. The companies also tried to create a climate in which it was legitimate to request and receive help with personal problems.

A common communications device is the attitude survey; half of the companies studied used it in one form or another. Regarded as an early warning system for spotting dissatisfaction, and a relatively objective way to study trends in employee attitudes, surveys are most effective when administered on a regular basis. The responses are anonymous, and confidentiality is strictly protected. Employees rate the company, their job, pay and benefit policies, and a variety of specific factors affecting the working climate. Managements follow up the results of surveys with varying degrees of commitment: those who formulate policy using survey results believe that the device is effective only if employees actually see changes taking place.

One disadvantage of surveys is that they are often resented by supervisors and low-level managers, who suspect either that employees don't take the questionnaires seriously or that surveys stir up unrest. Supervisors are also likely to feel that they are left out of the process. Supervisory concern about the surveys is probably one measure of their effectiveness, since if supervisors were indifferent toward or free to ignore survey results, employees would certainly regard surveys as meaningless.

Management also makes an effort to communicate with employees by means of counseling. The personnel staff frequently provides career counseling and also may be available to discuss personal problems. Two of the companies studied employed outside experts—social workers and ministers—to provide personal counseling.

At three of the companies studied, the employees elected representatives to serve on committees along with management and staff members. At several companies meetings between groups of employees and managers served to encourage communications. Annual "skip-level" interviews of employees by high-level managers are also used. (Managers "skip" a level or more to conduct interviews with employees two or three levels below them.) Finally, in many companies management responds formally to anonymous comments, complaints, and questions of employees.

These programs are frequently called "Speak-Out" or "Speak-Up" programs.

In addition to the variety of programs that encourage communications, the companies studied had formal grievance procedures. In contrast to many unionized companies, however, only two firms in the sample provided for outside, binding arbitration of grievance disputes. As an alternative to binding arbitration, these companies usually adopted an "open-door" policy—a series of discussions beginning with the employee's immediate supervisor and proceeding to higher levels of management if necessary. The goal of the open-door policy, which typically consists of formal, rigorous review and investigation, is to encourage supervisors and managers to resolve employee problems informally, before they reach the "official" avenues of solution. A principal finding with respect to formal grievance procedures in use at these nonunion companies was that they were rarely used. This is not to say, however, that they were unimportant. Analysis of the formal complaint procedures in use suggests that their main value is the encouragement they give to managers and supervisors to resolve employee problems before they become formal complaints. The formal procedures stimulate and enhance the effectiveness of informal problem-solving behavior, for their existence helps keep managers and supervisors "on their toes" with respect to the employee relations aspects of their jobs.

Careful Selection, Development, and Evaluation of Managers

An important way in which the nonunion companies studied achieved their personnel objectives was through the time and resources they devoted to the selection, development, and evaluation of managers. Of particular importance was the reward-and-punishment system as it was perceived by line managers, from division general managers to first-level supervisors. In order to convey to line management that effectiveness in dealing with employees is an important measure of their competence, for example, many of the companies avoided bonuses that rewarded short-term performance, believing that the pressure to meet short-run production and profit objectives often led to problems in the area of employee relations. In deliberate attempts to emphasize their long-run performance, including satisfactory employee relations, a company may offer managers stock options and other financial incentives that reflect the company's well-being over a continuous period of time.

Manager selection was a carefully considered procedure at the companies in the sample. "Panel" interviews, during which potential managers were subject to a series of interviews by examiners at various company levels, had been instituted in some cases. This procedure was intended to replace the traditional process where the boss picks his favorite for a promotion. Other companies sent candidates for managerial promotion to "assessment centers" for a series of rigorous tests. For example, candidates were given three hours to deal with a full "in-box," and they were judged on their ability to identify priorities and subdue management crises rapidly.

The ability to deal with people was weighted heavily in appraisals of managers' performance at these companies. Managers who were poor "people managers" might be removed from supervisory positions. Not only did management personnel regard the results of attitude surveys as indicators of their competence, but in many companies they believed that a union organizational drive or another major personnel problem would retard or even end their careers in the company. Given the companies' practice of associating promotion and job security with effective employee relations, it is not difficult to understand why line managers and personnel staffs kept their eyes focused on critical personnel issues. It also helps explain why personnel departments were listened to in these companies, and from whence they got their influence with line managers. This is obviously more true for some jobs than for others, and varied by company, but abilities in employee relations appeared to be very important in managerial selection and advancement at these companies.

At lower levels of the organization, many influences were brought to bear on the careers of supervisors. Considerable time, effort, and resources were devoted to supervisory training because it is the supervisors who deal with employees on a day-to-day basis. At best, employees have only occasional contact with top management, the personnel department, or a formal communications program. The nonunion companies studied maintained that well-trained supervisors who were sensitive to employees' problems, and who were working for managers with similar concerns, are essential.

Moreover, company programs, implemented by supervisors and managers, encouraged employee participation and involvement. Such programs included profit-sharing meetings, quality circles, and job-design and quality-of-worklife programs.

Because top management's personnel "vision" frequently focuses on the humblest employees, the supervisor may have the most difficult role of all in the nonunion companies studied. In some cases, the preoccupation of the founder with the welfare and security of the hourly workers appeared to have depreciated the role of the supervisor, who may not feel the security he believes is afforded to those he supervises. If supervisors come to experience too much insecurity or anxiety, this could be detrimental to the long-run health of the organization. This explains why the education and training of supervisors were considered critical by these companies.

Conclusion

While an understanding of the motivation and commitment of top management is essential, students of industrial relations should be interested in the institutionalization process as well. It is one thing for a company founder to declare that a worthwhile worklife is a company goal. It is another matter to put policies and practices into place which achieve that result after the founder has passed from the scene. Unless, through formal and informal processes, such goals, values, policies, and practices become part of the daily agenda of both line and staff managers, it is inconceivable that such philosophical statements can have a continuing impact.

It is frequently said that before something can be managed, it has to be possible to measure it. Some companies today, well aware of the importance of effective employee relations to business and competitive success, have found ways to measure and manage employee relations. The personnel programs and policies as well as the reward systems for managers are, accordingly, tailored to the bottom-line goal of achieving and maintaining the desired organizational climate. In such companies, the line manager whose company unit has many grievances or a union organizational drive does not distinguish himself within the corporation. Regular attitude or quality-of-working-life surveys help managers spot and deal with trends with respect to the human conditions of the organization. In one company the regular survey results in the color-coding of each organizational unit—either red, yellow, or green. If a manager's unit is coded either red or yellow, it is closely monitored and improvement is expected. Interestingly, in this company good employee relations and successful business performance correlated quite nicely.

My study convinces me that, barring a depression or major changes in company or environmental factors or union effectiveness, it is unrealistic to expect, at least in the private sector, any reversal of the trend away from unionization. This conclusion stems in part from the fact that many companies, especially large ones, have learned to manage their human resources very effectively, but even more from the observed desires of top managements to remain nonunion. Behind this motivation is both economic and noneconomic reasoning. Given a real commitment on the part of top management, appropriate policies and practices can be made effective. Thus, if unions are to effect any reversal in the strong trends I observed, drastic changes will be required.

The study also shows the impact that the union movement and the institution of collective bargaining has had on the policies of large nonunion companies. Unions have clearly done a lot of good for workers who are neither members or dues-payers to those organizations. Some of the large nonunion companies studied resembled the large unionized companies. Some, moreover, imposed upon themselves policies that are more restrictive than those that may emerge or be imposed under union contractual arrangements. This is true not only with respect to pay and benefits, but, more importantly, with respect to the plant's operating rules.

One cannot escape noting that one driving force behind the policies described is the fear of being unionized. To the extent that these approaches continue to be successful over time and spread to other companies, the portion of the U.S. workforce represented by organized labor will continue to decline, simply because these approaches seem to obviate the felt need on the part of at least a majority of the workforce for union representation.

A question with longer-run significance for students of industrial relations as well as for society is whether, eventually, the threat of unionization will be perceived as being so slight that some companies will lessen their commitment to effective human resources management.

Finally, and even though this chapter has been about the personnel policies and practices of a select group of large nonunion companies, the student of industrial relations should also consider the significance of some of the approaches discussed for improved employee relations in the organized sector. Employment security programs, effective upgrading, training and career development opportunities, improved communications, profit-sharing or other such equity-participation plans, and more sensitive supervisors and managers would contribute substantially to better employee relations and, with proper initiatives and good relationships with the union leadership at both the national and local levels, could result in better union-management relations as well.

CHAPTER 5

The Role of Law

THEODORE J. ST. ANTOINE
University of Michigan

I. Introduction

In the early New Deal days, workers' placards in the coal fields proudly proclaimed, "President Roosevelt wants you to join the union." [1] If not literally true,[2] that boast was well within the bounds of poetic license. After the brief interval of federal laissez-faire treatment of labor relations ushered in by the Norris-La Guardia Act of 1932,[3] the National Labor Relations (Wagner) Act of 1935 declared the policy of the United States to be one of "encouraging the practice and procedure of collective bargaining." [4] Employers, but not unions, were forbidden to coerce or discriminate against employees because of their organizational activities. Employers, but not unions, were required to bargain in good faith. Sparked by this government endorsement, the labor movement went on to enjoy the most spectacular decade of growth in its history.[5]

Only a dozen years after the passage of the NLRA, however, in the wake of the massive strikes that swept the country at the end of World War II, the national mood had changed dramatically. The House of Representatives was even prepared to repeal the

[1] Foster Rhea Dulles, *Labor in America* (New York: Thomas Y. Crowell, 1960), pp. 267–68.

[2] Roosevelt's initial indifference toward organized labor in general, and his lack of enthusiasm for the National Labor Relations Act in particular, are recounted in Irving Bernstein, *Turbulent Years: 1933–1941* (Boston: Houghton-Mifflin, 1969), pp. 2–7, 186, 190–91, 215–16, 324; Frances Perkins, *The Roosevelt I Knew* (New York: Viking, 1946), pp. 239–40, 325–27.

[3] 47 Stat. 70 (1932), 29 U.S.C. §101 (1976).

[4] 49 Stat. 449, §1 (1935), as amended 29 U.S.C. §151 (1976).

[5] Union membership increased from 2.9 million in 1933 to 14.8 million in 1945. Lloyd G. Reynolds, *Labor Economics and Labor Relations* (Englewood Cliffs, N.J.: Prentice-Hall, 1978), p. 339.

policy of "encouraging . . . collective bargaining," although cooler heads like Senator Taft ultimately prevailed and this language was left intact.[6] Taft's announced purpose was to redress the "balance" of power, so that "the parties can deal equally with each other." [7] So now unions were prohibited, like employers, from coercing or discriminating against employees. Unions became bound by a reciprocal duty to bargain. More to the point, unions were deprived of one of their principal organizing devices, the secondary boycott, with Senator Taft explicitly disavowing any distinction between "good" and "bad" boycotts.[8] Unions, along with employers, were made liable to suit in federal district court for breach of a labor contract, and subject to an 80-day federal injunction in the event of a strike or lockout imperiling the national "health or safety."

The Labor Management Relations (Taft-Hartley) Act of 1947[9] laid the foundations of the federal law that has governed union-employer relations (outside the railroad and airline industries[10]) during the past 30 years. In retrospect, union claims that Taft-Hartley was a "slave labor" law border on the paranoid. Yet the Act did signal a major shift in the predominant American attitudes toward organized labor, from sympathy and support to neutrality at best and increasing distrust or hostility at worst.[11] And passage of Taft-Hartley coincided with an abrupt halt in the forward progress of unionization throughout the country.[12] The reasons for

[6] See, e.g., H.R. 3020, 80th Cong., 1st Sess. §§1(b), 101 ["section 1"] (1947), as passed House; H. Conf. Rep. No. 510, 80th Cong., 1st Sess., pp. 30–31 (1947); 93 Cong. Rec. 3698 (daily ed. April 17, 1947) (remarks of Rep. Celler); 93 Cong. Rec. 7690 (daily ed. June 23, 1947) (remarks of Sen. Taft).

[7] 93 Cong. Rec. 7690 (daily ed. June 23, 1947) (remarks of Sen. Taft).

[8] 93 Cong. Rec. 4323 (daily ed. April 29, 1947) (remarks of Sen. Taft).

[9] 61 Stat. 136 (1947), as amended 29 U.S.C. §141 (1976).

[10] Rail and air, which are heavily unionized, are regulated by the much less controversial Railway Labor Act, 44 Stat. 577 (1926), as amended 45 U.S.C. §151 (1976). The RLA of 1926 was the product of a agreed-upon bill submitted jointly by the railroads and the rail unions. The Act has emphasized the use of permanent tripartite boards to resolve contract grievances and bargaining disputes. See generally *The Railway Labor Act at Fifty*, ed. Charles M. Rehmus (Washington: U.S. Government Printing Office, 1976).

[11] Opinion polls in the 1970s showed there is no other major institution in our society whose leadership so consistently lacks the confidence of the general public. Everett Carll Ladd, "The Polls: The Question of Confidence," *Public Opinion Quarterly* 40 (Winter 1976–77), pp. 544, 545.

[12] Except for a short-lived spurt during the Korean War, the trend of the percentage of unionized workers in the United States has been steadily downward since 1947, from a high of 23.9 percent of the total labor force in

this decline are manifold. Probably the most important is the continuing shift of jobs from the blue-collar to the white-collar sectors. Nonetheless, various studies, including comparisons of the superior membership gains of Canadian unions during the years 1947–1957, suggest that Taft-Hartley and amendments to it may have played a substantial role in impeding organization.[13]

This survey of the role of law in American industrial relations over the last three decades will first deal with the soundness of the power balance between unions and employers that has been struck by the federal government. The ouster of most aspects of state regulation in this field through the so-called "preemption" doctrine will be discussed next. Attention will then focus on the high priority accorded individual rights during the past 20 years, both in the workplace and within labor organizations. This focus on the individual employee will lead naturally to a consideration of the increasing emphasis of federal law on the substantive regulation of employment relationships, union and nonunion alike, as distinguished from the more traditional procedural regulation of collective bargaining. Finally, there will be a word on the elusive goal of "labor reform" at a time when Congress seems immobilized by pressure from conflicting interest groups, and when the political influence of organized labor has sunk to a new low.

II. Federal Neutrality and the Quest for An Appropriate Power Balance

One theory behind the Wagner Act was that collective bargaining was the workers' best hope, but that unions were weak and needed federal protection and assistance against entrenched, oppressive employers. The theory behind Taft-Hartley was that unions themselves had grown too powerful, and that workers, smaller employers, and the general public now needed protection against them. The result was a code of union unfair labor practices,

that year (33.1 percent of nonagricultural employment) to 19.7 percent (less than 25 percent of nonagricultural) today. Bureau of Labor Statistics, *Handbook of Labor Statistics—1978*, Bull. No. 2000, p. 507; *New York Times*, July 13, 1980, §3, p. 1, col. 1.

[13] See, e.g., Lester Spielman, "The Taft-Hartley Law: Its Effect on the Growth of the Labor Movement," *Labor Law Journal* 13 (April 1962), pp. 287, 290–91, 299–300; Harold M. Levinson, "Trucking," in *Collective Bargaining: Contemporary American Experience*, ed. Gerald G. Somers (Madison: IRRA, 1980), pp. 99, 135–36, 147.

including the prohibition of secondary boycotts, and federal sanctions against strikes in breach of contract and strikes that might cause a national emergency. While the official policy favoring collective bargaining was retained, the operative effect of Taft-Hartley was to transform the federal government from a promoter of unionism to something more like an impartial referee, enforcing a set of Marquis of Queensberry rules against two combatants, here, labor and management. Inevitably, however, the infinite variety of union and employer tactics, and the infinite variations in the economic power of the respective parties, have often made it difficult for government to determine a proper stance of neutrality.

SUPERSENIORITY, LOCKOUTS, AND "DISCRIMINATION"

Without any subjective antiunion animus, and with the wholly legitimate purpose of maintaining production in the face of a strike, an employer offered a 20-year "superseniority" credit to strike replacements and to strikers who would return to work. Violations of Section 8(a)(3) of the NLRA customarily require an "illegal intent," in this instance, "discrimination . . . to discourage [union] membership." In *NLRB* v. *Erie Resistor Corp.*,[14] the Supreme Court was prepared to sustain the National Labor Relations Board's unfair labor practice finding on the ground the grant of such superseniority was so "inherently discriminatory or destructive" that it "carried its own indicia of intent." Not unreasonably, the NLRB in two subsequent cases relied on this analysis to strike down employer resorts to a lockout as an offensive bargaining weapon. This time the Court reacted quite differently. In *American Ship Building Co.* v. *NLRB*,[15] it declared that the statute did "not give the Board a general authority to assess the relative economic power of the adversaries in the bargaining process and to deny weapons to one party or the other because of its assessment of that party's bargaining power." The Board's unfair labor practice rulings on lockouts were set aside.

One can appreciate the Court's thesis in the abstract. The referee does not change the rules because the heavyweight contender weighs in at 195 pounds while the champion tips the scales at 210.

---

[14] 373 U.S. 221 (1963).
[15] 380 U.S. 300 (1965). See also *NLRB* v. *Brown*, 380 U.S. 278 (1965).

But what then do we make of *Erie Resistor's* "inherently destructive" rationale? Or of the clear implications in *American Ship* that it might have made a difference if the employer had locked out prior to an impasse in the bargaining or if the employer had continued operations with permanent or even temporary replacements? In defining the Board's proper role, how does one distinguish in the concrete between its allowable appraisal of certain conduct as "inherently destructive" and its forbidden conclusion' that use of a certain weapon could give the employer "too much power"?

The Supreme Court in the superseniority and lockout cases enunciated general principles of scant predictive value. That would not be so bad if employers and unions were simply being informed that the deleterious impact of the diverse economic devices used by either side was intrinsically uncertain and that their categorization as "inherently destructive" of employee rights would have to turn on an ad hoc inquiry into the facts of each particular case. Unfortunately, in the classification process the Supreme Court seems to have relied on armchair speculation rather than on-site inspections. In the lockout cases, for example, the unions sought through "Brandeis briefs" to demonstrate the actual effect of the employers' action by presenting data on employee savings, the unions' war chests, and so on. The Court did not deign to dignify this approach with so much as a footnote reference.

These contrasting decisions highlight one of the dilemmas of legal administration in a field like labor. The NLRB must handle some 60,000 cases a year. Efficiency and economy of operation, as well as a concern for predictability, dictate a heavy stress on hard and fast rules and decision-making by categories. Yet drawing such subtle inferences as an employer's "illegal intent" from the "inherently destructive" nature of its conduct will surely result in frequent injustice unless there is the closest scrutiny of individual facts. To date the Supreme Court has not come close to resolving this dilemma.

SECONDARY BOYCOTTS AND INDUSTRY DIFFERENCES

Taft-Hartley, through Section 8(b)(4) of the amended National Labor Relations Act, outlawed the classic secondary boycott. That occurs when a union attempting to organize the Ace Manufacturing Co. proceeds to picket Black Retailers, asking the employees of Black to strike him as long as he continues to stock Ace products. The standard analysis is that Ace is the "primary" employer, and that the union is seeking to pressure it by enmeshing a neutral or "secondary" party, Black, in a dispute of no concern to the latter. The NLRB and the courts have spent the last three decades trying, with mixed results, to draw the line between allowable primary activity and forbidden secondary activity.[16]

The Supreme Court's most celebrated single essay at such line-drawing was *NLRB* v. *Denver Building & Construction Trades Council*.[17] Construction unions struck a job site when the unionized general contractor engaged a nonunion subcontractor to do electrical work. The unions contended they had a primary dispute with the general for failing to make the job all-union. The Supreme Court disagreed, holding in effect that the nonunion sub was the unions' "primary" target, that the sub and the general were independent contractors, and that to strike with an object of forcing the general to cease doing business with the sub was a violation of Section 8(b)(4). The Supreme Court may have flown in the face of reality by refusing to categorize the general contractor and the subcontractors on a building project as "economic allies," and thus to be treated as a single primary employer for statutory purposes. Indeed, since *Denver* was decided in 1951, every administration except President Ford's has favored legislation to overrule or modify it and to authorize "common situs" picketing in the construction industry.[18] But *Denver* remains the law.

Over the years a number of loopholes were exposed in the original Taft-Hartley ban on secondary boycotts. Probably the most serious was the so-called "hot cargo" or "hot goods" clause.

---

[16] A masterful analysis is performed by Howard Lesnick, "The Gravamen of the Secondary Boycott," *Columbia Law Review* 62 (December 1962), p. 1363. See also Raymond Goetz, "Secondary Boycotts and the LMRA: A Path Through the Swamp," *Kansas Law Review* 19 (Summer 1971), p. 651; Theodore J. St. Antoine, "What Makes Secondary Boycotts Secondary?" in *Labor Law Developments—Proceedings of the Eleventh Annual Institute on Labor Law*, ed. Southwestern Legal Foundation (Washington: BNA, 1965), p. 5.

[17] 341 U.S. 675 (1951).

[18] Ironically, the only time Congress mustered the votes to pass a common situs picketing bill was during the Ford presidency, and he vetoed it. Presumably, the Reagan Administration would also oppose a change in the *Denver* rule.

An essential element of a Section 8(b)(4) violation was a strike by employees. If a union went directly to an employer and got him to agree voluntarily, or even under a threat of violence or economic pressure, to cease dealing with another person, that would not be a violation, although the selfsame result effectuated by a strike would be prohibited.[19] The International Brotherhood of Teamsters made much use of "hot cargo" clauses to require union truckers not to handle freight that had been carried by nonunion firms. In the Labor-Management Reporting and Disclosure (Landrum-Griffin) Act of 1959,[20] Congress added Section 8(e) to the NLRA to prevent such arrangements.

Section 8(e) opened up another problem. By its terms it forbids an employer to agree "to cease or refrain from . . . using . . . the products of another employer, or to cease doing business with any other person." That would apply literally to an outright ban on subcontracting designed to preserve bargaining unit work, a result obviously not intended.[21] The problem gets sticky if the ban takes the form of an agreement not to use a particular product, like prefitted doors on a building project. In *National Woodwork Manufacturers Assn. v. NLRB*,[22] five Justices of the Supreme Court were prepared to say the union objective in such an instance was "preservation of work" traditionally done on site by carpenters, and it was thus primary. According to the majority, the "touchstone" was whether the challenged agreement was "addressed to the labor relations of the contracting employer vis-à-vis his own employees." Four dissenting Justices thought such a patent "product boycott," even for work-preservation purposes, was within both the "clear word" and the intent of the secondary boycott proscription.

The problem of reconciling work preservation and Section 8(e) becomes even stickier if, as so often happens, the work the union is trying to "preserve" has undergone some sort of transformation because of technological innovation. The Supreme Court confronted this situation in dealing with containerized shipping in

---

[19] E.g., *Carpenters Local 1976* v. *NLRB* [Sand Door], 357 U.S. 93 (1958).

[20] 73 Stat. 519 (1959), as amended, 29 U.S.C. §401 (1976).

[21] E.g., *Truck Drivers Local 413* v. *NLRB*, 334 F.2d 539 (D.C.Cir. 1964), cert. den., 379 U.S. 916 (1964).

[22] 386 U.S. 612 (1967).

NLRB v. *International Longshoremen's Assn.*[23] The ILA had agreed with a shippers association that ILA labor would have the job of "stuffing" or "stripping" all containers within a 50-mile radius of the port, and that a royalty would be paid on any containers passing over the piers intact. The NLRB concluded that since ILA members had never performed off-pier stuffing or stripping, it was engaged in illegal work acquisition rather than permissible preservation of work within its traditional jurisdiction. In another 5-4 decision, the Court disagreed that the determination that the work of the longshoremen had historically been the loading and unloading of ships was dispositive. Writing for the majority, Justice Marshall declared the question was how the parties "sought to preserve that work, to the extent possible, in the face of massive technological changes." The case was remanded to the Board for initial consideration of whether "the stuffing and stripping reserved for the ILA . . . is functionally equivalent to their former work," or whether "containerization has worked such fundamental changes in the industry that the work formerly done at the pier . . . has been completely eliminated." Although insisting the Board's answer was not preordained, Justice Marshall added pointedly: "This determination will, of course, be informed by an awareness of the congressional preference for collective bargaining as the method for resolving disputes over dislocations caused by the introduction of technological innovations in the workplace."

Justice Marshall's opinion apparently accepts, without explanation, the work preservation–work acquisition dichotomy as critical in boycott analysis. This is not a logical imperative. If an employer's labor relations "vis-à-vis his own employees" is the "touchstone" of primary activity, why is it so significant that he or his employees have never previously done the work he now has at his disposal?[24] Furthermore, deciding that a particular agreement, if accepted by an employer, does not run afoul of antiboycott strictures says nothing at all about whether the employer had any obligation under the NLRB to bargain about the matter in the first place. Perhaps he could have refused even to discuss it on the

---

[23] 100 S.Ct. 2305 (U.S. 1980).

[24] It is established that an employer must have the "right of control" over disputed work, or union pressure to secure it from him will be secondary. *NLRB* v. *Pipefitters Local 638* [Enterprise Assn.], 429 U.S. 507 (1977).

ground it was a managerial prerogative. That is an issue we shall consider later.[25] Beyond these legal conundrums lies the more fundamental policy question of how workers' interests in safeguarding their jobs should be balanced against employers' interests in increasing efficiency through technological improvements. Congress of course is the ultimate arbiter here, and, as Justice Harlan once put it, the Court should be cautious about outlawing union-employer arrangements to alleviate the problem "until Congress has made unmistakably clear that it wishes wholly to exclude collective bargaining as one avenue of approach to solutions in this elusive aspect of our economy." [26]

If the political climate were more propitious, it would be time for a thorough reexamination of boycott law in general. There has been entirely too much moralizing about what is essentially a device for exerting economic force. The boycott's allowance or disallowance should depend on a careful weighing, on the basis of empirical evidence, of union need against business and consumer injury. Some time ago I surveyed 99 cases in which the NLRB had found secondary boycott violations over a 28-month period.[27] Several conclusions emerged. First, the secondary boycott is largely a construction industry phenomenon. The building trades account for 70 percent of all violations. If the Teamsters were added in, only 15 percent of the secondary boycotts in my sample were left for the unions in all other industries combined. Quantitatively, this should greatly reduce apprehensions about the ravages of the secondary boycott. Picketing and strikes at a common situs in the construction industry would not even constitute violations of Section 8(b)(4) were it not for the much-criticized *Denver Building Trades* decision.[28]

Second, my study indicated that over three-fifths of all secondary boycotts had an organizational objective. It has been suggested elsewhere that as long as national policy officially favors collective

---

[25] See text at notes 64–67 *infra*.

[26] *National Woodwork Manufacturers Assn.* v. *NLRB*, 386 U.S. 612 (1967) (concurring opinion).

[27] Theodore J. St. Antoine, "The Rational Regulation of Union Restrictive Practices," in *Labor Law Developments 1968—Proceedings of the Fourteenth Annual Institute on Labor Law*, ed. Southwestern Legal Foundation (Washington: BNA, 1968), pp. 1, 11–14.

[28] See text at note 17 *supra*.

bargaining, boycotts for organizing purposes should be lawful.[29] The point has additional appeal now that union membership is down to only about one-fifth of the labor force.[30] But I am not ready to conclude, for this reason alone, that the restrictions on the boycott should be loosened. Against this evidence of union need must be set the evidence of damage caused by secondary boycotts to primary employers, secondary employers, and the public generally. Another empirical study conducted at the University of Oklahoma found that the injury to neutral parties was "negligible."[31] My own results were not quite so sanguine, although they did indicate that primary employers have a larger stake than secondary employers in the enforcement of boycott bans.[32] In any event, if it could be established that unions have a pressing need to use the secondary boycott for organizational purposes, and that neutrals suffer only small harm from it, Congress might be impelled to a more discriminating judgment than any rendered heretofore on the availability of this particular economic weapon.

Congress has already drawn some antiboycott lines on an industry-by-industry basis, and this may be a promising approach to pursue. For example, the garment industry is so highly integrated that collective bargaining could not exist if employers were able to subcontract to nonunion firms. Congress has responded by exempting that industry, in practical effect, from the antiboycott provisions of the statute.[33] Congress has also recognized the special relationships of general contractors and subcontractors at a construction site and has permitted building unions to seek agreements guaranteeing all-union jobs there.[34] In light of the massive power of the International Brotherhood of Teamsters vis-à-vis small individual truckers, on the other hand, one might always wish to

---

[29] Paul A. Brinker and William E. Cullison, "Secondary Boycotts in the United States Since 1947," *Labor Law Journal* 12 (May 1961), pp. 397, 403. See also Archibald Cox, "The Landrum-Griffin Amendments to the National Labor Relations Act," *Minnesota Law Review* 44 (December 1959), pp. 257, 273–74.

[30] See note 12 *supra*, and accompanying text.

[31] Brinker and Cullison, *supra* note 29, p. 403.

[32] In the 99 cases examined, primary employers sustained "substantial" damage to their businesses on 65 occasions, while secondary employers sustained such damage on only 46 occasions. St. Antoine, *Labor Law Developments—1968*, *supra* note 27, pp. 11–12.

[33] NLRA §8(e), 29 U.S.C. §158(e) (1976).

[34] *Ibid.*

retain bans on boycotts in the trucking industry, even if they were relaxed elsewhere.[35]

UNION ELECTION CAMPAIGNS—UNREALISTIC RULES AND INEFFECTIVE REMEDIES

A secret ballot election conducted by the Labor Board is probably the most dramatic manifestation of the rights accorded employees by Section 7 of the NLRA to organize and bargain through "representatives of their own choosing," [36] or to refrain from such activities. The importance of representation elections has been further enhanced by Supreme Court rulings that an employer who steers clear of unfair labor practices that might preclude a fair vote can ordinarily insist upon a union's filing a petition for an election, and need not grant recognition on the basis of signed authorization cards, which often exaggerate the support for the union.[37] Ideally, the vote that is finally registered should reflect the employees' free and informed choice, reached after careful consideration of the arguments for and against unionism. In the pursuit of this ideal, the NLRB has expended much time and energy perusing employer and union campaign communications for evidence of "coercive" statements that might have improperly influenced the voters' decision. There is now reason to believe, however, that all these years the Board may have been chasing a mirage in its efforts to ensure fair elections.

A recent empirical study of 31 NLRB elections could find no significant difference between voter behavior in "clean" and "dirty" campaigns.[38] Employees made up their minds on the basis of predispositions, their direct experience with the employer, and occasionally their personal contacts with the parties' representatives.

[35] See Cox, *supra* note 29, pp. 273–74; Robben W. Fleming, "Title VII: The Taft-Hartley Amendments," *Northwestern University Law Review* 54 (January-February 1960), pp. 666, 688. But at least one respected labor economist believes even the Teamsters have been adversely affected by hot cargo and other boycott restrictions. Levinson, *supra* note 13, pp. 99, 135–36, 147.

[36] NLRA §7, 29 U.S.C. §157 (1976).

[37] *Linden Lumber Div., Summer & Co. v. NLRB*, 419 U.S. 817 (1974); *NLRB v. Gissel Packing Co.*, 395 U.S. 575 (1969).

[38] Julius G. Getman, Stephen B. Goldberg, and Jeanne B. Herman, *Union Representation Elections: Law and Reality* (New York: Russell Sage, 1976). See also Derek C. Bok, "The Regulation of Campaign Tactics in Representation Elections under the NLRA," *Harvard Law Review* 78 (November 1964), p. 38.

But the actual content of the parties' speeches and other messages counted for relatively little. Coercion was rarely if ever a factor. The authors recommended that the Board "cease regulating speech," and that elections should be rerun only where employer conduct "interferes with union access to employees." [39] Shortly after this study, the NLRB was prompted to reexamine its rule concerning misrepresentations in a campaign. A 3-2 majority concluded that the Board generally would no longer set elections aside because of misleading statements.[40] Just a year later, however, a new 3-2 majority overruled that decision, returning to the position that an election should be invalidated if there is a substantial misrepresentation that the other side does not have time to refute.[41] A priori reasoning had apparently triumphed over the unsettling intrusion of hard fact.

There would be less concern about the substance of campaign propaganda if both parties, like opposing political candidates, had an equivalent opportunity to reach the voters. Unfortunately, the NLRB has seemed inhibited from any attempt to develop equal access rules by two other Supreme Court decisions concerning unfair labor practices. They held, first, that an employer could rely on its property rights to prevent entry to company premises by nonemployee union organizers as long as other channels of communication were reasonably available,[42] and, second, that an employer could use its supervisors to conduct an antiunion campaign on company time without allowing similar pro-union activity by employees, so long as this did not create "an imbalance in the opportunities for organizational communication." [43] Thus, the Board has expressly declined to set an election aside because an employer made an antiunion speech on company time shortly before an election and refused the union a chance to reply.[44] Yet these situations could readily have been distinguished. First, the Board undoubtedly has greater latitude in prescribing rules for the conduct of a fair election under Section 9 of the NLRA than it has

---

[39] Getman et al., *supra* note 38, p. 159.

[40] *Shopping Kart Food Market*, 228 NLRB 1311 (1977), *overruling Hollywood Ceramics Co.*, 140 NLRB 221 (1962).

[41] *General Knit of California, Inc.*, 239 NLRB No. 101 (1978).

[42] *NLRB v. Babcock & Wilcox Co.*, 351 U.S. 105 (1956).

[43] *NLRB v. United Steelworkers* [Nutone], 357 U.S. 357 (1958).

[44] *General Electric Co. and McCullock Corp.*, 156 NLRB 1247 (1966).

in finding a party guilty of an unfair labor practice under Section 8.[45] Second, empirical evidence is now available that an employer who addresses his employees at the workplace while denying those facilities to the union normally does reach a substantially larger proportion of his employees, thus producing the requisite imbalance in communication.[46]

The NLRB also appears to have been stymied in its efforts to fashion effective remedies for employer refusals to bargain by an unnecessarily broad reading of another Supreme Court decision. At the present time an employer who is willing to stand the heat of public opinion can forestall negotiations for several years. Eventually he will be subject to a judicially enforceable order to bargain, but in the meantime the employees will be denied the fruits of any contract that good faith bargaining might have produced. The Labor Board has refused union requests for a "make-whole" reimbursement remedy in these circumstances, even when the employer's violation is "clear and flagrant." [47] Prominent in the Board's thinking was the often-reiterated view of the Supreme Court that the Labor Act's philosophy of freedom of contract is antithetical to official compulsion of the actual terms of a collective bargaining agreement.[48] Thus, the Court has held contract terms may not be imposed even as a remedy for a proven violation.[49]

There is no gainsaying that a make-whole award would tend to place a floor under any settlement negotiated later. But technically it would not set contract terms for the future; it would merely be a measure of the employees' losses in the past. The Labor Board also claims that its expertise is not adequate to the task of calculating an appropriate amount. Courts have not been deterred, however, from estimating antitrust damages on the basis of a plaintiff's lost contracts,[50] and the availability of Bureau of Labor Statistics figures on union wage scales, comparable labor

---

[45] NLRA §§8, 9, 29 U.S.C. §§158, 159 (1976).

[46] Getman et al., *supra* note 38, p. 156.

[47] *Ex-Cell-O Corp.*, 185 NLRB 107 (1970), *enforced*, 449 F.2d 1058 (D.C.Cir. 1971); *Tiidee Products, Inc.*, 194 NLRB 1234 (1972), *enforced*, 502 F.2d 349 (D.C.Cir. 1974), *cert. den.*, 421 U.S. 991 (1975).

[48] NLRA §8(d), 29 U.S.C. §158(d) (1976) ("such obligation [to bargain collectively] does not compel either party to agree to a proposal or require the making of a concession").

[49] *H.K. Porter Co.* v. *NLRB*, 397 U.S. 99 (1970).

[50] See, e.g., *Bigelow* v. *RKO Pictures Inc.*, 327 U.S. 251 (1946).

contracts in the industry or area, and the like, should ease the Board's chore considerably. The egregious refusal to bargain would seem the paradigm case for application of the principle that if a wrongdoer has itself created the uncertainty, it should not be heard to complain when doubts are resolved against it.

Under the ill-fated Labor Reform Bill of 1978 Congress would have acted with regard to both the problem of union access to employer premises and the problem of inadequate bargaining remedies. The NLRB would have been directed to use its rule-making authority to establish guidelines providing unions an equal opportunity to reply to an employer's antiunion speeches on company property during an organizing drive. An employer would also have been subject to a make-whole remedy in favor of its employees if it unlawfully refused to bargain with a union prior to the execution of a first contract. Although the bill passed the House of Representatives easily, it ran afoul of a prolonged Senate filibuster that an unprecedented six attempts at cloture could not break. Subsequently, partisans of both management and labor were in agreement that business groups had organized "perhaps the most extensive and intense lobbying effort ever to hit Congress," [51] with an "all-time high of over three million . . . pieces of mail" pouring in on the Senate.[52] That is an extraordinary commentary on management hostility to a bill which had the general backing of every living ex-Secretary of Labor, Democrat and Republican, and which was designed not to alter the balance of bargaining power between unions and employers, but only to facilitate the organizing of the unorganized.[53]

DUTY TO BARGAIN

Whether imposing a statutory duty to bargain in "good faith" could ever amount to more than a pious exhortation has been the subject of much controversy. At the hearings on the original

---

[51] Gerald E. Rosen, "Labor Law Reform: Dead or Alive?" *University of Detroit Journal of Urban Law* 57 (Fall 1979), pp. 1, 8.

[52] Lester Asher, "Prospects for Labor Law Reform: Implications for Unions," in *New York University 31st Annual National Conference on Labor*, ed. Richard Adelman (New York: Matthew Bender, 1978), pp. 257, 264.

[53] Statements of Willard Wirtz and John T. Dunlop, *Hearings on H.R. 8410 [Labor Reform Act] before the Subcommittee on Labor-Management Relations of the House Committee on Education and Labor*, 95th Cong., 1st Sess., Pt. 2, pp. 326, 334, 346 (1978).

Wagner bill, Harvard's Sumner Slichter caustically likened it to enacting "that the lions and lambs shall not fail to exert every reasonable effort to lie down together."[54] As recently as 1961 a distinguished Labor Study Group branded the requirement "unrealistic," adding that "the provisions designed to bring 'good faith' have become a tactical weapon used in many situations as a means of harassment."[55] Over the years, however, there has been increasing evidence the statute has had practical effect, including voluntary compliance by management. Thus, one survey revealed that successful bargaining relationships were eventually established in 75 percent of the cases sampled that went through to a final Board order, and in 90 percent of the cases that were voluntarily adjusted after the issuance of a complaint.[56] Although a recalcitrant offender, as we have seen, can drag his heels with impunity, the majority of American employers and unions are law-abiding. However hard it may be to classify legally such particular tactics as "take-it-or-leave-it" bargaining,[57] it would seem almost perverse to deny at this late date that overall the statutory duty to negotiate in good faith has had a salutary impact.

Over the past 20 years, the most controversial issue concerning the duty to bargain has been the extent to which employers must negotiate about managerial decisions that result in a shrinkage of employee job opportunities. One approach could have been that the parties were simply under an obligation to deal in good faith with one another, whatever the subject might be. The Supreme Court may have made a serious misstep in the famous *Borg-Warner* case,[58] however, when it went in a quite different direction and endorsed the NLRB's classification of bargaining subjects

[54] Quoted in Russell A. Smith, "The Evolution of the 'Duty to Bargain' Concept in American Law," *Michigan Law Review* 39 (May 1941), pp. 1065, 1083.

[55] Labor Study Group, *The Public Interest in National Labor Policy* (New York: Committee for Economic Development, 1961), p. 82. Members of the Study Group were Clark Kerr, chairman, Douglas V. Brown, David L. Cole, John T. Dunlop, William Y. Elliott, Albert Rees, Robert M. Solow, Philip Taft, and George W. Taylor.

[56] Philip Ross, *The Government as a Source of Union Power* (Providence, RI: Brown University, 1965), pp. 180–230; Frank W. McCulloch, "The Development of Administrative Remedies," *Labor Law Journal* 14 (April 1963), pp. 339, 348.

[57] E.g., *General Electric Co.*, 150 NLRB 192 (1964), *enforced*, 418 F.2d 736 (2d Cir. 1969), *cert. den.*, 397 U.S. 965 (1970).

[58] *NLRB v. Wooster Div., Borg-Warner Corp.*, 356 U.S. 342 (1958).

as "mandatory" or "permissive." "Mandatory" is now shorthand for
the statutory itemization of "wages, hours, and other terms and
conditions of employment" about which the parties are obligated
to bargain.[59] Either union or employer may insist on seeking agreement on a given mandatory topic to the point of an impasse or
breakdown in negotiations. On the other hand, neither party may
demand bargaining on a permissive subject, that is, managerial
prerogatives or matters of purely internal union concern, if the
other party objects. Insistence on such an item as a condition of
contracting will be equated with an unlawful refusal to bargain
on mandatory subjects.

The existing rules suffer from several shortcomings. First, government becomes too much the arbiter of the appropriate subject
matter of collective bargaining. Why should a federal agency,
rather than the parties themselves, determine whether a particular
item is so important that it is worth a strike or a lockout? Second,
the current doctrine makes for hypocrisy in negotiations. If a party
deeply desires a concession on a nonmandatory subject that may
not legally be carried to impasse, what can it be expected to do?
It will hang the bargaining up on a fake issue that happens to
enjoy official approbation as a mandatory topic. Finally, the present mandatory-permissive rules are not logically necessary, and
are probably less likely than several possible alternatives to promote sensible collective bargaining.

At least two other tacks could have been taken in *Borg-Warner*.
One would have eliminated the mandatory-permissive distinction
entirely. Whatever either party wanted to put on the table would
have called for good faith negotiating. Candor would have been
enhanced, and unresolved disputes would have been recognized
for what they ordinarily become anyway, matters to be decided by
economic muscle. A second, middle course was advocated by Justice Harlan in *Borg-Warner*. He would have retained the mandatory-permissive distinction, but with a difference. Either party
would still be required to bargain to impasse about mandatory
subjects and not about permissive subjects. That is the existing
law. At the same time, however, either party under the Harlan
formulation could persist in pursuing any lawful demand, regardless of how the Board might categorize it, and refuse to contract

---

[59] NLRA §8(d), 29 U.S.C. §158(d) (1976).

absent agreement on that item. In short, Justice Harlan read Section 8(d) of the Labor Act to mean what it says, and only that. A party is obligated to bargain about wages, hours, and working conditions. But an insistence on bargaining about more is not the equivalent of a refusal to bargain about a mandatory subject. A union, for example, could dismiss out of hand an employer's demand for a secret-ballot strike vote procedure, but the employer would not commit an unfair labor practice if he remained adamant on it. Either of these two approaches might have comported better with the realities of collective bargaining than the law as now propounded.

Borg-Wagner is the accepted standard, however, and the parties must play the hand that has been dealt them. Under that rubric, it is crucial whether certain subjects are classified as working conditions or management rights. For a long time the NLRB held that in the absence of antiunion animus, employers did not have to bargain over decisions to subcontract, relocate operations, or introduce technological improvements, although they did have to bargain about the *effects* of such decisions on the employees displaced. Layoff schedules, severance pay, and transfer rights were thus bargainable, but the basic decision to discontinue or change an operation was not.[60] Under the so-called Kennedy Board, however, a whole range of managerial decisions were reclassified as mandatory subjects of bargaining. These included decisions to terminate a department and subcontract its work,[61] to consolidate operations through automation,[62] and to close one plant of a multiplant enterprise.[63]

In *Fibreboard Paper Products Corp.* v. *NLRB*,[64] the Supreme Court gave limited approval to this shift of direction. It sustained a bargaining order when a manufacturer wished to subcontract out its maintenance work. The Court emphasized this did not alter the company's "basic operation," or require any "capital investment." There was merely a replacement of one group of employees with

[60] E.g., *Brown McLaren Mfg. Co.*, 34 NLRB 984 (1941); *Brown-Dunkin Co.*, 125 NLRB 1379 (1959), *enforced* 287 F.2d 17 (10th Cir. 1961).

[61] *Town & Country Mfg. Co.*, 136 NLRB 1022 (1962), *enforced* 316 F.2d 846 (5th Cir. 1963).

[62] *Renton News Record*, 136 NLRB 1294 (1962).

[63] *Ozark Trailers, Inc.*, 161 NLRB 1294 (1966).

[64] 379 U.S. 203 (1964).

another group to do the same work in the same place under the same general supervision. Bargaining would not "significantly abridge" the employer's "freedom to manage the business." One court of appeals has elaborated on this rationale and held there is no duty to bargain about a "change in the capital structure." [65] Other courts of appeals, in cases of partial shutdowns and relocations, have balanced such factors as the severity of any adverse impact on unit jobs, the extent and urgency of the employer's economic need, and the likelihood that bargaining will be beneficial. [66] This has the attraction of maximizing fairness in individual situations, but it can lead to uncertainty and unpredictability. In recent years the Labor Board itself seems to have retreated somewhat from its former firm stand in favor of bargaining. For example, a 2-1 majority held an employer did not violate the statute when it totally terminated the manufacturing portion of its operations without bargaining over the question. [67]

Within the established framework of the mandatory-permissive dichotomy, the practical inquiry is whether imposing a duty to bargain about these "managerial" decisions will do more harm than good. It will obviously delay proceedings, and may interfere with the confidentiality of negotiations with third parties. In some instances bargaining will be doomed in advance as a futile exercise. Nonetheless, the closer we come to recognizing that employees may have something akin to a property interest in their jobs, the more apparent it may become that not even the employer's legitimate regard for profit-making or the public's justified concern for a productive economy should totally override the workers' claim to a voice in the decisions of ongoing enterprises that will vitally affect their future employment opportunities. [68] A leading management attorney of my acquaintance says he has "Fibreboarded" his unions for years, long before the decision itself, simply as a matter

---

[65] *NLRB* v. *Adams Dairy, Inc.*, 350 F.2d 108 (8th Cir. 1965), *cert. den.*, 382 U.S. 1011 (1966).

[66] *E.g., compare Brockway Motor Trucks* v. *NLRB*, 582 F.2d 720 (3d Cir. 1978), *with Midland Ross Corp.* v. *NLRB*, 617 F.2d 977 (3d Cir. 1980), *and NLRB* v. *Production Molded Plastics*, 604 F.2d 451 (6th Cir. 1979).

[67] *Summit Tooling Co.*, 195 NLRB 479 (1972). The latest word from the Supreme Court is *First National Maintenance Corp.* v. *NLRB*, 49 U.S.L.W. 4769 (1981) (employer has no duty to bargain about decision "to shut down part of its business purely for economic reasons").

[68] See text at note 136 *infra*. There is apparently no duty to bargain about a decision to go completely out of business. See *Textile Workers* v. *Darlington Mfg. Co.*, 380 U.S. 263, 267, n. 5 (1965).

of good personnel relations. In loftier terms, an ethical value is arguably at stake in determining whether employees may be treated as pawns in management decisions.[69] On a crasser level, unions will lose considerable leverage in bargaining even about the effects of a business change if the employer can present them with a fait accompli in the change itself. Occasionally, negotiations will produce a less drastic solution than a shutdown or a relocation. At the very least bargaining may serve a therapeutic purpose. As the Supreme Court put it in *Fibreboard*, the Labor Act "was framed with an awareness that refusals to confer and negotiate had been one of the most prolific causes of industrial strife." [70]

NATIONAL EMERGENCY DISPUTES

No provision of Taft-Hartley evoked a louder union outcry than the authorization for the Attorney General to seek an 80-day federal injunction against a strike or lockout when the President concludes, after receiving the report of a board of inquiry, that a work stoppage would imperil the "national health or safety." [71] In the eyes of the labor movement, this was a return to the dreaded days of "government by injunction" that existed prior to Norris-LaGuardia. But resort to these emergency procedures has declined through the years. They were invoked 27 times between 1947 and 1967, but only eight times since. After one early, heavy fine for contempt against John L. Lewis and the United Mine Workers, there has generally been compliance with the injunctions that were issued. On nine occasions (all involving maritime or longshoring disputes) there were major strikes after the 80 days expired.

Common criticisms of the Taft-Hartley procedure have been: (1) it discriminates against employees, since they must continue to work under the old contract terms; (2) the 80-day injunction period merely postpones the strike deadline and thus delays serious bargaining; (3) the secret vote the NLRB must conduct among the employees on accepting the employer's final offer during the last 20 days of the injunction is a waste of time (the offer is invariably rejected) and an impediment to late-hour negotiations; (4) denying the board of inquiry the power to make recommendations prevents it from rallying public opinion behind a fair settlement;

[69] E.g., Neil W. Chamberlain, *The Union Challenge to Management Control* (New York: Harper, 1948), pp. 8–9.
[70] 379 U.S. at 211.
[71] LMRA §§206–10, 29 U.S.C. §§176–80 (1976).

and (5) there is no provision for ultimate resolution of the dispute once the 80-day injunction is dissolved. Perhaps the very element of uncertainty introduced by the latter factor, however, is a spur to voluntary settlement. The absence of a definitive legislative solution may also reflect the reality that in today's world a genuine national emergency dispute is more a political than a legal problem.

ANTITRUST

Labor antitrust issues were quiescent in the Supreme Court during the 1950s and the early 1960s. A trio of major decisions in the forties had established guidelines that appeared to reduce substantially the antitrust implications of union activities. Strong dictum from Justice Stone in the *Apex Hosiery* case[72] indicated that the Sherman Act applies only to "some form of restraint upon commercial competition in the marketing of goods or services," and that it is not directed at "an elimination of price competition based on differences in labor standards." This was not a matter of a statutory exemption for unions; the Sherman Act, as written, would simply not cover a certain class of restraints. Employers, or employers in combination with unions, would presumably be as free as unions acting alone to halt competition grounded in labor market differentials.[73]

A year after *Apex*, a wholly new and different theory of union antitrust immunity was enunciated in *United States* v. *Hutcheson*.[74] Justice Frankfurter examined the anti-injunction provisions of the Clayton[75] and Norris-La Guardia[76] Acts, and pronounced the startling conclusion that activity immunized against injunctive relief by those two statutes, read together, was not to be deemed a substantive offense under the Sherman Act. The effect was to exempt from antitrust regulation peaceful, nonfraudulent union conduct in the course of a labor dispute, as long as a union acts in its own interest and does not combine with nonlabor groups.

---

[72] *Apex Hosiery Co.* v. *Leader*, 310 U.S. 469, 495, 503 (1940).

[73] *Id.* at 512. On the immunity of agreements among employers dealing with labor standards, see *Kennedy* v. *Long Island R.R.*, 319 F.2d 366 (2d Cir. 1963), *cert. den.*, 375 U.S. 830 (1963).

[74] 312 U.S. 219 (1941).

[75] 15 U.S.C. §17, 29 U.S.C. §52 (1976).

[76] 29 U.S.C. §101 (1976).

Unlike *Apex*, which focused on the nature of the restraint, regardless of who imposes it, *Hutcheson* created a genuine exemption from the antitrust laws for unions "acting alone." The corollary to this, as *Allen Bradley*[77] subsequently made clear, was that labor organizations lose their immunity when they "aid nonlabor groups to create business monopolies and to control the marketing of goods and services."

Hutcheson appeared at the time a nearly impregnable defense against union antitrust liability. What was overlooked was that it only applies to a union in the midst of combat, to a union engaged in striking, picketing, or similar concerted action against an employer. As soon as a union moves on to the more civilized phase of signing a peace treaty, and entering into collective bargaining, it is no longer "acting alone," and the *Hutcheson* antitrust exemption no longer applies. In 1965 the Supreme Court had to face up to this realization in a pair of landmark decisions.

In *UMW v. Pennington*[78] it was alleged that the Mine Workers and the major coal producers had conspired to drive smaller, less efficient operators out of business by establishing a uniform industry-wide wage rate higher than the smaller producers could afford. If true, the allegation would make it hard for a union to rely on the *Hutcheson* exemption for a union acting alone. Yet the competition that was to be eliminated was competition "based on differences in labor standards"—specifically, on wages, that core mandatory subject of bargaining under the NLRA—and thus arguably the *Apex Hosiery* doctrine came into play. A restraint confined to the labor market would not even be covered by the Sherman Act. Speaking through Justice White, the Supreme Court in *Pennington* added an important qualification to *Apex*. Even an arrangement concerning wages, hours, and working conditions could violate the antitrust laws if it had the "predatory purpose" of eliminating business competitors. The Court was little troubled by dissenting Justice Goldberg's objection that the proof of such unlawful purpose might turn on some local jury's determination that the union wage scale was "too high" for inefficient operators to meet.

The second 1965 case, *Meat Cutters Local 189 v. Jewel Tea*

---

[77] *Allen Bradley Co. v. IBEW Local 3*, 325 U.S. 797, 808 (1945).
[78] 381 U.S. 657 (1965).

Co.,[79] involved a much more direct restraint on the product market. A butchers' union compelled a grocery chain to limit its meat market hours from 9:00 a.m. to 6:00 p.m. The Court concluded (through two plurality opinions accepted by three Justices each) that this restriction, which in effect defined the butchers' working hours and their job content, was "intimately related" to working conditions. Hence the union's effort to secure the provision through arm's-length bargaining in pursuit of its own labor policies, and not in furtherance of some union-employer conspiracy, was exempt under the Sherman Act. Although the results of *Pennington* and *Jewel Tea* are understandable and defensible given the Court's reading of the facts, it is probably a confirmation of the inherent incompatibility of the antitrust laws and the labor field that a respectable argument can be made that both these cases were wrongly decided. *Pennington* may have given too much power to fact-finders to draw dubious inferences of union-employer conspiracies to destroy competition, and *Jewel Tea* may have failed to give sufficient weight to consumer interests in market access. In the latter case the butchers actually had a separate contract provision guaranteeing their job content and working hours; the further ban on night self-service operations would seem to have provided the butchers scant additional protection while causing substantial inconvenience to the shopping public.

The Supreme Court's *Connell* decision[80] in 1975 was a throwback to an earlier era of labor antitrust analysis. A plumbers' local had secured a commitment from a general contractor that it would subcontract mechanical work only to firms that had a collective bargaining agreement with the union. A 5–4 majority of the Court held the agreement subject to the antitrust laws, and remanded for consideration of the claim it violated the Sherman Act. Although nothing in the record indicated the union was conspiring with local mechanical contractors to exclude outsiders from the market by refusing to bargain with them, the Court concluded the arrangement with the general had "substantial anticompetitive effects, both actual and potential, that would not follow naturally from elimination of competition over wages and working conditions."[81]

---

[79] 381 U.S. 676 (1965).
[80] *Connell Construction Co.* v. *Plumbers Local 100*, 421 U.S. 616 (1975).
[81] *Id.* at 625.

What the Court in *Connell* did in effect was to classify the use of the union-only subcontracting clause, at least outside a direct bargaining relationship between the general contractor and the plumbers' local, as a restraint on the product market rather than as a restraint on the labor market. The majority erred in failing to realize that under established precedent,[82] the antitrust laws generally do not apply to agreements aimed at promoting union organization, as well as to agreements aimed at eliminating competition over other labor standards. *Connell* may foreshadow a stiffer standard for determining what constitutes wages and working conditions within the antitrust immunity afforded by *Apex Hosiery* and *Jewel Tea*. If so, that will be an unfortunate development. In dealing with labor abuses, primary reliance should be placed on the labor laws. Unions and the antitrust laws are premised on fundamentally opposing philosophies of competition. There will be anomalies at best, and grave distortions at worst, in attempting to regulate labor organizations through an instrument so at odds with their nature and purposes.

III. The Nationalization of Labor Law

The central achievement of the Warren Court in the labor field was a simple but basic restructuring of intergovernmental relations. In a series of decisions that were hotly controverted at the time but have quietly won general acceptance since, the Court largely succeeded in nationalizing the regulation of labor relations in industries affecting commerce. The importance in the Warren Court's eyes of "federal preemption"—the exclusion of state substantive law from areas regulated by Congress—can be shown to an extent simply in quantitative terms. About 110 labor decisions of the Warren era can be labelled as "important." Of these, almost 40, or over a third, deal either directly with the metes and bounds of the preemption doctrine, or with issues that would not have arisen but for the displacement of state law by federal. The cases will be discussed in two categories: those decisions concerned with the extent to which state law may still operate in areas subject to federal regulation, and those decisions concerned with the development of federal law to replace state law as the basis for enforcing collective bargaining agreements.

---

[82] E.g., *Hunt v. Crumboch*, 325 U.S. 821, 823 (1945).

STATE SUBSTANTIVE REGULATION

At the time Chief Justice Warren assumed office, the preemption doctrine in its application to labor relations was still in its adolescence. The well-nigh axiomatic principle had been established that a state could not directly impede the exercise of federal rights of self-organization, for example, by imposing onerous licensing requirements on union agents.[83] But states were still free to regulate such labor activities as "quickie" strikes, which technically were neither protected nor prohibited under federal law.[84] More important, no clear rationale had been evolved to justify conclusions that particular kinds of conduct fell either within or without the ambit of state regulation. And there had been little airing of the underlying policy considerations which go to the very heart of our federal system: the balancing of the need for a uniform national policy in matters affecting the country as a whole against the need to accommodate regional differences and desires for local experimentation.

The very first term of the Warren Court ushered in the vanguard of today's preemption theory. In *Garner* v. *Teamsters*,[85] the Court held that a state injunction could not duplicate a federal remedy by forbidding conduct proscribed under the National Labor Relations Act. Diversity of procedures was said to be as apt to produce conflicting adjudications as diversity of substantive rules. It soon became apparent, however, that a majority of the Court regarded a deficiency in the federal remedy as a sufficient reason for sustaining state jurisdiction. Thus, employees or employers suffering monetary losses through tortious conduct that was also an unfair labor practice could maintain a state court action for damages, since the National Labor Relations Board had no general power to award full compensatory relief.[86]

San Diego Building Trades Council v. *Garmon*,[87] decided in 1959, remains the Supreme Court's most nearly definitive statement on preemption. There the Court in handling the preemption

---

[83] *Hill* v. *Florida*, 325 U.S. 538 (1945).

[84] *UAW-AFL* v. *WERB* [Briggs & Stratton Corp.], 336 U.S. 245 (1949), *overruled Machinists Lodge 76* v. *WERB*, 427 U.S. 132 (1976).

[85] 346 U.S. 485 (1953).

[86] *Construction Workers* v. *Laburnum Construction Corp.*, 347 U.S. 656 (1954); *UAW* v. *Russell*, 356 U.S. 634 (1958).

[87] 359 U.S. 236 (1959).

issue shifted from an emphasis on the nature of the state relief sought (was it more adequate than the federal remedy?) to an emphasis on the nature of the activity in question (was it regulated under federal law?). The now-famous test was enunciated that if conduct is "arguably" protected by Section 7 of the LMRA, or "arguably" prohibited by Section 8, exclusive primary jurisdiction rests in the NLRB and state (or federal) courts are precluded from acting. Earlier decisions which had appeared to rely on the deficiency of the federal remedy were explained as upholding state court jurisdiction because violence or threatened violence was present, or because the activity was of "merely peripheral concern" to the federal statutory scheme.[88]

The soundness of that is surely not self-evident. Under the expansive preemption doctrine, states have been sharply limited in the role they can play as "laboratories" for social experiment. Numerous restrictions have been imposed on customary state functions. Thus, although the states can still assert their police power to maintain public order, they cannot take over a public utility to halt a strike.[89] Laws not dealing specifically with labor relations, such as state antitrust statutes[90] and even traditional common law libel doctrines,[91] may also run afoul of the preemption principle. This is so even though it is by no means clear that Congress was as eager as the Supreme Court would suggest to ensure the unsullied uniformity of federal regulation.[92] Indeed, the Burger Court has provided one major exception to *Garmon's* "arguably protected or arguably prohibited" formula. An employer may bring a trespass action in state court against a union engaged in peaceful picketing on private property, even though the picketing might be

[88] *Id.* at 241–43, citing *Laburnum, supra* note 86 (threatened violence); *Russell, supra* note 86 (mass picketing); *Machinists* v. *Gonzales*, 356 U.S. 617 (1958) (wrongful expulsion of member from union).

[89] *Street, . . . Employees Division 1287* v. *Missouri*, 374 U.S. 74 (1963).

[90] *Teamsters Local 24* v. *Oliver*, 358 U.S. 283 (1959).

[91] Cf. *Linn* v. *Plant Guard Workers Local 14*, 383 U.S. 53 (1966) (libel action maintainable only if defamation in course of labor dispute is malicious and actually injurious). Several members of the Burger Court, however, may now be ready to trim back the preemptive effect of federal labor law on state laws of "general applicability." See, e.g., *New York Telephone Co.* v. *New York State Department of Labor*, 440 U.S. 519, 533 (1979).

[92] When Congress enacted the Landrum-Griffin Act in 1959 to provide the first comprehensive regulation of internal union affairs, it specifically negated any general intent to exclude concurrent state regulation. See 29 U.S.C. §523 (1976).

either protected or prohibited under the NLRA.[93] The Court stressed that otherwise the employer would be helpless, since it itself could not get a definitive ruling on the legal issue from the Labor Board, and that in all likelihood such picketing is not federally protected.

On balance, the Warren Court acted wisely in most of its preemption rulings. Labor law continues to be one of our most divisive domestic issues, and much of the divisiveness runs along regional lines. Federally enforced uniformity thus seems peculiarly necessary, lest either unions or employers be unduly favored in particular states. Such regional variations could hardly fail to have an adverse impact on the nation's economy. For example, plants might be lured from place to place while labor bitterness constantly deepened. The present healthy trend toward a leveling of wage rates for similar jobs across the country could well be reversed. Of course, a different result in almost any given Supreme Court preemption decision would doubtless not have had dire consequences. But by now we probably have sufficient experience under the Court's preemption doctrine to conclude that vital local interests have in fact suffered no serious injury. This alone may be enough to indicate that the Court was right when it began to tip the scales, as a matter of general policy, in favor of national interests rather than local concerns.

One glaring break in the pattern of federal uniformity is attributable to Congress itself. Taft-Hartley's famous (or notorious) Section 14(b)[94] enables the states to outlaw union security agreements that would otherwise be permissible under the federal statute.[95] In 1947 this may have been a legislative compromise which was required in order to establish, as a matter of federal law, that a union was entitled to seek agreements preventing "free riders"—persons who reap the benefits of collective bargaining without paying their fair share of the costs.

By now, however, it is difficult to discern a principled basis for retaining 14(b). That the issue is highly charged is all the more reason for a single, federal solution. A national union engaged in

---

[93] *Sears, Roebuck & Co. v. San Diego County District Council of Carpenters*, 436 U.S. 180 (1976).

[94] NLRA §14(b), 29 U.S.C. §164(b) (1976).

[95] NLRA §8(a)(3), 29 U.S.C. §158(a)(3) (1976); *Retail Clerks Local 1625 v. Schermerhorn*, 373 U.S. 746 (1963).

bargaining for a national contract should not, even theoretically, have to impose the total financial burden on those employees who do not reside in a right-to-work state. And there are no longer any grounds for the "moral" argument that no person should be compelled to become a member of any organization as a condition of employment, or be forced to contribute to political causes in which he does not believe. Labor Board and Supreme Court decisions have established that under a union security arrangement an employee need not assume the status or obligations of union membership, and that the only mandatory financial exactions are the pro rata costs of collective bargaining, not the expenses of the union's political or social activities.[96]

ENFORCEMENT OF LABOR CONTRACTS

The Warren Court's vigor in furthering the primacy of federal law was demonstrated even more strikingly in its rulings on the enforcement of collective bargaining agreements. Labor contracts were traditionally enforced in accordance with state substantive law. It was often hard to sue a union in the state courts, however, because of the difficulty of obtaining jurisdiction over an unincorporated association. Therefore, in 1947, Congress wrote Section 301 into the Taft-Hartley Act[97] to provide that suits on contracts between unions and employers could be brought in the federal district courts. Unions were explicitly made competent to sue or be sued as entities.

But what was the substantive law to be applied in 301 suits— federal or state? If Section 301 were to be treated as merely procedural, with state substantive law applicable, the provision would be of dubious constitutionality; Article III of the Constitution confines the jurisdiction of the federal district courts to cases involving diversity of citizenship or a federal question. Yet Section 301 was silent on the question of applicable law, and Congress had furnished no clear guidance.

The Supreme Court came to grips with the problem in *Textile Workers Union v. Lincoln Mills.*[98] A union sued an employer in

---

[96] *Marlin Rockwell Corp.*, 114 NLRB 553 (1955); *Machinists v. Street*, 367 U.S. 740 (1961). Cf. *Abood v. Detroit Board of Education*, 431 U.S. 209 (1977).

[97] 29 U.S.C. §185 (1976).

[98] 353 U.S. 448 (1976).

federal court for specific performance of the arbitration provisions in the parties' collective contract. Jurisdiction was contested. Justice Douglas, for the Court, cut the constitutional knot with one swift stroke, declaring that "the substantive law to apply in suits under §301(a) is federal law which the courts must fashion from the policy of our national labor laws." Once this was established, jurisdiction could constitutionally be reposed in the federal judiciary. Perhaps the magnitude of the Court's undertaking in *Lincoln Mills* can best be gauged by the contemporaneous concern expressed by two distinguished scholars that this reading of Section 301 demanded of the federal courts a task to which they were "enormously unequal," and "its imposition on them is therefore capable of damaging their usefulness for the essential duties that they are suited to perform."[99]

The task shouldered by the Supreme Court, despite the grave apprehensions of some, was the task of fashioning a body of federal contract law to govern the enforcement of collective agreements. Its sources were to be the policies of the federal labor statutes, state contract law where appropriate, arbitrators' decisions, and so on. The scholars looked at these "bits and pieces" and were aghast; the Court had faith that "judicial inventiveness" would find a way.[100] Perhaps that is the difference between professors and practical men. By hindsight, at any rate, it is hard to find justification for the fears of the critics.

Possibly an explanation for the easy survival of the federal judiciary lies in the next maneuver executed by the Warren Court. Having boldly staked out a claim in *Lincoln Mills* to the whole of the labor contract domain, the Court then turned around in the *Warrior* trilogy[101] and delegated to arbitrators the principal responsibility for interpreting and applying collective bargaining agreements. Courts are to order arbitration of grievances under a contract "unless it may be said with positive assurance that the arbitration clause is not susceptible of an interpretation that covers

---

[99] Alexander Bickel and Harry H. Wellington, "Legislative Purpose and the Judicial Process: The Lincoln Mills Case," *Harvard Law Review* 71 (November 1957), pp. 1, 22–23.

[100] 353 U.S. at 457.

[101] *Steelworkers* v. *American Mfg. Co.*, 363 U.S. 564 (1960); *Steelworkers* v. *Warrior & Gulf Navigation Co.*, 363 U.S. 574 (1960); *Steelworkers* v. *Enterprise Wheel & Car Corp.*, 363 U.S. 593 (1960).

the asserted dispute."[102] Moreover, an arbitrator's award is to be enforced by a court without review on the merits, so long as the award is not the product of fraud or beyond the scope of the submission. Thus, through the *Warrior* approach, the Court may have finessed many of the problems envisaged by the critics of *Lincoln Mills*.

Even so, the Warren Court managed to build up a fairly substantial body of basic contract doctrine. For instance, a labor agreement may be binding on a successor employer even though he has not signed it.[103] Available grievance and arbitration machinery has to be exhausted before there can be resort to a court suit on a contract.[104] And in the absence of a federal statute of limitations, state statutes apply to Section 301 actions.[105] These are the kinds of questions one might have anticipated the Court would have to resolve. They hardly seem a threat to its institutional capacities.

One of the most nettlesome issues of labor contract enforcement was the impact of the Norris-La Guardia Act. The Act generally prohibits the federal courts from issuing injunctions against peaceful strikes. When Congress in Section 301 of the Taft-Hartley Act gave the federal courts jurisdiction over suits to enforce contracts, it deliberately rejected proposals to amend Norris-La Guardia to take account of this new development. In *Sinclair Refining Co.* v. *Atkinson*,[106] the Warren Court made the obvious, logical deduction. Even strikes in breach of contract remained covered by Norris-La Guardia's ban on federal injunctions. But there were evident policy deficiencies in this position. Most important, employers were deprived of what was often the most efficacious and sensible weapon against forbidden strikes. In the first year of the Burger era, the Supreme Court in *Boys Market, Inc.* v. *Retail Clerks Local 770*[107] managed to confound the logic of *Sinclair* (and probably the intent of Congress) and do justice at last. A crafty opinion by Justice Brennan declared that Con-

---

[102] 363 U.S. at 582–83.

[103] *John Wiley & Sons, Inc.* v. *Livingston*, 376 U.S. 543 (1964). But see text at notes 109 and 110 *infra*.

[104] *Drake Bakeries, Inc.* v. *Bakery Workers Local 50*, 370 U.S. 254 (1962); *Republic Steel Corp.* v. *Maddox*, 379 U.S. 650 (1965).

[105] *UAW* v. *Hoosier Cardinal Corp.*, 383 U.S. 696 (1966).

[106] 370 U.S. 195 (1962).

[107] 398 U.S. 236 (1970).

gress's refusal to amend Norris-La Guardia when enacting Taft-Hartley did not mean the injunction ban was left intact. It simply meant Congress was prepared to leave to the federal judiciary the task of working out an appropriate "accommodation" between the two statutes. Justice Brennan's solution was to authorize federal injunctions against strikes where the underlying grievance is subject to a "mandatory grievance adjustment or arbitration procedure" in a collective bargaining agreement. While it may offend purists in statutory construction, this rule has much to commend it in elementary fairness. Norris-La Guardia was designed to protect struggling unions against a biased and injunction-wielding judiciary, especially in organizing settings. When an established union has committed itself contractually not to strike, and has been provided an effective alternative means of redress through arbitration, it is hardly a desecration of Norris-La Guardia philosophy to grant the employer an injunction if the union goes back on its word and strikes.

In two cases involving "successor" employers, the Burger Court blurred, if it did not eradicate, major Warren Court teachings on the nature of the collective bargaining agreement. The earlier view was that it was "not an ordinary contract," but a "generalized code" setting forth "the common law" of a particular industry or of a particular plant.[108] A predecessor's labor contract, in the Warren period, could bind a successor employer where there was "substantial continuity of identity in the business enterprise," without regard to the existence of actual consent. In NLRB v. Burns International Security Services, Inc.[109] and Howard Johnson Co. v. Hotel & Restaurant Employees Detroit Local Joint Board,[110] the Burger Court refocused attention on traditional common law notions of the need for "consent" under "normal contract principles," and on the question of whether certain rights and duties were "in fact" "assigned" or "assumed."

On their facts, Burns and Howard Johnson held a predecessor's contract not binding on a rival company taking over through competitive bidding or on a purchaser who retained only a minority

---

[108] *John Wiley & Sons* v. *Livingston*, 376 U.S. 543 (1964).
[109] 406 U.S. 272 (1972).
[110] 417 U.S. 249 (1974).

of the seller's employees. This left open the possibility that the Warren successorship doctrine might still apply where there was a genuine link between predecessor and successor *and* a majority of the former's employees remained with the latter. What was more likely reflected here, however, was a clash of fundamental values in the labor field. The Warren majority was concerned about protecting employees against a sudden and unforeseen loss of bargaining and contract rights. There was also a concern about maintaining industrial stability and labor peace, through reducing the number of representation elections and sustaining the life of labor agreements. On the other hand, the Burger majority laid stress on the freedom and voluntariness of the collective bargaining process, on the importance of saddling neither unions nor employers with substantive contract terms to which they have not agreed. Stress was further laid on providing maximum flexibility in business arrangements, so that employers may respond to changing market conditions without being straitjacketed by the bargaining or contractual obligations that may have been assumed by imprudent predecessors. The future development of successorship law undoubtedly depends far more on the way the members of the Supreme Court ultimately balance out these competing values than on any logical deductions from the decisions to date.

IV. Individual Rights in the Workplace

Just as the federalization of labor regulation was the major preoccupation of the Warren Court in industrial relations, the overriding concern of the Court throughout the Burger decade of the seventies (perhaps to some persons' surprise) was the defining of individual rights in the workplace. The Burger Court has averaged over a dozen noteworthy labor decisions a term. Over half of these dealt with the rights of employees in relation to their employers or labor organizations.

Fair Representation

During World War II, in a case involving black railroad employees, the Supreme Court established the principle that a union exercising the power of exclusive representation under a federal statute had the concomitant obligation to represent all employees in the bargaining unit fairly and without discrimination.[111] An individual employee may now sue his employer for breach of contract, and may join the union or sue it alone if it has treated him arbitrarily, capriciously, or in bad faith.[112] An employee has no absolute right to have a grievance arbitrated,[113] however, and he must first pursue any remedies available under the contract before he can file suit.[114] At the same time a union may not "ignore a meritorious grievance or process it in perfunctory fashion."[115]

In *Hines v. Anchor Motor Freight, Inc.*,[116] the Burger Court held that an employer could not rely on the finality of an arbitration award as a defense against employee suits "if the contractual processes have been seriously flawed by the union's breach of its duty to represent employees honestly and in good faith and without invidious discrimination or arbitrary conduct." The standard enunciated in *Hines* can hardly be faulted in the abstract. Yet with the Supreme Court moving beyond the more clearcut instances of discrimination and bad faith to reach "arbitrariness" and "perfunctoriness," the lower courts may be tempted to go on to negligence, or at least gross negligence. This would undoubtedly mean greater justice for individual employees in a given case. But union business agents, not schooled in the niceties of due process, must often act quickly under pressure, and their customary aim has been the maximization of group interests, not the farthest pursuit of every individual claim. Moreover, decisions like *Hines* mean an employer cannot work out a grievance settlement with its employees' statutory bargaining representative which will have the same finality as an adjustment reached with a party's lawyer or other personally chosen agent. Unless carefully controlled, increasing judicial intervention and scrutiny of such union judgments may not bode well for the total collective bargaining process.

---

[111] *Steele v. Louisville & Nashville R.R.*, 323 U.S. 192 (1944). Fifteen years after Taft-Hartley was passed, the Labor Board for the first time concluded that a union's breach of the duty of fair representation was also an unfair labor practice. *Miranda Fuel Co.*, 140 NLRB 181 (1962), *enforcement denied*, 326 F.2d 172 (2d Cir. 1963). Cf. *Vaca v. Sipes*, 386 U.S. 171 (1967).

[112] *Humphrey v. Moore*, 375 U.S. 335 (1964); *Vaca v. Sipes*, 386 U.S. 171 (1967).

[113] *Vaca v. Sipes*, 386 U.S. 171 (1967).

[114] *Republic Steel Corp. v. Maddox*, 379 U.S. 650 (1965).

[115] *Vaca v. Sipes*, 386 U.S. 171, 191 (1967).

[116] 424 U.S. 554, 570 (1976).

UNION DEMOCRACY

One of the happier ironies of recent labor history can be found in the impetus given union democracy by the Landrum-Griffin Act of 1959.[117] At the time the Act was passed, the thinking of disinterested observers had not yet crystallized on the merits of running a union's affairs democratically.[118] It is probably fair to say that the main push in Congress for Landrum-Griffin and, particularly, its "bill of rights" title, came from a conservative coalition that was less concerned with promoting the individual rights of working people than with blunting the effectiveness of labor organizations.[119] There is hardly anything unique in such a situation; the purification of any well-established institution is likely to require a sizable (if unwitting) contribution by its enemies. Yet today most commentators would likely agree that the foes of unionism in the 1959 Congress performed their role in especially commendable style. By and large, the provisions of the Landrum-Griffin Act respecting internal union affairs have significantly advanced the cause of union democracy while doing little, if any, damage to the structure of organized labor.

Nevertheless, some reservations are in order about too hasty and naive an equation of ethical unionism with union populism. Unions are not merely debating societies. They are militant organizations that must act quickly and decisively in times of crisis. Real friends of the worker would not insist that every union decision be argued out and voted upon in town-meeting fashion. At the same time, however, both management and the public arguably stand to suffer from the irresponsibility in collective bargaining which is a possible side-effect of a massive injection of democracy

---

[117] Labor-Management Reporting and Disclosure Act of 1959, 73 Stat. 519 (1959), as amended, 29 U.S.C. §401 (1976).

[118] A number of respected American and English authorities could be cited in 1959 in support of the proposition that "democracy is as inappropriate within the international headquarters of the UAW as it is in the front office of General Motors." C. Peter Magrath, "Democracy in Overalls: The Futile Quest for Union Democracy," *Industrial and Labor Relations Review* 12 (July 1959), pp. 503, 525. The trend of opinion, however, has clearly been the other way. See, e.g., Archibald Cox, "Internal Affairs of Labor Unions Under the Labor Reform Act of 1959," *Michigan Law Review* 58 (April 1960), pp. 819, 830; Clyde W. Summers, "The Impact of Landrum-Griffin in State Courts," in *New York University 13th Annual Conference on Labor*, ed. Emanuel Stein (New York: Matthew Bender, 1960), pp. 333, 335.

[119] See Cox, *supra* note 118, pp. 820–21, 831–33.

into labor organizations. Two such savvy onlookers as Harvard's Derek Bok and John Dunlop have thus suggested, now that Landrum-Griffin has installed basic safeguards, that the issue of union democracy should move toward particular problems which vary from one organization to another.[120]

An example of the Supreme Court's efforts to balance membership claims and institutional interests can be seen in its handling of Landrum-Griffin's safeguards for internal union elections. The Court has approved the Secretary of Labor's pragmatic approach toward determining what are "reasonable qualifications" for elective union office under Title IV of the Act. If too many members (perhaps more than two-thirds) are disqualified by a particular rule or combination of rules, the provisions are presumed invalid. The Court agreed that a requirement of attendance at one-half of a local's meetings during the three years preceding an election was unreasonable, where the effect was that 96.5 percent of the local's 660 members were ineligible.[121] In an effort to assure unions an initial opportunity to police their own house, however, the Court has ruled that the Secretary of Labor may not sue to challenge an election on a ground that the complaining member, although aware of the facts, had not included   earlier in his internal protest to the union itself.[122]

EQUAL EMPLOYMENT OPPORTUNITY

In the 1960s Congress turned its attention to outlawing job discrimination by employers or unions because of race, color, religion, sex, national origin, or age. The most important of these statutes was of course Title VII of the 1964 Civil Rights Act.[123] In his second year of office Chief Justice Burger authored the most significant decision to date concerning the elements of a Title VII violation. In *Griggs* v. *Duke Power Co.*,[124] a unanimous Supreme Court held that the Act did not merely proscribe conscious, pur-

---

[120] Derek C. Bok and John T. Dunlop, *Labor and the American Community* (New York: Simon & Schuster, 1970), p. 91.

[121] *Steelworkers Local 3489* v. *Usery*, 429 U.S. 305 (1977).

[122] *Hodgson* v. *Steelworkers Local 6799*, 403 U.S. 333 (1971).

[123] 78 Stat. 241, 253–66 (1964), as amended, 42 U.S.C. §2000e (1976 & Supp. II 1978). See also the Equal Pay Act of 1963, 77 Stat. 56 (1963), 29 U.S.C. §206(d) (1976); Age Discrimination in Employment Act, 81 Stat. 602 (1967), 29 U.S.C. §621 (1976 & Supp. III 1979).

[124] 401 U.S. 424 (1971).

poseful discriminatory treatment. Employment practices entirely neutral on their face and even in their design, such as job qualifications or aptitude tests, were also barred if in actual practice they had a disproportionately adverse impact on protected classes like minorities and females and if they could not be justified by "business necessity."

One difficulty that has emerged in applying antidiscrimination legislation has been reconciling it with traditional labor relations values, such as seniority. In *Teamsters* v. *United States [T.I.M.E.– D.C.]*[125] the Supreme Court overturned a long, unbroken line of courts of appeals decisions in ruling that otherwise "bona fide" seniority plans do not violate Title VII even though they perpetuate the effects of pre-Act discrimination. The Court was almost surely correct as a matter of the original congressional intent. But coming as late as it did, *T.I.M.E.–D.C.* could be criticized for lack of judicial statesmanship in rekindling black-white antagonisms concerning seniority, and for failure to take adequate account of congressional acquiescence in the earlier approach of the courts of appeals when Title VII was amended in 1972.[126]

In the often frustrating struggle to eradicate the last, tenacious vestiges of centuries-old discrimination in employment, no weapon has proved more effective, or more controversial, than "affirmative action" programs instituted pursuant to Executive Order 11246.[127] Under this presidential directive, employers and unions must make "good faith" efforts to meet certain specified goals of minority and female hires as a condition for securing and retaining government contracts. Although the Supreme Court has not yet passed on challenges that this is "reverse discrimination" against white males under Title VII and a denial of their right to equal protection under the Constitution, the program has been upheld by the courts of appeals.[128] Furthermore, in *Steelworkers* v. *Weber*[129] the Supreme Court held (5–2) that Title VII did not prohibit a private,

[125] 431 U.S. 324 (1977).

[126] Equal Employment Opportunity Act of 1972, 86 Stat. 103 (1972).

[127] 30 Fed. Reg 12319 (1965), as amended by E.O. 11375, 32 Fed. Reg. 14303 (1967).

[128] E.g., *Contractors Assn. of Eastern Pennsylvania* v. *Shultz*, 442 F.2d 159 (3d Cir. 1971), cert. den., 404 U.S. 854 (1971); *Associated General Contractors* v. *Altshuler*, 490 F.2d 9 (1st Cir. 1973), cert. den., 416 U.S. 957 (1974).

[129] 443 U.S. 193 (1979).

voluntary race-conscious affirmative action job-training program initiated under a collective bargaining agreement between a union and employer in an attempt to eliminate segregated patterns of employment. And in *Fullilove* v. *Klutznick*[130] the Court sustained (6–3) the constitutionality of the provision in the Public Works Employment Act of 1977 that at least 10 percent of the federal funds granted for local projects must be set aside for minority business enterprises. Absent a change in the Court's membership, this would seem to ensure the validity of affirmative action under Executive Order 11246, unless a couple of Justices felt that the presence of congressional action in *Fullilove* was critical, and that the President was acting alone and with lesser authority in issuing the Order.

There is no blinking the fact that affirmative action and preferential treatment in favor of one race or sex raise grave moral questions, as well as questions going to the core of American traditions of individual merit and group neutrality. The essence of affirmative action is an effort to achieve justice among *groups*; in ordinary circumstances the essence of morality and law alike is justice among *individuals*.[131] The Appalachian white or the white ethnic from a ghetto may, personally, be far more disadvantaged by his background than the third-generation offspring of a professional black family, and yet it is the latter who will be favored under the usual affirmative action plan. I justify this, not without misgivings, on the ground we are dealing with no ordinary situation but with a national problem of staggering dimensions. A group wrong has been perpetuated for generation upon generation, and the wounds are deep, pervasive, and persistent. Heroic measures are called for in the treatment, specifically, a group remedy to cure this group wrong.

V. Employment Relations Law

This study has primarily concentrated on laws dealing with union-employer-employee relations in a collective bargaining set-

---

[130] 100 S.Ct. 2758 (U.S. 1980).

[131] See, e.g., *McDonald* v. *Santa Fe Transportation Co.*, 427 U.S. 273 (1976) (any individual, whether white or black, is protected under Title VII and 42 U.S.C. §1981 (1976)). See also *City of Los Angeles* v. *Manhart*, 435 U.S. 702 (1978) (female annuitants must be treated as individuals instead of components of a sexual class for Title VII purposes).

ting. But the Civil Rights Act of 1964 could be said to signal the beginning of a new era in government controls, which came to full flower in the 1970s. Previously, Congress was chiefly concerned with regulating the *procedural* aspects of union organizing, bargaining, and so on. It has now become increasingly concerned with the *substantive* aspects of the employment relationship, whether or not in a unionized situation. Space does not permit consideration of the enormous impact of such laws as the Occupational Safety and Health Act of 1970[132] and the Employee Retirement Income Security Act,[133] or the momentous implications they hold for the future directions of collective bargaining and arbitration.[134]

The malaise currently afflicting the labor movement[135] makes it likely that, at least for the foreseeable future, unorganized workers are going to constitute the great bulk of the labor force. Although they may be willing to forgo the full range of benefits provided by collective bargaining, it is inevitable they will come to demand that most elemental of job protections: protection against arbitrary, unfair discharge or discipline. The next major development in American industrial law may well be to prescribe "just cause" as a legal standard instead of leaving it simply as a standard imposed by union contracts.[136] Western Europe has already gone this route, and I am confident we will follow. Whether we shall do so by statute[137] or common law,[138] by judicial or administrative procedure, I do not know. In any event, the complex and some-

---

[132] 84 Stat. 1590 (1970), 29 U.S.C. §651 (1976).

[133] 88 Stat. 832 (1974), 29 U.S.C. §1001 (1976).

[134] See, e.g., John A. Fillion and Anne M. Trebilcock, "The Duty to Bargain Under ERISA," *William & Mary Law Review* 17 (Winter 1975), p. 251; David Feller, "The Coming End of Arbitration's Golden Age," in *Arbitration —1967*, Proceedings of the 29th Annual Meeting, National Academy of Arbitrators, eds. Barbara D. Dennis and Gerald G. Somers (Washington: BNA Books, 1976), p. 97; Harry T. Edwards, "Labor Arbitration at the Crossroads: The 'Common Law of the Shop' v. External Law," *Arbitration Journal* 32 (June 1977), p. 65.

[135] See note 12, *supra*, and accompanying text.

[136] See, e.g., Clyde W. Summers, "Individual Protection Against Unjust Dismissal: Time for a Statute," *Virginia Law Review* 62 (April 1976), p. 481; Cornelius J. Peck, "Unjust Discharges from Employment: A Necessary Change in the Law," *Ohio State Law Journal* 40 (No. 1, 1979), p. 1.

[137] Michigan and New Jersey legislators have bills under consideration.

[138] See, e.g., *Tamey v. Atlantic Richfield Co.*, 164 Cal. Rptr. 839 (Cal. 1980) (tort theory); *Toussaint v. Blue Cross & Blue Shield of Michigan*, 408 Mich. 579 (1980) (contract theory).

times cumbersome structure of our labor laws could hardly have a more fitting capstone.

VI. Conclusion

Ideally, our labor laws should be closely attuned to the needs of workers and unions in using persuasion and certain economic weapons to organize and bargain effectively, and to the competing interests of employers, employees, and the general public in being free from injurious pressures. Much evidence suggests that these needs and interests may differ significantly from industry to industry, even from firm to firm, and that different balances should be struck accordingly. Congress has recognized some of the disparity by loosening union security and hot cargo regulations in the construction industry and by exempting most of garment manufacturing from secondary boycott prohibitions. There should probably be more of these discriminating legislative judgments.

Even within the existing statutory pattern, the NLRB and the courts ought to pay less heed to armchair speculation and more to particular facts and empirical studies in assessing union and employer conduct. Thus arguably both sides have suffered as a result of administrative or judicial unwillingness to grub for a better sense of the real impact of such matters as superseniority, lockouts, employer communications and limited union access to employees in organizing campaigns, and union restrictive practices that allegedly restrain trade in the product market.

Grave procedural and remedial deficiencies remain in Taft-Hartley. The Labor Board's processes are clogged by an overwhelming number of cases and by lack of discretion to deny review of trial-level decisions. An intransigent employer can evade for years, if not indefinitely, its duty to bargain with a majority union, and the employees receive no monetary award for the contract benefits they presumably have lost. Legislation that would have gone far to cure these defects died in 1978 at the hands of one of the best engineered Senate filibusters of recent times. In today's conservative political climate, the likelihood that a beleaguered labor movement can revive support for such much-needed reforms seems nil.

The focus of public interest in labor relations, and the corresponding focus of our enacted legislation, has shifted dramatically over the decades. From the thirties through the fifties the emphasis was on workers' institutional rights, their freedom to organize or not without employer or union coercion, and their entitlement to democratically run unions. In the sixties and the seventies the emphasis was on workers' individual rights. They were entitled to equal employment opportunity, to a safe place to work, to various safeguards for their pensions and similar employee benefits. In the foreseeable future even the nonunionized worker may win protection against arbitrary and unjust discipline. Yet perhaps one may still harbor the hope that this quite healthy concern for individuals will not wholly obliterate concern for organizations. The post-industrial world, hardly less than the industrial world, may be a bleak place for the isolated individual. Whether a guild, a union, or a professional society, it has usually been through an institutional means that most working people have found the fullest expression of their common goals and the greatest capacity for realizing them. Neither the worker nor the law should be too quick to forget that lesson.

CHAPTER 6

Social Issues in Collective Bargaining[*]

PHYLLIS A. WALLACE
JAMES W. DRISCOLL
Massachusetts Institute of Technology

Introduction

This chapter examines how collective bargaining, especially in the last two decades, has responded to the challenge of three major social issues: equal employment opportunity, occupational safety and health, and the quality of work life. Further, the implication of this response for the future of collective bargaining as an institution is briefly explored.

The key events during the period in question were the social upheavals of the 1960s. This decade began with the crest of the civil rights movement. Sit-ins, freedom rides, and confrontations over jobs in the construction trades were highlighted by the passage of the Civil Rights Act of 1964. The latter half of the decade brought antiwar demonstrations, as well as demands from environmentalists, women, young people, and other groups in the society.

Although this social militancy took place largely outside the workplace, these demands were eventually reflected in the workplace. Title VII of the Civil Rights Act of 1964 prohibited discrimination in employment based on race, color, religion, national origin, or sex. Government contractors were obligated to develop affirmative action plans in order to improve their utilization of women and minorities. The Occupational Safety and Health Act of 1970 guaranteed to workers the right to a workplace free from

---

[*] We would like to thank our colleagues who commented on earlier versions of this chapter. Since we did not always take their advice, we alone are responsible for any errors or omissions that remain. We are grateful to Charles A. Myers, Thomas A. Kochan, Nicholas A. Ashford, James E. Jones, Jr., Herbert Hammerman, Charles Hecksher, Charles Markham, Harry Katz, and the editors of this volume.

hazards to life or limb. Finally, concern over worker apathy and distrust in institutions led to the establishment of employer programs to "improve the quality of work life."

A historical perspective on the institution of collective bargaining would predict its response to social issues. Unionism in the U.S. is usually labelled (with some exaggeration) both "business" and "job-centered." Certainly union demands in bargaining have emphasized economic protection for its membership over broader social and political concerns. However, workers in the U.S. did not simply choose and develop this particular style of unionism in a vacuum. Employers and all levels of government, consistently and often, violently opposed more radical forms of labor organization. Even during the period in question, a more sophisticated employer resistance (typified by consultants for a "union-free environment") and a new round of government regulation (state right-to-work laws and the Landrum-Griffin Act) contributed to the protectionist stance of American labor unions. Since this chapter assesses collective bargaining precisely on social issues, the reader should remember the contribution of all three actors in the industrial relations system—labor, management, and government—to the shape of unions in the U.S. and the scope of collective bargaining.

Equal employment opportunity is discussed in Part II, safety and health in Part III, and the quality of work life in Part IV. After reviewing the bargaining experience with these three major social issues, we comment on the future role of collective bargaining in dealing with expanding social demands. Each part of the chapter can be read separately, and the conclusion identifies themes cutting across the three issues.

Equal Employment Opportunity

Although equal employment opportunity emphasizes the role of women and minority workers, the collective bargaining issues examined in this section focus mainly on minorities. Minority workers bore the brunt of the adjustment on equal employment opportunities because during the first five years of the implementation of these federal rules and regulations, the overwhelming concern was racial discrimination. Since most women work in white-collar occupations in the nonunion sector, their involvement with unions has been limited. Even so, in 1977 women workers comprised 27.6 percent of employed wage and salary workers in labor organizations.[1]

The accommodation of unions to equal employment opportunity pressures has ranged from hostility and resistance to cooperation. Conflicts surrounding the referral and training policies of some craft unions in the construction industry, strategies used by several large industrial unions to protect seniority principles, and the enforcement of contract rights through arbitration, represent the areas of significant tension between unions and minority workers. During the past 15 years, the patterns and practices of collective bargaining were severely challenged by the stance of minority workers on these issues. Disputes that arose in the workplace over equal employment opportunity matters were resolved through external mechanisms. Contractual agreement and industrial self-government were pitted against independent statutory rights.

A brief review of the role of minorities in collective bargaining, the legal perspectives of fair representation, and the relationship of unions and the Equal Employment Opportunity Commission provide the background for the more detailed analysis of referral unions, seniority, and arbitration. Implicit in this discussion is an understanding that collective bargaining activities are not unilateral actions by unions; however, only the role of the union is discussed in this chapter.

ROLE OF MINORITIES IN COLLECTIVE BARGAINING

Until recently, blacks, the largest group of minority workers, shared an agenda of common objectives with unions only sporadically. Mutual suspicions on both sides contributed to the hostility and conflict. During the latter part of the nineteenth century, blacks were excluded from membership in many craft unions and, where there were fewer restrictions, were forced to operate in segregated locals.[2] As late as 1919 blacks were used as strikebreakers in the steel industry, thereby threatening the status of

---

[1] Linda H. Le Grande, "Women in Labor Organizations: Their Ranks Are Increasing," *Monthly Labor Review* (August 1978), p. 11.

[2] Ray Marshall, *The Negro and Organized Labor* (New York: John Wiley & Sons, 1965); Philip S. Foner, *Organized Labor and the Black Worker, 1619–1973* (New York: Praeger Publishers, 1974); Herberts R. Northrup, *Organized Labor and the Negro* (New York: Harper, 1944).

white union members. The gap between the perception by blacks of unions as discriminating organizations, and the reality of unions reflecting the social norms of the status quo, has been reduced over time.

The rise of the CIO and industrial unions in the 1930s greatly increased the number of black union members and helped to reduce some of the tension between unions and the black community. After the AFL-CIO merger in 1955, the rising militancy of black workers and, at times, the violent confrontations over construction jobs again intensified the conflict. During the deep recession of 1974–1975, tensions were exacerbated by the conflict between seniority issues and the implementation of affirmative action programs. The seniority provisions governing layoffs threatened to wipe out the gains made by affirmative action and other enforcement mechanisms of Title VII of the Civil Rights Act of 1964 during the previous decade.

By the end of the decade of the 1970s blacks had increased their membership in many of the largest unions, and they were more visible in union-leadership positions. Although blacks accounted for 11.2 percent of the civilian labor force, they contributed 14.2 percent of labor organization members in 1977.[3] About 33 percent of all blacks who earn wages and salaries were represented by unions, as compared with 26 percent for whites. The 1979 *Quality of Employment Survey* conducted by the Survey Research Center at the University of Michigan revealed that 67 percent of blacks who were not union members would vote to unionize, as compared with only a third of white nonunion members who would support such action.[4] This finding underscores what several researchers had noted earlier—that a receptive audience may have been found due to the fact that the earnings of black workers relative to white workers are consistently higher in unionized than in nonunion labor markets.

Nevertheless, the interests of black union members will frequently diverge from those of the union leadership and senior white union members, especially on discrimination issues at the

---

[3] U.S. Department of Labor, Bureau of Labor Statistics, *Earnings and Other Characteristics of Organized Workers, May 1977*, Rep. 556 (April 1979).

[4] Thomas A. Kochan, "How American Workers View Labor Unions," *Monthly Labor Review* 102 (April 1979), p. 25.

local level. This leadership, whether its purpose is to protect the interest of union members or to stabilize the political alignment within the union, resists external pressures to broaden the social perspective of their organizations. As recently as 1970 Bok and Dunlop commented, "It is hardly surprising, therefore, that many local unions include a substantial group of members who have strong prejudices on race issues." [5] They note further that, while the AFL-CIO has sought to persuade some national and local unions to change their policies on minorities, that organization has not been willing to support the drastic penalty of expulsion for fear of widespread secession from uncooperative unions: "As for the national and international unions, their leaders have chosen to reserve their limited powers of compulsion, such as trusteeship, for occasions involving political struggles for control of a local, corruption, and maintaining authority in disputes with employers." [6]

By 1978, however, 95 percent of the major collective bargaining agreements (covering 1,000 workers or more) had antidiscrimination clauses.[7] In another survey by the Bureau of National Affairs (BNA), discrimination on the basis of race, color, religion, sex, national origin, or age was banned in 84 percent of the sample contracts, which was up from 46 percent in the 1970 survey and only 28 percent in 1965.[8] The arbitration of discrimination grievances under a contract's general nondiscrimination clause may prove to be the most difficult objective to be achieved before black union members perceive unions in the same manner as do their white counterparts.

LEGAL PERSPECTIVES ON FAIR REPRESENTATION

Unions have met their obligations to minority workers under both the National Labor Relations Act and Title VII of the Civil Rights Act of 1964. Prior to the 1960s, unions grappled with the issue of the duty to represent fairly all of the workers within the bargaining unit. The fair representation doctrine established by

[5] Derek C. Bok and John T. Dunlop, *Labor and the American Community* (New York: Simon and Schuster, 1970), pp. 134–135.

[6] *Ibid.*, p. 135.

[7] U.S. Department of Labor, Bureau of Labor Statistics, *Characteristics of Major Bargaining Agreements,* January 1, 1978, Rep. 2065 (April 1980).

[8] Bureau of National Affairs, *Basic Patterns in Union Contracts,* 9th ed. (Washington: May 1979).

the Supreme Court in the *Steele* v. *Louisville and Nashville Railroad Co.* (1944) decision stipulated: "So long as a labor union assumes to act as a statutory representative of a craft, it cannot rightly refuse to perform the duty—to represent the entire membership of the craft—without hostile discrimination, fairly, impartially and in good faith."[9] This doctrine declared a statutory duty under the Railway Labor Act and was later applied to the National Labor Relations Act. The duty of fair representation applies to union conduct that involves the exercise of the union's power of exclusive representation in bargaining and grievance processing: "In those situations the individual employee has no power to protect his own best interests; rather, he must rely on the union to protect them in its actions as collective bargaining representative."[10]

The problem of fair representation as an unfair labor practice in a racial context was not treated until 20 years after the *Steele* case in the *Hughes Tool Company (1964)* case. The National Labor Relations Board held in this case that the refusal of a union to process a worker's grievance because of race was an unfair labor practice subject to certain remedies.[11] After the passage of Title VII of the Civil Rights Act of 1964 there was less reason to handle racial issues under the duty of fair representation.

TITLE VII OF THE CIVIL RIGHTS ACT OF 1964

Title VII of the Civil Rights Act of 1964, as amended by the Equal Employment Opportunity Act of 1972, seeks to rectify employment discrimination by employers, labor organizations, and employment agencies. A labor organization is not permitted under Section 703(c):

> (1) to exclude or to expel from its membership or otherwise discriminate against any individual because of his race, color, religion, sex, or national origin;
> (2) to limit, segregate, or classify its membership, or applicants for membership or to classify or fail or refuse to refer for employment any individual, in any way which would deprive or tend to deprive any individual of em-

---

[9] *Steele* v. *Louisville and Nashville Railroad*, 323 U.S. 192, 204 (1944).
[10] "The Union as Title VII Plaintiff: Affirmative Obligation to Ligate?" 126 *U. Penna. L. Rev.* 1402 (1978).
[11] *Hughes Tool Co.*, 147 NLRB 1573 (1964).

ployment opportunities or would limit such employment opportunities or otherwise adversely affect his status as an employee or as an applicant for employment, because of such individual's race, color, religion, sex, or national origin: or

(3) to cause or attempt to cause an employer to discriminate against any individual in violation of this section.[12]

Joint labor-management committees controlling apprenticeship or other training and retraining programs were also prohibited from discriminating against an individual because of his race, color, religion, sex, or national origin. Title VII applies to employers, labor organizations, and employment agencies employing or serving more than 15 people.

Two other sections of Title VII, Section 730(h) which exempts bona fide seniority systems, and Section 703(j) which prohibits preferential treatment, have been at the core of some of the most bitter disputes between unions and minority and women workers. Section 703(h) states in part:

Notwithstanding any other provision of this Title, it shall not be an unlawful employment practice for any employer to apply different standards of compensation, or different terms, conditions, or privileges of employment pursuant to a bona fide seniority or merit system—provided that such differences are not the result of an intention to discriminate because of race, color, religion, sex, or national origin.[13]

Section 703(j) states:

Nothing contained in this Title shall be interpreted to require any employer, employment agency, labor organization, or joint labor-management committee subject to this Title to grant preferential treatment to any individual or any group because of the race, color, religion, sex, or national origin of such an individual or group on account of an imbalance which may exist with respect to the total number or percentage of persons of any race, color, re-

---

[12] The Equal Employment Opportunity Act of 1972, Public Law 92-261, Approved March 24, 1972.

[13] Ibid.

ligion, sex, or national origin employed by an employer, referred or classified for employment by any employment agency or labor organization, or admitted to, or employed in any apprenticeship or other training program, in comparison with the total number or percentage of persons of such race, color, religion, sex or national origin in any community, state, section, or other area, or in the available work force in any community, state, section, or other area.[14]

Although the Equal Employment Opportunity Commission (EEOC) was given the major responsibility for administration of Title VII, federal district courts have broad discretionary powers to fashion remedies to overcome the effects of past and present employment discrimination.

Until the restructuring of the Equal Employment Opportunity Act in 1978, the federal effort was fragmented with jurisdictional disputes over which agency had the major responsibility for implementation of these laws and regulations. As of this writing the EEOC has become the super agency, but a greatly strengthened Office of Federal Contract Compliance Programs (OFCCP) in the Department of Labor still administers the antidiscrimination program for government contractors under Executive Order 11246.

Unions and the EEOC

Since the passage of Title VII of the Civil Rights Act of 1964, unions and the EEOC have endured a strained relationship. The main issue has been whether strenuous good-faith bargaining and grievance processing within the collective bargaining context satisfied the union's duty under Title VII. The courts have held both parties to a collective bargaining agreement responsible for the agreement. The difficulty is in distinguishing between those situations in which a union bargains for or tacitly accepts employment discrimination and those where the union actively resists discrimination but, because of inadequate bargaining strength, cannot force its position on the contractor.[15]

Since the *Steele* decision unions have been obliged to attempt to protect minority members from the discriminatory acts of em-

---

[14] *Ibid.*
[15] 126 *U. Penna L. Rev.* 1408–1409.

ployers. Under Title VII unions are liable for their role in negotiating, signing, and administering collective bargaining contracts containing discriminatory provisions. For example, until the *Teamsters* decision in 1977 unions were held liable for seniority systems that perpetuated past discrimination by locking blacks into undesirable jobs.[16] A note in the *Harvard Law Review* (February 1980) on union liability for employer discrimination concludes that "regardless of its pre-contract negotiating efforts, a union violates Title VII when it signs a collective bargaining agreement which discriminates in operation."[17]

Many union officials believed that unions could play a positive role in correcting discriminatory practices. However, some of these officials complained that the EEOC refused to recognize affirmative actions of unions and routinely named unions as defendants. In examining the role of unions in the early years of EEOC, Wolkinson noted sharp conflict between local unions and EEOC, and concluded that sometimes the nonconstruction international unions intervened in order to protect international authority or safeguard existing seniority arrangements. Wolkinson determined that in nearly 60 percent of the cases in his study, the international union's presence only hindered the Commission's compliance efforts.[18]

It was not until 1980 that the EEOC adopted a formal resolution agreeing to a discretionary legal strategy toward unions with "good faith" efforts on equal employment opportunity when made by parties in collective bargaining arrangements.[19] These efforts will be taken into account during the processing of investigation, conciliation, and enforcement.

REFERRAL UNIONS IN THE CONSTRUCTION INDUSTRY

The construction industry was the target of extensive confrontations between unions, contractors, and minorities, because the

---

[16] 431 U.S. 324, 14 FEP Cases 1514 (1977).

[17] "Union Liability for Employer Discrimination," *Harvard L. Rev.* (February 1980), p. 721.

[18] Benjamin W. Wolkinson, *Blacks, Unions and the EEOC: A Study of Administrative Futility* (Lexington, MA: D. C. Heath Lexington Books, 1973), pp. 118–120.

[19] "EEOC Background Paper and Resolution to Encourage Voluntary Affirmative Action in Collective Bargaining," *Daily Labor Report*, April 2, 1980, pp. D1–D2.

latter group perceived racial exclusion and discrimination to be widespread in the referral unions. From World War II to 1963, successive executive orders imposed an obligation on federal contractors not to discriminate on the basis of race, religion, or national origin, but these regulations lacked jurisdiction over labor unions. In 1963 Executive Order 11114 expanded the antidiscrimination program to include federally assisted construction contracts as well as procurement contractors. Construction unions became more directly involved in implementation of affirmative action objectives because these craft unions operate hiring halls from which workers are referred to employers. Construction hiring halls were mainly adopted immediately preceding and following the 1959 Landrum-Griffin Act.[20] By acting as employment intermediaries between their members and contractors, these unions are able to control the supply of labor, and this control was used to exclude minorities from membership, from apprenticeship training programs, and from many kinds of jobs in the skilled construction crafts. Although black construction workers accounted for slightly less than 10 percent of all workers in the construction trades, in 1978 they were still a small percent of electricians (4.8%), plumbers and pipefitters (2.8%), structural metal workers (4.3%), sheet metal workers (2.3%), and the highly skilled crafts. Nevertheless, these mechanical trades did increase their black membership from 1.6 to 4 percent of all referral members between 1969 and 1978.[21]

Initially, federal contractors were asked to obtain written statements from their unions pledging cooperation on nondiscrimination. Compliance was not easily achieved and eventually an operational procedure of great specificity was designed to assure implementation of the 1965 Executive Order 11246. The legality of goals and timetables established for an affirmative action program in the metropolitan Philadelphia labor market was upheld in *Contractors Association of Eastern Pennsylvania* v. *Secretary of Labor*.[22] Manning tables specifying the number of minorities to be employed in various crafts had been prescribed in the late

---

[20] Philip Ross, "Origin of the Hiring Hall in Construction," *Industrial Relations* 4 (October 1972), p. 367.

[21] Data provided by Herbert Hammerman.

[22] 442 F.2d 159 (3d Cir. 1971), *cert den.* 404 U.S. 854.

1960s in St. Louis (*U.S. v. Sheet Metal Workers Local 36, Building and Construction Trades Council*), Cleveland (*Ethridge v. Rhodes* and *Weiner v. Cuyahoga Community College*), and Seattle (*U.S. v. Ironworkers Local 86*).[23] All plans had been vigorously challenged in the courts by locals of craft unions or international unions, or briefs opposing the plans had been filed by the Building and Construction Trades Department of the AFL-CIO. The revised Philadelphia Plan of 1969 set specific goals to be achieved over a four-year period for the utilization of minority manpower in six selected skilled crafts: ironworkers, plumbers and pipefitters, steamfitters, sheet metal workers, and elevator construction workers. In these crafts minority representation was 1 percent as compared with an overall minority representation of 30 percent in the construction industry in the five-county Philadelphia area. The Philadelphia Plan required a good-faith effort by the contractors to achieve the goals. Failing that, sanctions could be imposed.

The Third Circuit court affirmed the ruling of the district court on the Philadelphia Plan, and noted that it did not violate the National Labor Relations Act, the Civil Rights Act of 1964, or the Fifth Amendment of the Constitution: "The Philadelphia Plan is valid Executive action designed to remedy the perceived evil that minority tradesmen have not been included in the labor pool available for the performance of construction projects in which the federal government has a cost and performance interest."[24]

U.S. District Judge Weiner had held:

> The heartbeat of 'affirmative action' is the policy of developing programs which shall provide in detail for specific steps to guarantee equal employment opportunity keyed to the problems and needs of minority groups, including, when there are deficiencies, the development of specific goals and timetables for the prompt achievement of full and equal employment opportunity. The Philadelphia Plan is no more or less than a means for implementation of the affirmative action obligations of Executive Order 11246.[25]

[23] 280 F.Supp. 719 (E.D.Mo. 1968); 268 F.Supp. 83 (S.D.Ohio 1967); 1 FEP Cases 618; 443 F.2d 544 (9th Cir.), *cert. den.* 404 U.S. 984 (1971).

[24] 442 F.2d 159 (3rd Cir. 1971).

[25] 311 F.Supp. 1002 (D.C.Pa. 1970).

This landmark decision validated the goals and timetables approach which became the standard operating procedure for non-construction federal contractors. Meanwhile, six plans similar to the revised Philadelphia Plan were imposed in other communities (St. Louis, San Francisco, Atlanta, Washington, D.C., Camden, and Seattle [imposed by the court], and after little success with its hometown plan, Chicago had an imposed plan). Also voluntary "hometown plans" were negotiated between construction unions, contractors, and minority and/or community interests in 70 other areas. Knowledgeable persons have disagreed over the reasons for the limited success of the efforts as a means of increasing minority employment where referral unions were in control. Ray Marshall and his colleagues at the University of Texas concluded that remedies for improving minority employment in the construction industry need to take account of the influence of union structure:

> Limited change is likely to occur where the pressure for change is concentrated on local building trades union leaders who have strong market control reasons for resisting change and, at the same time, are very vulnerable politically and can be responsible for only part of the labor market. National agreements are more effective because national union leaders are not as vulnerable politically, usually have better staffs to consider the implications of agreements, and are more responsive to pressures for change in unacceptable racial practices. National agreements, therefore, would be more effective than the local plans promoted by the Department of Labor.[26]

Godwin and Green indicated that, from their perspective, the most significant progress toward elimination of racial imbalance in the skilled building trades was achieved through federally financed apprenticeship outreach programs.[27] Hometown plans

---

[26] Robert Glover and Ray Marshall, "The Response of Unions in the Construction Industry to Antidiscrimination Efforts," in *Equal Rights and Industrial Relations* (Madison, WI: IRRA, 1977), p. 138. See also Ray Marshall et al., *Employment Discrimination: The Impact of Legal and Administrative Remedies* (New York: Praeger Publishers, 1978), Ch. 2, "Combating Employment Discrimination in Union Entry and Job Referral Through Litigation: The Case of Construction."

[27] Lamond Godwin and Ernest Green, "Selected Strategies to Increase Employment Opportunities for Nonwhites in the Construction Industry," unpublished paper for Workshop on Equal Employment Opportunity, M.I.T., 1974.

generally were not effective because they emphasized training and upgrading for journeymen rather than entry through regular apprenticeship. The outreach programs provided tutoring, counseling, and supportive services for entrants to apprenticeship training programs and to skilled jobs. In 1978 blacks were 10.3 percent of apprentices in the construction industry and 8.8 percent of the graduates from the apprenticeship programs.

The AFL-CIO, through its Human Resources Development Institute and local building trades union councils, sponsored many of the federally funded outreach programs. One of the key factors responsible for the success of the outreach program was support from the building trades unions, especially the AFL-CIO Building Trades Department. Grants were made to these organizations to support their training programs. The rest of the programs were sponsored either by civil rights (Urban League) or community-based organizations (Recruitment and Training Program) and were endorsed by local building trades councils.

In addition to the action against employment discrimination under Executive Order 11246, several significant legal decisions under Title VII of the Civil Rights Act of 1964 were focused on the construction industry. Three of the five cases examined by Marshall et al., *U.S.* v. *Sheet Metal Workers, Local 36* (St. Louis); *Local 53, Heat and Frost Insulators* v. *Vogler* (New Orleans); and *U.S.* v. *Ironworkers, Local 86* (Seattle), were filed on behalf of minorities as a result of dissatisfaction with progress made in entry and job referral in the construction trades.[28]

In the first case filed by the U.S. under Title VII, Local 36 and three other unions (Local 1 of IBEW, Plumbers Local 5, and Steamfitters Local 562) involved in building the St. Louis "gateway arch" were charged by the U.S. Attorney General with failure to admit blacks on a nondiscriminatory basis, failure to operate their respective hiring-hall referral systems in a nondiscriminatory manner, failure to inform blacks of opportunities to become members, and failure to organize employers who employed blacks.[29] Shortly after the Eighth Circuit court ruled against the union in 1969, the unions and contractors in the St. Louis area formulated

[28] Marshall, *Employment Discrimination.*
[29] 280 F.Supp. 719 (E.D.Mo. 1968); 416 F.2d 123 (8th Cir. 1969).

the St. Louis hometown plan which was replaced two years later with an imposed plan.

In the *Local 53, Heat and Frost Insulators and Asbestos Workers* v. *Vogler* case, employment was controlled through an exclusive bargaining agreement with firms doing insulation and asbestos work within the greater New Orleans area. Since membership in the union was restricted to sons and close relatives and was approved by secret ballot, Vogler, a white asbestos worker, filed a Title VII complaint that he was refused employment because of his nonunion status and his efforts to help a black friend attain union membership. The district court found that Local 53's nepotism policies denied blacks opportunities for employment referrals and union membership. An injunction issued against the union prohibited the use of family relationships and member endorsements and ordered that the union develop objective criteria for membership. The union was ordered to effectuate a referral system that alternated black and white prospective employees.[30]

This 1969 injunction was later upheld by the Fifth Circuit court. These activities provided the impetus to establish a hometown plan for New Orleans. The Fifth Circuit held, "The Court must be free to deal equitably with conflicting interests of white employees in order to shape remedies that will most effectively protect and redress the rights of the Negro victims of discrimination."[31]

In 1970 a Title VII suit was filed against Local 86, Ironworkers, and four other construction unions (sheet metal workers, and operating engineers who signed a consent decree prior to beginning of trial) and their Joint Apprenticeship Committees in the Seattle area. A comprehensive remedy to eliminate discrimination with respect to job referral and membership was specified by the district court. The union was ordered to recruit blacks into apprenticeship programs, to make immediate referrals of blacks, and to modify its apprentice/journeyman ratios.[32] The degree of desegregation of the union and improvement in the minority representation was overseen by the monitoring of the decree and various supplemental decrees by District Judge Lundberg.

---

[30] 294 F.Supp. 368 (E.D.La. 1968).

[31] 407 F.2d 1047 (5th Cir. 1969); 451 F.2d 1236 (5th Cir. 1971).

[32] 315 F.Supp. 1202 (W.D.Wash. 1970); 443 F.2d 433 (9th Cir. 1971).

At the end of the 1970s another major case (*Commonwealth of Penna.* v. *Local 542 of Operating Engineers*) was being litigated. After more than 15 years, the tensions between effective affirmative action programs and collective bargaining practices and procedures had become more exacerbated. The rates of unemployment were higher in construction than other industries, and in this environment of fewer jobs, a new allegation of reverse discrimination was made by many unions. Judge Higginbotham noted in the *Operating Engineers* case that:

> The facts of the instant case . . . demonstrate the complexity and subtlety of the interrelationship or race, collective bargaining, craft unions, the employment process and that ultimate goal . . . real jobs which offer adequate hourly compensation and reasonably consistent pay checks through the year. Here there are many contradictions between pronounced policies and actual practices. Also there are some aspects of viral nepotism at its worst which had a disproportionate impact against blacks but also affected many whites. Some of the practices cannot be categorized as exclusively beneficial to all whites or as exclusively harmful to all blacks. Thus there has to be a careful weighing of the relative racial impacts of many practices and policies.[33]

What is the present status of minority representation in the construction industry? After millions of dollars expended on outreach and training, implementation of executive orders, and Title VII litigation, the results are not overwhelming. Blacks accounted for 8.2 percent of the referral membership in 1978 as compared with 6.8 percent in 1969. In the fall of 1980 the OFCCP issued minority hiring goals for 285 major metropolitan areas and 183 largely rural surrounding areas. From 1968 to 1980 open-shop contractors tripled their share of the market (from 20 to 60 percent of all new construction).[34] It would be ironic if the efforts to increase minority participation in the unionized craft sector of the industry came to naught during the decade of the 1980s as that sector generates fewer jobs.

---

[33] 469 F.Supp. 329, 18 FEP Cases 1560 (D.C.Pa. 1978).

[34] Steven J. Donato, "A Comparison of Occupational Structure in Union and Non-Union Commercial Industrial Construction," Master's thesis, Alfred P. Sloan School of Management, M.I.T., June 1980.

SENIORITY ISSUES IN INDUSTRIAL UNIONS

Like the referral craft unions in the construction industry, some of the largest industrial unions have encountered major problems when attempting to deal with equal employment issues. Industrial unions mainly regulate the internal labor markets of companies through collective bargaining procedures, while employers retain control of hiring and initial assignments. The intervention of the government has led to restructuring of the senority provisions of collectively bargained agreements and has forced fundamental changes on the two parties to the agreement. Craft notes that since World War II seniority has become:

> an integral part of the institutionalized web of rules that affect the administration of human resources in the internal labor market. Specifically seniority has come to represent an enforceable priority under a collective bargaining agreement which qualifies an employee for benefits from the employer and provides a common basis for employees to estimate their relative status in terms of job security and opportunities for advancement.[35]

The treatment of seniority under equal employment opportunity laws is reflected in a series of major court decisions and consent decrees. During the past 15 years the courts have sought to reconcile remedies for past discrimination against minority workers with seniority expectations of majority workers. The definition of "rightful place" remedy, the restriction of compensation to specific employees, the seniority versus affirmative action tensions of layoffs, and the bona fide seniority system exemption from Title VII are discussed. The *Teamsters* decision in 1977 removed the seniority modification systems from the courts; however, consent decrees such as that reached with AT&T may temporarily override seniority provisions. With the *Weber* decision in 1979, the union in a voluntary agreement with employers modified the seniority arrangement.

During the first 12 years of implementation of Title VII, complex seniority issues arose in many southern plants over the merger of lines of progress that had previously been segregated by race,

---

[35] James A. Craft, "Equal Opportunity and Seniority: Trends and Manpower Implications," *Labor Law Journal* 26 (December 1975), p. 750.

the transfer rights of incumbent blacks to departments with better job progression, and layoff and recall procedures where there was a reduction of the workforce. Competitive-status seniority (time in a job, line, department) determines a worker's standing compared to others on transfer, promotion, layoff, and recall. Even in the more favorable economic environment of the late 1960s, black workers were on a collision course with seniority systems that were the product of collective bargaining by some of the largest industrial unions in steel, paper, telephone, and trucking. Judge Wisdom's decision in the Fifth Circuit on *Papermakers Local 189 v. United States* (1969) posed the significant questions:

> In this case we deal with one of the most perplexing issues troubling the courts under Title VII: how to reconcile equal employment opportunity *today* with seniority expectations based on *yesterday's* built-in racial discrimination. May an employer continue to award formerly white jobs on the basis of seniority attained in other formerly white jobs, or must the employer consider the employee's experience in formerly Negro jobs as an equivalent measure of seniority?[36]

Existing seniority systems did not credit time spent in black jobs, lines, or departments toward opportunities available in previously white lines, jobs, or departments. Minority workers may have been less inclined to transfer to lines with greater future earnings potential because they had to forfeit accumulated seniority as well as suffer a short-term wage reduction. Until the U.S. Supreme Court's *Teamsters* decision in 1977, which ruled that bona fide seniority systems were protected from the operation of Title VII, seniority systems which carried forward to the present the effects of former allegedly discriminatory practices were held to be unlawful (see discussion below). Earlier in *Quarles v. Philip Morris, Inc.* (1968) a district court stated: "A departmental seniority system that has its genesis in racial discrimination is not a bona fide seniority system."[37] Prior to the decision, blacks hired into formerly black departments before the employer ceased discriminatory hiring were not allowed to compete for future va-

---

[36] 416 F.2d 980 (5th Cir. 1969), *cert. den.* 397 U.S. 919 (1970).
[37] 279 F.Supp. 505 (E.D.Va. 1968), *cert. den.*

cancies in more desirable departments on the basis of their seniority.

Quarles and the *Local 189* case, in which the court abolished job seniority in favor of mill seniority for blacks hired prior to the 1966 merger of racial progression lines, set the pattern for seniority issues. Throughout this period, granting competitive-type seniority relief emphasized that innocent employees should not be penalized in order to remedy past acts of discrimination. The restructuring of seniority systems was based on the "rightful place" remedy.[38] Later, courts attempted to give special rights to "specifically harmed" individuals who were adversely affected by past discriminatory hiring or assignment. They would obtain their new position (rightful place) on seniority rosters, but not at the expense of other employees. Unions argued that the initial hiring and assignment to racial job slots had been intentional discriminatory acts by employers.[39]

However, the severe recession of 1974–1975, when the focus shifted from transfer and promotion via seniority systems to layoff and recall, produced the greatest conflict between antidiscrimination agreements and collective bargaining agreements. The *Jersey Central Power and Light Co.* v. *IBEW Local 327* case highlighted the tensions between these programs on seniority issues. Unions and civil rights groups who had formerly worked as members of a coalition seeking the passage of Title VII now appeared in court as adversaries. The issue was whether minority workers should maintain the same proportion in a reduced workforce as they held prior to a layoff. If the "Last In, First Out" (LIFO) procedures were followed, such workers would bear a disproportionate share of the burden of layoff. In the *Jersey Central* case the Third Circuit court reversed the lower court and held that a seniority clause providing for layoffs by reverse order was not subject to modification by court decree.[40]

The economic recession forced employers in the public sector as well as private employers to reduce their workforces. Violent confrontations erupted between minority workers and unions

---

[38] William B. Gould, *Black Workers in White Unions* (Ithaca, NY: Cornell University Press, 1977).

[39] *Franks* v. *Bowman Transportation Co.*, 424 U.S. 747, 12 FEP Cases 549 (1976), reversing and remanding 8 FEP Cases 66.

[40] 508 F.2d 687 (3d Cir. 1975).

representing police and firefighters when budgetary constraints forced a cutback in many municipal services. After 1972, state and local government employees were included under Title VII. In 1975 the Guardian Association and the Hispanic Society, organizations of black and Hispanic police officers of New York City, filed a Title VII suit alleging discrimination due to their disproportionate share of layoffs within the police department. They claimed that the hiring examinations and minimum height requirements in effect prior to 1973 barred the entry of many minorities into the police force, and effectively prevented those who were hired from accumulating enough seniority to withstand layoffs under the LIFO system. The district court granted a preliminary injunction barring New York City from hiring or recalling any of the nearly 3,000 police officers discharged until seniority lists were revised to eliminate the effects of past discrimination against minorities. At the present time there are still outstanding issues to be resolved in this case, *Guardians Association of New York City Police Department* v. *Civil Service Commission of New York.*[41]

The U. S. Supreme Court reversed lower court rulings in *International Brotherhood of Teamsters* v. *U. S.* (1977) and concluded that bona fide seniority systems which tend to perpetuate the effects of pre-Act discrimination were protected under Section 703(h) of Title VII. However, individuals are not barred from relief, including retroactive seniority, because of employer's post-Act hiring discrimination. In the *Teamsters* case local city drivers (mainly minority employees) of a nationwide common carrier of motor freight had to forfeit their accumulated competitive seniority if they wanted to transfer to more desirable jobs as over-the-road long distance drivers. The line driver positions were held mainly by white employees. Because minority employees had been denied the opportunity to become line drivers when they were initially hired, the lower courts had found that the seniority system in the collective bargaining contracts which did not allow carry-over of seniority from the bargaining unit for city drivers violated Title VII as it forced the transferees to start at the bottom of the line. The seniority systems operated to carry the effects of past discrimination into the present.

---

[41] 431 F.Supp. 526, 18 FEP Cases 63 (D.C.N.Y. 1977); 466 F.Supp. 1273, 19 FEP Cases 121 (D.C.N.Y. 1979); 21 FEP Cases 1467 (1980).

The Supreme Court, in reversing the lower courts, noted in awarding retroactive seniority to minority employees that the seniority system did not have its genesis in racial discrimination and that it was negotiated and had been maintained free of any illegal purpose. In fact, the placing of line drivers in a separate bargaining unit from other employees was rational and in accord with industry practice and consistent with NLRB precedents. The union's role of agreeing to and maintaining a seniority system that perpetuated pre-Act discrimination did not violate Title VII.[42]

How best to evaluate whether seniority systems are bona fide in accordance with the *Teamsters* doctrine was set forth in a later Second Circuit case, *James* v. *Stockham Valves and Fitting Co.* (1977). The criteria were: (1) whether the seniority system operates to discourage all employees equally from transferring between seniority units; (2) whether the seniority units are in the same or separate bargaining units (if the latter, whether that structure is rational and in conformance with industry practice); (3) whether the seniority system had its genesis in racial discrimination; and (4) whether the system was negotiated and has been maintained free from any illegal purpose. The United Steelworkers of America and Local 3036 (Birmingham, Alabama) were defendants in the *Stockham Valves* case, and it seems ironic that a majority of the local's grievance committee were black. Since 1970 the seniority system had been twice modified, through the collective bargaining process and through the union's having struck for five months seeking the company's agreement on plantwide seniority. Is the union liable for its ratification of a collective bargaining contract containing a seniority system which minority members wish to revise? Clearly, both parties to the collective bargaining process must be willing to modify and update a seniority system that was created under segregated procedures of the 1940s.[43]

Two other significant promotional seniority issues were raised by industrial unions in the late 1970s. Three telephone unions, the Communication Workers of America, the International Brotherhood of Electrical Workers, and the Alliance of Independent Telephone Unions challenged the 1973 AT&T consent decree. The telephone unions had not participated in the 1973 negotiated set-

---

[42] 431 U.S. 324, 14 FEP Cases 1514 (1977).
[43] 559 F.2d 310, 15 FEP Cases 827 (1977).

tlement which stipulated that over a six-year period the AT&T telephone operating companies would attempt to restructure their internal labor markets to meet specific goals for the better utilization of women and minorities. The technique of the affirmative action override of contractual seniority provisions was authorized where intermediate targets were not met in nonmanagement jobs. These unions, representing about 710,000 nonmanagement workers, with the Communication Workers of America representing about 600,000 employees, intervened to protect its collective bargaining agreement. The Supreme Court on July 3, 1978, let stand the decision of the lower courts that seniority systems may be modified in order to meet the target requirements of a consent decree, and that the use of the seniority override, as a remedial measure to correct underutilization of women and minorities in nontraditional jobs, is lawful. The override permits members of target groups to "leap frog" incumbents with greater seniority and/or better qualifications. The override does not affect seniority with respect to layoff and recall of employees.[44]

For nearly 15 years, management, the United Steelworkers, and black workers in the basic steel industry wrangled over the issue of the incumbent black employee who wished to transfer from previously segregated seniority lines to better paying jobs in other departments. Prior to the civil rights era, the duty of fair representation doctrine under the National Labor Relations Act dealt with discriminatory seniority arrangement in the steel industry. In *Whitfield* v. *United Steelworkers* (1959), segregated seniority lines were abolished, but black employees could enter the previously all-white lines only at the bottom and they forfeited previously acquired seniority rights in the black line. In 1967 under the antidiscrimination law, the OFCC found a number of discriminatory practices at the Sparrows Point facility of Bethlehem Steel. The issue was not resolved until 1973 with an order that permitted black workers to transfer with rate retention (so that wage cuts were not required) and to carry forward seniority credits. Meanwhile numerous complaints were filed against the union and employers by black workers who were extremely dissatisfied with the seniority arrangements (*U.S.* v. *Bethlehem Steel,* Lackawanna

---

[44] 556 F.2d 167, 14 FEP Cases 1210 (1977); *cert. den.* 17 FEP Cases 1095 (1978).

Plant, *U.S.* v. *United States Steel,* Fairfield Plant, *U.S.* v. *H. K. Porter*). The rule of preference for job openings in departments and units within those departments being retained for those already in these work areas started to be modified with the circuit appeals decision of the *Lackawanna* case in 1971.[45]

The trend in the modification of seniority arrangements by judges induced the union to negotiate an industrywide solution with nine basic steel companies and representatives of the federal government. The Steel Consent Decree was signed in April 1974. Under this agreement, plantwide seniority would be used for promotion, transfer, layoff, and recall, but the lines of progression within departments would not be altered. Since vacancies within a department would still be filled from below, transferees could enter only at the bottom. The rate retention option was available to encourage some employee transfers. The consent decree was upheld in *U.S.* v. *Allegheny-Ludlum Industries* (1975).[46]

The Steel Consent Decree had an effect on the collective bargaining process and equal employment which reached far beyond the basic steel industry. The terms of the consent decree were included in the Master Agreement of the Steel Industry in 1974. The United Steelworkers union represents the aluminum industry as well, and an identical provision of affirmative action for skilled craft jobs was included in the 1974 Master Agreement between the United Steelworkers and aluminum producers. Under the aegis of a joint company-union committee, goals were to be established for reducing racial imbalances in skilled jobs. Fifty percent of the slots in the on-job training program for craft workers were reserved for minority and/or female employees. A dual seniority roster based on plant seniority was created to fill the training vacancies.

Brian Weber, a white employee at the Gramercy plant of Kaiser Aluminum challenged these agreements (*Kaiser Aluminum and Chemical Corporation* v. *Brian F. Weber et al.*) under Title VII of the Civil Rights Act of 1964. The Steelworkers Union opposed Weber, and the Supreme Court (June 1979) reversed the decisions of the lower courts that provisions of the Kaiser affirmative action program violated proscriptions of Title VII against preferential treatment. The *Weber* decision is seen to be a victory

---

[45] 312 F.Supp. 994 (W.D.N.Y. 1970); 446 F.2d 652 (2d Cir. 1971).

[46] 553 F.2d 451, 15 FEP Cases 935, *cert. den.* 16 FEP Cases 1093 (1978).

for collective bargaining as a means of accommodating diverse interests in the workplace. *Weber* emphasized that voluntary compliance is preferable to court action, and that private settlement without litigation is central to Title VII.[47]

A keen observer of the evaluation of EEO seniority law, James E. Jones, Jr., has noted that:

> The critical role of seniority in determining who should work and its priority position in trade union ideology insured that efforts would be made by its supporters to immunize it from the emerging EEO law and the attempts of civil rights advocates to curb its effect. It is no wonder that the AFL-CIO's legislative support of the Civil Rights Act of 1964 included efforts to insure that previous seniority rights would not be adversely affected by the new civil rights. That the trade union objectives in this regard were less than clearly successful is attested to by two factors: (1) the ambiguity of sections 703(h) and (j) of the Civil Rights Act of 1964, and (2) extensive litigation of seniority issues over the past 12 years.[48]

The dual aspects of competitive seniority, the promotion and transfer as separate from layoff and recall issues, will probably experience quite different outcomes in the future. During the first years of implementation of the antidiscrimination laws, the problem of the "incumbent black" and past discrimination produced much of the controversy. Today these "incumbent blacks" are older workers who may prefer the security of remaining in their old departments where they have accumulated seniority. Younger blacks are entering integrated lines along with their white counterparts. Thus, with the retirement of the older black workforce, the issues of promotion and transfer will fade away. Layoff and recall will generate controversy as long as the economic climate is not very healthy. Those same younger black workers who may benefit from the new rules of the seniority game in terms of promotion and transfer may be prime candidates for layoff under LIFO rules. As fairly new entrants to many types of jobs, they

---

[47] 415 F.Supp. 761, 12 FEP Cases (D.C.La. 1976); 563 F.2d 216, 16 FEP Cases 1 (5th Cir. 1977); and 443 U.S. 193, 20 FEP Cases 1 (1979).

[48] James E. Jones, Jr., "The Transformation of Fair Employment Practice Policies," in *Federal Policies and Worker Status Since the Thirties* (Madison, WI: IRRA, 1976).

may not have acquired enough plant seniority to protect themselves in their jobs. Unions have been major actors in the evolution of the seniority policies. They have been forceful advocates of maintaining the seniority principles that are imbedded in the American industrial relations system.

ARBITRATION

Since the *Steelworkers Trilogy* cases,[49] arbitration was declared to be the preferred means of industrial dispute settlement. The arbitral decision was final and binding on the parties, and the court could not review the merits of an arbitration award. George Hildebrand sees the emergence of multiple avenues of relief for adjudication of claims based on individual rights in the workplace as adverse to the traditional collective bargaining process. In his view, the exclusivity and finality of voluntary arbitration have been weakened. He notes:

> In the earlier history of collective bargaining the dominant view was that the contracting parties were the employer and the union. The employee in the bargaining unit stood in the position of third-party beneficiary of the agreement. The union bargained to gain employee rights, and it also protected its employees in the breach or observance of these rights. At the apex of the relationship were the grievance procedure and arbitration, with arbitration as the terminal step in which decision by a neutral, after a proceeding between the parties in which the union represented the grievant, brought the issue to a final determination.[50]

The Supreme Court attempted to define the proper relationship of the grievance-arbitration machinery of collective bargaining to equal employment opportunity under Title VII. In the *Alexander v. Gardner-Denver Company (1974)* case it held that an adverse decision in arbitration would not prohibit subsequent Title VII litigation and that employees are not required to exhaust their

---

[49] *United Steelworkers* v. *American Mfg. Co.,* 363 U.S. 564 (1960); *United Steelworkers* v. *Warrior and Gulf Navigation Co.,* 363 U.S. 574 (1960); *United Steelworkers* v. *Enterprise Wheel and Car Corp.,* 363 U.S. 593 (1960).

[50] George Hildebrand, "Prospects Regarding the Administration of Collective Bargaining," in *The Shrinking Perimeter,* eds. Hervey A. Juris and Myron Roomkin (Lexington, MA: D. C. Heath Lexington Books, 1980), p. 105.

arbitration remedy before pursuing a claim of employment discrimination in court. In its famous footnote 21, the Court indicated that in some cases arbitral findings of fact may be accorded great weight if certain specified conditions have been met: (1) existence of provisions in the collective bargaining agreement that conform substantially with Title VII; (2) the degree of procedural fairness in the arbitral forum; (3) adequacy of the record with respect to the issue of discrimination, and (4) the special competence of particular arbitrators.

Nevertheless, Justice Powell of the Supreme Court was forceful in stating that "The rights conferred by Title VII can form no part of the collective bargaining process since waiver of these rights would defeat the paramount congressional purpose behind Title VII." [51] Thus, the Supreme Court did not adopt the deferral to arbitration rules that usually prevail under the National Labor Relations Act. In resolving employment discrimination grievance disputes, the Court relied on a judicial forum rather than arbitration. An employee's right to trial de novo under Title VII could not be foreclosed by prior submission to arbitration under a collective bargaining agreement.

After the *Alexander* v. *Gardner-Denver* decision, a number of experts suggested ways in which arbitration might serve as a viable alternative in equal employment disputes. Professor Harry T. Edwards (now a federal judge in the District of Columbia Circuit Court) proposed a two-track arbitration system that would accommodate and reconcile the conflicting interests of the parties:

> Employers and unions want the speedy and inexpensive resolution of disputes that arbitration has traditionally supplied. Employers wish to avoid being subjected to litigation in several forums on the same claim, whereas unions want to ensure that they comply with their duty of fair representation. Employees who have been subjected to employment discrimination desire full relief.[52]

Edwards suggests that his proposal be limited to those cases in which the grievance alleges an act that might be considered a violation of both the collective bargaining agreement and Title

---

[51] 415 U.S. 36 (1974).

[52] Harry T. Edwards, "Arbitration as an Alternative in Equal Employment Disputes," *Arbitration Journal* (December 1978).

VII. It would specifically exclude from arbitration all grievances (1) alleging only a breach of law; (2) charging both the union and the employer with discrimination; (3) seeking a reformation of the contract; (4) claiming inconsistency between the collective bargaining agreement and a court or administrative order; (5) constituting a class action, or (6) involving unsettled areas of the law.[53] These screening criteria would limit the substantive jurisdiction of the arbitrator in a way designed to minimize or eliminate the necessity of court review. This special procedure for employment discrimination cases would be handled by a panel of lawyer-arbitrators with expertise in Title VII law.

Gould, law professor and arbitrator, has noted that "an exclusion of employment discrimination cases from the grievance arbitration machinery and their relegation to the courts would have a deleterious impact inasmuch as it would segregate the claims of racial minorities and women from the mainstream of plant level adjudication." [54] Some unions have adopted antidiscrimination programs that include arbitration of discrimination grievances, as in the UAW and General Motors contract.

The *W.R. Grace Company v. Local 759, International Union of the United Rubber, Cork, Linoleum and Plastic Workers of America* case, decided in the district court of the Northern District of Mississippi in July 1980, reflects the confusion that still surrounds seniority, conciliation, and arbitration in the employment discrimination context. In 1974 the employer had entered an EEOC conciliation agreement that conflicted with the seniority provisions of its collective bargaining contract. These seniority provisions were superseded by a system to determine layoffs so that the percentage of women employed by the company would never be reduced by a layoff. The union objected to the change, and the company refused to arbitrate. By 1975 the court ordered the conciliation agreement binding on both company and union. By the time the union's appeal reached the Fifth Circuit, the *Teamsters* case (1977) had changed the seniority law. One arbitrator ruled in 1978 that W. R. Grace was acting in concurrence with the district court's order and did not have to prosecute grievances which occurred during the appeal proceedings. A sec-

---

[53] *Ibid.*, p. 24.
[54] Gould.

ond arbitrator reversed this ruling because the first arbitrator "had exceeded the scope of his jurisdiction, going outside of the plain, written terms of the contract between the union and the company."[55] The district judge vacated the arbitration award of the second arbitrator because the collective bargaining contract also provided that if any provision of the agreement was found to be in conflict with any state or federal law, such law would supersede the conflicting provisions. During the time of the appeal and before the reversal based on the *Teamsters* decision, the conciliation agreements had the effect of nullifying the seniority provisions in the collective bargaining contract.[56]

Finally, the issue of arbitration has become moot as far as the EEOC is concerned. In 1977 the Commission established a Rapid Charge Procedure (RCP) in order to reduce the backlog of Title VII complaints and also to expedite the process. The RCP was essentially a face-to-face factfinding conference for the settlement of individual claims, and it swiftly resolved many claims where the facts were at issue.[57] It is likely that most of these charges originated in the nonunionized sector. Whether the arbitral forum will be considered a viable way to resolve discrimination disputes will depend to some extent on how minorities perceive the outcomes of such action. One observer has noted that all is not lost: some employment discrimination cases may now be processed under the grievance-arbitration procedure when they originate as just cause, discipline, or seniority claims.[58]

CONCLUSION

Equal employment opportunity requirements (including laws, executive orders, administrative regulations, affirmative action plans, consent decrees, and judicial decisions) have altered some important rules of the workplace. We have examined three areas—referral and training programs of craft unions, seniority systems, and arbitration—where the antidiscrimination efforts have been in

---

[55] 23 FEP Cases 852 (1980).

[56] 23 FEP Cases 588 (1980).

[57] Interview with official from EEOC, January 1980.

[58] Harry T. Edwards, "Arbitration of Employment Discrimination Cases: An Empirical Study," in *Arbitration—1975*, Proceedings of the 28th Annual Meeting, National Academy of Arbitrators (Washington: BNA Books, 1976), p. 69.

conflict with collective bargaining agreements. Our analysis indicates that adjustment has been painful for all parties: (1) employees who differ by race, sex, skill level, and expectations; (2) unions attempting to restructure in order to survive; and (3) employers who may have had to modify their management strategies in order to avoid being adversely affected. The role of unions has not been an easy one.

It may be that the extent of the positive commitment of some unions to the full participation of women and minorities has yet to be researched. We do not know how many unions have supported their minority and women members through lengthy litigation on EEO matters. For example, the Newspaper Guild of New York financially supported both the women and minority employees of *The New York Times* in a seven-year legal battle.[59] When the consent decree was signed for the minority employees, Judge Metzger ordered the attorneys' fees for the plaintiffs doubled from $250,000, stating that the original amount was "extremely modest in light of the complexity of proof."[60] Further research on these neglected areas of industrial relations deserves high priority.

Occupational Safety and Health

The second major social issue to confront collective bargaining in the 1960s, occupational safety and health, was also heralded by federal legislation: the Coal Mine Health and Safety Act of 1969 and the Occupational Safety and Health Act of 1970 (OSHAct). These laws, according to Ashford, resulted from an increased injury rate (up 29 percent in the decade), the discovery of new occupational diseases (coal miners' black lung and cancers caused by asbestos and vinyl chloride), rapid technological change especially in chemical processing, the environmental movement's concern over toxins and pollution in general, and a better-educated, more affluent workforce.[61]

The Scope of the Problem

Whatever the cause of recent legislation, safety and health pose

---

[59] *Boylan* v. *New York Times* (1978); *Rosario* v. *New York Times*, 24 FEP Cases 994 (S.D.N.Y. 1980).

[60] *Daily Labor Report*, December 29, 1980.

[61] Nicholas Askounes Ashford, *Crisis in the Workplace: Occupational Disease and Injury, a Report to the Ford Foundation* (Cambridge, MA: M.I.T., 1976).

a major problem in the workplace. Accidents killed 13,100 people at work in 1980, according to the National Safety Council (NSC).[62] Workers also die from diseases caused by working conditions—possibly as many as 100,000 each year according to the (then) Department of Health, Education, and Welfare (HEW).[63] While the magnitude of such disease-related deaths due to cancer, respiratory, and heart diseases is in dispute, there is little disagreement about the growing problem of occupational disease.[64]

In addition to deaths, the NSC estimated that there were 2.2 million disabling accidents in 1979, at a cost to the economy of $23 billion.[65]

Subjective reports by workers confirm the magnitude of the problem. Forty-six percent of all blue-collar workers in the 1977 Quality of Employment Survey reported unpleasant working conditions; 40 percent of all workers are exposed to air pollution at work, 29 percent to dangerous equipment, and 29 percent to dangerous chemicals.[66] Fifteen percent reported an injury or illness made more severe by conditions at work. Seventy-six percent of all workers surveyed felt workers should have "complete" or "a lot of" say over safety equipment and practices as opposed to 30 percent desiring such influence over wages and salaries.

Despite their importance, safety and health issues have been slow in calling forth significant legislative or bargaining activity.

HISTORY OF REGULATION

Early industrialization in the U.S. left safety and health to the play of market mechanisms. Workers either accepted the risk of hazards or quit. Employers could be sued for negligence, but common law defenses of contributory negligence limited employer ex-

---

[62] *Accident Facts*, 1979 ed. (Chicago: National Safety Council, 1979). Data for 1980 given in telephone conversation. The Bureau of Labor Standards estimate is lower (5,000), but it is based on employer reports from less than the total population.

[63] Ashford.

[64] Herbert P. Northrop, Richard L. Rowan, and Charles R. Perry, *The Impact of OSHA* (Philadelphia; Industrial Research Unit, Wharton School, University of Pennsylvania 1978).

[65] National Safety Council.

[66] Robert P. Quinn and Graham L. Staines, *The 1977 Quality of Employment Survey* (Ann Arbor: Institute for Social Research, University of Michigan, 1979).

posure.[67] After the turn of the century, President Theodore Roosevelt urged the states to pass workingmen's compensation laws. In return for guaranteed (and limited) payments for injuries from an employer fund, workers gave up their right to sue under these laws. Finally, in 1970, the federal government shifted the emphasis from compensation after the fact, to prevention.

The OSHAct, as it will be abbreviated, imposed a general duty on employers to provide a "place of employment . . . free from recognized hazards . . . causing death or physical harm." [68] The National Institute of Occupational Safety and Health was set up in HEW to do research on hazards, the Occupational Safety and Health Administration to issue and enforce standards, and an Occupational Safety and Health Review Commission to monitor enforcement. Each worker in the U.S. was granted certain rights, namely to: (1) complain about violations of specific standards of the employer's general duty; (2) retain anonymity; (3) have a representative accompany the government official on any subsequent inspection; and (4) be protected against reprisals.

Implementation of this fundamental shift in employment relations has sparked controversy. According to the AFL-CIO, the Nixon Administration provided lax enforcement, appointed a weak staff, and used the agency for political fund raising.[69] Only under Labor Secretary Ray Marshall, according to AFL-CIO President Lane Kirkland, "have our unions been able to work with a Labor Department which believes in OSHA and is doing its best to make it work."[70] On the other hand, according to management representatives, the law from the beginning has meant petty harassment, costly wasted investment, and distraction from effective safety and health programs.[71]

Secretary Marshall initiated several reforms to meet management criticism: dropping some 1,000 standards, targeting inspections on high-hazard industries, and emphasizing consultation with employers. Nonetheless, Congress found such reforms insufficient

---

[67] Ashford.

[68] Ashford.

[69] Lane Kirkland, "OSHA: A 10-Year Success Story," *The AFL-CIO American Federationist* 87 (July 1980), p. 1–4.

[70] Kirkland, *ibid.*

[71] Fred K. Foulkes, "Learning to Live with OSHA," *Harvard Business Review* 51 (November-December 1973), pp. 57–67.

and exempted small businesses in low-injury industries from most inspections.[72] The Reagan Administration brings to OSHA a general determination to "get the government off the backs of industry."

Given the different interests of the two parties, no objective assessment of the OSHAct is possible. While the Supreme Court ruled that the economic cost of one specific standard for exposure to benzene was too great,[73] the labor movement cites an overall decrease due to the Act, of 10 percent in fatalities and 15 percent in injuries.[74] Academic evaluations of a single standard have ranged from net negative to net positive and reflect the assumptions of the authors.[75]

Against this larger societal debate, the question addressed here is how collective bargaining responded on safety and health.

COLLECTIVE BARGAINING ACTIVITIES

Contract Negotiations. Although no empirical evidence exists, it is our experience that union and management representatives spend relatively little time in negotiations discussing safety and health and rarely, if ever, do negotiations go to impasse solely or primarily over these issues. A rare example is, according to Ashford, the 1973 negotiations between the Oil, Chemical, and Atomic Workers and Shell Oil, which resulted in a work stoppage in part over safety.[76]

Local walkouts are undoubtedly more frequent in some unions such as the United Mine Workers or in extreme conditions such as the highly publicized sterilization of seven workers in the production of DBCP.[77]

Kochan has assembled reports from several sources to describe the results of these negotiations in actual contract language (Table

---

[72] "Comparison Between the Schweider Rider (FY '80 Appropriations) and Byron Rider (FY '81 Appropriations)," U.S. Department of Labor, Occupational Safety and Health Administration, October 8, 1980 (mimeo).

[73] *Industrial Union Department, AFL-CIO, Petitioner v. American Petroleum Institute et al.,* and *Ray Marshall, Secretary of Labor, Petitioner, v. American Petroleum Institute et al.,* 48 LW 5022.

[74] Kirkland.

[75] John Mendeloff, *Regulating Safety: An Economic and Political Analysis of Occupational Safety and Health Policy* (Cambridge, MA: M.I.T., 1979).

[76] Ashford.

[77] "Song of the Canary," broadcast by Public Broadcasting System.

1).[78] Most contracts have some provision dealing with safety and health, and the frequency of such provisions has increased since the passage of the OSHAct.[79] Also such provisions are concentrated in manufacturing and in specific industries such as mining where the hazards are greatest. However, the rights and benefits conferred on workers are relatively limited, most generally taking the form of a general statement of responsibility. Less frequently do contracts guarantee the workers' right to refuse hazardous work, and rarely do they impose more stringent standards for exposure than does the law.

TABLE 1

Collective Bargaining Provisions
On Safety and Health

	Percent in all contracts	Percent in mfg. industry contracts	Percent in mining industry contracts
Some provision on safety	82	87	100
General statement of responsibility	50	58	75
Company to comply with laws	29	29	50
Company to provide safety equipment	42	46	92
Company to provide first aid	21	26	50
Physical examinations	30	30	75
Hazardous work provisions	22	19	67
Accident investigations	18	24	58
Safety committees	43	55	92
Dissemination of safety information to employees	16	18	38
Dissemination of safety issues to union	19	21	44
Employees to comply with safety rules	47	50	67
Right of inspection by union or employees safety committees	20	30	56
Wage differentials for hazardous work	15	6	6

Sources: First nine items, "Safety and Health Patterns in Union Contracts," Daily Labor Report #178, September 13, 1978, p. E-1; last five items, "Major Collective Bargaining Agreements: Safety and Health Provisions," BLS Bulletin #1425-16 (Washington: 1976). Reproduced from Thomas A. Kochan, Collective Bargaining and Industrial Relations (Homewood, IL: Richard D. Irwin, 1980).

[78] Thomas A. Kochan, Collective Bargaining and Industrial Relations (Homewood, IL: Richard D. Irwin, 1980).

[79] "Safety and Health Patterns in Union Contracts," Daily Labor Reports, September 13, 1978, pp. E1–E2.

The Right to Refuse Hazardous Work. Under the National Labor Relations Act workers in the U.S. have a general right to strike as a "protected concerted activity."[80] A union can strike to win contract provisions on safety and health. However, based on the Supreme Court's *Gateway Coal* decision, if a contract provides for the arbitration of grievances, safety and health complaints must be brought to that forum[81] and strikes are prohibited.

There are two exceptions to this prohibition on work stoppages during the contract. Paragraph 502 of the National Labor Relations Act defines the quitting of labor in good faith because of abnormally dangerous conditions *not* to be a strike. In *Redwing Carriers,* the NLRB interpreted this exception narrowly.[82] The conditions must be *unusually* dangerous (even in a usually dangerous job) and supported by *objective* evidence (not beliefs). In 1980, the Supreme Court added a second exception when it upheld a controversial regulation from the Secretary of Labor in its *Whirlpool* decision.[83] If a worker reasonably believes a threat of death or serious bodily harm exists, *and* if there is no time to call for a government inspection, *and* if the employer has been notified and refuses to change the condition, then the worker may refuse to work.

The legal implication of this tangled web is paradoxical. Non-union workers have the full protection of the NLRA to conduct a work stoppage over any threat to safety and health, even if only subjectively perceived. Union workers covered by an arbitration clause have the right to quit work over safety and health only under the two exceptional conditions mentioned. Of course, the union workers have the more general political and economic protection of the union as well.

Arbitration. Grievances over safety and health are relatively rare.[84] Nonetheless, they form an exception to the general arbitral

---

[80] The following section relies heavily on Nicholas A. Ashford and Judith I. Katz, "Unsafe Working Conditions: Employee Rights Under the Labor-Management Relations Act and the Occupational Safety and Health Act," *Notre Dame Lawyer* 52 (June 1977), pp. 802–836.

[81] *Gateway Coal* v. *UMW,* 414 U.S. 368 (1974).

[82] *Redwing Carriers,* 130 NLRB 1208, 1209, 47 LRRM 1470 (1961).

[83] *Whirlpool Corporation, Petitioner* v. *Ray Marshall, Secretary of Labor* 48 LW 4189 (1980).

[84] Thomas A. Kochan, Lee Dyer, and David B. Lipsky, *The Effectiveness of Union-Management Safety and Health Committees* (Kalamazoo, MI: W. E. Upjohn Institute for Employment Research, 1977.

principle that the union member should "follow orders first and grieve later." How much protection arbitration provides depends on the language of the contract and the beliefs of the arbitrator. Generally, arbitrators have *not* held the subjective belief of the worker to be an adequate justification for refusing work.[85] Where a contract specifies such subjective fear as adequate, then arbitrators have ruled more frequently in favor of the grievant.[86] A serious problem with arbitration of safety and health disputes was highlighted by a review of published cases. The median time from disciplinary action for refusing hazardous work until the arbitrator's decision was more than six months.[87] Such delays, all too typical of arbitration, leave the discipline or discharge in place pending resolution, with a chilling effect on other potential complaints.

Labor-Management Committees. As indicated in Table 1, 43 percent of the major contracts provide for a joint committee on safety and/or health, again more frequently in manufacturing and high-hazard industries, and again more frequently since the passage of the OSHAct.[88] However, some committees, for example in the mining industry, long predate the 1970 Act. The typical committee is composed of 50 percent union and 50 percent management, meets monthly, and has advisory power. The committee can inspect accidents, tour the facilities, and make recommendations to management. To bind management to action, however, the union has to resort to a grievance, a work stoppage, or calling for a government inspection.

The effectiveness of such committees is a matter of debate and some skepticism.[89] Kochan, Dyer, and Lipsky, in a survey of International Association of Machinists locals in upstate New York, found that only a half of the joint committees had met as often as once a month; they also found wide variation in levels of com-

---

[85] Joseph B. Summa, "Criteria for Safety and Health Arbitration," *Labor Law Journal* 26 (June 1975), pp. 368–374.

[86] John Listinsky, "Arbitration and Refusing Hazardous Work" (Buffalo: New York State School of Industrial and Labor Relations, Cornell University) (OSHA Programs mimeo).

[87] *Ibid.*

[88] "Safety and Health Patterns," *Daily Labor Report.*

[89] George G. Robinson, "Voluntary Committees Function Effectively Only Because OSHA Is There," *The AFL-CIO American Federationist* 87 (July 1980), pp. 9–10.

mittee activity.[90] Those committees which were active and involved in problem-solving behavior were associated with a lower issuance of citations following an OSHA inspection, thus indicating greater enforcement between inspections. High levels of committee continuity and activity were found where OSHA pressure was perceived as strong, where the local union was perceived to be vigorous, where rank-and-file involvement was substantial, and where management approached safety issues in a problem-solving manner. The researchers also emphasized the importance of separating the committee from other bargaining activity.

INNOVATIVE JOINT EFFORTS

A similar pattern of forces for success emerges when overall joint programs are examined in detail. For example, in 1973 United Auto Workers and General Motors agreed on one full-time union health and safety representative in each plant.[91] Picked by the international union, the representative is trained and paid by the company. The jointly acknowledged success of the program depends in large part on the ability of the representatives to work effectively with management counterparts.

Likewise, the contract between the United Rubber Workers and B. F. Goodrich also calls for a full-time safety and health representative for the union in each plant, paid for by the company.[92] Plant-level, union-management committees also meet monthly, tour the plant, and identify hazards for high-priority correction by the company maintenance department. What is unique in this relationship is an independent study of safety and health in the company's working environment funded with a contribution of 1 cent an hour and conducted by the Harvard School of Public Health.

In addition to strong local unions, a committed management, and specialized staff, the existence of problem-solving forums appears helpful. For example, the Joint Labor-Management Committee of the Retail Food Industry worked together on a safety prob-

---

[90] Kochan, Dyer, and Lipsky.

[91] Lawrence S. Bacow, "Bargaining for Job Safety and Health" (Cambridge, MA: M.I.T., 1980).

[92] Harry C. Herman Associates, "A Journalistic Study of Labor-Management Safety Committees," Report to Occupational Safety and Health Administration, U.S. Department of Labor, June 1980.

lem.[93] One of the consensus standards for the retail food industry required meatcutters to wear protective mesh gloves when cutting meat. If the meatcutter is using a knife, the glove protects fingers from amputation. However, if the same meatcutter is using a power saw, he or she is liable to lose an *arm*, because the mesh glove catches in the saw where a piece of flesh would not.

The industry-wide, general-purpose committee recognized this shortcoming, undertook a national survey of local experience, and obtained a clarification of the standard from OSHA (not a change which would have triggered an elaborate rule-making process).

INNOVATIONS BY THE LABOR MOVEMENT

Education. A major problem facing the unions is the lack of skilled people in health and safety. In 1975, Ralph Nader's Health Research Group found only a handful of union experts.[94] Even today, one high-level union official estimates only 65 safety and health professionals are working for unions, and these include only 40 industrial hygienists. The New Directions program of the Occupational Safety and Health Administration is supporting, in one way or another, practically every safety and health professional now working for the labor movement.[95] Both the Oil, Chemical, and Atomic Workers and the United Steelworkers, among other international unions, are seeking to identify hazards in local workplaces around the country and to educate members on hazard recognition. Likewise, the Building Trades Department of the AFL-CIO has established a national safety and health resources center in Washington and is organizing 16 regional centers for intensive training in high-hazard construction. The Labor Department has also made grants to university-based labor education programs to develop training on safety and health.

Coalitions for Occupational Safety and Health (COSHs). In 1972, activists in the Chicago area came together to form a local coalition for occupational safety and health, the first of what are

---

[93] James W. Driscoll, "Labor-Management Panels: Three Case Studies," *Monthly Labor Review* 103 (June 1980), pp. 41–44.

[94] "Occupational Health Efforts of Fifteen Major Labor Unions," *Union Labor Report—Weekly Newsletter*, October 28, 1976.

[95] U.S. Department of Labor, Occupational Safety and Health Administration, "Institutional Competency Building Program in Occupational Safety and Health, Project Summaries for Second Year Grants (FY '80)," December 17, 1979, mimeo.

now about a dozen across the nation. Typical of such efforts, the Massachusetts COSH is funded by dues from unions and individuals and a grant from the New Directions program of OSHA.[96] Massachusetts's COSH provides education, training, and technical assistance to unions and workers including, in 1979, answers to over 300 telephone requests for information, typically questioning the impact of some chemical on humans.

MANAGEMENT PROGRAMS

The primary legal and practical responsibility for occupational health and safety rests with management. Not only is management the classic initiator of action in industrial relations, but action on occupational diseases, in particular, requires such information as types of substances used in production, potential health hazards, and worker health records.

The elements of a successful management program all emphasize commitment: top level support, assignment of a specialized representative, delegation of significant decision-making power to that representative, formulation of written procedures, training for managers and first-level supervisors, and inclusion of safety and health in formal performance evaluations.[97] In addition, management must train individual workers in hazard and accident prevention. Unless individual workers have the knowledge and motivation to avoid hazards, then efforts to provide safe and healthy working conditions are limited. It is a truism in accident prevention that both the environment and the worker are potential causes.

Lack of management commitment to safety and health poses a potential problem, given the relatively limited collective bargaining and union initiatives described above. The petrochemical industry provides the most discouraging example. Epstein virtually accused the industry of criminal conspiracy and neglect in concealing health hazards from it workers.[98] Yet, even today, informed observers of the industry cite no management programs to identify

[96] "MASSCOSH Report to Membership, November 22, 1980," Massachusetts Coalition for Occupational Safety and Health, Boston, MA.

[97] Kochan, Dyer, and Lipsky.

[98] Samuel S. Epstein, *The Politics of Cancer* (Garden City, NY: Anchor Books, 1974).

worker risks, such as a review of company medical records for clusters or patterns of disease.

In the U.S. industrial relations system, significant improvement in safety and health will depend largely on management action. Nonetheless, within that context, it is possible to offer an assessment of collective bargaining's contribution to that end.

ASSESSMENT OF COLLECTIVE BARGAINING AND OCCUPATIONAL SAFETY AND HEALTH

No direct comparisons have as yet been made between union and nonunion organizations in safety and health performance. According to Kochan, union members report more serious problems with hazards on their jobs, but there were no significant differences in injuries.[99] He also cites suggestive evidence that union workers receive higher compensating wage differentials for hazardous work. Subjectively, union members report reasonable levels of satisfaction with their union's efforts on safety and health.[100] They are less satisfied with safety and health performance of the union than with traditional bread-and-butter issues, but more satisfied than with nontraditional quality-of-work issues such as providing "interesting jobs."

Some high-level union officials say that future success lies not in collective bargaining, but in stricter legislation and grassroots education of workers regarding hazards. Indeed, when asked in the Quality of Employment Survey "To whom do you report health and safety hazards?" only one union member in 20 cited a union representative.[101] Likewise, unorganized workers in the same survey did not see collective bargaining as a way to improve safety and health at work. Only 1 percent of nonunion workers who would vote for a union if given the opportunity gave improved safety and health as a reason for their vote.

Despite the objective magnitude of the safety and health problem at work and the strong desire of workers for influence over its resolution, safety and health takes a distinct second place to traditional economic concerns such as wages, fringe benefits, and job security in both collective bargaining activity and impact. Safety and health are middle-range issues in collective bargaining.

---

[99] Kochan, 1980.
[100] Quinn and Staines.
[101] Ibid.

and health are middle-range issues in collective bargaining. The reasons for this subordination are many and interrelated.[102]

1. The problem is ambiguous. Even the number of deaths is uncertain and the causes of occupational disease are difficult to disentangle. It may be that bargaining is ill-suited to deal with such an amorphous issue.[103]

2. Bargainers have other priorities. Since the OSHAct, stagflation has highlighted wage increases and job security.[104]

3. The median voter is often assumed to determine priorities in an elected leadership, and most safety and health problems affect only a minority.[105]

4. Unions fear liability for negligence damages if they take responsibility for safety and health. In *Helton* v. *Hake* (1978), the Missouri Court of Appeals held an Ironworkers local liable for $150,000 for a steward's failure to enforce a contractual safety rule.[106] That particular contract had unusual language absolving the employer from responsibility for the rule in question. Based on other cases, unions appear to have no liability in the safety and health area beyond the usual duty to fair representation.[107] However, the possibility raised by the *Helton* case has led some national unions to instruct their locals to avoid *any* safety and health language.

5. Negotiators, especially on the union side, lack access to relevant expertise and information.

6. Much of the labor movement's activity has taken place at the central level, testifying at OSHA hearings and challenging standards in the courts, while bargaining is decentralized.

7. The federal government has preempted union action by setting standards and providing an alternative complaint mechanism to the union hierarchy.

---

[102] Bacow.

[103] My colleague, Tom Kochan, made a related point in personal discussions.

[104] Ashford.

[105] Henry S. Farber, "Individual Preferences and Union Wage Determination: The Case of the United Mine Workers," *Journal of Political Economy* 86 (October 1978), pp. 923–942.

[106] *Helton* v. *Hake*, 564 S.W.2d 213, 98 LRRM 2905 (Mo.Ct.App. 1978).

[107] Morris David and Lawrence Drapkin, *Workplace Safety and Health: Recent Development in Union Liability* (Berkeley: Labor Occupational Health Program, Institute of Industrial Relations, University of California, June 1980).

8. The Administrative Procedures Act of 1946 encourages an adversarial rather than a cooperative approach to solving safety and health problems.[108] Both labor and management usually present the most extreme possible arguments about each hazard and almost never have a forum to explore creative solutions and compromises.

9. Because of the costs involved, aggravated by this adversarial process, management has resisted most of the legislative and bargaining initiatives on safety and health.[109]

10. Collective bargaining, according to Ashford,[110] could have allowed union and management jointly to develop specific solutions to particular industry and local conditions. However, based on our review of negotiations, contracts, arbitration, and committees, most parties have not felt sufficient pressure on safety and health to develop effective mechanisms to solve these problems.

The Quality of Work Life

The third major social issue to confront collective bargaining in the period was the popular conception that U. S. workers had grown increasingly bored and alienated by simple, routine jobs. The general term, the Quality of Work Life (QWL), has come to mean any process of increased worker participation in decision-making to counter such feelings. The participation may be based either on the individual or the work group, and focuses on job-centered issues ranging from more interesting or responsible job content, to scheduling and setup, on up to traditional issues for collective bargaining, such as the development of payment systems. In Europe, the term implies much greater worker control, often the result of national legislation, culminating in worker representation on the boards of directors. Unlike the other two issues discussed in this chapter, no federal legislation dealt with QWL in the U. S. and the American experience has followed a tradition of job-conscious unionism with a job-centered worker participation in decision-making.

---

[108] John T. Dunlop, "The Limits of Legal Compulsion," *Labor Law Journal* 27 (February 1976), pp. 67–74.

[109] W. Edward Stead and Jean G. Stead, "Cancer in the Workplace: A Neglected Problem," *Personnel Journal* (October 1980), pp. 847–849.

[110] Ashford.

ALIENATION, MILITANCY, AND THE DESIRE FOR PARTICIPATION

In other countries, most notably France and Italy, the world-wide social disturbances of the 1960s struck the workplace directly. Over the last decade the result has been a marked increase in shop-floor unionism throughout Europe to supplement the tradition of centralized unions, centralized bargaining, and political activity.

Although no parallel upheaval shook U. S. industrial relations, for a short time in the early seventies government and the media reacted as if the revolution was imminent. The Department of Health, Education, and Welfare released its famous report, *Work in America*, which advanced the thesis of debilitating and widespread alienation.[111] Rank-and-file rejection of contract proposals increased during the late sixties to wide fanfare, and a local wildcat strike at the General Motors assembly plant in Lordstown, Ohio, was widely interpreted by the media to demonstrate increased worker militancy.

With the benefit of hindsight, the crisis was shown to be greatly exaggerated. Major national surveys showed no decline in job satisfaction through the early seventies.[112] Satisfaction with specific facets of the job (pay, supervision, etc.) did increase between 1973 and 1977, after the crisis,[113] but overall measures of satisfaction remained high and unchanged from the earliest available surveys.[114] Disruptive worker behavior—strikes, absences, turnover—seem to have reflected underlying economic conditions such as the boom in the late 1960s, rather than a fundamental shift in militancy.[115]

The desire for participation is less well-documented, but again falls far short of crisis proportions. The 1977 Quinn and Staines

[111] Special Task Force on Work in America, *Work in America, Report* (Cambridge, MA: M.I.T., 1973).

[112] George Strauss, 'Quality of Work Life and Participation as Bargaining Issues," in *The Shrinking Perimeter*, eds. Hervey A. Juris and Myron Roomkin (Lexington, MA: D. C. Heath Lexington Books, 1979). See also Graham C. Staines, "Is Worker Dissatisfaction Rising?" *Challenge* 22 (May-June 1979), pp. 38–45, and Charles N. Weaver, "Job Satisfaction in the United States in the 1970s," *Journal of Applied Psychology* 65, No. 3 (1980), pp. 364–367.

[113] Staines.

[114] Charles Heckscher, "Directions in the Democratization of Work," (Cambridge, MA: The Group for Work Democracy, mimeo).

[115] Robert Flanagan, George Strauss, and Lloyd Ulman, "Worker Discontent and Workplace Behavior," *Industrial Relations* 12 (May 1974), pp. 1–23.

survey showed U. S. workers wanting much more say over safety and health than over how the work is done.[116] In the same survey, union members gave low priority to increasing the worker's say over the job, or providing more interesting work.

GOVERNMENT REACTION

The federal government initiated action that might well have culminated in major legislation over QWL, but the economic troubles beginning with the 1973 oil embargo both diverted national attention and demonstrated the limited nature of the crisis. In 1972, the Senate held well-publicized hearings on worker alienation.[117] In 1975, the National Center for Productivity and Quality of Working Life was established by Congress,[118] but was allowed to lapse three years later. The Congress did authorize the Federal Mediation and Conciliation Service in 1978 to encourage labor-management cooperation, but another two years passed before any funds were appropriated.[119]

MANAGEMENT REACTION

By contrast to the brief and abortive governmental program to improve the quality of work life, the U. S. management community during the early seventies intensified and has since sustained an interest in "employee participation" programs, as they are often called, which began in the 1950s. These programs included:[120]

1. *Job enrichment.* New job descriptions allowed workers to exercise more responsibility on individual tasks, e.g., completing a subassembly or a service. AT&T was best known for such programs, but many others, including IBM, did likewise. The technique appeared most often in batch manufacturing and manual assembly.

---

[116] Quinn and Staines.

[117] U.S. Congress, Senate Committee on Labor and Public Welfare. *Worker Alienation, 1972, Hearings* before the Subcommittee on Employment, Manpower, and Poverty.

[118] National Center for Productivity and Quality of Working Life, *Directory of Labor-Management Committees.* 1st and 2d eds. (Washington: 1976).

[119] Kochan, 1980, pp. 413–414.

[120] This section relies heavily on Heckscher. For a survey of current practices, see "Special Report: The New Industrial Relations," *Business Week*, May 11, 1981, pp. 84–98.

2. *Semi-autonomous work groups.* Team production with greatly reduced supervision originated in process industries like oil refining, but General Motors has adopted it for manufacturing in its new southern plants.

3. *Problem-solving groups.* These department meetings to discuss production problems characterize Japanese quality circles and Scanlon Plan committees. Assembly-line operations have utilized these groups where the technology limits fundamental shifts in job design.

4. *New plant design.* Increasingly managers are avoiding the constraints of technology by designing new facilities from the ground up to facilitate group production and meetings.

It has been estimated that one-third of the companies in the *Fortune 500* have such participation programs under way. Enough companies have designed participative new plants that a formal network of such plant managers meets regularly.

The current era of participative management represents the latest evolution in management strategy to motivate and direct the workforce. At the turn of the twentieth century, Taylor's "scientific" management replaced the "laissez-faire" of early industrialization with job descriptions, production standards, and individual incentive payments. The rise of industrial unionism in the thirties limited management's unilateral control over production. As management developed as a profession after World War II, complete with graduate schools and associations, the emerging behavioral sciences contributed two new techniques for the management of people at work. First, the importance of human relations skills for supervisors had been highlighted by the Hawthorne studies. Second, participation in decision-making was identified not as a concession to worker demands, but as a leadership technique to increase motivation and commitment to decisions.

The resulting philosophy of participative management, called "bureaucratic paternalism" by the left or "positive employee relations" by the right, depends critically on stable employment and requires the resources of a large firm to support personnel professionals and supervisory training.[121] Increasingly in the 1960s and 1970s, large employers in the U.S. have come to rely on partici-

---

[121] Heckscher.

pative management of which QWL programs are but an extension. Much participative management has an antiunion component in practice, if not in concept. At a minimum, effective managers are assumed now to identify and satisfy worker needs, thus eliminating the need for labor union representation. At a maximum, participative management forms one prong in an antiunion attack, along with reprisals against union sympathizers and delaying tactics in legal proceedings. The success of participative management, even at its most benign, was a major factor in the success of managers during the sixties and seventies in keeping unions out of highly visible nonunion manufacturing companies, new facilities of formerly all-union manufacturers, and entire growth industries such as high-technology manufacturing.

Union Reaction to QWL

Before presenting the union perspective on QWL in employment relations, a brief aside is in order on the quality of *union* life. The 1977 Quinn and Staines surveys identified two serious problems for the labor movement.[122] First, many workers have a negative image of "big labor." Surprisingly, a majority believed that unions were more powerful than employers. Second, as mentioned already, current union members put a higher priority on improving the internal administration of the union than on basic bread-and-butter issues in bargaining. While the mass media and public education shape popular stereotypes of unions, the findings suggest the need for some analogue to "participative management" for internal union administration.

With respect to QWL, the mainstream union position is skeptical of QWL programs given their largely nonunion locus, and emphasizes instead the outcomes of collective bargaining.[123] Union leaders rightly remind psychologists that union members with comparable backgrounds receive more pay and more fringe benefits than nonunion workers. They point to the fundamental due-process protection provided by the grievance procedure and arbitration to a unionized worker with a complaint against management. And finally, they emphasize the proportionately much

---

[122] Quinn and Staines.
[123] Thomas R. Donahue, "Collective Bargaining, Co-determination, and the Quality of Work," *World of Work Report* 1 (August 1976), pp. 1, 6.

greater impact of union membership in increasing the wages of
black and female workers compared to white males. Indeed, if the
broad definition of QWL popularized by Walton is accepted as a
criterion, then no QWL program yet reported approaches the impact of collective bargaining.[124]

A small minority of union leaders have pushed joint QWL
programs as another union strategy to "enhance human dignity,"
as retired UAW Vice President Irving Bluestone put it.[125] Their
efforts have created some significant QWL programs under collective bargaining.

QWL UNDER COLLECTIVE BARGAINING

Under collective bargaining, QWL is defined here as programs
to increase worker participation in job-centered decisions beyond
the traditional mechanisms of contract negotiation and the grievance procedure. Three currents characterize the evolution of such
efforts: small-scale demonstration projects stimulated by government or foundation spending, large-scale corporate initiatives, and
joint labor-management committees growing out of traditional
bargaining.

Demonstrations. The American Center for the Quality of Work
Life (ACQWL) was founded in 1974, with funding from the
Department of Commerce and the Ford Foundation. Its objective
is to stimulate QWL demonstration projects. Seven projects persisted through 1978.[126] The program aimed only at unionized
employers, and has involved, among others, the United Mine
Workers, the United Automobile Workers, the Bakers and Con-
fectioners, the Office and Professional Employees, and the American Federation of State, County, and Municipal Employees. So
far the projects have been confined to relatively small companies
or small subunits within large organizations.

The structure of the projects was roughly similar. A joint union-
management committee oversaw the project and hired a be-

[124] Richard E. Walton, "Quality of Working Life: What Is It?" *Sloan
Management Review* 15 (Fall 1973), pp. 11–22.

[125] Irving Bluestone, "How Quality of Work Life Projects Work for the
United Auto Workers," *Monthly Labor Review* 103 (July 1980), pp. 39–41.

[126] Edward E. Lawler and John A. Drexler, "Dynamics of Establishing
Quality of Work Life Projects," *Daily Labor Report*, March 31, 1978, pp.
B2–B6.

havioral-science consultant to advise the project and guide the organizational changes once work was under way.[127]

The particular organizational changes varied across projects. In the best-documented project, an experimental section of a small coal mine in Rushton, Pennsylvania, adopted semi-autonomous groups for getting coal.[128] At the Bolivar, Tennessee, car-mirror manufacturing plant of Harmon Industries, the UAW agreed to an earned-idle-time program. There the workers, if they reached their production standard,[129] could go home early or take part in educational courses. In the Tennessee Valley Authority, the local engineering association agreed to performance appraisal with merit bonuses and a four-day workweek for some.[130]

The demonstration projects have had limited impact, although results vary from failure to moderate success. At Rushton, the participative production system resulted in no certain productivity gains or decreases in absenteeism or turnover.[131] Safety practices improved, but did not reduce already low accident rates. The participants in the experimental section liked the new organization, but miners outside the experiment (who envied the top wage rate paid to all participants in the experiment regardless of seniority or skill) carried a union vote and terminated the project. The Bolivar project fared better. Macy estimated a net present value of savings to the company of $3,000 per worker.[132] Although the workers showed some increases in satisfaction, they have not yet shared financially in these productivity gains.

Some projects have simply failed. Driscoll interviewed representatives from management and all the worker associations in a QWL project in a large, private medical center and found no indication of any substantial impact, either positive or negative.[133]

    [127] Ibid.
    [128] Paul S. Goodman, *Assessing Organizational Change: The Rushton Quality of Work Experiment* (New York: John Wiley & Sons, 1979).
    [129] Margaret Molinari-Duckler, Robert Duckler, and Michael Maccoby, "The Process of Change at Bolivar," *Journal of Applied Behavioral Science* 13 (July-August-September 1977), pp. 387–399, and Barry A. Macy, "The Quality of Work Life Project at Bolivar: An Assessment," *Monthly Labor Review* 103 (July 1980), pp. 41–43.
    [130] Barry A. Macy and Aaron J. Nurick, "The Tennessee Valley Authority Quality of Working Life Experiment," paper presented to the Academy of Management, August 1977, mimeo.
    [131] Goodman.
    [132] Macy, "Quality of Work Life Project at Bolivar."
    [133] Driscoll, 1980.

Few of the projects have spread beyond the experimental sub-unit in the company or agency. The choice of consultants may have contributed to the failures and limited diffusion. All the consultants practiced organizational development and learned collective bargaining while on the job. Questionable industrial relations judgments appear in several cases. At Rushton, the new joint committee processed traditional grievances as well.[134] On the eve of the vote to terminate the project, the committee spent most of its time discussing a non-QWL grievance. In the hospital project, the QWL consultants sought to continue the project even as the administration systematically undermined two participating employee associations.[135]

Organization-Wide Projects. By contrast with these isolated demonstrations, General Motors and the UAW, as of 1980, had some 50 separate plant projects, at some level of development, to improve QWL.[136] The program of union involvement was preceded by unilateral management attempts at organizational development using participative management. Indeed, the most innovative departures from traditional personnel practice occurred in new-plant-design projects in southern parts-manufacturing facilities which GM opened and originally operated nonunion. In 1973, Bluestone, as chief negotiator with GM, demanded a formal role for the union. In a Letter of Agreement, the two parties agreed to undertake local projects with the aid of corporate and international-union staff.

As in the ACQWL's projects, the specific local changes vary, but the projects follow general guidelines agreed to nationally:[137]

1. A joint union-management committee oversees the project.
2. Production standards cannot increase.
3. No jobs will be lost due to the project.
4. The collective bargaining agreement will not be changed.
5. Individual participation is voluntary.

---

[134] Goodman.
[135] Driscoll, 1980.
[136] Bluestone.
[137] *Ibid.*

6. The union is represented in all aspects of the project.

7. Either side may terminate the project at any time.

The best known local project helped turn the assembly plant at Tarrytown, New York, from a low-rated production facility with a poor labor relations climate into one of the sites chosen by GM for its new energy-efficient front-wheel-drive model.[138] The Tarrytown project emphasized problem-solving groups. Originally applied in the redesign of the layout for two trim departments, problem-solving group techniques were subsequently the object of a $1.6 million company-funded training program.

Other than Tarrytown, no objective evaluation of the GM-UAW projects is available or envisioned. However, both the company and the union have expressed satisfaction with their results.

Compared to the demonstration projects, the parties here have shown more sensitivity to collective bargaining. For example, the union insists on keeping grievances out of the QWL forums. In addition, only union officials sit on the QWL committees to ensure the exclusion of grievances and maintain control over the project.

In 1980, two potentially major programs appeared on the U.S. QWL scene. First, the United Steelworkers and the ten basic steel companies agreed on demonstration projects.[139] Next, AT&T agreed with each of its major unions, namely the Communications Workers, the International Brotherhood of Electrical Workers and the Telecommunications International, on national joint committees to deal with the quality of work life.[140]

The Dana Corporation, a billion-dollar supplier of parts to the slumping automobile industry, has maintained its commitment to the Scanlon Plan, a more venerable approach to QWL.[141] In 1980, Dana had 19 plants following separate plans. Originally developed by a local Steelworker Union leader, Joe Scanlon (later a lecturer at MIT) to aid failing plants during the Depression, the plan in-

---

[138] Robert H. Guest, "Quality of Work Life—Learning from Tarrytown," *Harvard Business Review* 57 (July-August 1979), pp. 76–87.

[139] Bureau of National Affairs, *Selected Contracts in Text in Collective Bargaining Negotiations and Contracts: Techniques and Trends, Curent Settlements* (Washington: 1980), pp. 271–72.

[140] "A New Bell Pact Everyone Likes," *Business Week*, September 1, 1980, p. 56F.

[141] James W. Driscoll, "Working Creatively with a Union: Lessons from the Scanlon Plan," *Organizational Dynamics* 8 (Summer 1979), pp. 61–80.

cludes: departmental worker-management committees to generate productivity suggestions and a monthly bonus based on labor-cost savings. Schuster has recently provided econometric evidence of the productivity gains from Scanlon and the absence of employment losses,[142] a conclusion supported by a U.S. General Accounting Office survey of current experience.

Labor-Management Committees. Without using the term QWL, or employing a high-priced organizational-development consultant, negotiators in collective bargaining have a long history of discussing job-centered QWL topics apart from contract negotiations and the grievance procedure.[143] (The obvious effect of negotiations and the grievance procedure on QWL as benefits to workers was emphasized earlier.) Five thousand labor-management committees to improve productivity and morale formed during World War II and 20 percent remained in effect as late as 1948.[144] Indeed, cooperation to supplement contract negotiation began at TVA 30 years before the QWL demonstration.[145]

Subsequent reviews have revealed widespread problem-solving projects. In a study of northern Illinois, Minneapolis, and St. Paul, Shirom found labor-management committees in virtually every local relationship.[146] More recently, the National Center for Productivity and Quality of Working Life found hundreds of joint committees around the U.S.[147] Derber and Flanigan, based on informal inquiry, found 115 committees in the state of Illinois.[148]

---

[142] Michael Shuster, "Labor-Management Cooperation Effects on Production and Employment" (tentative title), doctoral dissertation, Syracuse University. U.S. General Accounting Office, "Productivity Sharing Programs: Can They Contribute to Productivity Improvement?" (Gaithersburg, Md.: U.S. G.A.O., AFMD-81-22, 1981).

[143] Milton Derber and Kevin Flanigan, "A Survey of Joint Labor-Management Cooperation Committees in Unionized Private Enterprises in the State of Illinois, 1979: Part One," Institute of Labor and Industrial Relations, University of Illinois, January 4, 1980. See also the 1977 Conference Board Survey cited by Kochan, 1980, p. 424.

[144] Dorothea de Schweinitz, *Labor-Management Cooperation in a Common Enterprise* (Cambridge, MA: Harvard University, 1949), and Ernest Dale, "Union-Management Cooperation," in *Industrial Conflict*, eds. Arthur Kornhauser and others (New York: McGraw-Hill, 1964).

[145] Macy, Quality of Work Life Project at Bolivar."

[146] Arie Shirom, "Industrial Cooperation and Adjustment to Technological Change: A Study of Joint Management Union Committees," doctoral dissertation, University of Wisconsin, 1968, cited in Derber and Flanigan.

[147] National Center for Productivity and Quality of Working Life, *Directory of Productivity and Quality of Working Life Centers* (Washington: 1978).

[148] Derber and Flanigan.

Committees deal with a variety of subjects, many paralleling the changes developed in designated QWL projects. Derber and Flanigan list the following subjects in order of frequency: safety and health, apprenticeship and training, employee benefits, charitable contributions, and equal employment opportunity.[149] Of those committees, 30 percent dealt with productivity and technological change; 14 percent reported tackling job redesign directly.

The committees present a different picture from the QWL demonstrations. Most start and meet without the help of a third party. Contract negotiators serve on almost every committee. The committees meet frequently (monthly at the mode) and have continued in most cases for many years. Usually, the parties have more than one committee. Although their usual role is advisory to management, the committees possess substantial authority in a large majority of cases. At least by their own descriptions, the members engage more in problem-solving behavior than negotiating, and they also feel moderately successful in meeting their objectives.

The objectives and accomplishments of these committees (and for that matter of QWL projects) require careful attention. In a survey of the committees identified by the National Center, the participants claimed their major purpose as well as their major accomplishment was to improve the interpersonal relationships among members of the committee.[150] As their major contribution, then, committees may facilitate indirectly the traditional process of contract negotiation and administration.

The committees are described by participants as more successful under certain conditions:[151] First, there is pressure on the parties to take action beyond contract negotiation. Second, the bargaining power of both sides is relatively equal. Third, the bargaining history is long and relatively positive. And fourth, the parties succeed in adopting a different style, emphasizing problem-solving over adversarial negotiating.

---

[149] *Ibid.*

[150] James W. Driscoll, "Labor-Management Committees in the U.S.: A National Survey" (Cambridge, MA: M.I.T. Sloan School of Management, August 23, 1979), mimeo.

[151] James W. Driscoll, "Problem-Solving Between Adversaries: Predicting Behavior in Labor-Management Committees," *International Journal of Applied Psychology* (forthcoming).

ASSESSMENT OF COLLECTIVE BARGAINING AND QWL

Neither the labor movement nor the institution of collective bargaining has responded well to quality of work life issues, narrowly defined. Of all the issues considered (bread-and-butter, QWL, and internal union administration), union members expressed the least satisfaction with union efforts on QWL issues in the Quality of Employment Surveys.[152] Potential union members never mentioned the possibility of union membership bringing them either more interesting jobs or more say in how the work is done.[153]

Collective bargaining has primarily reacted to initiatives for QWL programs from outside the bargaining process. The highly publicized demonstration projects by the American Center for Quality of Work Life (ACQWL) were government or foundation stimulated and have usually not spread beyond the experimental sites. While exceptions exist, these projects have had little impact.

The major corporate programs (e.g., GM, Dana) have spread widely. However, it would appear that management stimulated most of these QWL efforts as part of a major evolution in management strategy to deal with worker needs, unrelated to collective bargaining.

Labor-management committees represent the most encouraging prospect for collective bargaining, since they grew out of the process. However, these committees are a form of indirect participation in job-centered decision-making, not direct worker involvement. The scanty evidence suggests that their primary impact may be improved relationships between the bargaining representatives rather than direct effects on workers.

The future will almost certainly bring a vast expansion of QWL projects in large firms as managers apply their latest wisdom on human resource management. Large nonunion firms, especially high-technology firms, have led the QWL movement from the start. With GM, AT&T, and basic steel, unionized management is clearly moving in the same direction.

The QWL movement, or more generally participative management, represents a fundamental challenge to collective bargaining. Participative management means the resolution of industrial con-

---

[152] Quinn and Staines.
[153] *Ibid.*

flict on a continuous basis at the individual or work-group level, by problem-solving discussions with the facilitation of a behaviorally sensitive management representative. By contrast, collective bargaining has evolved as a conflict-resolution process based on episodic exchanges between representatives of large, formal organizations using negotiating tactics, with only occasional resort to government or neutral third parties.

While QWL may be appropriate for some shop-floor production questions, major economic and political conflicts will be less amenable. What happens to the distribution of corporate income between wages and other claimants such as stockholders? How are economic crises weathered? The inability of QWL projects to deal with wage levels and wage demands has hampered some of the best known projects,[154] and it is unclear how a plant shutdown would be handled.

Three alternative scenarios are possible. First, participative management may be capable of handling such fundamental conflicts at least in the core of the economy (leaving disturbances and their resolution to the periphery). Second, participative management may not deal with such conflicts, but may undermine the ability of collective bargaining to deal with resulting worker dissatisfaction. Or third, collective bargaining may incorporate participative structure and retain its ability to address macro-level conflicts. Only the third scenario is optimistic for collective bargaining and requires innovation by its practitioners.

In unionized settings, both management and union representatives must recognize the preeminence of collective bargaining (unless they intend to handle all conflicts in a cooperative mode). That perspective will occasionally restrain a QWL program. For example, keeping union stewards off of QWL joint committees may increase the likelihood of fruitful, cooperative problem-solving (and most departmental Scanlon committees exclude stewards). However, such separation weakens the ability of the union to control the direction and content of a QWL program.

A final word is appropriate on QWL in nonunion settings.

---

[154] Richard E. Walton, "The Diffusion of New Work Structures: Explaining Why Success Didn't Take," *Organizational Dynamics* 3 (Winter 1975), pp. 2–22. See also Paul S. Goodman, "Realities of Improving the Quality of Work Life: Quality of Work Life Projects in the 1980's," *Labor Law Journal* 31 (August 1980), pp. 487–494.

There, management is presumably satisfied with their programs. However, the labor movement has not capitalized on an opportunity. First, QWL projects identify natural leaders for an organizing campaign. And second, most QWL programs in a nonunion environment probably violate Section 8(a)(2) of the National Labor Relations Act by establishing, in effect, "a company union" and dealing with it as a bargaining agent.[155] The filing of an unfair labor practice would force the employer either to terminate a desirable program or to extend full bargaining rights to the worker representatives on the project.

Conclusion

These three "social issues"—equal employment opportunity, occupational safety and health, and the quality of work life—raise serious questions about the continued viability of collective bargaining as the dominant mode of resolving industrial conflict in the United States. Such issues were not simply challenges to collective bargaining, but a new range of employment conditions being given substantial societal attention for the first time in the 1960s. The message running through the discussion from the perspective of an advocate of "voluntary collective bargaining" so far has been on the negative side, with some positive experiences.

Given the difficulty created for collective bargaining by these issues, it is striking how little research has been done by industrial relations scholars on their empirical impact. There is a wealth of behavioral science interest in the quality of work life, but the research neglects labor relations implications. On the remaining two issues the dominant mode is legal analysis or informed speculation. Despite this shortcoming of the research, several conclusions deserve mention.

First, all three issues in large measure forced change on unions from outside. Federal legislation on equal employment opportunity and on safety and health, although passed only with the support of the labor movement, required modification in existing collective bargaining contracts. But the laws also established complaint mechanisms in addition to and in potential conflict with the existing grievance procedures. Management has initiated quality

---

[155] Kent F. Murrman, "The Scanlon Plan Joint Committee and Section 8(a)(2)," *Labor Law Journal* 31 (May 1980), pp. 299–304.

of working life in the U.S. Moreover, QWL emphasizes individuality, flexibility, and worker participation in decision-making in direct conflict with the emphasis in labor agreements on consistency, precedence, and management's right to direct the workforce.[156]

Second, the institutions of collective bargaining have not usually made a major impact on these issues, and none of the actors in the industrial relations system (management, government, union, or workers) has defined collective bargaining as the major mechanism to address the issues. Even in safety and health, where workers desire substantial input, neither union members nor nonmembers define collective bargaining as the means of influence. The priority for collective bargaining appears to be traditional economic issues.

Third, the central body of the labor movement clearly has played the leading role in equal employment and safety and health. As for QWL, at the UAW where projects have spread the furthest, the international union has taken the lead. Indeed, local union leaders, in discussions of all three issues, are often criticized for subservience to member prejudices on equal employment, willingness to trade off the safety and health concerns of the minority for economic concessions, and a predisposition to sit back and watch management initiatives in QWL. Unless the local grass roots membership of the labor movement is educated and mobilized on these social issues, collective bargaining will lack the stimulus to take significant action.

Fourth, government action on equal employment, safety, and health may well have undermined the role of collective bargaining on these issues. In the thirties and early forties, U.S. society seemed committed to collective bargaining as the primary means of dealing with industrial conflict. Some important questions remained about the impact of bargaining and its regulation. But in that era, one could have conceived of government action encouraging *collective bargaining* to resolve conflicts over equal employment or safety. For example, elected delegates in union and

---

[156] Leonard A. Schlesinger and Richard E. Walton, "Work Restructuring in Unionized Organizations," Proceedings of the 29th Annual Meeting, Industrial Relations Research Association (Madison, WI: IRRA, 1977), pp. 345–351. See also Strauss.

nonunion shops could have been empowered to bring complaints on both issues or stop operations (over safety and health).

Instead, the actual legislation guaranteed worker rights of a peculiar sort. Individual workers, not their collective representatives, had the right to action. Litigation in courts rather than the use of economic power in a work stoppage was specified as the immediate remedy. By one interpretation, this legislative strategy recognized the minority status of labor unions within the workforce; by an alternative interpretation, such legislation contributed to its decline.

Fifth, and perhaps most importantly, legislation over equal employment, safety and health, and management-initiated QWL projects has greatly increased the complexity of collective bargaining by creating a separate institutional mechanism for resolving conflict. The individual complaint mechanisms of equal employment and of safety and health put both union and management negotiators in the middle. If they subordinate an individual or minority concern to the majority interest, they can be circumvented and overruled no matter how good their intention and their judgment. Moreover, representatives on union-management committees are subject to conflicting expectations in their roles as problem-solvers and interest-group representatives.[157] Even Edwards's separate EEO tracks imply a committee to assign cases either to arbitration or to the courts. Therefore, keeping bargaining representatives (e.g., stewards and contract negotiators) off joint committees should increase the quality of problem-solving.[158] However, such separation limits the ability of the union to use social issues to raise the consciousness of its membership and similarly increases the threat to management's contractual prerogatives. Making these judgments and managing these conflicts requires increasingly sophisticated and flexible representatives to oversee a continuous process of both bargaining and problem-solving.[159]

Finally, the limited collective bargaining response to these

[157] James W. Driscoll, Paul McKinnon, and Marvin Israelow, "Coping with Role Conflict: An Exploratory, Field Study of Union-Management Cooperation," *International Journal of Applied Psychology* (forthcoming).

[158] Driscoll, "Problem Solving Between Adversaries."

[159] James W. Driscoll, "A Behavioral-Science View of the Future of Collective Bargaining in the U.S.," *Labor Law Journal* 30 (July 1979), pp. 433–438.

social issues suggests some broader conceptualization of the problem. Much of industrial relations research focuses on the latest court rulings in each area or on narrow topics such as union-management committees. The important question is what do these three social issues and the limited response of collective bargaining imply for the conflict between labor and management in the U.S, Do these three social issues signal the decline of collective bargaining in favor of government regulation of working conditions? Does participative management represent a successful management strategy to deal with industrial conflict on the individual and small group level at the expense of collective bargaining? These are the important and generally neglected industrial relations questions raised by these social issues in the last two decades.

Chapter 7

Will the Real Industrial Conflict Please Stand Up?*

Peter Feuille
University of Illinois

Hoyt N. Wheeler
University of Minnesota

Performing a comprehensive analysis of the practice of and the research about industrial conflict in the United States during the past 30 or so years, all in one thin chapter, is a lot like inscribing a union-management contract on the head of a pin: such a comprehensive engraving can be done (and no doubt would be much admired), but the value of the final product would be highly uncertain. Accordingly, we will selectively focus on a variety of practical and analytical topics and will offer our own normative judgments where appropriate, especially regarding what we perceive as some research shortcomings. Because the public sector was thoroughly analyzed in a recent volume in this series (see especially Kochan, 1979), we will focus primarily on the private sector, and space constraints prevent us from giving more than a passing nod to the industrial conflict practices and research in other countries.

What is Industrial Conflict?
What is Industrial Conflict Research?

Industrial conflict is an elusive concept with unclear boundaries, and thus the phenomena and research that fits within its rubric are subject to some debate. One of the key definitional problems is that the same word, "conflict," can be used to describe a con-

* The authors are very grateful to Ken Hillary, Mark Phillips, Herman Theeke, and Roger Wolters for their research assistance in the preparation of this chapter, to Thomas Kochan for recently writing a book which facilitated the writing of this chapter, and to Tom Kochan, Robert McKersie, and Jack Stieber for some helpful comments.

dition of opposing interests, methods, or goals and also used to describe occurrences that are reflections or symptoms of that condition. For example, strikes can be viewed as conflict and also as symptoms of an underlying condition of conflict. Since most practitioners and researchers seem to use the observable events approach (that is, conflict exists when workers take actions to oppose management's methods or goals), a second and related definitional problem is the difficulty of specifying the occurrences which qualify as conflict. For instance, strikes, grievances, slowdowns, and sabotage appear readily acceptable as indicators of workplace conflict. But what about union representation election victories? Union decertification? The use of "union-free" consultants? Collective bargaining itself? Union or employer political activity? Mediation? Interest arbitration? Absenteeism? Quits? Discharges? Worker-manager personality conflicts? Safety and health complaints? Racial/sexual/religious discrimination charges? How is conflict detected in employment contexts where the power distribution is so uneven that the weaker party fearfully acquiesces to the interests of the stronger party? These examples suggest two conclusions. First, some conflict indicators are easier to obtain and analyze than others. For instance, strikes are easy to measure, there is a great deal of strike data available, and consequently it is hardly surprising that strikes appear to be the standard and even preferred indicator of industrial conflict. Second, various workplace phenomena tend to fall within the territories of different academic disciplines, with the result that industrial or workplace conflict is approached and researched differently across disciplinary boundaries.

A very important reason for these different approaches involves differing views about the inevitability and desirability of workplace conflict. We can identify, within generally accepted limits of oversimplification, two schools of normative thought on this topic (we have borrowed heavily from Barbash, 1980, and Nightingale, 1974). The pluralists, or what we call the "Conflict School," believe that employees and managers have opposing interests: employees want to avoid an unreasonable amount of effort and maximize their compensation, while managers want to maximize output and minimize cost. In addition, Dahrendorf (1959) and Wheeler (1980) argue that the employer-dominated hierarchical authority structure in the workplace creates tensions which can produce aggressive responses by employees. Given this assumed opposition of goals and methods, the potential for conflict is always present. In addition, the pluralists believe that the occurrence of some overt conflict is desirable, for it demonstrates that neither side has overwhelmed the other. Further, a balanced distribution of power is desirable because of the assumption that society has an interest in *both* the efficient production of goods and services and reasonable levels of income and working conditions for employees.

A second and contrary view is expressed by what we call the "Cooperation School." This view assumes a basic similarity of interests between managers and employees, largely because they are members of and dependent upon the same organizations. Conflict is dysfunctional and even harmful because it interferes with the efficiency and effectiveness of organizations, creates unpleasant encounters between human beings, and may lead to violence against persons and property. It occurs less from opposing interests and more from breakdowns in communication, understanding, or trust. In short, conflict is avoidable and should be avoided because the costs clearly exceed the benefits.

There is some impressionistic evidence that these two schools of thought are correlated with academic disciplines. Most labor economists and industrial relationists belong to the Conflict School, while many organizational behaviorists and especially organizational development specialists appear to accept the tenets of the Cooperation School (Strauss, 1977). OB-OD researchers' interests focus on such topics as job satisfaction, job performance, organization-environment relations, superior-subordinate relations, job design, responses to organizational change, etc., without any apparent assumption that organizational members are or will have opposing interests. In contrast, industrial relations researchers tend to focus on various aspects of carefully selected employer-employee relationships based upon an assumed divergence of employer and employee interests (Kochan, 1980). In the remainder of this chapter we focus on research done by people who fit this second description. In so doing, we will be meeting the expectations of most of our readers, but these same readers should recognize that we will be ignoring a large amount of research and writing which clearly deals with workplace conflict but which does not fit within the phrase "industrial conflict" as it is usually defined.

Within the Conflict School of researchers and practitioners, industrial conflict is defined largely by some implicit parameters. Perhaps the most obvious, judging from the published writings, is that industrial conflict is almost always synonymous with union-management conflict. This emphasis on conflict in unionized workplaces (or workplaces attempting to become unionized) creates the impression that a heavy majority of the employees and managers in the United States work under conflict-free conditions because no unions exist in their workplaces. The most likely explanation for the focus on union-management conflict is visibility and concomitant ease of measurement. American IR scholars have displayed a tendency to study visible issues, and strikes certainly are more visible (and dramatic) than most other forms of workplace conflict.

This leads to a second and equally obvious parameter, the heavy reliance on strikes as *the* preferred indicator of industrial conflict. This strike emphasis creates the impression that conflict is muted (or at least hidden from view) when there are no strikes. The industrial relations research community's dependence on strikes should not be interpreted, however, as deriving solely from researcher myopia, but rather as a particular example of the Gresham's Law of Social Science Research which states that the presence of low cost and readily available data tends to drive out the collection of high cost and hard-to-obtain data. The U.S. Bureau of Labor Statistics annually publishes large amounts of strike statistics, and computer technology has provided the means to analyze these data at nominal costs. Combine these data and data processing availabilities with the increased pressures in social science disciplines for quantitative research, and the result has been an almost irresistible set of incentives to equate industrial conflict with strikes.

The emphasis on strikes leads to a more general third parameter, the almost exclusive research focus on worker actions in opposition to management's methods or goals. As Hyman (1980) has persuasively pointed out, "industrial conflict" as an analytical construct apparently is based on the assumption that worker actions represent departures from the "normal" workplace situation in which employees conform to the objectives and expectations of employers. Consequently, there is little or no recognition that actions taken by management against employee interests, such as speed-ups, lockouts, discharges, plant closings, unsafe working conditions, etc., represent departures from the "normal" objectives and expectations of employees and as such are equally deserving of attention as industrial conflict. Although almost all of the events and research reviewed in this chapter focus on actions taken by unionized employees against management's methods or goals, there is no necessary reason why industrial conflict should be defined in this one-way fashion.

Public Policy and Industrial Conflict

The strategies that various societies have used to cope with industrial conflict (however defined) have ranged from total suppression to almost unlimited toleration. There has been a mixture of suppression and toleration in the United States, as is reflected in the two basic American strategies of conflict handling, namely, conflict management and conflict resolution. We use conflict management to mean the authoritative establishment, by the state, of the rules of the labor-management game within which the parties are allowed to seek their own resolutions to the substantive issues which divide them. In contrast, conflict resolution refers to the mandatory intervention of a third party who definitively resolves any dispute the parties cannot resolve. Perhaps the easiest way to distinguish between these two strategies is to focus on the role of third parties. A conflict resolution strategy requires a third party to have the authority to dictate the terms of a settlement, while the third party under a conflict management strategy is limited to facilitating agreement between the disputants or establishing the boundaries of their dispute.

The conflict management strategy is reflected in Section 8 and in Title II of the Labor-Management Relations Act. Section 8 establishes a set of employer and union unfair labor practices and other rules and definitions. Within these constraints, as applied by the National Labor Relations Board and the courts, unions and managements in the private sector are allowed to resolve their differences via collective bargaining and concerted activities. Similarly, Title II provides a forceful method for the federal government to intervene in "national emergency" disputes, but this authority is limited and does not provide for government imposition of settlement terms. In contrast, many states have given public employees the right to bargain, prohibited them from striking, and imposed interest arbitration as a resolution procedure which must be used if the parties cannot or will not settle their own disputes. As these examples imply, conflict management has been the most visible strategy in the private sector, while conflict resolution is prominent in public-sector thinking on the subject.

The two preceding paragraphs present an oversimplified distinction which implies more rationality among public policymakers and practitioners than actually exists. Unions and employers in both sectors use a variety of conflict management and conflict resolution techniques. For instance, as a society we have followed a conflict management policy regarding the negotiation of union-management contracts in the private sector, while at the same time we have adopted a conflict resolution policy regarding the handling of grievances. Similarly, the parties seek a determinative third-party resolution whenever they test the limits of the rules of the conflict management game. In the public sector, most states have opted for a de jure third-party resolution policy by prohibiting strikes and imposing factfinding, arbitration, and legislative determinations, but in practice many of these same states de facto tolerate more overt conflict (via strikes and job actions) than the official policy allows. In addition, during the past 15 or so years, the federal government has decided that such substantive issues as equal employment opportunity, occupational safety and health, and pension standards should be authoritatively determined by third parties, that is, governments, rather than by employer and employee representatives.

The Management of Industrial Conflict

STRIKE ACTIVITY

As a result of the U.S. Bureau of Labor Statistics' collection and reporting of strike activity, we know that during the 1950–1980 period (1) the annual number of strikes fluctuated between 3,000 and 6,000, though during 1968–1977 this annual figure consistently exceeded 5,000; (2) in any given year the number of workers involved in strikes ranged from one million to 3.5 million (that is, from about 1 percent to 7 percent of the total employed in each year); (3) average strike duration ranged between 15 and 27 days, though in recent years average duration consistently remained near the high end of that range; (4) total worktime lost due to strikes consistently remains in the range of one-tenth to one-half of 1 percent; (5) there are a few very large strikes which have disproportionate impacts on the economy (for example, in 1970, 34 strikes [of 5,710 that year] accounted for 50 percent of all workers involved in strikes and 53 percent of all days idle due to strikes); (6) wages are consistently the major issue in 40 to 65 percent of all strikes (although the data on this point are of questionable accuracy); and (7) there is considerable variation in strike activity across industries, occupational groups, and regions. These raw figures may not help us predict very accurately where and when strikes will occur, but they convincingly demonstrate that the strike is in no danger of withering away (Ross and Hartman, 1960).

The BLS also keeps us well informed on strike activity in the public sector. Major strike activity is relatively more recent in the government service, as evidenced by the contrast between 1965, when there were only 42 public-employee strikes across the entire country, and 1979, when there were 593 such strikes. Public-employee strikes are typically shorter in duration than private-sector strikes and they typically account for a smaller proportion of time lost due to strikes, two unsurprising results considering that most such strikes are illegal. However, public employees seem to have motivations which are similar to those of private employees, as wages are the major issue in most strikes in both sectors. One difference between the two sectors: teachers account for 25 to 50 percent of all public-employee strikes, while no single occupation in the private sector plays such a dominant role.

Aggregate strike statistics tell us almost nothing about the probability of a strike in any specific round of contract negotiations, or the "propensity to strike." The difficulty in determining such a propensity is due to the absence of precise data on the number of contract negotiations in any given year. Kochan (1980, p. 249), using Federal Mediation and Conciliation Service data, calculates that during the 1968–1975 period strikes occurred in 2 to 3 percent of the bargaining units for which 30-day contract expiration notices were filed by the parties (Section 8(d) of the National Labor

Relations Act requires that these notices be filed with the FMCS). Kaufman's (1978) analysis of large bargaining units in manufacturing (those including at least 1,000 workers) during the 1954–1975 period shows that in these manufacturing establishments annual strike propensities ranged from 5 to 30 percent around a median of 13 percent. Consequently, we know that the likelihood of strikes is significantly greater in large rather than small bargaining units (at least in manufacturing) and in certain years compared to others. However, the knowledge that strikes are not totally random events does not carry us very far in our quest for predictive power.

STRIKE DETERMINANTS

Academic researchers have been and still are absorbed in the quest for a general explanation of strike behavior. Researchers have been telling each other for decades that strikes are positively correlated with the business cycle (Hansen, 1921; Yoder, 1940; Rees, 1952; Weintraub, 1965; Scully, 1971; etc.). The theoretical basis for this positive correlation is inherently plausible, namely, that during prosperous times unions have more bargaining power —due to employer unwillingness to forgo sales and profits during strikes—and therefore can press employers for more favorable terms than during recessionary periods.

In addition, during the past dozen or so years, researchers have been examining the correlation between real wage changes and strikes (Ashenfelter and Johnson, 1969; Hibbs, 1976). The theoretical basis for this relationship focuses on worker wage expectations and employer wage offers. A decline in real wages or real wage growth is a proxy for an increase in worker wage expectations (to improve their relative economic position). Strikes supposedly result when these expectations outrun employer willingness to pay. In turn, strikes induce employers to offer more and induce workers to moderate their expectations to the point where a settlement can occur. In this view, then, the strike serves to moderate the opposing expectations and bring them into alignment, but it is not clear who does most of the moderating. It also is not clear if this explanation retains its validity during periods of continuous high inflation.

More recently, noneconomist researchers have contended that

the focus on economic explanations for U.S. strikes is appropriate only for the period after World War II (Britt and Galle, 1974; Snyder, 1977). They argue that prior to that war (that is, prior to the institutionalization and maturation of collective bargaining on a large scale) strikes can be more accurately explained by a favorable political climate for unions and the degree of union organizational strength (measured by membership) than by traditional economic variables. Most of the postwar U.S. strike research assumes that strikes occur during negotiations for a new contract. This assumption, and the research based on it, is appropriate for the postwar period, but is clearly out of place for the prewar period when many and sometimes most strikes occurred over union organization issues (Snyder, 1977). Snyder's and Hibbs's (1976) research suggests that in some other countries a politically based strike model is more appropriate than an economic model, which in turn suggests that U.S. strike research may have little or no applicability outside our borders.

More recently, Shalev (1980) has focused on strike opportunities, tactical advantages, and workers' economic frustrations as explanations for U.S. strikes during the 1954–1975 period. His econometric results suggest that strikes can be explained by focusing on expectations (or dissatisfactions or frustrations), strike opportunities, and the tactical ability to inflict damage on the bargaining adversary. In other words, workers are more likely to strike when they are dissatisfied *and* when they perceive the strike to be an effective mechanism to alleviate their dissatisfaction. This view is corroborated by Kochan's (1980) findings that strike rates are positively correlated with successful bargaining outcomes, that is, wages and nonwage contractual provisions (measured on a favorableness-to-the-union scale).

There are a variety of other factors which various researchers have found to be systematically correlated with strikes. Stern (1976), for instance, found that community strike rates varied around the country according to a set of variables which could be used as indicators of prounion and antiunion attitudes or climate. In a case study, Snorr (1975) found some interesting demographic differences between strikers and nonstrikers in a small plant in a small Midwestern city, but his limited sample precludes any general conclusions. Eisele (1974) found that strike frequency increases as plant size increases up to a certain level (about 750 employees), and as plant size increases beyond that level strike frequency declines. Roomkin (1976) found that strike frequency is positively associated with decentralized decision control within unions, with the building trades unions as the best examples. Bok and Dunlop (1970) emphasized the importance of strikes to change the structure of bargaining (rather than strikes over substantive employment terms) as an important explanation of the lengthy duration of many strikes during the 1960s.

Most of the research discussed so far has been quite aggregate in nature, for it typically includes economy-wide strike data. In contrast, there are a few industry-specific studies which yield particularistic results. These results are less generalizable, but are useful for understanding the nonrandom distribution of strikes. For instance, Lipsky and Farber (1976) showed that during the 1949–1971 period in the construction industry strike activity increased compared to most other industries. Many of these strikes resulted from jurisdictional and union organizing disputes (which are much less important as causes of strikes in most other industries). They also found that federal wage controls were associated with a decrease in strikes over wages but an increase in strikes over working conditions. Similarly, Northrup and Foster (1975) sought to explain the (often violent) turbulence in construction labor relations by focusing on the growth of the open-shop share of the industry. In the electrical equipment manufacturing industry McLean (1977) found an increase in strikes during the 1966–1974 period (compared to the 1950–1965 period), but this increase was not attributable to the introduction of coalition bargaining (as claimed by others, such as Chernish (1969)). Eschewing the multiple regression analytical methods which characterize much of the above cited research, James and James (1965) presented an extremely insightful analysis of the late Jimmy Hoffa's use of contract strikes, grievance strikes, secondary boycotts and hot cargo clauses, and centralized bargaining to achieve increased benefits for Teamster members and to win control of the Teamsters union and the U.S. trucking industry. Their research suggests that industrial conflict may be shaped considerably by a single person, and this implication stands in sharp contrast to the focus on aggregate market, political, and institutional forces in most of the strike research published during the past 10 to 15 years.

STRIKE PREDICTIONS

As the foregoing review implies, the industrial relations research community has done a considerable amount of strike research, and this research supports a variety of conclusions about strike activity in the United States. We know that there are many market, political, and institutional forces which are systematically associated with strike activity, as seen in the brief review in the preceding section. However, it is not at all clear that this research, taken in pieces or in the aggregate, has substantially improved our 1980 ability to predict where and when strikes will and will not occur compared to that same predictive ability in 1950. As Shalev (1980) and Stern (1978) have noted, most strike research is conducted on a highly aggregated basis using multiple regression analysis. Statistically significant results may simply be the averaged responses which differ by industry, occupation, location, firm, bargaining unit, etc. Further, this research often employs different indicators of strike activity and rather weak proxies to capture the effects of the main variables of interest, either because these proxies represent the only available data or because they exist in a form which can be easily inserted into the computer. Finally, the data (Bok and Dunlop, 1970; Shalev, 1980) show that only slightly more than half of all strikes occur during contract negotiations (though these negotiation strikes may account for 80 to 90 percent of all person-days idle due to strikes). To the extent that quantitative strike research is based upon a conceptualization of strikes as contract negotiation events, the error term is destined to remain forever large.

These data and analytical limitations inherent in the standard strike studies become even more apparent when we consider some research which illustrates the kinds of variables or phenomena which often are not investigated in "mainstream" studies of industrial conflict. As mentioned above, the James and James (1965) investigation of Hoffa suggests that much overt industrial conflict may result from the policies and actions of one person, and this "great man" (or "great person") notion of conflict causality emerges strongly from many biographies and case studies of union and management leaders and single unions and companies (Ozanne, 1967; Uphoff, 1966). This emphasis on individual participants in union-management relations also emerges from some recent research on bargaining and dispute resolution in the public sector.

For instance, Kochan and Baderschneider (1978) found that the probability of an impasse developing in police and firefighter bargaining in New York was strongly correlated with the presence of hostility between the parties. Also, Walton and McKersie (1965) reported instances of conflict which seemed to result primarily from the strongly negative attitudes that union or management negotiators had toward their adversaries.

The variables investigated in "mainstream" strike studies can be quite different from those looked at in studies of wildcat strikes. Brett and Goldberg (1979) investigated wildcats in coal mining and found that the key differences between two high-strike mines and two low-strike mines were the differential abilities of foremen to resolve miners' complaints promptly and the presence or absence of a problem-solving relationship between local mine management and the local mine committee. Their study is an excellent example of the value of disaggregated strike research, and their results suggest micro-organizational variables may be as important in explaining strikes as the macro economic and political variables used in other studies. More generally, wildcat strikes have received comparatively little research attention during the past 30 years (Kerr and Siegel, 1954; Gouldner, 1954; Slichter, Healy, and Livernash, 1960), and the amount of this research interest seems to have declined over this period as wildcats have become less common in most industries (with the obvious exception of coal mining). Brett and Goldberg's research also indicates that wildcats are comparatively expensive to study, and therefore we may expect that the Gresham's Law mentioned earlier will serve to hold down the amount of wildcat strike research in the future.

It may be impossible (or possible only at prohibitive cost) to predict where and when strikes will occur, evidence from the stock market notwithstanding (Neumann, 1980). It is almost certain that researcher attempts to paint strike explanations with extremely broad brushes will continue to produce rather fuzzy portraits which are of little or no value to policymakers (Dunlop, 1977), practitioners, or teachers. For instance, to discover that strikes and real wage declines are positively correlated is not the same as saying that a strike is likely in a firm whose workers have suffered a real wage decline during the life of the expiring contract. Also, the discovery of a positive correlation between the length of airline strikes and the existence of the former Mutual Aid Pact (Unterberger and Koziara, 1980) is insufficient evidence upon which to predict that future airline strikes will be short because of the prohibition of such pacts. Further, suggesting to a policymaker that strike frequency will be reduced by a set of economic policies which provide for real wage increases does not seem to be a particularly useful piece of advice during periods of high inflation.

In short, the mountain of strike research since World War II and the continuing strike record during that same period suggests that we should content ourselves with (1) post hoc explanations of aggregate strike behavior which contain some significant generalizable variables and some large residuals (that is, unexplained behaviors), and (2) post hoc explanations of strike behaviors in particular circumstances which are highly idiosyncratic and therefore of limited generalizability. Expecting more will cause serious frustration and disappointment, at least until some general theory is developed which is capable of providing us with a framework for understanding and prediction. Such a theory should deal with industrial conflict generally and should posit a set of contingencies which constitute the conditions for its occurrence, whether or not in the form of a strike (Wheeler, 1980).

COPING WITH CONFLICT: DISPUTE INTERVENTION

There is a long history of governmental regulation of industrial conflict. In this and the next section we look at governmental efforts to facilitate the settlement of labor disputes and to shape the rules of the conflict game.

Starting with the Railway Labor Act in 1926, the federal government has statutorily given itself increasing authority to intervene in selected bargaining disputes. Both the RLA (covering railroads and airlines) and the 1947 Taft-Hartley Act (covering other industries) give the President the power to invoke procedures which will postpone the start, or interrupt the continuation, of overt conflict if such conflict creates or threatens to create an emergency. These statutes do not give the government the authority to impose the terms of the settlement, but they do provide clear-cut mechanisms to postpone strikes while third parties intervene and facilitate the search for an acceptable outcome. Thus, both statutes provide for a combination of temporary strike restraint, mediation, and factfinding.

Space constraints prevent us from offering detailed assessments of the impacts of these procedures, but we can draw upon some research (notably Cullen, 1967; Cullen, 1977; Kahn, 1980) to summarize their performance. The Railway Labor Act's emergency board procedures (provided for in RLA Section 10) came under increasing criticism during the 1940s, 1950s, and 1960s for being used too frequently, chilling the bargaining process, and providing too few resolutions of the substantive issues in dispute. This criticism perhaps reached its peak with President Nixon's 1970 proposed transportation disputes legislation which would have eliminated RLA Section 10, and with the 1971 publication of a "Labor Relations in Transportation" symposium in the *Industrial and Labor Relations Review* in which most contributors were critical of the RLA's intervention procedures.

During the 1970s there has been a rather remarkable turnabout in prevailing opinion about the RLA's intervention procedures. As Cullen (1977) documents, emergency boards have been almost eliminated from airline bargaining and have been used less frequently in railroad bargaining than in earlier decades. President Nixon's first Secretary of Labor, George Shultz, fostered this change with his repeated insistences that the government should stay out of negotiating disputes whenever possible.

A capsule summary of the impact of Title II of Taft-Hartley is more difficult to provide because of the wide variety of circumstances in which it has been invoked. There have been 31 apparent invocations of the Taft-Hartley emergency procedures in the 34 years the law has been on the books, but since 1972 the procedure has been applied only once (in early 1978 in the longest coal strike in the nation's history). Cullen's (1967) conclusion that the Taft-Hartley record provides ammunition to both supporters and detractors is as valid today as it was 14 years ago. Some strikes have been settled during the 80-day cooling-off period, while others have resumed after the temporary cessation of hostilities. During the 1950s there were several attempts to determine precisely which disputes posed genuine "emergencies," but these efforts failed to produce a "definition of emergency strikes that is scientifically objective or commonly accepted" (Cullen, 1967, p. 47). However, the historical record suggests that it is hard to quarrel with Acker-mann's (1979) conclusion that selected strikes create virtually irresistible political pressures to be labeled and handled as "emergencies" regardless of their actual impacts, and consequently some type of emergency dispute intervention procedures are inevitable.

Over the years the federal government has used three other methods to intervene more forcefully into bargaining disputes. During the 1960s, Congress established itself as the arbitrator in a few protracted railroad labor disputes and imposed settlement terms on the parties (Kilgour, 1971). This practice does not appear to have become a habit, however, for Congress apparently has not arbitrated a private-sector dispute since 1971. During an almost century-long period, several U.S. presidents (starting with Lincoln) have seized (or attempted to seize) different industries on 71 different occasions to keep them operating, primarily during wartime (Blackman, 1967). After the U.S. Supreme Court in 1952 rather emphatically removed President Truman from the seizure business, no more seizures have occurred and subsequent presidents have relied upon presidential "arm-twisting" as a form of intervention to supplement or even supersede the statutory interventions under the Railway Labor and Taft-Hartley Acts. Apparently the personal involvement of presidents ceased after Lyndon Johnson left office, though all presidents have used high level officials to intervene on their behalf.

The Railway Labor Act, Taft-Hartley, and a large number of public-sector bargaining statutes provide for mediation and fact-finding interventions (though not always using those labels) to facilitate the settlement of negotiating disputes. Congress created the Federal Mediation and Conciliation Service in the Taft-Hartley Act, and it annually provides mediation services in thousands of cases. Similarly, the Railway Labor Act provides that the National Mediation Board can mediate in railroad and airline disputes. Similarly, both acts provide for factfinding in their emergency disputes procedures, and the 1974 Taft-Hartley amendments provided for FMCS factfinding in health-care negotiating disputes.

Public-sector bargaining statutes have relied heavily on mediation and factfinding to serve as substitutes for the right to strike (which usually is prohibited), and thus these nonbinding procedures are designed to replace rather than supplement strike threats as settlement devices (as in the private sector). These statutes are administered by various state agencies and thus the relevant data are more fragmented, but it appears that thousands of public-sector negotiating disputes each year receive the attention of mediators and factfinders (including FMCS mediators in some states).

The labor relations conventional wisdom is that mediation is an effective and desirable intervention device while factfinding is much less effective and hence less desirable. Researchers and practitioners alike praise mediation because it is a noncoercive procedure (the mediator has no authority to impose a settlement) which seems to work (many disputes are settled with the assistance of mediators). In other words, it is an effective third-party intervention device which is quite compatible with "free" collective bargaining. One recent study reports that union and management representatives in several countries have a high degree of satisfaction with mediation (Krislov and Galin, 1979). It is not clear why or how the process works to bring about a settlement, for most mediators insist that their work is much more "art" than "science," but Rehmus (1964), Simkin (1971), Kressel (1972), Kochan and Jick (1978), Gerhart and Drotning (1980), and Kolb (1981) use different analytical methods to provide us with some insights.

Although it is probably best viewed as a formal and written version of mediation, factfinding is much less well regarded than mediation. The name itself earns little respect, for researchers and practitioners alike realize that rarely are any facts ever found. Instead, the low opinion of this process results from a deadly mixture of high expectations and low performance. Settlement expectations are high because the procedure appears quasi-adjudicative (with its hearing room, formally anointed factfinder, witnesses, exhibits, and written report which often contains settlement recommendations), yet performance may be low because either party is free to reject the factfinder's report. Further, the experiences with Railway Labor Act emergency boards (Cullen, 1977), health-care boards of inquiry (Tanner, Weinstein, Ahmuty, 1980), and public-sector factfinding (Kochan, 1980) show that many negotiating disputes are unsettled after the completion of the factfinding process, sometimes with the parties farther apart than they were when the dispute started, and that many post-factfinding strikes occur. In the public sector this disillusionment is reflected in the 1973–1979 decline in the number of bargaining statutes that provide for fact-finding as the terminal procedure step (Schneider, 1979). However, research by Gallagher and Pegnetter (1979) indicates that factfinding may be a very useful device when used in conjunction with arbitration, and Wolkinson and Stieber (1976) found that union and management representatives in Michigan believed that factfinding was effective in resolving impasses. It may also have served as a stepping-stone to compulsory arbitration in the development of public-sector laws.

As a society we have long recognized the tension between socioeconomic stability and "free" collective bargaining, and our labor relations laws reflect this tension. On the one hand, we prohibit some kinds of overt conflict and provide for third-party resolution (to be discussed later), and we assist union and management representatives in their quest for mutually satisfactory terms. On the other hand, we allow the disputants, within limits, to inflict pain on one another in their quest for desirable terms, recognizing that this ability can cause considerable damage to innocent bystanders. To date we have resolved this tension by giving primary importance to "free" collective bargaining and thereby legitimizing overt industrial conflict. Perhaps this is relatively easy to do in a country such as the United States where only a small proportion of the labor force is organized for collective action. Further, there is no evidence to suggest that during the 1950–1980 period the industrial relations community has reduced its overall reliance on concerted activities. As a result, the government's protection of and the private-sector practitioners' reliance upon concerted activities will probably continue, even though these activities may inflict significant costs on uninvolved others. In the public sector we likely will continue our eclectic (or quixotic, depending upon your point of view) experimentation with a variety of conflict management and conflict resolution strategies, and this experimentation simultaneously may involve more strike rights for some groups and arbitration rights for other groups.

COPING WITH CONFLICT: RULES OF THE GAME

The primary thrust of public policy interventions into labor disputes has not been to settle substantive negotiating disputes but to regulate the parties' bargaining and coercive interactions. The visible illustration is seen in the very short statement in NLRA Section 7 of employees' rights to bargain and engage in concerted activities and the lengthy wordings in Section 8 which defines bargaining and specifies the types of activities which are prohibited. Similarly, the Railway Labor Act and various public-sector bargaining statutes contain a variety of "thou shalt nots" which restricts the activities in which the parties may legally engage during the search for favorable terms. These laws, and their subsequent administration by agencies and courts, are an attempt to channel industrial conflict within boundaries which are acceptable to a variety of groups with different normative labor relations perspectives.

There are three key indicators of the extent to which conflicts emerge over the application of the rules and over what the rules should be. The first is the annual intake of unfair labor practice cases at the National Labor Relations Board. In fiscal 1950, 5,809 ULP cases were filed with the Board. By fiscal 1979 that figure had increased to 41,259. It is not readily apparent what this sevenfold increase in finger-pointing represents (other than more work for more lawyers). Since most of these cases are withdrawn or dismissed, and since only about one-third of the total charges have merit (Roomkin, 1981), the number of actual labor law violations is considerably less than the number of case filings indicates. Consequently, it is not clear if there is more real conflict over rules violations than there was 30 years ago. The parties may simply have become more litigious over time, they may have become more adept at manipulating NLRB procedures to their own advantage (Roomkin, 1981), or they may be using NLRA Section 8 to harass each other more. A respected group of labor scholars in 1960 decried the trend toward more litigation and recommended that the law be substantially revised (Committee for Economic Development, 1961), but nothing ever came of their recommendations. There has been no revision of the statutory rules of the game since 1959, and it is rather unlikely that there will be any in the foreseeable future.

The second key indicator is the extent that labor, management, and the government seek to change the rules in some particular direction. The 1950–1980 period was marked by a more or less continuous series of contests for favorable rules. The most visible contests were legislative: the 1958–1959 Landrum-Griffin battle over internal union regulation and fine-tuning of Taft-Hartley, the 1965–1966 attempts to get Taft-Hartley Section 14(b) repealed, the 1970–1971 proposals for transportation disputes regulation, the 1975–1976 attempts legislatively to permit common situs picketing, and the 1977–1978 Labor Law Reform contest to amend the organizing and bargaining provisions of Taft-Hartley. The unions lost most of these engagements. Legislative contests are often matched with equally vigorous contests over nominations and appointments to the NLRB and the Supreme Court, as unions and managements have sharply differing preferences about desirable regulators. Finally, there is a constant stream of NLRB and federal court cases in which unions and managements seek favorable interpretations of the legislative rules which they can use in their search for favorable terms.

The 1950–1980 record indicates that: (1) unions and employers are constantly seeking more advantageous rules and rulemakers; (2) it is very difficult to change the legislative rules without a strong groundswell of supportive public opinion (Cohen, 1961); and (3) unions have failed to achieve major improvements in the rules from their perspective. It is not clear if these political contests absorb union-management tensions which might otherwise erupt as overt industrial conflict or if these political contests represent an additional layer of industrial conflict on top of the concerted activities which occur in the workplace. The peaceful processing of thousands of unfair labor practices and representation cases, and the energies devoted to seeking advantageous rules and rulemakers peacefully support the "absorption" interpretation, but the rhetorical hostility surrounding the Landrum-Griffin and Labor Law Reform legislation supports the "additional layer" interpretation.

This takes us to our third key conflict indicator, and that is the shape of labor relations rhetoric offered for public consumption. The "hostility quotient" of labor relations rhetoric has varied considerably during the past 30 years. Recognizing the hazards of making these interpretations on the basis of limited and impressionistic evidence, it appears to us that this hostility quotient was rather high during the late 1950s and late 1970s and much lower during the rest of that period. The rhetorical peaks coincide with

(1) a successful attempt by the government, acting with the support of employers, to regulate union affairs more tightly than ever before (via Landrum-Griffin) which occurred as 20 years of organizational momentum had run out of steam, and with (2) an unsuccessful attempt by the unions (the Labor Law Reform bill) to amend the NLRA to eliminate what they perceived as legislative inequities which work to the employers' advantage (Prosten, 1978; Roomkin and Juris, 1978). In addition, the 1970s were characterized by what the unions perceived as an active employer campaign to resist unionization which included: closing unionized plants and shifting operations to new plants operating on a nonunion basis, often in parts of the country which have antiunion climates; seeking and following the advice of growing numbers of "union-free" consultants on how to resist unions; encouraging workers to decertify their unions; and turning the Labor Law Reform contest into some kind of labor relations "holy war."

As this chapter is being written, it is apparent that we are witnessing a continuation of this recent high level of rhetorical hostility between labor and management compared to the situation that prevailed during most of the 1950–1980 period. The unions argue that this hostility derives from the employer actions just described. Further, there is additional evidence (Kochan, 1980, Ch. 6) which suggests that most U.S. employers have not philosophically accepted unions and collective bargaining 45 years after the passage of the Wagner Act. Consequently, the phenomena described in these past few paragraphs may indicate that there is more conflict than there was, say, ten years ago. However, it is not clear if these events will translate into increased conflict as measured with such standard indicators as strikes, grievances, organizing attempts, and so forth (in fact, there were considerably fewer strikes in 1978 and 1979 than in the preceding few years). In addition, it is here that the onesidedness of our (and the traditional) definition of conflict as *worker* action shows a tendency to obfuscate the reality of conflict between managers and workers, for it leads us to neglect aggressive action by management.

COPING WITH CONFLICT: INSTITUTIONALIZED COOPERATION

Ever since the 1946 strike wave, industrial relations practitioners, academicians, and policymakers have been searching for the key to "industrial peace." Some managers seem to think that industrial peace is best obtained by operating on a nonunion basis, some unionists seem to think that overwhelming bargaining power reduces conflict, and some observers have argued that compulsory arbitration will do more than anything else to guarantee industrial peace. In addition, throughout the 1950–1980 period there has been a more or less continual search for mechanisms which will replace adversarial interactions between unions and managements with a process (and spirit) of cooperation. During the 1960s, several productivity bargains received considerable attention (Healy, ed., 1965), as did some cooperative arrangements to cope with the impact of technological change. During the 1970s, other productivity agreements received publicity (McKersie and Hunter, 1973; Goodman, 1979), but it is hard to quarrel with Kochan's (1980) conclusion that all the publicity given to specific productivity agreements over the years suggests that these agreements are clear exceptions to "normal" collective bargaining.

During the 1970s, productivity bargaining has emerged in some workplaces under the "quality of worklife" (QWL) label. The various QWL programs involve a variety of specific practices to increase worker involvement and participation in work, to make work more interesting, and to improve the quantity or quality of products produced. Some impressive results have been reported from some of these QWL programs, but most of the reports have been issued by people or organizations who have a vested interest in a successful outcome. Further, unions tend to view these programs with a wary eye, and it is clear that union leaders and members do not want these programs to replace normal collective bargaining (Dyer, Lipsky, and Kochan, 1977; Ponak and Fraser, 1979).

The latest wrinkle in efforts to institutionalize cooperation is labor-management committees. These committees, composed of union and management representatives, are designed to meet frequently outside the collective bargaining process and deal with mutual problems in a cooperative manner. These committees apparently have become fairly numerous during the 1970s, they have received explicit public policy support (via the Labor-Management Cooperation Act of 1978), and a few of them have been touted as highly successful (e.g., in Jamestown, New York). However, it is not very clear what these committees actually do (besides hold meetings), and there is little or no evidence that these committees have had any significant impact on collective bargaining processes and outcomes.

There seems to be widespread agreement that a problem-solving approach to various employment issues results in more cooperation and less conflict than an adversarial or win/lose approach. However, there is little in the experience and research records of the past 30 years that suggest how a problem-solving, cooperative approach can be institutionalized successfully. Further, there is absolutely nothing in the record of the past three decades to suggest that some form of institutionalized cooperation will replace the adversarial relationship known as collective bargaining. Collective bargaining is based upon the assumption of divergent worker and employer interests, yet successful labor-management cooperation efforts seem to require that these divergent interests be forgotten (or at least temporarily set aside). This may be feasible in a genuine crisis which threatens both sides (for example, the New York City and Chrysler bankruptcies), but adversarial self-interest seems to achieve more desirable results during "normal" times (Kochan, 1980).

The Effectiveness of Conflict Management

If we assume, as the pluralists or Conflict School members do, that employees and employers should be able to seek and press for advantageous employment terms and that bystanders should be protected from the more inimical impacts of these employment contests, the 1950–1980 industrial conflict experience in the United States suggests that our conflict management system works reasonably well. Annual strike frequency appears within tolerable bounds. Since 1946, there has been no strike wave to provoke a public outcry to "do something" about strikes. The emergency dispute intervention procedures of Taft-Hartley and the Railway Labor Act have been used rather sparingly during the past decade considering how many large-scale strikes occur each year and how frequently these procedures were invoked prior to 1970. Further, there was only one serious legislative proposal to modify these procedures during the entire period (President Nixon's 1970–1971 transportation disputes legislation), and it received little support from any quarter. In general, there has been no broad-based public pressure to modify significantly the U.S. conflict management system during this entire 30-year period, for the groundswell of public opinion which emerged in the late 1950s was directed at the regulation of internal union affairs. Consequently, if we use the absence of widespread pressure for change as our primary measure of effectiveness, the U.S. system of industrial conflict management is working well.

This conclusion, however, is qualified by three concerns. First, the 1977–1978 Labor Law Reform debate corroborated earlier research findings (P. Ross, 1965) that our conflict management system contains rather weak penalties for determined noncompliance (weaker, say, than penalties for EEO noncompliance), and as a result it is too easy for some employers and some unions to violate the conflict management rules with relative impunity. Second, using bargaining outcomes as a measure of bargaining power, it is abundantly clear that there are large differences in union abilities to press the claims of their members (Kochan, 1980; Feuille, Hendricks, and Kahn, 1981). These outcome differences imply that the regulatory system may work well for some groups and less well for other groups. Third, there is still no consensus over how much pain third parties should bear as a result of union-management warfare. Union-management conflict which creates hardship or merely inconvenience for third parties usually creates a strongly negative reaction among these third parties, with the result that there is continuing pressure to limit and isolate the third-party damage caused by industrial conflict.

The Resolution of Industrial Conflict

The public policy emphasis in the United States on the management of industrial conflict has not prevented unions, employers, and the government from adopting explicit third-party mechanisms to resolve some kinds of employment disputes in a binding manner. As we shall see below, the number and use of these binding third-party procedures has increased substantially during the past 30 years, and they have absorbed and resolved many employer-employee conflicts which otherwise would have emerged in costlier form.

GRIEVANCE ARBITRATION

Contract interpretation disputes have been settled in two ways: (1) the strike (or, much less frequently, the lockout), and (2) adjudication by neutral third party. The strike has historical primacy, is legally permissible (except where it has been waived), and is still commonly available as a grievance settlement mechanism in some industries such as paper, trucking, and construction (although arbitration is gaining favor in construction). In most industries, however, unions have been willing to trade off their right to strike during the term of the contract in return for the quid pro quo of the right to arbitrate. Prior to World War II grievance arbitration was rare, but the National War Labor Board's insistence on arbitration to resolve contract interpretation disputes dramatically reversed that situation. By 1949, 83 percent of a large sample of union contracts contained grievance arbitration provisions, and today about 95 percent of BLS-sampled contracts contain such provisions. During this same period, the volume of grievance arbitration work has grown substantially, judging from requests for arbitration assistance: in fiscal 1950, the Federal Mediation and Conciliation Service received 801 requests for arbitration panels; in fiscal 1977 it appointed 11,985 arbitrators to cases, but the total number of cases closed was 6,935 (U.S. FMCS, 1950, 1977). The American Arbitration Association's referral service also shows a very large increase in use during this period (Killingsworth, 1972), and by 1980 approximately 8,000 AAA awards were being issued each year (American Arbitration Association, 1981). In addition, of course, many thousands of arbitration appointments were made directly by unions and managements, and thus these cases do not show up in the referral agency statistics.

The federal and state governments have gone out of their way to encourage the use of arbitration. In a variety of case decisions, the Supreme Court (*Steelworkers Trilogy*, 1960; *Boys Market*, 1970) and the National Labor Relations Board (*Spielberg*, 1955; *Collyer*, 1971) have said that grievance arbitration is *the* preferred method for resolving most contract interpretation disputes. This same encouragement has been occurring in the public sector; in fact, a few states (for example, Florida, New Hampshire, Pennsylvania, New Jersey, Minnesota) have statutorily mandated that collective agreements negotiated for public employees in those states *must* contain a grievance procedure, and these same statutes often explicitly permit grievance arbitration (Pennsylvania and Minnesota go farther and require it). However, many state courts appear to have adopted the view that the scope and use of grievance arbitration ought to be narrower in the public sector than in the private sector. This presumably reflects a judicial response that collective bargaining in government cannot and should not operate in a manner identical to the private sector (Grodin, 1979). Nevertheless, in a 1975 survey the BLS found that 90 percent of the public-sector agreements surveyed contained a grievance procedure, and 79 percent of these (or 71 percent of the total sample) culminated in binding arbitration.

The conventional wisdom about grievance arbitration (at least in the private sector) is that it is one of the clear success stories in American union-management relations. This view is hardly surprising, given that most commentators on the subject are professors who also work (or aspire to work) as arbitrators. The very widespread use of the process suggests that grievance arbitration serves the interests of employees, unions, and managements (as well as arbitrators, arbitration referral agencies, arbitration reporting services, etc., etc.), as it provides for a binding resolution of contract interpretation arguments while relieving the parties of the costs and uncertainties of strikes over small-scale disputes. Arbitration has some defects, but proposals to replace the grievance arbitration system with the use of concerted activities, with labor courts, or with some other procedure usually are received with deafening silence.

The 1950–1980 experience with grievance arbitration also has demonstrated a variety of specific shortcomings. The procedural category of defects focuses in part on the length of time and amount of money involved in obtaining an arbitrator's decision. Over the years the amount of time and money necessary to obtain an arbitrated resolution of a grievance has increased substantially: the parties often prefer to wait (sometimes for several months) for the most popular arbitrators to hear their cases; there has been an increase in the use of lawyers, legal briefs, and transcripts; and arbitration fees have increased substantially. However, throughout the 1970s various unions, managements, and referral agencies have developed a variety of "expedited" arbitration programs to reduce the time and monetary costs without sacrificing employee or employer rights under the contract (Kochan, 1980). The growing use of expedited arbitration suggests that it has successfully served the parties' interests.

A second criticism of arbitration is that it can be used as a mechanism by one side to harass the other and thus can increase rather than reduce conflict. Perhaps the most visible example is the over-used grievance procedure in which cases are rarely settled short of arbitration, and each side views arbitration either as a mechanism to "get" the other side or as a tactical maneuver designed to negotiate favorable grievance settlements. The conventional wisdom suggests that the number of "distressed" grievance procedures is low (A. Ross, 1963), and that such procedures are symptoms of more fundamental union-management hostility than simply differing opinions on how to process and settle grievances. In short, most of the time arbitration effectively resolves contract interpretation conflicts, but on occasion the parties' hostility may be at such a high level that arbitration becomes an additional source of conflict.

A third criticism is that arbitration and its quid pro quo counterpart, the no-strike/no-lockout clause, do not guarantee that arbitrable disputes will be resolved procedurally instead of concertedly. Each year a significant fraction of all strikes occur during the life of an agreement, and while some occur because both parties have chosen to resolve such disputes via concerted activities rather than arbitration, many are wildcat walkouts over subjects that are supposed to be taken to arbitration. The data (Kochan, 1980) suggest that the underground bituminous coal mining industry has had more problems with wildcats than any other industry, and that during the past 30 years the overall proportion of strikes occurring during the life of the contract has declined (except in coal mining). Consequently, the wildcat strike issue may be far more important in coal mining than in any other industry (Brett and Goldberg, 1979), but other research suggests that there is a common set of conditions associated with wildcats in different industries (Gouldner, 1954; Kerr and Siegel, 1954).

A fourth criticism is that arbitration cannot deal effectively with an increasing number of employment issues, such as equal employment opportunity, occupational safety and health, and pension standards. As the federal government legislates more statutory employment rights (presumably because other means are insufficient to cope with these problems), there is the potential for an increasing amount of jurisdictional conflict between arbitration and other regulatory forums for resolving disputes involving statutorily based rights. So far there is little hard evidence that this potential has been translated into actual conflict, and the increasing demand for arbitral services suggests that unions and managements may not yet be aware that the "golden age" of grievance arbitration is coming to an end (Feller, 1977).

However, it is true that grievance arbitration's near impregnable finality, which has existed ever since the *Trilogy* decisions in 1960, has shown signs of loosening during the 1970s. The Supreme Court said in 1974 (in *Alexander* v. *Gardner-Denver*) that statutory EEO rights continue beyond an arbitrator's resolution of the merits of the case, and in the public sector management has shown a greater willingness to appeal arbitration awards than in the private sector (for instance, one arbitrator estimated that 17 percent of federal arbitration awards are appealed to the Federal Labor Relations Authority versus a 1 to 2 percent court appeal rate of private-sector awards (Bureau of National Affairs, 1980)). The rising tide of judicial intervention may also be found in the burgeoning number of duty of fair representation cases (for example, *Hines* v. *Anchor Motor Freight*, 1976) through which many arbitral decisions have been overturned. However, during this entire period the vast majority of arbitration awards have been accepted by unions and management as final and binding resolutions of their contract interpretation conflicts. We see no evidence that this state of affairs has changed substantially during the past five to ten years, but there is increasing evidence that grievance arbitration may be a somewhat less final conflict-resolution device for selected issues (for example, EEO) and in government employment.

Grievance arbitration and the arbitration reporting services have contributed to the spread of the Gresham's Law mentioned earlier by providing researchers with a large body of low cost data about the terminal resolution step in most grievance procedures.

The unsurprising result of this data availability is that we have accumulated a great deal of arbitration research results which dwarfs the comparatively small amount of research on the pre-arbitration processing of grievances. Some very useful grievance processing studies have been performed, such as Peach and Livernash's (1974) examination of grievance filing and resolution in five basic steel firms. They found several factors which distinguished high grievance rate departments from low rate departments, and they found other factors which contributed to the prompt resolution of grievances in some departments and not in others. However, their finding that each department had its own grievance processing characteristics does not offer much solace to those researchers or practitioners looking for conclusions which can be generalized to other workplaces. In short, we know a lot about the issues, the costs, the time, and the decisions involved in arbitration, but we have much less knowledge about why or how grievances are resolved short of arbitration. Also, we have seen little examination of the quality or the impacts of the decisions rendered by arbitrators. The 1950–1980 research experience suggests that this situation, in which there are gaping holes in our knowledge of grievance processing and arbitration, is unlikely to change in the foreseeable future.

We also have no general explanations for why some unions prefer to retain the right to strike over grievances (as in trucking), why some unions are embroiled in numerous wildcats over issues which are supposed to be arbitrated (as in coal mining), or why some employers exclude some bargaining subjects from arbitral determination (as with production standards in the auto industry). We do know that Jimmy Hoffa was a master at using the threat of grievance strikes to extract concessions from trucking employers (James and James, 1965), that many eastern coal miners have been very dissatisfied with their grievance procedures (Brett and Goldberg, 1979), and that the famous 1972 Lordstown auto assembly plant strike occurred over production standards during the life of a collective bargaining agreement. These pieces of particularistic information, however, do not tell us much about how these same subjects are handled in other contexts, and the high cost of this kind of research suggests that we may need to be content with this fragmentary knowledge.

VOLUNTARY INTEREST ARBITRATION

The longstanding and deeply held opposition by private-sector unions and managements to compulsory arbitration of new contract terms (Northrup, 1966) has been largely responsible for the traditional view that the government should not impose substantive employment terms upon employers and employees. This view is reflected in Supreme Court decisions reversing NLRB orders to the parties to agree to specific terms (*H. K. Porter*, 1970), in the absence of any statutory authority to impose settlements in emergency disputes, and in the reluctance of Congress to arbitrate only a small number of festering disputes on the railroads. As a result, unions and managements which prefer to avoid strikes must voluntarily adopt and enforce their own interest arbitration procedures.

The most visible (measured by column inches of print media attention) voluntary arbitration procedure in the country (and perhaps the world) is the Experimental Negotiating Agreement (ENA) adopted in 1972 by the United Steelworkers and the major steel producers. This agreement provides that issues unresolved after the completion of a specified period of negotiations would be settled by a three-person panel of arbitrators rather than by a strike or lockout. The parties must be pleased with the ENA, for they have renewed it twice; they negotiated the 1974, 1977, and 1980 steel contracts without recourse to arbitration; and they have avoided the boom-and-bust production cycle caused by pre-1972 strike hedge buying which in turn imposed heavy costs on both sides (that is, the ENA has served the special needs of the steel industry (Craft, 1976)). However, a substantial share of USW leaders and members opposed and still oppose the relinquishment of the right to strike, and some management representatives perceive that the dollar cost of negotiated agreements (to avoid arbitration) has been too high.

The steel arbitration experience helps explain why voluntary arbitration is used in only a small fraction of all bargaining relationships in this country. As the name implies, the procedure will be adopted only when *both* sides perceive that they will reap net benefits from giving up the right to strike or lockout and allowing a third party to impose a settlement. Voluntary arbitration has a long history of use in the transit, printing, flat glass, and electrical contracting industries and more recently in a few airlines and in major league baseball (for individual salary disputes). The available research (Bernstein, 1954; Miller, 1967; Stieber, 1970; Cole, 1974; Myers, 1975; Holly and Hall, 1977) suggests that voluntary arbitration of new contract terms may have been used more frequently during the 1950–1980 period than the conventional wisdom suggests. However, this same research does not really tell us why both parties in these arbitration relationships decided that they would relinquish their decision authority to third parties, and as a result we have little specific knowledge with which we can predict when and where voluntary arbitration will be adopted. Further, there is little evidence that voluntary arbitration is more frequently used now than it was 30 years ago (but see Holly and Hall, 1977), and the 1972 predictions that other large unions and employers would follow the lead of the steel union and steel producers has not been borne out. Stieber's survey (1970) found that union and management representatives were more enthusiastic about ad hoc interest arbitration than arbitration by prior agreement. Consequently, it seems safe to conclude that most American unions and employers will not entrust their negotiating interests to third parties unless there are compelling reasons to do so.

COMPULSORY INTEREST ARBITRATION

There has been limited use of voluntary arbitration in the private sector and there has been much less use of compulsory arbitration. Unions, managements, and the federal government appear as ideologically opposed to compulsory arbitration in 1980 as in 1950, though over the years various government units have experimented with it or proposed it. For instance, Congress imposed settlement terms in a few protracted and complex railroad disputes during the 1960s (Kilgour, 1971), but the 1970–1980 experience suggests that Congress did not adopt arbitration as a habit. Also, the National Labor Relations Board experimented with the limited imposition of settlement terms as a new remedy in selected refusal-to-bargain unfair labor practice cases until the Supreme Court issued clear instructions to the contrary (in the 1970 *H. K. Porter* case). In 1970 former Secretary of Labor George Shultz proposed that the President have the statutory authority to order the arbitration of emergency disputes in the transportation industries, but this proposed legislation received little support and became a casualty of electoral politics. Congress refused to impose interest arbitration in the 1974 health-care amendments to Taft-Hartley, and in 1978 the Senate refused to adopt the Labor Law Reform bill which contained "make whole" remedial authority for the NLRB to use in selected refusal-to-bargain cases. In sum, we appear to be no closer to the adoption of compulsory arbitration in the private sector than we were in 1950, and there is nothing on the horizon that suggests this situation will change in the foreseeable future.

The conflict resolution scene in the public sector in 1980 is remarkably different from that in the private sector. The steady expansion of collective bargaining rights for public employees has been accompanied by the steady expansion of compulsory arbitration, to the point that by 1980 at least 20 states require that arbitration be used to resolve negotiating conflicts between unions and employers for one or more occupational groups (primarily police and firefighters). Further, this governmental experience has demonstrated that compulsory arbitration is not a monolithic process, for there has been a great deal of procedural experimentation across these various states (for two reviews, see Feuille, 1979; and Kochan, 1979). Space constraints prevented a detailed examination of the operation and impacts of compulsory arbitration in government, except to note briefly that it has not destroyed collective bargaining but has reduced negotiating incentives in particular union-management relationships, has been constitutionally acceptable most of the time but has been a source of sharp political conflict, and has not resulted in excessively generous settlements for employees but has provided them with moderately larger wage increases than they would have negotiated otherwise (Stern, et al., 1975; Olson, 1980). Militant unions, such as the International Association of Fire Fighters and the American Federation of State, County, and Municipal Employees, have come to accept and even prefer arbitration as a means of resolving their negotiating disputes. Perhaps most important, compulsory interest arbitration in government has demonstrated that collective bargaining can function effectively without the right to strike. It is not clear, however, that this demonstration effect will change the anti-arbitration attitudes of private-sector practitioners and commentators.

Conclusions

INDUSTRIAL CONFLICT EXPERIENCE

It is not clear that there has been a long-run increase in the propensity to strike during the past 30 years. Any conclusion on this point must be tempered by the fact that while the actual number of strikes can be counted with some precision, the opportunities to strike can only be estimated. There does seem to be a long-run decline in wildcat strikes (with the obvious exception of the coal industry), and unions and managements have been increasingly exposed to administrative procedures to handle recognitional, organizational, and jurisdictional disputes. Consequently, most time lost due to strikes occurs because of contract negotiation strikes, but other types of strikes still account for a large proportion of all strikes.

Second, the steady increase in unfair labor practice charges filed with the NLRB suggests either that the parties are increasingly willing to resolve their rules-of-the-game disputes via third-party resolution instead of economic coercion, or that the NLRB simply represents an increasingly important arena for union-management conflict.

Third, the apparent increase in grievance arbitration procedures and cases during the past 30 years suggests that both sides seem to prefer this method of resolving contract interpretation disputes to other available methods. Further, the fact that the arbitration caseload appears to have grown faster than the number of contracts and the number of unionized employees may suggest that contracts are becoming ever more complex, thus creating more and more opportunities for interpretation disputes. Alternatively, the increase in arbitration cases may result from an increase in the proportion of grievances which are not settled at the prearbitration steps, or the increase may result from the incentives (that is, fees, status) that union and management advocates have to arbitrate. In addition, there are few generalizable explanations of how or why most grievances are settled short of arbitration, though the Peach and Livernash (1974) and Brett and Goldberg (1979) studies indicate that low level managerial discretion to settle grievances leads to reduced strife.

Fourth, there has been little or no discernible increase in the substitution of binding or nonbinding procedures for strikes as the preferred method of resolving otherwise unresolvable contract negotiation disputes in the private sector. To be sure, some unions and managements have voluntarily adopted interest arbitration, but we have been unable to determine if the proportionate use of interest arbitration has increased or decreased during the past three decades. Similarly, statutory emergency dispute procedures have been used throughout this period, but there seems to be a downward trend in the reliance upon these procedures to resolve negotiating disputes. Further, the comparatively passive form of mediation apparently practiced by the FMCS (Kolb, 1981) can hardly be considered as a substitute for strikes. In short, there seems to be no greater willingness today among unions and managements in the private sector to forswear economic coercion and allow third parties to dictate contract terms than there was 30 years ago, and the public-sector developments during the past 15 years have not yet had any noticeable carryover into private industry.

Fifth, the absence of any changes in the statutory management of the industrial conflict rules since 1959 clearly suggests that during most of the period under consideration the amount and types of overt industrial conflict generally have been tolerable. Conflict-prone industries, such as coal mining and construction, seem to be recognized as exceptions to the more general state of conflict stability which exists throughout most of the economy, and these exceptional cases do not seem to have produced any serious proposals for general changes in public conflict management policy. At the same time, the data clearly show that the strike has not "withered away" as an instrument of private or public policy, either in the United States or in other countries (Ross and Hartman, 1960; Hibbs, 1976). Consequently, the experience of the past 30 years suggests that there will be few, if any, major changes in conflict occurrences or conflict policy in the foreseeable future. This presumes, of course, no major change in the political milieu.

Sixth, the increasing amount of direct substantive regulation by the federal government of various employment issues (EEO, safety and health, pensions, import impact assistance, incomes policies) suggests that we have been in the midst of a move away from national labor policy as process regulation toward national labor policy as employment standards regulation. However, the government's increasing regulation of employment terms has done little to narrow the scope of actual collective bargaining, and there is no reason to expect that any such narrowing process will increase in the foreseeable future. Consequently, we may expect unions and managements to continue to have an ample supply of employment issues over which conflicts may occur, including administrative conflicts with regulatory agencies. If there is a reversal of the trend toward employment standards regulation, the parties to collective bargaining may have to devise new ways of dealing with some of these issues to which regulation has given high visibility.

Finally, until there is a consensus regarding the appropriate objectives of policy, it will be difficult to evaluate its effectiveness intelligently. We suggest that the proper function of conflict management mechanisms is not the suppression of all conflict, but rather its creative use to serve the interests of workers, employers, and society. This means that conflict-handling mechanisms should facilitate the pursuit of legitimate interests of workers and employers, while simultaneously holding the inconvenience and costs to society within reasonable bounds. These criteria are obviously susceptible to debate. Given the conflict of interests among the debaters (that is, employers and employees, producers and consumers, regulators and regulatees, etc.), any genuine consensus may be difficult to achieve.

INDUSTRIAL CONFLICT RESEARCH

The "all is (relatively) well" implication in the preceding section cannot be applied to the research on industrial conflict. As we noted earlier, industrial conflict research seems to follow the path of least-cost myopia where research quality often is measured by the amount of numerical data which is processed and the degree of rigor and elegance in the analytical methods used rather than by the extent to which the results assist researchers, policymakers, or practitioners to understand where, when, and why conflict occurs. To be sure, the strike research of the past 15 or so years has informed us of the impact of such factors as business cycles, political climate, plant size, bargaining unit size, union structure, real wage changes, and community attitudes on strike occurrences. However, the aggregate nature of most of this research is based upon three implicit assumptions: a worker is a worker is a worker, a union is a union is a union, and a management is a management is a management (that is, these assumptions ignore the great diversity among employees, unions, and managements). In light of the tremendous variation in strike activity across industries, occupations, firms, unions, and locations, these implicit research assumptions are naive, condescending, and often erroneous. There is some other research based upon the explicit assumption that strike activity varies widely, but the recognition and acceptance of this fact has not stayed researchers from their quest for the All-Encompassing Model of Strike Behavior which will explain everything worth explaining about strike activity. While such a model could be useful, current research does not appear to be leading in the direction of developing one that is adequate to the task. The research is at once too narrow and too broad—too narrow in that it tends to deal with only one form of industrial conflict, the strike; too broad in that each study tends to attempt a general explanation rather than taking on the more modest task of adding one more stone to a pyramid of knowledge.

In addition, the research concentration on strikes as the preferred indicator of industrial conflict (and sometimes the only indicator) does not seem to have changed very much during the past 30 years. Events such as grievances, job actions, sabotage, and turnover are sometimes used as conflict indicators, but we have very sketchy understandings of the conflict importance and meaning of these phenomena. For instance: Are grievances primarily indicators of conflict between specific employees and specific managers, between the union as an organization and the employer as an organization, or between different employees competing for scarce rewards? What kinds of nonstrike job actions occur in various workplaces, and why do they occur? Further, collective bargaining itself can be regarded as an indicator of industrial conflict. Organization of a group of employees represents an employee decision to institutionalize an adversarial interaction mechanism with the employer, and the carrying out of bargaining is the operation of such a mechanism. Yet for at least the past 30 years the IR research community seems to have regarded the peaceful absorption and resolution of employment disputes as nonconflict. Perhaps this is because collective bargaining is at once conflict and co-operation or, as E. Wright Bakke labeled it, antagonistic coopera-tion. There is nothing in the research record of the past three decades to indicate that this view has changed, but there ought to be explicit recognition that the published results of most industrial conflict research focus on a rather small slice of the conflict uni-verse.

If there is a theme to this chapter, it is that "industrial conflict" is a multifaceted phenomenon which is conceptually defined in broad terms but actually researched in narrow terms. As our anal-ysis suggests, the working definition of industrial conflict (at least in the United States) is rooted in the practice and regulation of collective bargaining. We suggest that this working definition may have been very appropriate for the 1930s, 1940s, and 1950s, but it is becoming increasingly outmoded in the 1980s. The events of the 1970s suggest that for millions of U.S. workers and managers: wages are determined by macroeconomic events and incomes pol-icies; job security is determined by monetary policy and corporate investment strategy; hiring, promotion, firing, pensions, and safety are regulated directly by the government; job satisfaction is de-termined by management's organization of the workflow process; and collective bargaining plays little or no visible role in any of these issues. Further, there are many divergent interests and hence conflict over the implementation of these issues (does anyone be-lieve that EEO and workplace safety complaints represent ex-amples of industrial harmony?), yet there has been little incor-poration of these issues into the IR community's research agenda. In other words, "industrial conflict" needs to be redefined to keep up with the changing employment scene, and that redefinition should include the use of a wider range of conflict indicators than presently occurs.

Recently one of our colleagues commented that "if a genuine epidemic of industrial peace developed, there would be many arbitrators jumping out of windows," and we think this same pre-diction could be applied to numerous union and management prac-titioners, regulatory agency staffers, and industrial relations aca-demicians. This assessment reflects the fact that the authors and readers of this chapter have a vested interest in the existence of industrial conflict (and more rather than less of it). Given this vested interest, and given the Conflict School's assumption of the inevitable potential for conflict between employees and employers, it is somewhat dismaying that industrial relations researchers have used the "iceberg" approach and concentrated their research efforts on only the most visible part of the conflict universe. We hope that the industrial conflict chapter written 30 years hence for this series will reflect a much broader range of research interests than has occurred during the past 30 years.

References

Ackerman, John A. "The Impact of the Coal Strike of 1977–1978." *Industrial and Labor Relations Review* 32 (January 1979), pp. 175–88.
American Arbitration Association. Letter to Labor Arbitrators, July 17, 1981.
Ashenfelter, Orley, and George E. Johnson. "Bargaining Theory, Trade Unions and Industrial Strike Activity." *American Economic Review* 59 (March 1969), pp. 35–49.
Barbash, Jack. "Collective Bargaining and the Theory of Conflict." *British Journal of Industrial Relations* 18 (March 1980), pp. 82–90.
Bernstein, Irving. *The Arbitration of Wages.* Berkeley: University of California Press, 1954.
Blackman, John L., Jr. *Presidential Seizure in Labor Disputes.* Cambridge, MA: Harvard University Press, 1967.
Bok, Derek C., and John T. Dunlop. *Labor and the American Community.* New York: Simon and Schuster, 1970.
Brett, Jeanne M., and Stephen B. Goldberg. "Wildcat Strikes in Bituminous Coal Mining." *Industrial and Labor Relations Review* 32 (July 1979), pp. 465–83.
Britt, David, and Omer T. Galle. "Structural Antecedents of the Shape of Strikes: A Comparative Analysis." *American Sociological Review* 39 (October 1974), pp. 642–51.
Bureau of National Affairs. *Government Employee Relations Report*, No. 885 (October 27, 1980), p. 33.
Chernish, William N. *Coalition Bargaining: A Study of Union Tactics and Public Policy.* Philadelphia: University of Pennsylvania Press, 1969.
Cohen, Sanford. "An Analytical Framework for Labor Relations Law." *Industrial and Labor Relations Review* 14 (April 1961), pp. 350–62.
Cole, David L. "Focus on Bargaining: The Evolving Techniques." *AFL-CIO American Federationist* 81 (May 1974), 14–20.
Committee for Economic Development. *The Public Interest in National Labor Policy.* New York: CED, 1961.
Craft, James A. "The ENA, Consent Decrees, and Cooperation in Steel Labor Relations: A Critical Appraisal." *Labor Law Journal* 27 (October 1976), pp. 633–40.
Cullen, Donald E. "Emergency Boards Under the Railway Labor Act." In *The Railway Labor Act at Fifty*, ed. Charles M. Rehmus. Washington: National Mediation Board, 1977. Pp. 151–86.
———. *National Emergency Strikes.* ILR Paperback No. 7. Ithaca: New York State School of Industrial and Labor Relations, Cornell University, 1967.
Dahrendorf, Ralf. *Class and Class Conflict in Industrial Society.* London: Routledge, 1959.

Dunlop, John T. "Policy Decisions and Research in Economics and Industrial Relations." *Industrial and Labor Relations Review* 30 (April 1977), pp. 275–82.

Dyer, Lee, David B. Lipsky, and Thomas A. Kochan. "Union Attitudes Toward Management Cooperation." *Industrial Relations* 16 (May 1977), pp. 163–72.

Eisele, C. Frederick. "Organization Size, Technology and Frequency of Strikes." *Industrial and Labor Relations Review* 27 (July 1974), pp. 560–71.

Feller, David E. "Arbitration: The Days of Its Glory Are Numbered." *Industrial Relations Law Journal* 2 (Spring 1977), pp. 97–130.

Feuille, Peter. "Selected Benefits and Costs of Compulsory Arbitration." *Industrial and Labor Relations Review* 33 (October 1979), pp. 64–76.

Feuille, Peter, Wallace E. Hendricks, and Lawrence M. Kahn. "Wage and Nonwage Outcomes in Collective Bargaining: Determinants and Trade-offs." *Journal of Labor Research* 2 (Spring 1981), pp. 39–53.

Gallagher, Daniel G., and Richard Pegnetter. "Impasse Resolution Under the Iowa Multistep Procedure." *Industrial and Labor Relations Review* 32 (April 1979), pp. 327–38.

Gerhart, Paul F., and John E. Drotning. "Dispute Settlement and the Intensity of Mediation." *Industrial Relations* 19 (Fall 1980), pp. 352–59.

Goodman, Paul S. *Assessing Organizational Change: The Rushton Quality of Work Experiment.* New York: Wiley, 1979.

Gouldner, Alvin. *Wildcat Strikes.* Yellow Springs, OH: Antioch Press, 1954.

Grodin, Joseph R. "Judicial Response to Public-Sector Arbitration." In *Public-Sector Bargaining,* eds. Benjamin Aaron, Joseph R. Grodin, and James L. Stern. Industrial Relations Research Association Series. Washington: Bureau of National Affairs, 1979. Pp. 224–53.

Hansen, Alvin. "Cycles of Strikes." *American Economic Review* 11 (December 1921), pp. 616–21.

Healy, James J., ed. *Creative Collective Bargaining.* Englewood Cliffs, NJ: Prentice-Hall, 1965.

Hibbs, Douglas A., Jr. "Industrial Conflict in Advanced Industrial Societies." *American Political Science Review* 70 (December 1976), pp. 1033–58.

Holly, J. Fred, and Gary A. Hall. "Dispelling the Myths of Wage Arbitration." *Labor Law Journal* 28 (June 1977), pp. 344–54.

Hyman, Richard. "Pressure, Protest and Struggle: Some Problems in the Concept and Theory of Industrial Conflict." Paper presented at the conference, Industrial Relations and Conflict Management: Different Ways of Managing Conflict, June 29–July 3, 1980, at The Netherlands School of Business.

James, Ralph, and Estelle James. *Hoffa and the Teamsters: A Study of Union Power.* Princeton, NJ: D. Van Nostrand, 1965.

Kahn, Mark L. "Airlines." In *Collective Bargaining: Contemporary American Experience,* ed. Gerald G. Somers. Industrial Relations Research Association Series. Madison, WI: IRRA, 1980. Pp. 315–72.

Kaufman, Bruce E. "The Propensity to Strike in American Manufacturing." *Proceedings* of the 30th Annual Meeting, Industrial Relations Research Association. Madison, WI: IRRA, 1978. Pp. 419–26.

Kerr, Clark, and Abraham Siegel. "The Inter-industry Propensity to Strike—An International Comparison." In *Industrial Conflict,* eds. Arthur Kornhauser, Robert Dubin, and Arthur M. Ross. New York: McGraw-Hill, 1954. Pp. 189–212.

Kilgour, John G. "Alternatives to the Railway Labor Act." *Industrial and Labor Relations Review* 25 (October 1971), pp. 71–84.

Killingsworth, Charles C. "25 Years of Labor Arbitration—and the Future." In *Labor Arbitration at the Quarter Century Mark,* Proceedings of the

25th Annual Meeting, National Academy of Arbitrators. Washington: BNA Books, 1972. Pp. 11–27.

Kochan, Thomas A. *Collective Bargaining and Industrial Relations.* Homewood, IL: Richard D. Irwin, 1980.

———. "Dynamics of Dispute Resolution in the Public Sector." In *Public-Sector Bargaining*, eds. Benjamin Aaron, Joseph R. Grodin, and James L. Stern. Industrial Relations Research Association Series. Washington: Bureau of National Affairs, 1979. Pp. 150–90.

Kochan, Thomas A., and Jean Baderschneider. "Dependence on Impasse Procedures: Police and Firefighters in New York State." *Industrial and Labor Relations Review* 31 (July 1978), pp. 431–49.

Kochan, Thomas A., and Todd Jick. "The Public Sector Mediation Process: A Theory and Empirical Examination." *Journal of Conflict Resolution* 22 (June 1978), pp. 209–38.

Kolb, Deborah M. "Roles Mediators Play." *Industrial Relations* 20 (Winter 1981), pp. 1–17.

Kressel, Kenneth. *Labor Mediation: An Exploratory Survey.* Albany, NY: Association of Labor Mediation Agencies, 1972.

Krislov, Joseph, and Amira Galin. "Comparative Analysis of Attitudes Toward Mediation." *Labor Law Journal* 30 (March 1979), pp. 165–73.

Lipsky, David B., and Henry S. Farber. "The Composition of Strike Activity in the Construction Sector." *Industrial and Labor Relations Review* 29 (April 1976), pp. 388–404.

McLean, Robert A. "Coalition Bargaining and Strike Activity in the Electrical Equipment Industry." *Industrial and Labor Relations Review* 30 (April 1977), pp. 356–63.

McKersie, Robert B., and Lawrence C. Hunter. *Pay, Productivity, and Collective Bargaining.* London: Macmillan, 1973.

Miller, Richard U. "Arbitration of New Contract Wage Disputes: Some Recent Trends." *Industrial and Labor Relations Review* 20 (January 1967), pp. 250–64.

Myers, Charles A. "Voluntary Arbitration of Disputes Over New Labor Contracts." *Sloan Management Review* 18 (Fall 1976), pp. 73–79.

Neumann, George R. "The Predictability of Strikes: Evidence from the Stock Market." *Industrial and Labor Relations Review* 33 (July 1980), pp. 525–35.

Nightingale, Donald. "Conflict and Conflict Resolution." In *Organizational Behavior: Research and Issues*, eds. George Strauss, Raymond E. Miles, Charles C. Snow, and Arnold S. Tannenbaum. Industrial Relations Research Association Series. Madison, WI: IRRA, 1974. Pp. 141–64.

Northrup, Herbert R. *Compulsory Arbitration and Government Intervention in Labor Disputes.* Washington: Labor Policy Association, 1966.

Northrup, Herbert R., and Howard G. Foster. *Open Shop Construction.* Philadelphia: Industrial Research Unit, Wharton School, University of Pennsylvania, 1975.

Olson, Craig A. "The Impact of Arbitration on the Wages of Firefighters." *Industrial Relations* 19 (Fall 1980): 325–39.

Ozanne, Robert. *A Century of Union Management Relations.* Madison: University of Wisconsin Press, 1967.

Peach, David, and E. Robert Livernash. *Grievance Initiation and Resolution: A Study in Basic Steel.* Boston: Graduate School of Business, Harvard University, 1974.

Ponak, Allen M., and C. R. P. Fraser. "Union Members Support for Joint Programs." *Industrial Relations* 18 (Spring 1979), pp. 197–209.

Ponak, Allen M., and Hoyt N. Wheeler. "Choice of Procedures in Canada and the United States." *Industrial Relations* 19 (Fall 1980), pp. 292–308.

Prosten, Richard. "The Longest Season: Union Organizing in the Last Decade, a/k/a How Come One Team Has to Play with Its Shoelaces Tied Together?" *Proceedings* of the 31st Annual Meeting, Industrial Relations Research Association. Madison, WI: IRRA, 1979. Pp. 240–49.

Rees, Albert. "Industrial Conflict and Business Fluctuations." *Journal of Political Economy* 60 (October 1952), pp. 371–82.

Rehmus, Charles M. "The Mediation of Industrial Conflict: A Note on the Literature." *Journal of Conflict Resolution* 9 (March 1965), pp. 118–26.

Roomkin, Myron. "A Quantitative Study of Unfair Labor Practice Cases." *Industrial and Labor Relations Review* 34 (January 1981), pp. 245–56.

———. "Union Structure, Internal Control, and Strike Activity." *Industrial and Labor Relations Review* 29 (January 1976), pp. 198–217.

Roomkin, Myron, and Hervey A. Juris. "Unions in the Traditional Sectors: The Mid-Life Passage of the Labor Movement." *Proceedings* of the 31st Annual Meeting, Industrial Relations Research Association. Madison, WI: IRRA, 1979. Pp. 212–22.

Ross, Arthur M. "Distressed Grievance Procedures and Their Rehabilitation." *Proceedings* of the 16th Annual Meeting. National Academy of Arbitrators. Washington: BNA Books, 1963.

Ross, Arthur M., and Paul T. Hartman. *Changing Patterns of Industrial Conflict.* New York: Wiley, 1960.

Ross, Philip. *The Government as a Source of Union Power.* Providence, RI: Brown University Press, 1965.

Schneider, B. V. H. "Public-Sector Labor Legislation—An Evolutionary Analysis." In *Public-Sector Bargaining,* eds. Benjamin Aaron, Joseph R. Grodin, and James L. Stern. Industrial Relations Research Association Series. Washington: Bureau of National Affairs, 1979. Pp. 191–223.

Scully, Gerald W. "Business Cycles and Industrial Strike Activity." *Journal of Business* 44 (October 1971), pp. 359–74.

Shalev, Michael. "Trade Unionism and Economic Analysis—The Case of Industrial Conflict." *Journal of Labor Research* 1 (Spring 1980), pp. 133–73.

Simkin, William E. *Mediation and the Dynamics of Collective Bargaining.* Washington: Bureau of National Affairs, 1971.

Slichter, Sumner, James J. Healy, and E. Robert Livernash. *The Impact of Collective Bargaining on Management.* Washington: Brookings Institution, 1960.

Snarr, D. Neil. "Strikers and Nonstrikers: A Social Comparison." *Industrial Relations* 14 (October 1974), pp. 371–74.

Snyder, David. "Early North American Strikes: A Reinterpretation." *Industrial and Labor Relations Review* 30 (April 1977), pp. 325–41.

Stern, James L., Charles M. Rehmus, J. Joseph Loewenberg, Hirschel Kasper, and Barbara D. Dennis. *Final-Offer Arbitration.* Lexington, MA: D. C. Heath, 1975.

Stern, Robert N. "Intermetropolitan Patterns of Strike Frequency." *Industrial and Labor Relations Review* 29 (January 1976), pp. 218–35.

———. "Methodological Issues in Quantitative Strike Analysis." *Industrial Relations* 17 (February 1978), pp. 32–42.

Stieber, Jack. "Voluntary Arbitration of Contract Terms." *Daily Labor Report* 85 (May 1, 1970), pp. 1–21.

Strauss, George. "The Study of Conflict: Hope for a New Synthesis Between Industrial Relations and Organizational Behavior." *Proceedings* of the 29th Annual Winter Meeting, Industrial Relations Research Association. Madison, WI: IRRA, 1977. Pp. 329–37.

Tanner, Lucretia Dewey, Harriet Goldberg Weinstein, and Alice L. Ahmuty. "Collective Bargaining in the Health Care Industry." *Monthly Labor Review* 103 (February 1980), pp. 49–53.

U.S. Federal and Mediation Service. *Third Annual Report, Fiscal Year 1950.* Washington: FMCS, 1950.
———. *Thirtieth Annual Report, Fiscal Year 1979.* Washington: FMCS, 1977.
Unterberger, S. Herbert, and Edward C. Koziara. "The Demise of Airline Strike Insurance." *Industrial and Labor Relations Review* 34 (October 1980), pp. 82–89.
Uphoff, Walter H. *Kohler on Strike.* Boston: Beacon Press, 1966.
Walton, Richard E., and Robert B. McKersie. *A Behavioral Theory of Labor Negotiations.* New York: McGraw-Hill, 1965.
Weintraub, Andrew. "Prosperity Versus Strikes: An Empirical Approach." *Industrial and Labor Relations Review* 19 (January 1966), pp. 231–38.
Wheeler, Hoyt N. "Roots of Industrial Conflict: Consequences for Conflict Management." Paper presented at the conference, Industrial Relations and Conflict Management: Different Ways of Managing Conflict, June 29–July 3, 1980, at The Netherlands School of Business.
Wolkinson, Benjamin W., and Jack Stieber. "Michigan Fact-Finding Experience in Public Sector Disputes." *Arbitration Journal* 31 (December 1976), pp. 225–47.
Yoder, Dale. "Economic Changes and Industrial Unrest in the United States." *Journal of Political Economy* 48 (April 1940), pp. 222–37.

CHAPTER 8

A View from Abroad*

ANDREW THOMSON
University of Glasgow

Introduction

The purpose of this chapter is to evaluate the American industrial relations system between 1950 and the present day in the context of developments in other systems, primarily those in Western Europe. The perspectives are those of a Briton who has spent some years in the States, and analysis will thus reflect this viewpoint. In the space available, the chapter cannot in any sense be a detailed comparative study, so some important dimensions, such as those in labor economics and the behavioral sciences, will be either omitted or treated in cursory fashion. Moreover, comparative analysis in industrial relations has not been notably successful:[1] statistics are notoriously difficult to match, cultural diversity cannot be explored adequately, and so on, but the greatest danger in the present chapter is perhaps in portraying European industrial relations systems as much more homogeneous than is in fact the case for the purpose of contrast with the United States. There is a further issue of the appropriate criteria of comparison; this chapter proposes to use the strength and vitality of the pluralist institutions of industrial relations, together with a crude estimate of their appropriateness within their national context.

The primary topic of the chapter will be the ostensible relative stability or, some would argue, stagnancy of the U.S. industrial relations system as compared with flux and change in Europe over

* Thanks are due to Tom Kochan, Laurie Hunter, Phil Beaumont, and the editors for helpful comments on an earlier draft of this paper.

[1] Michael Shalev, "Industrial Relations Theory and the Comparative Study of Industrial Relations and Industrial Conflict," *British Journal of Industrial Relations* 18 (March 1980), p. 26. For the best approaches to comparative analysis, see *Collective Bargaining in the Industrialised Market Economies* (Geneva: International Labor Office, 1973), Part I, by John P. Windmuller; and John T. Dunlop, *Industrial Relations Systems* (Carbondale: Southern Illinois University Press, 1958).

the last 30 years, viewed largely in terms of two interrelated themes, namely, the structure of collective bargaining and the relative political roles of the labor movements. The positive aspect of this stability was well expressed by Strauss in 1976:

> By the mid 1950's, the American system of industrial relations was well established and working. Strikes had not been eliminated—on the contrary—but we had learned to live with them. Indeed during the 1960's and 1970's our IR system was one of the few relatively stable institutions in American life. Except for those on the extreme left and right, few questioned its premises or even its workings.[2]

The negative view was put by Cullen, writing in 1970:

> A generation ago in the United States collective bargaining was viewed as an instrument of change by its friends and critics alike. . . . In recent years, however, many critics have charged that American unions have lost their earlier zeal for reform and that today their bargaining activities are more often aimed at preserving rather than attacking the status quo. According to this indictment neither the process nor the structure of bargaining in the United States has shown the flexibility necessary to cope with the problems emerging after the Second World War such as inflation, structural unemployment, the civil rights revolution, the persistence of poverty and the advent of automation.[3]

In the very recent past the latter view has tended to dominate, with concern that the role and legitimacy of unions, and hence collective bargaining as an institution, are being seriously challenged by a combination of interrelated factors—changing industrial structure, public hostility, loss of political power, and a new managerial aggressiveness.[4]

---

[2] George Strauss, "The Study of Conflict: Hope for a New Synthesis Between Industrial Relations and Organizational Behavior," *Proceedings of the 29th Annual Winter Meeting, Industrial Relations Research Association,* 1976, p. 330.

[3] Donald E. Cullen, "Recent Trends in Collective Bargaining in the United States," in *Collective Bargaining in Industrialised Market Economies,* p. 330.

[4] Books and articles have recently begun to appear highlighting this decline: Hervey A. Juris and Myron Roomkin, *The Shrinking Perimeter: Unionism and Labor Relations in the Manufacturing Sector* (Lexington, MA: D. C. Heath, 1980), and R. Schlank, "Are Unions an Anachronism?" *Harvard Business Review* (September/October 1979).

In contrast, the position in Europe is one where unions have everywhere gained social, economic, and political power over the last 30 years, where collective bargaining has frequently moved into a central position in macroeconomic decision-making and where indeed the democratic state itself seems under challenge from the activities of the unruly industrial parties.[5] Almost everywhere there has been legislative change and experimentation with new modes of industrial relations going beyond collective bargaining, such as codetermination, social contracts, and corporatism. Moreover this has taken place in the framework of an intensifying ideological debate about the industrial system and class relations, in which union-management relations are at the core.[6] It can be argued that some of the changes are more of form than substance, and that much of the debate is empty rhetoric, but there can be no gainsaying the enhanced importance of industrial relations as an issue in Europe.

Thirty years ago these relative positions were far from true. In 1950 the industrial relations system in the United States played a highly important part in political debate, in the economic policies, and in the shifts in social structure. In spite of the Taft-Hartley Act, the unions were seen as rampant, exerting power over the whole economy and polity. The questions that were being asked of the labor movement were those of responsibility, as by Drucker:

> Never before, it seems, has organized labor been as strong, as powerful and as accepted, in this country, as today. Yet the American labor movement faces its most serious crisis. It is a crisis of success, not of failure, but that may make it all the more severe. Our union leaders still live in the days when they had to fight for recognition if not existence. But the problems they really face are those of labor's power and responsibility as a ruling group in industrial society.[7]

In Europe in 1950, by contrast, although there were challenges by

[5] B. Peper, "Tradeoffs and Politicization," in *Collective Bargaining and Government Policies* (Paris: OECD, 1979), and Solomon Barkin, ed., *Worker Militancy and its Consequences* (New York: Praeger, 1975).

[6] C. Crouch and A. Pizzorno, eds. *The Resurgence of Class Conflict in Western Europe Since 1968* (London: Macmillan, 1978), 2 vols.

[7] Peter Drucker, "Labor in Industrial Society," *Annals of the American Academy of Political and Social Science* 274 (March 1951), p. 145.

the unions both in their political and economic guises, these were muted for the most part by a general consensus within the European economies that the primary objective was to redevelop the economy after the years of war. Unions shared these objectives, most markedly in the Netherlands, but elsewhere also. The German system of codetermination was not only an indication of a distrust of big business, but also a genuine willingness to work together. In Britain, this period could be seen as the highwater mark of a responsible, voluntary, mature system.[8] Major questions about industrial relations systems therefore did not really begin for some time thereafter.

There are, of course, many common features in the development of the industrial relations systems of the United States and Europe over the past 30 years, especially in consequence of similar changes in industrial and labor market structures, and in the encroaching role of the state, especially in its regulatory guise. Nevertheless, the reversal of the relative positions of the industrial relations systems as sketched out above is striking, and furthermore, broadly speaking, developments elsewhere in the world outside these two areas have been closer to the European model than to the American one. The reasons for the change cannot, of course, be explained entirely in terms of the industrial relations systems and their relation to the larger society, but much can.

There are very considerable strengths in the American system, but they are largely at the lower day-to-day levels, reflecting the strength of institutional structure, the comprehensiveness and codification of the system at the local levels, the professionalism of the actors, the relatively closely defined links between levels and organizations on both sides. These are very important benefits and they continue and have been built upon. But, it will be argued, they do not make up for the weaknesses of the system at the higher levels, such as the lack of any coherent philosophy within the union movement, the apparent complacency about questions of union structure and level of organization, the loss of political power and credibility of unions within American society, and consequentially the fact that there are few issues of social significance being channeled through the industrial relations system. Thus, from

---

[8] O. Kahn-Freund, "Intergroup Conflicts and Their Settlement," *British Journal of Sociology* 5, No. 3 (1954).

a European social democratic, never mind Marxist, perspective, the system is not carrying out its primary function of social change agent. Instead it remains a means of setting the terms and conditions of employment for an increasingly narrow group of American workers, creating no social dynamic as it does so and posing no challenge to the established order. The net result is that European unions have had the range of activities to be able to adapt to and, indeed, to promote changes in economic structure and decision-making, whereas American unions have not been able to adjust to change outside industrial relations, with stagnating results for the industrial relations system as a whole. The conclusion is that the American model of collective bargaining as the predominant means of giving effect to an industrial relations system may not be enough.

The outline of the chapter from this point is to present the basic hypothesis of differences in bargaining structure, and follow this by an examination of structure in practice, the roles of the industrial parties, and a look at the operation of collective bargaining. Thereafter we will look at the role of law in the systems, the extent of conflict, and industrial democracy before returning to evaluate the relative efficiencies of the American and European systems. Penultimately, it is proposed to examine the important political context within which the industrial relations system operates before proceeding to the conclusions.

The Hypothesis

The underlying hypothesis builds on that of Clegg,[9] who saw the structure of bargaining as an important determinant of union roles and behavior. Clegg argued inter alia the following propositions:

1. Union government is relatively centralized where agreements are made at an industry or national level and relatively decentralized where they are made at regional or plant level.

2. Factionalism in unions is linked with decentralization in union government and hence with the level of bargaining.

3. Where the scope for plant bargaining is narrow, or where its independence is limited by the law or by the joint action of the parties, workplace organization plays a minor part in union

---

[9] H. A. Clegg, *Trade Unionism Under Collective Bargaining* (Oxford: Blackwell, 1976).

government. Conversely, where plant bargaining is important, it will affect the extent and nature of union organization at this level.

4. Strikes are expected to be few where collective bargaining is conducted at higher levels, and numerous where there is plant bargaining.

5. Where bargaining is at a high level, there has been a development of schemes of worker-directors and consultative arrangements to supplement collective bargaining, but these are not felt to be so necessary by unions where there is decentralized bargaining.

Clegg was dealing with aspects of union organization and behavior under collective bargaining, but it is possible to extend his approach to other aspects of industrial. relations.

6. Bargaining, and therefore organization, at a national or centralized level is likely to give much better access to the political and macroeconomic decision-making processes than in a decentralized bargaining structure. This is both because the industrial parties are more capable of delivering results for the policy-makers than in a decentralized system and also because the industrial relations system tends to become meshed into the economic and political systems.

7. From this it follows that national labor policies are easier to carry out under a centralized than a decentralized system and that there is more likely to be co-option of the industrial parties in some form of shared decision-making. Terms such as bargained corporatism and the social contract are associated with this tendency.[10]

8. It also follows that centralized bargaining is more compatible with the direct participation of the industrial parties, and especially unions, in politics. Moreover it leads to what Barbash has called economic policy unionism, which in his terms is characterized by "a union undertaking to relate its protective demands in collective bargaining and legislation to specified national policy goals."[11]

9. Under centralized bargaining, recognition of unions as a

[10] C. Crouch, *Class Conflict and the Industrial Relations Crisis* (London: Heinemann Books, 1977); Solomon Barkin, "The Total Labor Package from Wage Bargain to Social Contract," *Journal of Economic Issues* 11 (June 1977).

[11] Jack Barbash, *Trade Unions and National Economic Policy* (Baltimore: Johns Hopkins University Press, 1972), p. 161.

prerequisite for collective bargaining is only of limited significance once a certain threshold density has been achieved. This is because the reach of collective bargaining is more determined by the extent of employer association membership than by the unionization of any one plant or firm, and since employers adhere to the terms of the agreement in any case,[12] they have no reason not to permit or even encourage unionization. Under a decentralized structure, on the other hand, recognition is a vital issue at every plant in an industry. Even allowing for pattern-setting, there will be differences in terms and conditions between plants, and if the nonunion sector is or becomes sizable, it may significantly affect union bargaining power in the organized plants.

10. Centralized bargaining is likely to be less intensive or detailed than decentralized bargaining, which can be geared much more easily to the needs of particular workplaces. In this sense, decentralized bargaining may be intrinsically more satisfying to the workers and managers who have to live under the agreement.

11. Centralized bargaining is likely to be associated with rather different forms of law than is decentralized bargaining. Because centralized bargaining cannot have great depth or detail and because political consensus is easier to achieve, there will be a tendency to set legislative regulations over some of the areas that might otherwise be covered by collective bargaining. By contrast, decentralized bargaining, because it is likely to have a higher level of conflict, as noted in (4) above, is likely to have law which deals in more detail with the behavioral aspects of bargaining.

The above propositions are intended as a starting point for discussing differences in American and European trends, but of course political, economic, and social factors not directly related to the industrial relations system have also had a considerable impact.[13]

---

[12] In some cases employers took the initiative in creating wage boards without recognizing unions (A. Flanders, "Collective Bargaining," in *The System of Industrial Relations in Great Britain*, eds. Flanders and Clegg (Oxford: Blackwell, 1954), p. 269).

[13] Some writers have stressed these factors rather than the internal structural aspects espoused by Clegg. Thus Shalev: "I would argue that collective bargaining arrangements are reflections of the distribution of power and the outcome of conflicts between labour movements, employers and the state at the time these arrangements came into being. In so far as they subsequently acquire a degree of 'functional autonomy,' the institutions of industrial relations should still occupy no more than the position of intervening variables in comparative theories, the task of causal explanation being reserved for factors in the social, political and economic environment" (Shalev, p. 29).

And much more immediately for the industrial relations system, the propositions beg the very important question of how the structure of bargaining developed in the first place and how it changes over time. Clegg argues that:

> In most instances the answer is that the structures and attitudes of employers' associations and management are the main direct influences. Collective bargaining has its regulatory effect by restricting and controlling managerial decisions. Consequently it has its best chance of being effective when it operates at the points where managerial decisions are taken and employers' associations reach their collective conclusions.[14]

This is not accepted by Livernash,[15] who has seen unions as the major determinant of structure in the American context, and in any case it begs the further question of why employers have different structures and attitudes in different countries. However, these are issues beyond the scope of this paper.

Bargaining Structure

It is well accepted, in spite of the difficulties of definition, that the North American systems of collective bargaining are the most decentralized in the world. This is illustrated in Figure 1, which was produced in the late 1970s, but if a similar figure had been produced for 1950, it would certainly show an even larger disparity between the North American systems and the others, since the broad tendency has been for decentralization to take place in the European systems and some moderate centralization in the North American ones. According to the Bureau of Labor Statistics in 1974, the United States has some 194,000 collective agreements, and this is up from some 150,000 a few years earlier.[16] By comparison, the numbers of agreements in Europe range from a few hundreds to the lower thousands, although the process of supplementation makes the counting of separate agreements very difficult. Nevertheless, the coverage of collective bargaining is very

---

[14] Clegg, p. 10.

[15] E. Robert Livernash, "The Relation of Power to the Structure and Process of Collective Bargaining," *Journal of Law and Economics* 6 (October 1963).

[16] Quoted in Thomas A. Kochan, *Collective Bargaining and Industrial Relations* (Homewood, IL: Richard D. Irwin, 1980), p. 85.

Figure 1

RELATION OF CENTRALISATION OF STRUCTURE
TO LEVEL OF BARGAINING

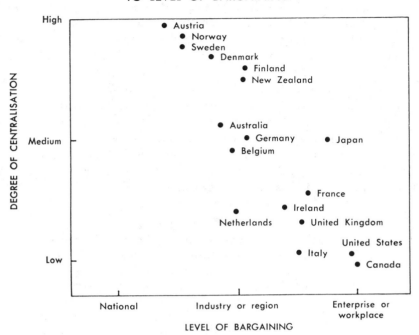

Source: C. A. Blyth, "The Interaction Between Collective Bargaining and Government Policies in Selected Member Countries," in *Collective Bargaining and Government Policies* (Paris: OECD, 1979), p. 92.

much greater in the more centralized European systems, where it is only distantly related to union membership. Although accurate figures are not available, coverage probably ranges from 70 percent to well over 90 percent, as compared to the 27 percent of the United States and 31 percent in Canada.[17] Inevitably, this very large discrepancy between the two sides of the Atlantic makes for a very different significance of collective bargaining in the economy.

The considerable differences between bargaining structures have

_____

[17] OECD, *Collective Bargaining and Government Policies in Ten OECD Countries.* It will be noticed that there is some difference union membership and collective bargaining coverage in the U.S. as well as Europe, although nothing like as much. See Kochan, Table 5-2, p. 129.

been best characterized by Ulman,[18] who postulated two distinctive models: (A) reflecting the system generally in the U.S. manufacturing sector, and (B) reflecting the model found in much of Europe. Model (A) involves the negotiating of wages, fringes, and some working conditions between the company and one or more national unions, the latter connecting the company-wide wage settlements in the industry via pattern bargaining. Working conditions and, to a lesser degree, some pay questions are also negotiated at the plant level with local unions, and local and national unions are sequentially involved in grievance handling. Ulman saw this model as giving management "an arrangement designed to connect the wage setting and productivity determining activities as closely as possible" and as permitting the national union, for its part, "to perform vital and highly visible services for local officers and members alike in processing their grievances and policing the contract." [19] Model (B) on the other hand

> is characterised by wider separation of the centres of decision-making and more overlap in the determination of pay. Pay is determined by formal industry-wide bargaining and again, less formally at plant level by management activity either unilaterally or under pressure from shop stewards or local shop committees; the company-wide level tends to drop out as a visible locus of wage determination. The role of the national union in the determination of non-pecuniary conditions and in the disposition of grievances is minimal; these functions tend to be discharged by management and/or local work groups, as in the determination of local wage supplements, and also by legislative enactment and labour courts.[20]

Ulman concluded by arguing "(a) that connective bargaining under model (A) might make for less inflationary and less restrictive settlements and that (b) that under certain circumstances company level bargaining under model (A) need not result in fatter settlements than industry-wide bargaining under model (B)." This result would be because "the closer linkage of working conditions, security, grievance settlement, and wages makes model (A)

[18] Lloyd Ulman, "Connective Bargaining and Competitive Bargaining," *Scottish Journal of Political Economy* 21 (June 1974).

[19] *Ibid.*, pp. 99–100.

[20] *Ibid.*, pp. 100–101.

a presumptively more efficient system of industrial relations than model (B)." [21] We shall examine this hypothesis later.

The continued relevance of Ulman's models should not, however, conceal the extent of structural change. That in the American system over recent years has been relatively small, and its origins have been largely economic in nature, with such factors as the widening of product or labor markets, the growing size of companies, and coalition bargaining being important influences. There has also been a certain amount of governmental pressure to increase the size of units in areas where whipsawing has been frequent, as in some parts of the construction industry. [22] But, on the whole, the configuration of bargaining structure in the United States in 1980 is not vastly different from that in 1950, although there are of course significant changes in the balance of individual sectors, most notably the public sector. By comparison, changes in European systems have been more substantial, usually less planned or even intended, and not always embodied in formal institutional structures. The Donovan Commission noted in 1968 that:

> Britain has two systems of industrial relations. The one is the formal system embodied in the official institutions. The other is the informal system created by the actual behaviour of trade unions and employers' associations, of managers, shop stewards and workers. . . . The formal and informal systems are in conflict. The informal system undermines the regulative effect of industry-wide agreements. . . . Nevertheless, the assumptions of the formal system still exert a powerful influence over men's minds and prevent the informal system from developing into an effective and orderly method of regulation. [23]

The situation in Italy has been similar to that in Britain, and even in a centralized country such as Sweden there has been widespread wage drift, while in the Netherlands the highly centralized

---

[21] *Ibid.*, p. 107.

[22] Lewin notes that John T. Dunlop resigned as Secretary of Labor when the picketing bill for the construction industry was vetoed, because he felt that this would have helped reduce the degree of decentralization in the industry (David Lewin, "The Impact of Unionism on American Business: Evidence for an Assessment," *Columbia Journal of World Business* (Winter 1978), p. 103).

[23] Royal Commission on Trade Unions and Employers' Associations, Chairman Lord Donovan (London: Her Majesty's Stationery Office, Cmnd 3623, 1968), p. 12.

bargaining system of immediate post-World War II period was destroyed in the mid-1960s by powerful centrifugal forces, due to the different economic circumstances of different industries, and industry-wide bargaining once again became the most general pattern. France is probably the country where there has been less change than elsewhere, and the cautious approach found there is well expressed by Reynaud:

> Several large firms have elaborated a policy of decentralization for social problems, giving more authority to the local managers. . . . But this policy is at best applied very gradually by those who advocate it and has had little echo among the great bulk of medium-sized companies. The trend toward plant or shop bargaining and toward some degree of direct expression of work groups found no institutional expression, and it was severely constrained by the economic crises.[24]

Employers

Compared with Western Europe, where employer cooperation has a history which often predated unionism, American employers have never organized to the same extent for any purposes, and there are no significant signs of change. There is, of course, a considerable amount of multi-employer bargaining in the U.S., although very little at industry level, and there are powerful employer lobbies in Washington, as the labor movement has discovered in recent years. But the differences between America and Europe are arguably much more significant on the employer side than on the union side, and are worth some attention.

The sheer size of America has something to do with the difference, but two other factors are probably much more important. One is the rapid emergence of large companies under American industrialization, which did not need to be serviced by employer associations; this was particularly true given that the extensive unionization of American manufacturing was not until the 1930s. By contrast, European employers at a relatively early stage of economic development saw an advantage in taking costs out of the sphere of competition and of forming associations to respond to the growth of unions. The other factor, which partly results from

---

[24] J. D. Reynaud, "France," in *Towards Industrial Democracy*, ed. B. C. Roberts (London: Croom Helm, 1979), p. 76.

the preceding one, is the antitrust ethos which has always been strong in America, and which resulted in large part from populist reaction to the growth of the large companies. But once American industrial relations had taken on its special characteristics of decentralized organization, there was no real reason for employers' associations to form. European employer organizations essentially exist to protect the marginal firm; large firms increasingly act outside of or even leave their associations in order to pay higher rates for higher performance and to co-ordinate and professionalize their industrial relations. There was no need to protect the marginal firm in America because in some cases the unions have never been powerful enough to threaten it by imposing unacceptable standards,[25] in others because pattern bargaining performed some of the same functions. There has, of course, been a good deal of informal cooperation even in large-scale industry, and in small-scale industries employer associations have been the norm. The implications of employer structure in America are twofold. One is that there has never been a central focus for employer dealings with government on macroeconomic issues, and this has been one important missing factor in the possible development of corporatist tendencies.[26] The other is that there was a necessity for professionalism in industrial relations at the plant and company levels, and for all the perceived ambiguities of the personnel function in the U.S.,[27] it was and is better trained and possesses a more clearcut role and higher status than in Europe. We now look more explicitly at how companies handle labor relations in the U.S.

Most large American employers have been able to develop wellorganized routines for industrial relations and, as a Conference Board report has put it,[28] to "manage" coexistence. Labor relations has become highly centralized within the company, with control of bargaining at the corporate level even where bargaining is ostensi-

---

[25] Even beyond the reach of employers' associations, many European countries have a capacity for legal extension of industry-wide collective agreements.

[26] But cf. Robert J. Flanagan, "The National Accord as a Social Contract," *Industrial and Labor Relations Review* 34 (October 1980).

[27] G. Ritzer and H. Trice, *An Occupation in Conflict: A Study of the Personnel Manager* (Ithaca: New York State School of Industrial and Labor Relations, Cornell University, 1969).

[28] Audrey Freedman, *Managing Labor Relations* (New York: The Conference Board, 1979).

bly at plant level. In three-fifths of the Conference Board companies, the Chief Executive Officer has final authority over the labor-cost terms of bargaining, but beyond this there are a wide number of activities primarily carried out by specialized staff functions. The survey interestingly reports that on wage and benefit targets, one quarter of the companies achieved their target, one quarter negotiated a package below the target cost, and the other half settled above their target. Even in this latter instance, however, the extent of overshoot was less than 1 percent for more than half the companies. With some caveat about the target-setting process, this indicates not only a capacity to plan, but also power to achieve targets; it is also significant that 88 percent thought that agreements, when reached, would stick. But the basic criteria for evaluation of the labor relations function are economic; as the survey concluded: "The Wild West imagery of labor relations is no longer appropriate. . . . Labor relations now occupies a much more complex world of economic production functions." [29] The companies themselves seemed well satisfied with the outcomes and, indeed, the system as a whole, although less satisfaction was expressed with those aspects relating to individuals, such as morale and productivity, than with those concerned with bargaining.

The overall picture is therefore one in which American employers feel that their labor relations are manageable, predictable, and stable and that this will continue into the future. Often the union performs useful quasi-managerial functions for them and even if most would rather do without unions and resist organization at new plants, from this picture it is only at the margin that there is a threat to established relationships as a result of employer withdrawal. This margin is important, however, because it must be seen in conjunction with what Kochan has called "the growth of aggressive, sophisticated, and generally successful attempts to avoid unions," [30] while Raskin has also warned that many companies are questioning whether their investment in union good will pays dividends. [31] Such developments are especially connected with

[29] *Ibid.*, p. 72.

[30] Thomas A. Kochan, "An American Perspective on the Integration of the Behavioural Sciences into Industrial Relations," in *The Behavioural Sciences and Industrial Relations: Some Problems of Integration*, ed. A. Thomson and M. Warner (Farnborough: Gower Press, 1981), p. 8.

[31] A. H. Raskin, "Management Comes Out Swinging," *Proceedings of the 31st Annual Meeting, Industrial Relations Research Association*, 1978, p. 228.

the geographical changes in American industry, as Rosow has noted:

> Expansion of plants to the Sunbelt and other areas with little unionization is usually preceded by plans to build a non-union fence around the new facilities. This includes offering attractive wages, benefits and working conditions, as well as establishing selection procedures and training to ensure a union-free organization. These employer efforts are not consistent or failsafe, yet the willingness to anticipate employee needs and to offer as much or more than the unions before they can get in is stronger than ever.[32]

Another reason for the growth of antiunion activities has undoubtedly been the economic pressures of the last decade, of inflation, low profitability, greatly increased foreign competition, and the consequent desire on the part of management to have as free a hand as possible. Decentralization has been a disadvantage to the unions here because of the competitive posturing required and the implication that union recognition is a comment on managerial human relations skills.

Managements and employer associations in Europe have developed along very different lines than those in the United States. There has until recently been far less professionalism at the company and plant, and indeed a 1954 study by Harbison and Burgess of France, Italy, and Belgium found an attitude of autocratic paternalism, with an undermanned but highly centralized management structure.[33] Communication was from the top down with little or nothing in the reverse direction. Most industrial relations issues in this period were in any case left to the employers associations.

Management has now changed a great deal in Europe, both in terms of increased professionalism, and especially in the extent to which they have been forced to accept unions as an integral part of the socioeconomic system. A perspective of Italy published in 1980 is particularly illustrative:

> Management, so far largely inactive in shaping industrial

---

[32] Jerome Rosow, Industrial Relations Research Association Newsletter, 1979, p. 1.

[33] Frederick Harbison and G. Burgess, "Management in Post War Europe," American Journal of Sociology 60 (September 1954).

relations policies, is preoccupied by the decreasing legitimacy of its power within the enterprise and also within the socio-political system. . . . On the other hand, the management of large companies in particular realizes that sheer resistance to the encroachment of trade unions is not enough. Positive solutions need to be offered. . . . The leadership of Confindustria appears also to agree that the objective of more stable industrial relations cannot be attained simply by going back to the rigid bargaining structure of the sixties or by reducing the scope for industrial conflict through legal regulations. It seems aware of the need to form a consensus on unresolved issues . . . in order to foster more rational industrial relations.[34]

Similarly, Reynaud reports that employers are one of the groups that has altered most in French society,[35] with the CNPF taking initiatives in similar areas to Confindustria such as redundancy, consultation, and working conditions. In Germany there has always been a high degree of sophistication in the BDA, but after their immediate postwar lack of popular trust, the employers have become more aggressive, as the constitutional challenge to the new Codetermination Act indicates; nevertheless, the felt need for consensus by Germany employers has always been strong. In Britain there has been a decline in the significance of industry associations as bargaining has become increasingly decentralized, but to counter this there has been the creation in 1965 and rise to a position of major significance (but still less than the TUC) of the Confederation of British Industry.[36]

Large European companies have also generally been forced to consider the overall policy of their enterprises apart from their association membership.[37] Since the employer association is geared to the marginal firm, the large firms have been under pressure to pay more and to seek higher standards and efficiencies. Some firms have resigned from their associations, but more have developed supplementary policies or agreements over and above the industry

---

[34] T. Treu, "Italy," in Roberts, ed., *Towards Industrial Democracy*, p. 93.

[35] Reynaud, p. 56.

[36] This was a classic case of an institution being created for corporatist purposes, since the Labor Government of that period badly needed an employer organization with which to negotiate its ill-fated National Plan.

[37] W. Brown and M. Terry, "The Changing Nature of National Wage Agreements," *Scottish Journal of Political Economy* 25 (June 1978).

agreement. These trends are somewhat toward the American model, but in terms of their changing relative position vis-à-vis the unions European employers stand in very considerable contrast to the picture of American employers outlined above. It is true that in many European countries the strike record is much better than in the U.S., but the foundations of the whole system have been much less stable both in relation to the immediate challenges of the unions and the underlying political system. There has been no equivalent study in Europe to the Conference Board survey from which attitudes can be gauged, but employers everywhere have seen institutional and legislative advances by the unions and a growing challenge from the political system, with unions playing a leading role, to the principles of the capitalist system. It is paradoxically in those countries with the most outwardly stable systems of industrial relations that the challenge has been most coherently pressed through proposals such as the Meidner Plan in Sweden and the union proposals for the extension of codetermination in West Germany.[38] In other countries the challenge for employers has been that of more immediate firefighting resulting from the decentralization of bargaining, but ideological issues are not far from the surface. Moreover, unlike American employers escaping to the Sunbelt, European employers have nowhere in their own countries to hide, and it is an interesting comment that at least some of the European capital which has recently flowed into the U.S. is reported to have done so to avoid unions.

Unions

There is no space available to do justice to the diversity of characteristics both within and between the labor movements in the United States and Europe; this is especially so of the very important organizational, coverage, and ideological differences to be found within Europe.[39] It is therefore proposed to review the three main common characteristics of European unionism and use these as a base with which to compare the American situation.

---

[38] R. Meidner, *Employer Investment Funds* (London: George Allen and Unwin, 1978); *Mitbestimmung in Unternehuen* (Bundestags-Drucksache VI/334—The Biedenkopf Report, 1970); B. Wilpert, "Research on Industrial Democracy: The German Case," *Industrial Relations* 6 (Spring 1975).

[39] W. Kendall, *The Labour Movement in Europe* (London: Allen Lane, 1975).

First, the European unions have the benefit of a wide coverage of collective bargaining based on employer association coverage, and even beyond that in many countries there are legislative means for extending the operation of collective agreements. This means that union membership is not the crucial factor that it is in the United States, although, of course, it is far from unimportant.[40] Union memberships in the period under review have generally grown, if not dramatically, but more importantly they have managed to respond to changing industrial and labor force structures, especially in the white-collar field. In some countries the growth of the white-collar labor force has been taken up by separate confederations, in others within the blue-collar confederations, but everywhere the barriers of status which have appeared to make unionism less relevant to the salariat have been breached, in part due to the very high coverage in the public sector.

Second, European unions have been centralized in structure, at least until recently. Their focal point of operation was generally industry-wide bargaining, which meant that there was no strong reason for an organizational presence at plant level. Indeed, in several countries this was effectively precluded by the legislative provision of works councils. However, over the period under review there has been a considerable move on the part of the unions, and often backed by legislation, to establish themselves at the plant level as various aspects of bargaining have appeared at this level. Even so, such moves are far from complete, perhaps especially in Britain and Italy where plant bargaining developed more spontaneously and strongly, and quasi-autonomous bodies with less than complete allegiance to the parent unions grew up. At the same time, changes in the focus of national economic policy in many European countries have resulted in the strengthening of the confederation level for the purpose of corporatist bargaining with governments and national employer bodies.

Third, European unions are political,[41] often in the sense of

---

[40] No comparative union membership statistics are provided because statistics for key countries such as France and Italy are considered unreliable to the point of meaninglessness, and, of course, American statistics are provided elsewhere in this volume. The most comprehensive discussion of comparative union statistics is in G. S. Bain and R. Price, *Profiles of Union Growth: A Comparative Statistical Portrait of Eight Countries* (Oxford: Basil Blackwell, 1980).

[41] See the symposium on European unions and politics in *Industrial and Labor Relations Review* 28, Nos. 1 and 2 (October 1974 and January 1975).

being associated with a political party, but also in the sense of having ideological objectives of more or less radical change in society. Over the period this ideological dimension has become more pronounced in most European unions, although very few have gone to the lengths of defining their alternative society in any rigorous way.[42] It is noticeable that in countries such as Sweden and Britain, where the main union groupings are closely associated with the socialist parties, that the unions have moved from being on the right wing of their party to the left wing, and that in those countries where Catholic unionism has been strong there has been a tendency to become more overtly political and less religious. These ideological movements are not necessarily shared by the union membership, but the economic and materialist aspirations of the membership have tended to produce a degree of militancy in bargaining since the late 1960s which can be portrayed as having ideological significance.[43]

After this all-too-brief thumbnail sketch, we now turn to the considerable contrast presented by the American labor movement. The first striking feature of contrast between the American and other industrial relations systems has been the diminishing proportion of union membership in the United States, which has fallen from approximately one-third of nonagricultural workers in 1950 to less than a quarter at the present time.[44] But the overall figures hide the major structural differences between America and other countries. American unionism is entrenched in the areas of the economy which are declining or likely to grow, at best, slowly, namely, in white, male, private-sector, manufacturing, northern, urban, large-scale industry. Almost all these are areas of decline within the context of the total labor force. Only in the public sector has there been union vitality and growth over the last couple of decades, but from an extremely low base, and even here there seems to be a levelling off now.[45] By comparison, European

---

[42] But see the series of major publications by the Swedish LO, including T. L. Johnston, ed. and trans., *Economic Expansion and Structural Change: A Trade Union Manifesto* (London: Allen and Unwin, 1963); and Meidner.

[43] Crouch and Pizzorno.

[44] Kochan, *Collective Bargaining*, Tables 5-1 and 5-2, and for the most detailed analysis, Richard B. Freeman and James L. Medoff, "New Estimates of Private Sector Unionism in the United States," *Industrial and Labor Relations Review* 32 (January 1979).

[45] Thus Cohen argues that there has been a public reaction against

countries do not have the massive gaps that are apparent in American union coverage, or the big differences even within categories. It must also be remembered that most of Western Europe, with the major exception of Britain and Denmark, has no union security provisions to enforce union membership.[46]

Moreover, the loss of American union membership has not only been a function of the massive structural changes in the labor force from manufacturing to nonmanufacturing, significant though these have been. There has also been a considerable drop in the percentage organized both within manufacturing and within nonmanufacturing separately. The losses are not large and they are by no means irreversible, but they illustrate a worrying momentum for labor. As Roomkin and Juris put it: "Because bargaining power is still strongly related to union penetration and union penetration is declining, we expect to see significant changes in the industrial relations systems in manufacturing and construction."[47] Unions are not only winning smaller and, indeed, less than half the numbers of certification elections, but are now beginning to lose very significant numbers of decertification elections.[48] The growth of antiunion consultancy has been a feature of the last decade, and a 250 percent growth in illegal discharge for union activity between 1961 and 1976 has been reported.[49]

The reasons for American union growth have tended to be more dependent upon external factors than in almost any other

---

public-sector unions and denies the argument that they are inherently powerful (Sanford Cohen, "Does Public Sector Unionism Diminish Democracy?" *Industrial and Labor Relations Review* 32 (January 1979).

[46] It is a moot point as to the effect of union security provisions. Some have argued that the right-to-work laws in some 20 states have had little effect (Frederic Meyers, *Right-to-Work in Practice* (New York: Fund for the Republic, 1959)). But this is rather different from estimating the effect had there never been any union security clause in the Wagner Act. It is also to be noted that a case has been brought before the European Human Rights Court to decide whether the union shop is an infringement of personal liberty and a preliminary hearing has decided that it is. (*Industrial Relations Europe* 11 (March 1981), p. 1.)

[47] Myron Roomkin and Hervey A. Juris, "Unions in the Traditional Sectors: The Mid-Life Passage of the Labor Movement," *Proceedings of the 31st Annual Meeting, Industrial Relations Research Association*, 1978, p. 221.

[48] The numbers of decertification elections rose from 234 in 1967 to 849 in 1977, and the percentage lost by unions rose from 70.5 percent to 76.0 percent (Kochan, *Collective Bargaining*, p. 140).

[49] W. Tillery, "Conventions," *Monthly Labor Review* 101 (March 1978), p. 36.

country;[50] by external is meant the pressures of war, inflation, the business cycle, or the impact of favorable legislation, rather than personal motivation because the cultural drives which encourage collectivist and group action in other countries seem in the United States to be replaced by a pervasive individualism. There are no external events such as produced the periods of growth of unionism in the past which are at all discernible on the horizon today. Recent attempts to use political power to gain a better legislative mechanism for organization have merely led to a public exposure of union lack of power, and hence an enhanced loss of credibility. Recent legislation may in fact have had the paradoxical effect that the expansion in legislated job rights may have diminished the grievance-handling protective function which was always a major appeal of American unionism. The only economic pressure which seems favorable is the world recession, but this by itself would seem to be an unlikely source of union growth without some other trigger such as governmental action; indeed, the recession both internationally and nationally may have increased the union wage differential and increased the likelihood of nonunion substitution.[51] This appears to have happened in construction. We therefore turn to look within the union movement for sources of growth.

The organizational structure of the union movement itself has several possible dimensions relating to membership growth. One is the absence of any strategy for developing a structure which might facilitate growth in the key white-collar sector. There is no union which appears likely to be able to organize white-collar workers in the private sector; the jealousy of the unions within the AFL-CIO makes it unlikely that such a union can be chartered, and it is also unlikely that the predominantly manual unions will have sufficient attraction for white-collar workers to be able to encompass them within the existing structure. Moreover, American legislation has proved to be of little use to white-collar workers;

---

[50] G. S. Bain and F. Elsheikh, *Union Growth and the Business Cycle* (Oxford: Blackwell, 1976); Woodrow L. Ginsburg, "Union Growth, Government, and Structure," in *A Review of Industrial Relations Research*, Vol. 1 (Madison, WI: Industrial Relations Research Association, 1970).

[51] The widening of the union differential in periods of recession is a well observed phenomenon (H. Gregg Lewis, *Unionism and Relative Wages in the United States* (Chicago: University of Chicago Press, 1963)). This result would also follow from union pushfulness (Kochan, *Collective Bargaining*, p. 139).

supervisors and those in authority are excluded, while the need for a majority in an election has proved too much for most other white-collar groups.

Second, the AFL-CIO as the central confederation is less able than its counterparts elsewhere to bargain nationally as the acknowledged representative of the total labor force or, more importantly for membership purposes, to give strong central leadership to the labor movement. This is in part due to low coverage and a fissiparous labor force, in part to political forces, but also because its affiliates are unwilling to delegate power to it. This lack of delegation follows in turn from the degree of decentralization of bargaining, and it is indeed arguable that the single central federation is weaker than either of its components were separately, since each separate labor movement required a strong center for defensive purposes, but now the national unions can be more self-sufficient. In an international survey,[52] Windmuller concluded that the AFL-CIO was among the weakest of the national centers on the basis of three criteria: the confederation's share of total income; the degree of interaction in affiliate union affairs; and participation in setting the terms of employment.[53] The only criterion on which the AFL-CIO was given less than the lowest marking in Windmuller's categorization was intervention in the affairs of affiliates, and this on the basis of its disciplining and expelling of unions for corruption. These events, however, took place quite soon after the merger, and it is arguable that the Federation would not repeat such actions, especially since a significant proportion of union members lie outside its ranks. The other reasons for the weakness of the AFL-CIO are essentially to do with the fact that Washington is relatively less important in the economic process than the capitals of other countries, that

---

[52] John P. Windmuller, "The Authority of National Trade Union Confederations: A Comparative Analysis," in *Union Power and Public Policy*, David B. Lipsky, ed. (Ithaca: New York State School of Industrial and Labor Relations, Cornell University, 1975).

[53] Some of the centers which also ranked low on Windmuller's scale may well have increased their relative ranking since he wrote, in line with the general argument about the increased politicization of industrial relations in recent years. One such example would be the increased involvement of the British TUC in national-level bargaining over wages under the Wilson and Callaghan Labor Governments. (A. W. J. Thomson, "Trade Unions and the Corporate State in Britain," *Industrial and Labor Relations Review* 33 (October 1979), p. 51.)

legislation is relatively less central to American labor's interests, and that labor does not exert much influence there anyway.

Third, a strategy for growth would require considerable investment. But a good deal of research has shown that American union members view their unions in a fairly narrow instrumental way,[54] and this does not include using union funds for organizational purposes. Members want services directly related to themselves, and unless new organization is likely to add to the existing members' bargaining power, the existing members see no reason why it should be carried out. This is partly connected to the individual decision to join or not join a union. Many of the pressures to join unions in Europe and Japan result from collectivist or class-based pressures. By contrast, American workers tend to view unions as means of achieving their job-related objectives. A union is therefore not taken as part of a total social philosophy, but rather in order to achieve improved terms and conditions of employment. In the most thorough recent study,[55] Kochan has however noted that there are relatively few distinctions between categories of workers with respect of their propensity to join unions, although nonwhite workers were much more willing to organize than whites. Even among southern and white-collar workers there appeared to be no uniform antiunion orientation except in the managerial and administrative areas. This suggests that the problem is one of tapping instrumental objectives in competition with management, rather than facing an ideological barrier. But one further interesting feature of Kochan's study was that there was less orientation to join unions in very large establishments than there was in medium-sized ones; he suggests that this may be due to the ability of larger employers to offer sufficiently high wages and other benefits to reduce the incentive to join the unions. This illustrates the dilemma for unions of high organizing costs per member gained, since there are high fixed costs and low variable costs in any organizing situation.

Nevertheless, within the framework of what they see as their role, American unions appear to do a good job for their members.

---

[54] Thomas A. Kochan, "How American Workers View Labor Unions," *Monthly Labor Review* 102 (April 1979); T. V. Purcell, *The Worker Speaks His Mind on Company and Union* (Cambridge, MA: Harvard University Press, 1956).

[55] Kochan, *ibid.*

They always have been, and still are, relatively professional by world standards, and their nonwage contribution is probably at least as important as the economic contribution. Their structure maintains a reasonable balance of power between the various levels within unions and internal communications seem generally to be better than in Europe. There seems to be no evidence that the membership wants any different kind of representation, or that the leadership believes that there are radical new directions to pursue. We shall discuss the political dimension later, but at the day-to-day level of industrial relations, American unions must be judged as successful.

Collective Bargaining

Many of the trends in collective bargaining in the United States and Europe over the past 30 years have been in the same direction. In both there has been a widening of the scope of bargaining, although this has paradoxically been associated with a wider range of state regulations covering aspects of the employment relationship as well. The widening scope of bargaining has been much more marked in Europe than the U.S., largely because Europe started from a lower base. The period has also seen a major development of bargaining at the plant and company level in Europe, thus creating the basis for the type of detailed agreements which have been the hallmark of American bargaining. But the collective agreement still remains the cornerstone of the American relationship in a way which it has not yet generally achieved in Europe, where there is still more informality, more vagueness. However, the widening of scope in the United States has predominantly taken the form of fringe benefits, procedures, seniority, and job and union security, whereas that in Europe, while encompassing some of these items and obtaining others via legislative means, has tended to make more challenges to management rights, in keeping with the broader philosophy of antimanagerialism which suffuses European unionism. Nevertheless, it is probably still true that the net effect of collective bargaining in America is to give a greater degree of immediate job control than in Europe, although the total impact of collective bargaining in Europe is certainly greater at the level of the economy, and there are some cases in Europe, such as instances of resistance to layoffs or changes in technology, where European unions have exerted more control of a negative kind. One noticeable development in the U.S. which has had no real parallel in Europe has been the shift to the longer term contract since 1950, such that the great majority of contracts last three years. This has given an additional amount of predictability to the employer. This has held up remarkably well during inflation, although the widespread COLA clause does help here.

There are also much greater differences in Europe between establishments in relation to the scope of bargaining; industry-wide agreements cannot be as detailed as plant agreements, and there are wide variations within Europe as to the effectiveness of collective agreement coverage depending on whether the employer accepts his association's agreement, engages in supplementary bargaining, or has certain aspects of the industry agreement extended to him. In many instances in Europe, collective bargaining still has little relation to what actually happens at the plant, especially if there is no union presence at this level. In this sense, the impact of collective bargaining is much more uniform in the United States.

A second common development has been the rise of problems in public-sector bargaining. Although many of the American difficulties in this area in the last two decades have been about union organizational issues, others have been about the political dimensions of much public-sector bargaining, the ambiguities of structure on the employer side, and problems of setting criteria for the supply, demand, productivity, and financing of services.[56] All these latter issues have been at least equally important in Europe, and in fact with a larger and more densely unionized public sector in a period where a reaction to increasing public expenditure is setting in, these problems have brought the public sector into the forefront of concern about the impact of collective bargaining on the economy.

---

[56] The American literature on public-sector bargaining is too voluminous and too well known to require citing. The European literature is much less extensive. See Charles M. Rehmus, ed., *Public Employment Labor Relations: An Overview of Eleven Nations* (Ann Arbor: Institute of Labor and Industrial Relations, University of Michigan–Wayne State University, 1975); J. Schregle, "Labour Relations in the Public Sector," *International Labour Review* (November 1974); A. W. J. Thomson and P. B. Beaumont, *Public Sector Bargaining* (Farnborough: Saxon House, 1978).

A third dimension of collective bargaining common to both continents has been the growing complexity, formality, and multiplicity of grievance and negotiating procedures. Europe has tended to have more parallel procedures,[57] given the general supplementation of grievance procedures with a system of labor courts, and these latter have tended to become more influential as new regulatory legislation has accumulated. The internal grievance procedure has, however, tended to become more significant as well, especially where the decentralization of bargaining has taken place. In Britain in particular the grievance procedure has moved much closer to the American model, with several stages and sometimes a conclusion in arbitration. But even so, nowhere in Europe is the grievance procedure as important as in America, not least because the concept of contract administration through the procedure is not as well developed and there is not the same differentiation between rights and interests issues. Voluntary grievance arbitration is also far better developed in America and is indeed the ultimate guarantee of impartiality which makes the grievance system acceptable. However, the grievance process in the U.S. is not without problems. One aspect is that it has become much more formal over the period, much more concerned with the narrow interpretation of the language of the contract, much less with extending its scope. This has been inevitable as the parties themselves have become more sophisticated and as the contract itself has been fleshed out to codify most areas of uncertainty. But at the arbitration level the use of other cases as precedent, the almost court-room style of presenting evidence, and the increasing use of lawyers have made the process more rigid and remote than hitherto.[58] A second aspect for concern is that the traditional dominance of the internal grievance procedure has been challenged by external legal procedures permitting individuals or sometimes parties to bring cases under the agreement. We shall refer to this later in examining legal developments. On the negotiating procedure front, there has been more development in America than in Europe in the search for new negotiating procedures to diminish the likelihood of damaging strikes, with

---

[57] Benjamin Aaron, ed., *Labor Courts and Grievance Settlement in Western Europe* (Berkeley: University of California Press, 1971).

[58] R. W. Fleming, *The Labor Arbitration Process* (Urbana: University of Illinois Press, 1965).

proposals such as continuous negotiations, no-strike strikes, the experimental negotiation agreement in steel, and so on, but although imaginative, these have done little to change traditional patterns of bargaining.

Another area where there has been some growth of interest on both sides of the Atlantic is in the development of consultation and the creation of joint committees for specific purposes. In part this reflects growing economic problems, and a joint recognition of the need to face up to them. But again there is probably some difference in emphasis, with the American approach being to concentrate on the problem without it having any significant effect on the wider relationship, while the European approach on the union side at least is to see it as a contribution to joint decision-making. *Work in America* began,[59] or at least signalled, an impetus to move beyond traditional collective bargaining to new types of programs whereby almost two-thirds of one sample of bargaining units had at least one such committee, with health and safety the favorite topic.[60] Dyer, Lipsky, and Kochan found that there was indeed some willingness among unionists to consider joint programs in the quality-of-working-life area, some limited willingness in the productivity area, and very little in the traditional areas of collective bargaining.[61] But if, on the whole, Americans' goals in the development of new institutions are hardly radical, the same cannot be said of Europe, and we now turn to an examination of industrial democracy.

Industrial Democracy

The possibility of a greater involvement of employees and their union representatives in decision-making over and above that obtained in collective bargaining is one of the clearest distinctions between the United States and Europe since it has evinced an immense amount of interest and a fair amount of implementation in Europe, but very little indeed of either in the U.S.[62] There is

---

[59] *Work in America: Task Force Report for the Secretary of Health, Education, and Welfare* (Cambridge, MA: MIT Press, 1971).

[60] Kochan, *Collective Bargaining*, p. 423.

[61] Lee Dyer, David Lipsky, and Thomas Kochan, "Union Attitudes to Management Cooperation," *Industrial Relations* 16 (May 1977).

[62] Perhaps the most comprehensive review is "Industrial Democracy in International Perspective," *Annals of the American Academy of Political and Social Science* 431 (May 1977). Important American works are P. Blumberg,

no space to explore the various institutional dimensions of industrial democracy or its success or failure in Europe,[63] but the reasons for the disparity between the two sides of the Atlantic are of considerable interest. Part of the European interest is happenstance. West Germany wanted some institutional bulwark against the power of Hitler-tainted big business in the immediate postwar period, and codetermination fitted well with this goal. Thereafter codetermination became Germany's contribution to the Common Market, and it was incorporated into EEC policy in 1972.[64] The other big European countries, Britain, France, and Italy, only then began to respond.[65] But industrial democracy also satisfied the growing feeling that collective bargaining was not enough to enable unions to come to terms with many other corporate decisions which affected the labor force, or to provide unions with an ideological rationale as organizations rather than as part of a wider political movement. This was the genesis of some of the most developed thinking in the area, which has been mainly by the Swedish LO among the union movements, and it has been pursued by many left-wing groups distrustful of the centralized state and seeing unions as the most available vehicle for radical social change. The political dimension of industrial democracy is undoubtedly of the greatest significance. No union has or is likely to achieve industrial democracy in the sense of power-sharing over a wide range of company decisions purely by its economic power, but the political route to compulsory industrial democracy is a very real challenge to existing systems of industrial relations and one taken very seriously by employers.[66]

But underlying these two threads of development is the struc-

Industrial Democracy (London: Constable, 1968); G. Hunnius, G. Carson, and J. Case, eds., *Workers Control* (New York: Vintage Books, 1973).

[63] See Biedenkopf Report (note 38); Industrial Democracy in Europe–International Research Group, *European Industrial Relations* (London: Oxford University Press, 1980); and Industrial Democracy in Europe–International Research Group, "Participation: Formal Rules, Influence and Involvement," *Industrial Relations* 18 (Fall 1979).

[64] Proposal for a Fifth Directive on the Structure of Limited Liability Companies (EEC Doc. COM 172/887 fin, 1972).

[65] *Report of the Committee of Inquiry on Industrial Democracy*, Chairman Lord Bullock (London: HMSO Cmnd 6706, 1977); Rapport du Comité d'Étude pour la Reforme de l'Enterprise, Chairman Pierre Sudreau (Paris: La Documentation Française, 1975).

[66] H. G. Myrdal, "The Swedish Model—Will It Survive?" *British Journal of Industrial Relations* 18 (March 1980).

tural point articulated by Clegg, namely, that the pressure for industrial democracy is a function of the structure of bargaining. In those countries with centralized bargaining systems, there is little access to managerial decision-making at company and to a lesser extent at plant level, and industrial democracy is a logical means of achieving such success.[67] It is worth noting, however, that in both Britain and Italy, the two European countries where decentralization has proceeded furthest, many unions have tended to back away from a codetermination-type system and have sought to extend collective bargaining because they see the two approaches as conflicting with each other.[68] This explanation does not, however, indicate why American unions have not also sought to extend collective bargaining to areas such as investment, and here one must fall back partly on the limitations of Section 8(a) of LMRA but more on the culturally induced willingness of unions to leave the job of managing to management. In the now widely quoted words to Thomas Donahue of the AFL-CIO: "We do not seek to be a partner in management—to be most likely the junior partner in success and the senior partner in failure. We do not want to blur in any way the distinctions between the respective roles of management and labor in the plant." [69] A few examples of movement in the direction of more institutionalized participation in the United States can be adduced, but they are the exception that proves the rule.[70]

The Role of Law

Before assessing the role of law in the industrial relations systems of America and Europe, it is perhaps best to try to distinguish various different kinds of law in the industrial relations system. Kahn-Freund has suggested a taxonomy of auxiliary,

[67] Clegg, p. 83.

[68] TUC, The Trade Union Role in Industrial Policy (1977).

[69] Quoted in John T. Dunlop, "Past and Future Tendencies in American Labor Organizations," Daedalus 107 (Winter 1978), p. 91.

[70] G. Lodge and K. Henderson, "The United States," in Roberts, ed., Towards Industrial Democracy. They argue, contrary to most commentators, that there has been a growth of collectivist or communitarian values and an erosion of the Lockean values of individualism, property rights, competition, specialization, and a limited state. This may, of course, be so in relation to the eighteenth century, but it is certainly not true in relation to Europe, nor can one see that the growth of communitarian values is having a major impact on labor-management relationships in the United States.

restrictive, and regulatory law:[71] auxiliary law is that which helps the industrial parties to come together in a bargaining relationship; restrictive law essentially represents the Queensberry rules of collective bargaining behavior; and regulatory law covers the definition by legislation of substantive areas of the employment relation. Almost all countries now have elements of each of these three different kinds of law, but the balance, the history, and the approaches between them are often significantly different. In broad outline, America has concentrated much more upon the auxiliary and the restrictive aspects of law than the regulatory aspect, although it must also be noted that regulatory law has been an increasing feature of the American industrial relations system over the last two decades. By contrast, the European approach has had a much higher ratio of regulatory law.

The best rationale for American labor law has been provided by Bok,[72] who argued that the law was derived from the pre-existing industrial relations system and also from the wider culture. A permissive auxiliary law was eventually required because American society, with its highly individualistic slant, was not disposed to grant easy recognition to collective bodies such as unions. But the already decentralized nature of the system at the time of the passage of the Wagner Act also contributed to some of the unique features of American labor law. Exclusive representation was made necessary by the existing degree of interunion competition, but it also made more difficult the development of larger bargaining units, as evidenced by the great length of time that it has taken for coalition bargaining to develop in the United States. Again, the very detailed provisions for recognition, including the issues of unit determination and the unfair labor practice of failure to bargain in good faith, were made necessary by the unwillingness of employers to have any truck with unionism. These provisions further cemented the decentralization of the system, and the battles over unit determination between narrow and wide units never meant anything more than occupational groupings within the same employer. Thus once the auxiliary laws were created in order to take account of the existing system, they ex-

---

[71] O. Kahn-Freund, "Industrial Relations and the Law—Retrospect and Prospect," *British Journal of Industrial Relations* 7 (November 1969).

[72] Derek Bok, "Reflections on the Distinctive Character of American Labor Law," *Harvard Law Review* 84 (April 1971).

acerbated the decentralized aspects of that system and made it very difficult for it to change, even if there had been a willingness on the part of the industrial parties to develop much wider units. Moreover, once the decentralized system had been set up, once agreements had been made which amounted to the full rate of wages and not merely a minimum wage, it followed that there would be some considerable need for a battery of constraints on bargaining activities, because the stakes were extremely high and conflict for purely economic reasons tended to be extremely hard fought. As Bok again put it: "There is a price to be paid for decentralization and competitive rivalry in terms of the burden of government regulation needed to achieve the standards of behavior that society requires."[73] Moreover, once the laws were created, there was a process of judicial development: "An early articulation of simple standards is typically followed by a constant embellishment of exceptions, qualifications, complex reformulations and ad hoc decision-making."[74]

In Europe the law played a less significant role in the development of industrial relations. Much of the early recognition of unions took place outside any legal framework in France, Germany, Sweden, and Britain, and the common-law-based clashes between the law and the unions over bargaining behavior were as fierce in Britain as in the U.S., but they were ended by legislation in 1906. Moreover, a centralized bargaining system was unlikely to require much auxiliary or restrictive legislation because employers were likely to regard such a development as desirable and also because state attempts to impose on such large-scale relationships would have run a risk of rebuff not so likely in decentralized units. Changes in European law over the last two decades have been aimed at primarily three sets of objectives: first, the expansion of union rights, especially at the plant level; second, the expansion of union rights in respect of sharing in management decision-making; and third, the expansion of individual rights in respect of job security and welfare provisions.[75] The

---

[73] *Ibid.*, p. 1460.

[74] *Ibid.*, p. 1462.

[75] ILO, *Collective Bargaining*. In some respects individual rights and union rights merge in that the expression of individual rights can sometimes be vested in unions (M. Moran, "Citizens and Workers," *Political Quarterly* 50 (January-March 1979)). Moran has also argued that the expansion of

changes have been a function of two factors: the political power of labor and its allies, and the desire of governments to relate the law to what seems to be the balance of economic power in industry. These taken together have resulted in a considerable shift in the legal balance toward unions, in spite of occasional moves in the reverse direction such as the British acts of 1971 and 1980.[76]

In the postwar period, American law has moved in two rather separate directions. On the one hand the auxiliary and restrictive aspects of law are still essentially geared to achieving a satisfactory implementation of the 1935 principles. The arguments have become much more detailed, but in essence the debate has not moved forward from 1935 at a time when European issues are now much more concerned with the nature of control in industrial society.

On the other hand there has been an enormous expansion of regulation in the United States. Between 1960 and 1975 the number of regulatory programs administered by the Department of Labor tripled from 43 to 134, and Kochan has therefore argued that the basic premise underlying the National Labor Relations Act, the promotion and regulation of the process of collective bargaining but neutrality with respect to its substantive outcome, should be viewed as "mere historical rhetoric" rather than as an accurate description of present day reality.[77] He also argued that the regulation has been needed because collective bargaining has been inadequate. For that matter, the adequacy of the legislation can be questioned; as Bok has pointed out, American regulatory legislation is often restricted in coverage, and those excluded are arguably the most in need of coverage.[78] Unlike European unions, moreover, American unions have not strongly pursued legislation. As Barbash has noted: "The union in America employs law and its administration mainly as an auxiliary strategy. It is subordinate

---

industrial rights has been such as to place them on a par with the individual's political, civil, and social rights. It should also be noted that in Europe the changing balance between legal regulation and collective bargaining has not all been in the direction of the former; the gain for collective bargaining has been particularly true of France (Reynaud, p. 70).

[76] Industrial Relations Act C 72 1971; Employment Act C 42 1980. Both pieces of legislation were passed by Conservative Governments desirous of reducing the power of the unions.

[77] Kochan, *Collective Bargaining*, p. 478.

[78] Bok, p. 1417.

to collective bargaining because, by comparison (a) its effects on the terms of the employment relation are less clearly perceived by union people, (b) it is not necessarily as responsive to union influence and (c) it is not as adaptable to *particular* union interests." [79]

Many of the pieces of regulatory legislation which have been introduced in recent years create much more difficulty than earlier legislation in setting standards and need a great deal of judgment with which to operate them; this is the case with the equal employment legislation, the Occupational Health and Safety Act, and the various pieces of employment and training legislation. Some of these have been heavily criticized, as for example by Smith: "The confusion, uncertainty, constant change of regulation, and unstable body of law the past has produced in the pursuit of equal employment opportunity should not be a model for the future." [80]

Not only is the welter of legislation causing problems in its own right, but it is causing a major impact upon existing voluntary institutions, especially grievance and arbitration procedures. The *Trilogy* cases of 1960 had appeared to set arbitration decisions above the normal scope of review of the judicial system,[81] but the *Alexander v. Gardner-Denver* case of 1974 moved away from this by arguing that an arbitrator's decision in a case involving discrimination should not preclude judicial review of the substantive merits of the claim.[82] A further important result has been the growth of multiple remedies offered by overlapping jurisdictions in the industrial relations area. One company, Sears Roebuck, filed a suit against the government charging that the regulations to combat discrimination are impossible to comply with in the sense that compliance with one regulation is hindered by compliance with others.[83] Certainly choice of jurisdiction is now an important issue in deciding where the best chance of success

---

[79] Barbash, p. 193.

[80] A. Smith, "The Law and Equal Employment Opportunity: What's Past Should Not Be Prologue," *Industrial and Labor Relations Review* 33 (July 1980), p. 505.

[81] *United Steelworkers* v. *American Manufacturing Co.*, 363 U.S. 564 (1960); *United Steelworkers* v. *Warrior & Gulf Navigation Co.*, 363 U.S. 574 (1960); *United Steelworkers* v. *Enterprise Wheel & Car Corp.*, 363 U.S. 593 (1960).

[82] 415 U.S. 36 (1974).

[83] Kochan, *Collective Bargaining*, p. 480.

lies in an American industrial relations suit. As a result of public policy and public laws impinging in this way upon the previous autonomy of the industrial parties, the concept of a separate industrial system of justice for the shopfloor is no longer appropriate, which detracts to a very significant extent from one of the major strengths of the American system of industrial relations, that the parties could create and monitor their own industrial relations system. This growth of regulation has not unnaturally led to considerable dissatisfaction and also to concern for the bargaining system. Thus Dunlop has argued that regulatory legislation does many types of damage to the existing system, such as offering over-simplistic remedies to complex problems, being too rigid to apply to diverse settings, being extremely slow in adjudication, producing unintended consequences, creating side-effects which are as severe as the problems they are intended to cure, discouraging mutual accommodation and compromise, encouraging legalistic gamesmanship, creating a mass bureaucracy, and inevitably producing regulatory overlap.[84]

It can thus be argued that law in the United States is encroaching upon collective bargaining, with a net impact detrimental to the unions, both because it carries out labor's protective job for it, and also because many aspects of law are aimed at controlling unions as well as employers in their relations with individuals. At the same time American labor's strength depends upon the law, lacking sufficient inherent economic or political power, and although a policy set up in 1935 can sustain the industrial relations system for so long, eventually it requires further backing from the political system. However, this backing seems unlikely to be forthcoming. In 1961 Cohen suggested that shifts in national policy occur in response to major changes in the political access of interest groups and the ideology toward property rights in the larger society, which is a proxy for the ideology of society toward labor.[85] Both these aspects tend to be drifting against American labor, in contrast to what is happening in Europe.

Toward a Comparison of Relative Efficiencies

It will be recalled from the section dealing with bargaining

---

[84] Quoted in Kochan, *Collective Bargaining*, p. 430.

[85] Sanford Cohen, "An Analytical Framework for Labor Relations Law," *Industrial and Labor Relations Review* 14 (April 1961).

structure that Ulman has argued that the decentralized system of bargaining as found in the American manufacturing sector is presumptively more efficient than the centralized system found in Europe.[86] We now look at three criteria for testing this proposition, namely, wage inflation, productivity, and conflict, although Ulman was primarily interested only in the inflationary consequences. There are considerable dangers beyond shortage of space in trying to be too definitive about the results of such an examination, because not only are many potentially relevant variables omitted even within the industrial relations system, but factors external to the system may have a major impact on it. Nevertheless, Table 1 provides the most comprehensive set of comparative economic data over the period, covering the wage and productivity aspects for 11 countries in manufacturing industry. Data for the period 1950–1960 are unfortunately not available in directly comparable form; however, for the broad purposes of this essay, the patterns during that decade were sufficiently similar to those of the period 1960–1973 for the points made to be extended to the earlier decade also.

WAGE INFLATION

Table 1 suggests that the contribution of wages alone to inflation has been less in the United States than elsewhere, in that hourly compensation increased less than in any other country over all the three time periods recorded. American rates of inflation have themselves been well below the European average over the period, and American average wages, from being vastly higher than anywhere else in the world in 1950, have now been caught by several European countries such as Germany, Sweden, Denmark, and the Netherlands.[87] Although part of this catching-up process is due to exchange rate changes, most of it is real. In fact, if the various social welfare costs directly tied to employment are added to wages, American labor costs per hour become lower than the countries mentioned.[88]

Some considerable part of this lower rate of wage increase must be attributed to the collective bargaining system, thus en-

---

[86] See the section on "Bargaining Structure," above.

[87] Institute of the German Economy, *Wage Costs in Manufacturing Industry*, 1979.

[88] *Ibid.*

TABLE 1

Annual Percentage Change in Manufacturing 1960-1979: Selected Indicators for Eleven Countries

	Output			Output Per Hour			Hourly Compensation			Unit Labor Costs			Unit Labor Costs in US$		
	1960-79	1960-73	1973-79	1960-79	1960-73	1973-79	1960-79	1960-73	1973-79	1960-79	1960-73	1973-79	1960-79	1960-73	1973-79
U.S.	3.8	4.7	2.0	2.6	3.1	1.4	6.3	5.0	9.4	3.7	1.8	7.9	3.7	1.8	7.9
Canada	5.1	6.4	2.2	3.8	4.6	2.2	8.1	6.2	12.4	4.1	1.5	10.0	3.1	1.3	7.1
Japan	10.4	12.8	5.3	9.2	10.3	6.9	14.4	15.1	12.8	4.7	4.4	5.5	7.5	6.7	9.4
France	5.4	6.7	2.6	5.5	5.8	4.8	11.7	9.8	15.8	5.9	3.8	10.5	6.7	4.6	11.3
Germany	4.2	5.2	1.9	5.4	5.5	5.3	10.1	10.2	10.0	4.4	4.4	4.5	9.0	8.1	11.1
Italy	5.8	7.0	3.2	6.1	7.2	3.7	16.0	13.6	21.2	9.3	5.9	16.9	7.6	6.5	10.1
U.K.	1.8	3.0	-0.7	2.9	4.0	0.5	11.8	8.6	19.2	8.7	4.4	18.6	7.1	3.3	15.7
Belgium	5.0	6.7	1.4	6.7	7.0	6.0	11.7	10.9	13.5	4.7	3.6	7.1	7.7	5.8	12.2
Denmark	4.8	6.1	2.0	6.1	7.0	4.4	12.2	11.5	13.5	5.8	4.2	8.7	7.2	5.4	11.3
Netherlands	4.6	6.0	1.6	6.7	7.4	5.3	12.6	13.1	11.5	5.5	5.3	5.9	9.0	7.8	11.7
Sweden	3.8	5.5	0.3	5.3	6.7	2.4	11.8	10.4	15.0	6.2	3.5	12.3	7.2	4.8	12.5
Eight European countries	4.3	5.5	1.8	5.2	5.8	4.0	11.6	10.4	14.1	6.1	4.3	9.7	8.0	6.4	11.6
Ten Foreign countries	5.7	7.0	2.9	6.0	6.5	4.8	11.6	10.6	13.7	5.3	3.8	8.5	7.3	5.8	10.6

Source: Arthur Neef and Patricia Capdevielle "International Comparisons of Productivity and Labor Costs," *Monthly Labor Review* (December 1980), pp. 32-38.

dorsing Ulman's contention that a decentralized system of bargaining need not be more inflationary than a centralized one. In spite of pattern bargaining, the American system produces a good deal of competitive cost-consciousness on the part of individual firms, whereas in Europe, firms must accept a base wage and due to lack of detailed information about earnings, often allow supplemental bargaining to increase this. In neither aspect of bargaining does the firm exercise the degree of control that is true in the U.S. Two potential caveats, however, require to be made on this issue. One is that the very limited coverage of American collective bargaining is a strong deterrent to wage inflation in the covered sector. Second, U.S. real wage rates have actually declined since the early 1970s, which may be a function of the weakness of the unions as much as a comment on the structure of the system.

PRODUCTIVITY

All industrialized countries have become worried by falling productivity, but nowhere has this concern been more strongly expressed than in the U.S., even though GDP per employee is still higher than anywhere else in the world. As can be seen, American productivity growth over the whole period has been lower than in any other country. Such a trend runs counter to the concept of a more efficient bargaining system, and in particular to Ulman's argument that a higher rate of productivity growth due to more detailed bargaining would offset a tendency to higher wage increases. In fact, as we see, the reverse is the case: the U.S. has lower wage increases and lower productivity increases. Productivity, of course, includes many factors other than labor input, including the rate of technological change, which in turn is associated with investment and profitability. The fact remains that American productivity levels are very poor by international standards and, in fact, dropped under 1 percent over the 1977–1979 period. It is debatable, however, to what extent this can be attributed to industrial relations. Brown and Medoff found that unions were associated with a positive productivity effect of the same order of magnitude as the wage effect.[89] Moreover, American

---

[89] C. Brown and J. Medoff, "Trade Unions in the Production Process," *Journal of Political Economy* 86 (June 1978).

unions have been on the whole cooperative in achieving technological change,[90] while managements have certainly used the bargaining process to achieve objectives of their own, as opposed to providing higher wages with little in return, as has tended to be the case with industry-wide bargaining in Europe.

Taking productivity and wages together in unit labor costs, the United States again comes out very well, with the lowest rate of increase over the whole period, even if not since 1973, although it still remains below the overall average. Moreover, the key statistic is the exchange rate adjusted figure rather than the absolute increase, and the decline of the value of the dollar in relation to strong currencies such as the mark and the yen has maintained the American advantage after 1973 vis-à-vis all overseas countries. By these standards, therefore, the American industrial relations system has certainly not significantly reduced American competitiveness.

CONFLICT

North America and Europe differ very considerably in patterns of strikes, and a good deal of attention has been given to these.[91] Although groups of variables have been used, such as political, structural-institutional, and economic, there is considerable agreement that the bargaining structure is significant. The strike plays a very important part in the American bargaining process; it tends to be economic, professional, and calculated in nature, and its conduct is usually within the rules of the industrial relations game. By contrast, strikes in Europe are relatively rare at the formal level of industry bargaining, but when they do occur can have an economy-wide impact. But strikes do not last as long and are often intended as much to be a protest, sometimes a political protest, as to inflict economic damage on management. The European system also tends to generate more wildcat strikes, although these are of course far from unknown in the U.S.

---

[90] Sumner Slichter, James Healy, and E. Robert Livernash, *The Impact of Collective Bargaining on Management* (Washington: The Brookings Institution, 1960).

[91] A. Ross and P. Hartman, *Changing Patterns of Industrial Conflict* (New York: Wiley, 1960); D. Hibbs, "Industrial Conflict in Advanced Societies," *American Political Science Review* 70 (December 1976); D. Snyder, "Institutional Setting and Industrial Conflict," *American Sociological Review* 40 (June 1975); Shalev.

Hibbs took 15 advanced economies over the period 1950–1969, divided them into structural groupings, and examined them according to strike activity in terms of man days lost per 1,000 wage and salary earners, with the following results:[92]

	Bargaining Structure	*Strike Activity*
1.	Decentralized systems, characterized by company and plant bargaining, e.g., U.S.	425
2.	Centralized systems, characterized by industry-wide, multi-employer bargaining, e.g., U.K.	172
3.	Highly centralized systems, characterized by economy-wide bargaining, e.g., Sweden.	67

However, it should also be noted that when Hibbs introduced structure in a multiple regression analysis which controlled for real wages, unemployment, and profits, it did not achieve statistical significance.

Hibbs was dealing with the period up to 1969, and there have been significant changes in Europe since then, even though patterns in the U.S. have held relatively constant. The strikes in France in the wake of the student revolt of May 1968, the "long hot summer" in Italy in 1969, the coal strikes in Britain in 1972 and 1974 all had a profound influence on the industrial relations and, indeed, the political systems of those countries.[93] Even in Sweden and Germany the strike became a more significant factor than in the earlier postwar decades. Although that strike wave has diminished, all European nations are aware of the potential challenge of the strike to existing social and political institutions, in a way which does not seem remotely likely of the U.S. with its decentralized system. In other words, if there is a price to pay for the decentralized type of bargaining in terms of higher strike activity,[94] it is not a price which includes the potential social challenge of more centralized bargaining.

The implications to be drawn from this brief review of relative efficiencies must be inconclusive; but even if Ulman's thesis is not substantiated, there is nothing to suggest that the United States suffers any significant economic disadvantage from its industrial

[92] Hibbs.
[93] Crouch and Pizzorno. The Polish union, Solidarity, is certain to have a major impact on state-union relations in the Communist bloc.
[94] For the costs, see Neil W. Chamberlain, "Strikes in Contemporary Context," *Industrial and Labor Relations Review* 20 (July 1967).

relations system on the basis of the data provided. Efficiency, however, may not only be a statistical concept. It might be suggested that a decentralized system of bargaining tends to breed an adversarial relationship, and that there seems to be a growing recognition of the economic advantages of consensus at several levels in the industrial relations system.[95] But whatever the balance of advantage at the lower levels, account must also be taken of the higher levels. In particular, the industrial relations system interacts with and depends on the political system for its development and maintenance, and it would be unrealistic to attempt any final conclusions without setting it in its sociopolitical context.

The Political Context

Of all the differences between the European and American systems of industrial relations, perhaps the most immediately noticeable is the political and cultural context in which they operate.[96] Almost all European unions are ideological in the sense that they see their representational role as extending beyond the workplace into the political system for the purpose of radically changing the social and economic structure. All European countries have unions which are associated with, often very closely, political parties of a socialist or communist persuasion, and politics can generally be seen on a left-right ideological spectrum in which economic philosophy and social class play a very important role.

By contrast, the United States has never had a close connection between unionism and the political parties, nor have the parties themselves been formulated along the ideological spectrum which is general in Europe. The reasons for the absence of a labor party in the United States have often been examined: the absence of class structures, the small industrial labor force when the vote was obtained, the problem of organizing new parties within the complex federal structure, and, most importantly of all, the political attitudes of individualism, of pragmatism, almost of antiphilosophy which has permeated American political thought have all been put forward as partial explanations.[97] Bargaining struc-

---

[95] See, for example, *Business Week*, June 30, 1980.

[96] *Industrial and Labor Relations Review* Symposium (note 41); for the United States, the most recent book on the political role of unions is G. K. Wilson, *Unions in American National Politics* (London: Macmillan, 1979).

[97] Wilson, *ibid.*

ture has also played a not insignificant part, since it has not only contributed to the particularism of business unionism and its lack of claim to represent interests outside work, but also to weak central institutions. We are, however, here less concerned with the reasons than the implications of this situation.

In 1951 Avery Leiserson quoted the adage that "if an organization is to maintain its economic power it must be able to exert political power also" in respect of the American labor movement.[98] The truth of this adage is one of the major arguments of the present chapter, and the implication is that, for reasons to some extent outside its own control, the American labor movement is being undercut in terms of the backing it needs to maintain its strength and vitality. By contrast, most European unions have become increasingly important within their political systems and have made the industrial relations system a matter of major political significance. Following on the adage above, Leiserson went on to say, "Apparently determined to reject the road of independent party action, organized labor in 1950 has never before seemed so much involved in politics, so committed to raising funds for political and campaign activity, or so active on the congressional and national publicity stages."[99]

The situation seems far different now; labor was unable to exert enough influence in the 1970s to gain even limited objectives such as the 1978 labor law reform, and it played a very minor role in the 1980 election, whose result seems likely to reduce its influence further still. Yet as Raskin has noted, "Labor's most consequential battles in the 1980s are likely to be fought out in the political arena."[100] Lewin has argued that labor's political strength is considerable when acting in concert with other pressure groups, and that it is only when it is pursuing objectives of fairly narrow union interest that it has failed.[101] It is the contention put forward here that the political system has changed and that labor, as an old political bloc, has been able to do relatively little about it, although its own lack of cohesiveness, its inability to organize

[98] Avery Leiserson, "Organized Labor as a Pressure Group," *Annals of the American Academy of Political and Social Science* 274 (March 1951), p. 108.
[99] *Ibid.*, pp. 115–116.
[100] Raskin, p. 232.
[101] Lewin.

much beyond the traditional manual working class, and its continued taint of excessive power and corruption as far as the general public is concerned have certainly not helped.

King has suggested two major changes in political ideas within the American political system:[102]

> The first is the decline of the idea of the New Deal as the principal organizing themes of American political life. The central idea of the New Deal was a simple one; that the federal government could and should solve the country's economic and social problems. . . . The second outstanding change in the realm of ideas is the altogether new emphasis on the value of participation in politics. In the 1960's it came to be thought good for both the participating individuals and the polity that ordinary men and women should have a direct say not merely in the choice of public office holders but in the making of public policy.

Both these trends have tended to reduce the political power of labor: the New Deal ideology was essentially based upon economic issues in which labor could pose as the defender of the underdog and, as for the second, labor is effective only if acting as a monolithic bloc. To quote King again: "The politics of the 1930's and 1940's resembled a 19th century battlefield, with two opposing armies arrayed against each other in more or less close formation; politics today is an altogether messier affair, with large numbers of small detachments engaged over a vast territory and with individuals and groups frequently changing sides." [103] The new style politics has several other characteristics detrimental to labor. One is the decline of party structures; it is indeed an open question, posed by King, whether there are effectively any such things as parties any longer. The breakdown of party has also meant the breakdown of discipline in Congress; it is now very difficult even for Presidents to transact business with that institution because the party bloc no longer exists. The decline of party also means that there is no manifesto, no program to enable the broader pressure groups such as labor to influence policy over

---

[102] A. King, "The American Polity in the Late 1970's: Building Coalitions in the Sand," in *The New American Political System*, A. King, ed. (Washington: American Enterprise Institute, 1978), p. 371.

[103] *Ibid.*, p. 372.

a large spectrum. As Barbash noted: "Where the Europeans tend to think in terms of the economy and social policy, the Americans characteristically think in terms of specific programs and pieces of legislation." [104]

As a result, by the late 1970s voters have been less willing to be guided in their voting behavior by partisan cues, whether of a party nature or reflecting one major pressure group. [105] Pressure groups themselves have changed. Previously pressure groups were almost entirely self-interested; business, labor, agriculture, and the professions all pursued their own objectives, and coalitions and deals were the everyday stuff of politics. Now many interest groups are idealistic and self-interest is much more indirect. The rise of dozens of competing issues and groups does not, however, mean that the interest groups are building blocks toward larger coalitions—they tend to be single-interest and cross-voting. As a result, coalitions of the kind which labor needs to be able to spread its political power over a range of different activities cannot easily be built. In short, American politics have become to a high degree atomized.

In these developments it is not altogether easy to see what would have been the appropriate course of events for the labor movement, short of the massive difficulties of starting a new political party or at least trying to take over the Democratic Party. [106] The same, however, is not true of Europe. Leiserson's argument of the United States that "the potential forms of labor's political activity—union, class, and party, involve conflicts of interest and choice," [107] is not as true of Europe because in respect of Europe there is not the same necessity for conflict and choice; all three dimensions can be subsumed within the same philosophy and mode of action. As King also noted: [108]

> . . . the proliferation and disintegration of American political structures would not appear to represent the work-

---

[104] Barbash, p. 193.
[105] Geographical patterns have added to these other factors. Bok and Dunlop note that more than half of all union members now live in the suburbs, which are the main focus of low party allegiance (Derek Bok and John T. Dunlop, *Labor and the American Community* (New York: Simon and Schuster, 1970), p. 433).
[106] Michael Piore, "Unions and Politics," in Juris and Roomkin, eds.
[107] Leiserson, p. 112.
[108] King, p. 394 (The splitting away of the Social Democrats in Britain may split up the old political structure, but this remains to be seen.)

ing out in the United States of large social and political forces that are also present in other countries. Many of the sources of atomization appear to be peculiarly American. In Great Britain by contrast most of the old political structures survive more or less intact; and the major interest groups in particular have recently tended to form themselves into larger and stronger units. . . . In Europe generally, not just in countries like Sweden and the Netherlands, the trend seems to be towards centripetal politics and concertation.

Not only has European politics been increasingly oriented toward concertation, or corporatism as it is perhaps more frequently called, but the origins of this corporatism lie in the centrality of economic relations within the European political systems.[109]

Industrial relations in particular has become increasingly politicized, mainly as a result of the felt need of governments to control bargaining for macroeconomic policy reasons. It is presumed that the effectiveness of such policies depends in considerable part on bargaining structure, with advantages in a centralized system.[110] In Europe the process has led to enhanced power for the parties, especially the unions, as they have been able to bargain for a quid pro quo in return for restraint, and the concept of a social contract has frequently been used to describe this. The sequence of events can be a dangerous one, potentially leading to loss of control by either the union leadership or the government. Indeed Peper has argued that there is an irreversible process of politicization in which: "It will become more difficult for the political system to shirk the responsibility—even a derived responsibility—for the outcome of more or less unobstructed negotiations by the social partners. And it is equally impossible for the social partners not to be affected by the consequences of government policy for the bargaining process and its results."[111] One important consequence of politicization is the growth of what Peper calls "a democracy of interest groups" in which "[t]here is now a strong impression that the independent power of the gov-

---

[109] Crouch.

[110] Lloyd Ulman, "Report on the Conference," in OECD, *Collective Bargaining*, p. 31.

[111] Peper, p. 147.

ernment has not grown in proportion to the display of power outside the sphere of government." [112] The big difference between Europe and the United States lies in the relatively monolithic nature of the major interest groups in Europe; they are large enough to be a serious constitutional threat, as several countries have discovered in this century. This is not to say that there are not many single-interest groups in Europe, but they tend to be subordinate to the major interest groups of labor and capital. As a result, coalitions which are difficult to create in America are relatively easy to formulate in Europe and this has been enormously helped by the maintenance of party boundaries and disciplines.

In short, American unions are losing political significance not only because of their own deficiencies but because centrifugal forces have tended to prevail in the American political scene, whereas, with strong central institutions to start with, centripetal forces have been dominant in Europe, and this has added to the power of the economic parties.

Conclusions

The great advantage of the American system of industrial relations for the worker covered by collective bargaining is that he is provided with a highly professionalized system of industrial self-regulation; for the unionized employer there is a high degree of predictability that he is getting what he pays for; and for the society at large the system provides an excellent, if limited, example of competitive pluralism whilst keeping well within the fundamental philosophical tenets of capitalism. But the system is limited in a number of ways—in coverage, scope of interaction, flexibility in response to changing industrial and occupational patterns, popular acceptance, and political significance—and moreover the limitations look more obvious from the perspective of 1980 than they did from that of 1950. Since that time the system has become assimilated and institutionalized, progressively reducing the status of unions as major actors on the economic and social scene. It can be argued that it is precisely because "unions in America have been unswerving in their affirmation of private property, the capitalist system, and the prevailing system of government," [113]

[112] *Ibid.*, p. 143.
[113] Bok and Dunlop, p. 485.

that they can be taken for granted by politicians and outflanked by managements, since they offer no alternatives and pose no threats. Their social role is being pre-empted by other institutions and they appear to have become increasingly instrumental agencies to their members. In spite of this, they are still viewed as contrary to the American ethos and have provided a convenient scapegoat for America's doubts about itself and its role.

It is, of course, true that: "Reports of organized labor's death are, as were those of Twain's, greatly exaggerated," [114] and even on a pessimistic prognosis there is no indication that the basic functions of unionism are under challenge. But the situation in the United States does contrast with that in Europe, where many of the philosophical, social, and economic changes in the societies are being channeled through the industrial relations system, and where the unions pose perhaps the major threat to the stability of governments. Much depends on what a society expects from its industrial relations system—a limited but stable institution or a social change agent and challenge to the existing order. One suspects that there are those on both continents who wish that each could borrow from the other.

---

[114] Peter J. Pestillo, "Learning to Live Without the Union," in *Proceedings of the 31st Annual Meeting, Industrial Relations Research Association*, 1978, p. 233.

CHAPTER 9

Summary and Conclusions

JACK STIEBER
RICHARD N. BLOCK
Michigan State University

The authors of the several chapters in this book have given us their assessment of various aspects of the U.S. system of industrial relations. Clearly, while the system is functioning reasonably well in many respects, it falls short of what the authors regard as its potential in a number of other respects. This chapter summarizes some of the major conclusions of the authors and adds our own perspective on some of the issues discussed as well as others that have not been addressed in this volume.

Economic Impact of Unions

The first two chapters deal with the economic effects of unions and collective bargaining. Mitchell examines the impact of collective bargaining on the economy as a whole, while Freeman and Medoff look at union/nonunion differentials at the plant or firm level.

Mitchell notes the existence of a significant and sizable union/nonunion wage differential that has widened over the last 25 years. He believes that the evidence shows such wage premiums have been caused by unions operating through collective bargaining and points out that nonunion employers, by their vigorous resistance to unionization, apparently also accept this view. However, this does not mean that there is a direct relationship between unionism and inflation. Mitchell believes, with most economists, that collective bargaining has not been the initiating cause of inflation during the post-World War II period. But the relationship between unionism and efforts to combat inflation is less clear.

Mitchell argues that union-induced wage changes are subject to two contradictory influences: the growth in importance of long-

343

term contracts which reflect the influence of the past; and the escalator clauses, often included in such agreements, which are sensitive to recent price movements. Thus, if economic conditions when a long-term contract was negotiated were more (less) inflationary than current conditions, the agreement would likely serve to aggravate (moderate) the current inflation. The effect of escalator clauses depends on the current rate of price increase, and this may also serve to aggravate or moderate inflation. The existence of an escalator clause would contribute to a successful anti-inflation policy but would aggravate the ineffectiveness of an unsuccessful policy or price increases caused by exogenous forces. Mitchell does not consider the effect of "caps" on escalator clauses, which have become quite common during periods of rapid price increases. Placing a "cap" or ceiling on cost-of-living increases would, of course, serve to moderate their effect.

Mitchell regards nontraditional anti-inflation policy (i.e., direct government intervention through incomes policy, wage-price controls or guidelines) as an effort to force wage and price setters to respond to the "signals" of the market. Since the unionized sector attenuates the response to these signals, it is the focus of government policies. He regards the difficulty with direct intervention more one of technique than rationale because of the problems associated with the myriad complexities of wage determination, attaining credibility for such a program, and obtaining at least tacit support from the labor movement. Finally, Mitchell ties the phenomenon of strikes to the discussion of the impact of collective bargaining. He sees the strike or the threat of one as the ultimate cause of union/nonunion wage and nonwage differentials. It is the desire to avoid strikes which motivates employers (and unions also) to negotiate long-term contracts—less frequent negotiations mean fewer strike opportunities. Long-term contracts, as noted above, contribute significantly to the insensitivity of union wages to labor market conditions. The main impact of the strike, according to Mitchell, is not the disruption to production, but the reinforcement of union/nonunion differentials in the labor market.

Complementing Mitchell's macroeconomic analysis, Freeman and Medoff examine some of the micro effects of unions. They conclude that the union/nonunion wage differential is roughly 15–20 percent. Furthermore, recent evidence indicates that unions also have significant nonwage effects. Comparisons of unionized and nonunionized workers and firms show higher fringe benefits, lower labor turnover, less job satisfaction, higher "human capital," higher productivity, and lower rates of return on capital accompanying unionism. Economists have long debated whether these apparent union effects are "real" or "illusory." The "real" effect school of thought believes that unions and collective bargaining fundamentally alter economic behavior by operating through imperfections in labor and product markets and via institutional routes. The "illusory" school contends that union effects found by researchers can be explained by such "pre-union characteristics" as quality of labor, workers' preference structures, and firm production functions; and that firms, once unionized, can make relatively costless adjustments to unionism through substitution between capital and labor, hiring workers of varying quality, and readjusting the compensation and noncompensation aspects of jobs.

Freeman and Medoff provide a comprehensive explanation of union/nonunion differences based on previous research, including their own, and an in-depth analysis of the "real" vs. "illusory" arguments. They also discuss the extent to which deficiencies in econometric research designs may have affected the perceived impact of unions. Their conclusion: union effects are "real."

We suspect that the Freeman-Medoff findings will be subjected to critical review by economists and other social scientists. In the course of such research, we hope that more attention than was possible in this brief and pioneering paper will be accorded to the extent to which union effects operate through institutional routes as opposed to market imperfections.

Management's Response to Unions

Whatever positive effects unions may have, as evidenced by research explored by Freeman and Medoff and earlier by the Slichter-Healy-Livernash study,[1] management is not persuaded that the benefits of unionism (if indeed there are any) are greater than the disadvantages of being organized. Mills cites three overall industrial relations objectives of management: to hold down labor

---

[1] *The Impact of Collective Bargaining on Management* (Washington: The Brookings Institution, 1960).

costs, to encourage high employee productivity, and to preserve nonunion status wherever possible. He presents evidence that U.S. unit labor costs in manufacturing compare favorably with those in other industrialized nations and that, despite recent productivity decreases, U.S. workers are more productive than those of its major trading partners.

Mitchell has argued that union wages have not caused inflation, though they have tended to attenuate anti-inflationary weapons. U.S. management doesn't accept the view that unions are not an important contributing cause of inflation or that they have a positive effect on productivity. (Neither do the American people generally, according to a 1981 Louis Harris Survey.[2]) This is shown by the overriding importance attached by management to keeping as many of their employees as possible nonunion.

Management pursues this objective by a strategy which has come to be known as "union-avoidance"—a term unions regard as a euphemism for anti-unionism. In 1955 Brown and Myers wrote that the growth of a professional managerial group was one of the factors leading to the greater acceptance of unions by management during the preceding 25 years.[3] The ensuing 25 years has seen continued growth in professionalization of the managerial function. But, unlike the earlier period, this has not been accompanied by an increased willingness of management to accept unionization of their employees. As Mills notes, while executives may have become less emotional in their attitudes toward unions, they are not less determined in their opposition to unions than they were 25 years ago.

This attitude does not come out of a careful cost/benefit analysis of unionism as is true of many other management functions. Rather, it grows out of a prevailing view that unions exist as a reflection of management's failure to manage their human resources properly. Managers see unions as complicating their lives through inefficient work practices, contributing to the decline in productivity, and opposing corporate interests in the legislative and judicial arenas. To the extent that one accepts the Slichter-

---

[2] *Daily Labor Report* No. 106, June 3, 1981, Bureau of National Affairs, Washington.

[3] "The Changing Industrial Relations Philosophy of American Management," in *Annual Proceedings*, Industrial Relations Research Association (1956), pp. 84–99.

Healy-Livernash and Freeman-Medoff findings, the first two conclusions are at least doubtful. As for the third, unions more often than not have been on the opposite side from management. However, unions have on occasion joined with management to lobby Congress and to appear before regulatory bodies and in state legislatures in support of protective legislation, steel trigger prices, loans for Chrysler, quotas on Japanese auto imports, and other common interests.

In assessing the quality of union-management relations, Mills notes that, based on time lost due to strikes, relations between unions and companies appear to be satisfactory. But this positive indicator is overshadowed by the widespread opposition, even among companies with good union-management relations, to the growth of unionism. One aspect of management organizational structure, noted by Mills, is the allocation of responsibility in many companies for both union relations and union avoidance to the same executive. This would appear to contradict the widely accepted view among industrial relations specialists that "trust" between bargaining partners is a prerequisite to harmonious labor relations. How can there be "trust" on the part of the union in an individual who is also seen as responsible for containing union growth? Mills believes that "by and large, management has been successful" in compartmentalizing these contradictory functions so that conflict over union organizing does not affect collective bargaining.

There is, however, some evidence to the contrary. Unions are increasingly demanding and a few have succeeded in obtaining "neutrality pledges" from companies with respect to organizing efforts in their nonunion plants. Furthermore, the Industrial Union Department of the AFL-CIO has urged corporate leaders to weigh the ultimate effects of trying to overturn existing collective bargaining relationships on the basic relationship between labor and management.[4] These developments suggest that unions do not regard union-avoidance policies of companies as separable from collective bargaining.

Nonunionized Employers

In a country whose labor force is only 25 percent unionized,

---

[4] *AFL-CIO News*, August 15, 1981, p. 3.

any assessment of industrial relations without consideration of the nonunionized sector would be incomplete. Unfortunately, information regarding employment policies and practices in nonunionized companies is not as readily available as for those covered by collective bargaining agreements. The chapter on nonunionized employers is limited to 26 large companies whose names, according to the author, are "household words" and "impressive." Most readers of this book would probably be able to make a reasonably good educated guess as to some of the companies that were included in Professor Foulkes's study. However, it is not necessary to identify the companies in order to draw conclusions regarding their personnel policies.

A profile of the typical large nonunionized company would include most of the following factors, according to Foulkes: a corporate philosophy that unions are unnecessary to employee welfare; plants limited to 200–1200 employees, including a substantial proportion of women and professionals; plant locations in non-urban areas and not in close proximity to large unionized firms; a dominant market position in a profitable high-technology growth industry; a centralized personnel office with considerable influence on corporate policy; being either privately owned or having a close relationship between ownership and management.

While staying nonunion is not the primary objective of most of these companies, it occupies a central role in determining company policies. Employee relations policies which have been found conducive to staying nonunion include: a no-layoff policy, or at least a strong commitment to providing employment security; strong adherence to seniority in layoff (when necessary) and recall, promotion, and transfer; promotion from within and posting of job openings; pay and benefit programs as good as or better than those of comparable unionized companies; effective communications and feedback mechanisms; a formal grievance procedure without arbitration. Foulkes notes that a "driving force" behind these policies is the fear of unionization and wonders whether the commitment to effective human resources management would continue in the absence of a perceived threat from unions.

Except for the absence of grievance arbitration and guaranteed employment security, these policies can also be found in many large unionized companies. Indeed, they have been copied from such companies in many instances. However, the difference between the unionized and nonunionized employers following these policies may be in whom the employees credit for their generally satisfactory earnings and working conditions. In the unionized firm, the union claims and usually gets the credit. In the nonunionized company, the employer uses its communications network to persuade employees that they already have everything and more than a union could offer.

Foulkes believes that, barring a major turn-around, it is unrealistic to expect a reversal of the trend away from unionism in the private sector. He may be right, though his study of the personnel policies and practices of 26 large "better-standard" nonunion employers seems a rather limited sample on which to base such a sweeping conclusion. However, to the extent that nonunion companies provide the advantages and follow the policies of companies included in the Foulkes study, bringing them into the union fold will be a formidable task.

Labor Law

Union-management relations in the United States are conducted pursuant to a plethora of legislation, National Labor Relations Board decisions, and court rulings. The sole lawyer among our authors, Professor St. Antoine assesses the role of law and how well legislation has performed during the three decades under study.

The 50-year period 1930–1980 might be divided into two periods: the first 30 years during which Congress fashioned the laws governing labor-management relations, and the last two decades when the courts were busy telling us what the laws meant. In considering important court decisions, St. Antoine suggests that the courts should pay more attention to the facts and indulge in less "armchair speculation." He cites with approbation the Getman-Goldberg-Herman study of NLRB representation campaigns which found no significant difference between voter behavior in "clean" and "dirty" election campaigns and consequently recommended that the Board cease regulating speech.[5]

---

[5] *Representation Elections: Law and Reality* (New York: Russell Sage, 1976). However, a recent study found that the minority of voters who are influenced by election campaigns may cast enough votes to affect the outcome

St. Antoine's suggestion is elaborated in a paper prepared by Professor Goldberg on empirical research in labor law. Goldberg notes that because "few lawyers are capable of designing or conducting empirical research," the "obvious solution" is multidisciplinary research. However, as Goldberg notes and many industrial relations institutes have discovered, such research is easier to conceptualize than to carry out.[6]

In examining developments in labor law during the past three decades, St. Antoine makes the following observations and recommendations:

1. In dealing with secondary boycotts, the Congress, the NLRB, and the courts should do less moralizing and pay more attention to balancing union needs against business and consumer interests. The law on secondary boycotts needs a thorough reexamination, preferably on an industry-by-industry approach as was done for the construction and garment industries.

2. The ability of employers to avoid negotiations for years after losing an NLRB election, which is encouraged by the refusal of the Board to direct "make-whole" remedies for refusal to bargain, is a serious shortcoming which calls for bolder Board action, though there is doubt that such action would be sustained by the courts.

3. The overall effect of the "good faith" bargaining requirement has been salutary. However, the distinction between "mandatory" and "voluntary" issues, first made by the Board in *Borg Warner* in 1958, is unrealistic and too easy for both parties to evade. He suggests some alternative approaches to this issue.

4. The primary reliance in considering antitrust cases involving unions should be on labor laws rather than antitrust laws because statutes in these areas are premised on opposing philosophies of competition.

5. The major accomplishment of the Warren Court in the labor field was the nationalization of the regulation of labor relations by promulgating the "federal preemption" doctrine. While this approach has limited social experimentation by the states,

---

of an election. See Myron Roomkin and Richard N. Block, "Case Processing Time and the Outcome of Representation Elections: Some Empirical Evidence," *University of Illinois Law Review*, Vol. 1981, No. 1.

[6] Stephen Goldberg, "Empirical Research in Labor Law: Some Practical Problems," unpublished paper.

which could be useful, federal uniformity is necessary to keep states from competing with each other by weakening labor laws in order to attract business.

6. The difference between the Warren Court and the Burger Court is evident in their different approaches to "successor" employers. The Warren Court decisions reflect a primary concern with protecting employees against sudden and unforeseen loss of bargaining and contract rights, and sustaining the life of the labor agreement. The Burger Court has stressed the freedom and voluntary nature of collective bargaining and has evinced concern that neither unions nor employers be saddled with contract provisions which they have not negotiated. These differences reflect a clash of fundamental values in the labor field.

7. Contrary to union fears and the probable intentions of its proponents in Congress, the 1959 Landrum-Griffin Act has advanced the cause of union democracy without seriously damaging unions.

8. Where the emphasis in legislation during the 1930s through the 1950s was on institutional rights, the last two decades have seen a shift in emphasis to individual rights in labor relations. St. Antoine sees this trend continuing into the 1980s with the prospect that nonunionized workers may be afforded protection against unjust discipline and discharge.

Social Issues in Collective Bargaining

Wallace and Driscoll address three relatively new issues that have already had a significant impact on collective bargaining and may pose serious problems for unions and employers in the 1980s. One of these issues—equal employment opportunity—is the result of legislation which grew out of the civil rights movement and had union support; another—occupational safety and health—is the product of legislation initiated by the labor movement; and the third—quality of worklife—is largely a nonunion phenomenon which has profound implications for union-management relations, but has not been the focus of legislation.

Government intervention to prohibit discrimination and promote affirmative action in employment has led to a restructuring of seniority provisions and has altered some important rules of the workplace. Though supported by the labor movement, EEO legislation has often pitted the government against unions as well as employers. The adjustment has been difficult because it has affected one of the most cherished benefits of collective bargaining—seniority. While the conflicts generated some bad feeling between unions and minority and women's organizations, on the whole unions have accepted the results of the legislation and incorporated necessary changes into their collective bargaining agreements. Unlike many employers, who have welcomed the Reagan Administration's promise to get the EEOC and the OFCCP "off their backs," the labor movement has not supported deregulation in the field of equal employment opportunity and affirmative action.

An interesting aspect of the second social issue discussed by Wallace and Driscoll is their observation that, although more than twice as many workers indicated that they want a "say" over occupational safety and health as over wages and salaries, little time is spent on these issues in contract negotiations. Among the reasons cited by the authors for this cursory treatment of such an important issue in negotiations is that the federal government has preempted the field by setting standards and establishing an alternative complaint mechanism to that available through collective bargaining. We would note, however, that this reason was not valid before 1970 when the OSHAct was passed. Why, then, did unions give a relatively low priority to safety and health in bargaining before the law was enacted? Indeed, since the OSHAct, the frequency of contract provisions on safety and health has increased, suggesting that federal legislation may have had a positive effect on the inclusion of this issue in negotiations.

The importance assigned by the labor movement to federal regulation of occupational safety and health is indicated by its strong opposition to the Reagan Administration's commitment to deemphasize government involvement in this area. Unions obviously believe that collective bargaining cannot do the job that needs to be done to protect workers against occupational hazards. Unlike the EEO, which created conflicts between different groups of union members, thereby posing problems for even those union leaders who are most committed to the cause of equal employment opportunity, occupational safety and health is desired by all workers.

In contrast to the great interest by workers in safety and health, Wallace and Driscoll found little evidence of workers wanting a "say" in decision-making regarding their jobs. This attitude is reflected in the failure of unions to raise quality-of-work-life issues in negotiations. Indeed, with the exception of a few unions, the labor movement generally has evinced considerable skepticism, if not outright opposition, to QWL. The reasons are not hard to fathom. The fact that QWL has been pressed most vigorously by nonunion companies and has been used as a union-avoidance technique is sufficient reason for unions to be on their guard when such programs are suggested.

Perhaps even more important is the suggestion by the authors that participative management schemes represent a fundamental challenge to U.S. style collective bargaining. Where QWL is directed at the resolution of industrial conflict on a continuous basis at the level of the individual or small workgroup, collective bargaining deals with such conflict on a periodic basis and is directed at reaching solutions which will satisfy a majority of the membership. Can the two approaches overcome this barrier?

Some union leaders believe they can and have cooperated with management in the installation of QWL programs. During the 1980s a clearer picture should emerge regarding the compatibility of QWL and collective bargaining.

Industrial Conflict

The major thrust of the Feuille-Wheeler chapter is that industrial conflict needs to be more broadly defined and that research in this area should look beyond strike statistics and arbitration awards to other kinds of conflict between employees and unions, on the one hand, and management on the other. The authors make the interesting observation that scholars trained in different disciplines have different perspectives on conflict in the workplace. The "conflict" school, made up largely of labor economists and industrial relations specialists, believes that the fundamental interests of employees and employers differ, making conflict inevitable and, some would say, even desirable. The "cooperation" school, coming from a background in organizational behavior and development, assumes more common interests between employees and

employers and regards conflict as harmful to efficiency and productivity.

The narrow focus on conflict as strikes and other forms of concerted action carries with it the implication that industrial conflict
does not exist in nonunionized firms and that conflict is more or
less synonymous with, if not caused by, unions. How then should
we classify speed-ups, plant shutdowns, employee discharge for
cause, unsafe working conditions, and other employer-initiated
actions which give rise to conflict in both organized and unorganized companies?

Despite the considerable amount of research conducted on
strikes, we are no closer to a general theory capable of predicting
where and when strikes will or will not occur than we were 30
years ago. The problem is that most research uses aggregate strike
data which tell us nothing about the predictability of individual
strikes. While the incidence of strikes has shown no discernible
increase since 1950, the constant efforts of employers and unions
to gain an advantage by changing the rules governing labor-
management relations via legislation and to secure appointees to
key government agencies and the courts indicate that more conflict exists than might be inferred from strike statistics. The absence of any major changes in the laws governing labor-management relations during the 1950–1980 period suggests that there
is no ground swell to modify the U.S. system of conflict management in the direction sought by either labor or management.

Further evidence that researchers tend to follow where the
data lead is found in the published work on grievance arbitration.
We know a great deal about the issues, elapsed time, costs, and
disposition of arbitration cases, but very little about the resolution
of the much larger number of grievances that are settled in the
pre-arbitration steps of the grievance procedure. Except for a few
studies on what has happened to discharged employees who have
been reinstated as a result of arbitration decisions,[7] we also know
practically nothing about the effect of awards on the parties' future relationship or on their agreements.

[7] J. F. Holly, "The Arbitration of Discharge Cases: A Case Study," in
Critical Issues in Labor Arbitration, Proceedings of the 10th Annual Meeting,
National Academy of Arbitrators (Washington: BNA Books, 1957), pp. 1–17;
A. A. Malinowski, "An Empirical Analysis of Discharge Cases and the Work
History of Employees Reinstated by Arbitrators." *The Arbitration Journal* 36
(March 1981), pp. 31–46.

The Feuille-Wheeler dissatisfaction with the dearth of research on many important aspects of grievance arbitration is understandable. However, it cannot be easily remedied because of the voluntary and private nature of the arbitration process in the United States. Employers and unions have generally been reluctant to release grievance records, where they exist, to outsiders. Thus researchers are of necessity limited to analyzing arbitration decisions in their quest for information about grievances. However, the reliability of published decisions as indicators of the outcomes of arbitrated grievances is doubtful, since only a small proportion of all arbitration decisions are released by the parties for publication and even the released decisions are published only on a selective basis. Thus, there is no reason to believe that published arbitration decisions are representative of the thousands of decisions made by arbitrators each year. Yet, it is this more or less randomly selected sample upon which all grievance arbitration research is based. Such research should carry the warning "caveat emptor."

The grievance arbitration caseload of the Federal Mediation and Conciliation Service and the American Arbitration Association, the two major arbitrator referral agencies, has grown much more rapidly than either the number of agreements or the number of organized workers. In addition to a large increase in public-sector cases, Feuille and Wheeler ascribe the different growth rates to more complex agreements leading to more interpretation disputes, the tendency for the parties to settle fewer cases in the pre-arbitration steps of the grievance procedure, or the desire of union and management advocates to gain higher status and fees from taking more cases to arbitration.

We would note that the proportion of grievances over discipline and discharge has remained fairly stable over the years at about one-third of the total.[8] Since discipline and discharge cases are little affected by the complexity of contract provisions, this suggests that more complex and detailed agreements have not been a significant cause of the increase in the arbitration caseload. The influence of union and management advocates also does not strike us as a logical explanation since the decision to go to arbitration is usually made "in-house" before outside advocates become involved in the process. This leaves the greater willingness

---

[8] Annual Reports of the Federal Mediation and Conciliation Service.

of the parties to resort to arbitration rather than settle in earlier steps of the grievance procedure as the most likely cause for the increase in the arbitration caseload. This would be consistent with the increased litigiousness which has characterized our society generally during the past two decades. Whatever the reasons for it, the increase in grievance arbitration would seem to indicate more labor-management conflict than is suggested by strike statistics.

A View from Abroad

The chapters of this book were organized to assess U.S. industrial relations in its various aspects, first through the eyes of American scholars and then from an international perspective as seen by a foreign commentator. Thomson's essay has touched on almost every subject dealt with in the other chapters and for the most part his findings coincide with those of the other authors. However, these findings often look different in a comparative perspective than they do when considered solely within the U.S. industrial relations framework.

Thus, while agreeing with Freeman and Medoff that American unions have done well for their members through collective bargaining, Thomson notes the limited scope of bargaining, the minority of workers directly affected, and the decreasing significance of collective bargaining for some of the major issues of the 1970s and the coming decade.

Buttressing Mitchell's findings that U.S. unions have not been responsible for inflation, Thomson points out that while U.S. productivity has decreased relative to other countries, so also have wage increases. The two measures taken together have given the U.S. a lower rate of increase in unit labor costs than other industrialized nations during the past two decades.

The antipathy of U.S. employers to unions and their aggressive measures to avoid unionization, which were highlighted by Mills, has no counterpart in West European countries. Thomson explains the contrast largely in terms of the greater decentralization of collective bargaining in the United States which fosters an adversarial relationship between unions and employers at the plant or company level. Under the more centralized bargaining structures that exist in most West European countries, unions have little access to managerial decision-making at the plant level, and consequently have sought the extension of industrial democracy through various types of codetermination schemes at the corporate level. It is anomalous that American unions which support the capitalist system are less accepted by employers than European unions which, for the most part, reject capitalism and are committed to changing the economic order.

On the role of law in industrial relations, Thomson notes that in the United States the emphasis is on "auxiliary law," which is designed to bring the parties together, and "restrictive law," which sets forth rules of conduct to govern labor-management relations. In Europe, "regulatory law" dealing with the substantive areas of employment relations is much more important. In general, the law plays a less important part in other countries because union recognition has long since ceased to be a battleground and was accomplished outside the legal framework, in contrast to the U.S. where recognition remains an important issue and is highly regulated by the National Labor Relations Act. As St. Antoine and others have noted, U.S. law has taken a turn toward more regulation during the last two decades, with significant effects on collective bargaining.

Regulatory law is not a new phenomenon in U.S. industrial relations. Mine safety legislation, laws prohibiting child labor, the Fair Labor Standards Act, and others have been on the books for many years. With the advent of the National Labor Relations Act in 1935, the emphasis has been on the procedural aspects of labor relations. However, there are limits to what collective bargaining can accomplish, and during the 1960s and 1970s U.S. labor sponsored or supported the enactment of laws to deal with such national problems as unemployment, occupational safety and health, discrimination in employment, protecting the environment, and others. This legislation has generally gone beyond what other countries have done, although the Reagan Administration is committed to reducing the federal role in these areas.

A social issue which has been of much greater interest to European unions than to American unions is worker participation in decision-making in its various forms. The U.S. approach has been to establish joint labor-management committees at the plant level to deal with specific problems such as health and safety or productivity and, to a much more limited extent, for labor and management to cooperate in quality-of-worklife programs. The European approach has been much more radical, in keeping with the more ideological philosophy underlying unionism in those countries. Where the U.S. unions shy away from being a "partner with management" in order to avoid blurring the respective roles of labor and management, European unions have, in varying degrees and in differing forms, espoused the concept of advancing industrial democracy through legislation designed to give them a role in corporate decisions affecting employees. This has taken the form of codetermination, works councils, and other less formal structures to provide worker participation in corporate decision-making.

Personnel policies in nonunionized firms, a subject which is integral in any discussion of U.S. industrial relations, would have little significance in an assessment of European industrial relations. This is understandable in countries where collective bargaining coverage extends to a substantial majority of the labor force as compared with less than 30 percent in the United States. Thomson notes a number of reasons for the greater acceptance of unions by European employers. Under centralized bargaining, union recognition on a plant or company basis is of little importance since employers will adhere to agreements reached by their associations. Therefore, they have little reason to oppose or even discourage unionization. The greater class distinction in European countries and the absence of the individualistic philosophy prevalent in the United States lead to greater acceptance of the need for collective action by different interest groups, including unions. The much lower degree of professionalism at the plant and company level in Europe would make it more difficult to mount the sophisticated union-avoidance campaigns which have become characteristic in the United States. Finally, there is the simple fact that, unlike American employers who can escape to the Sun Belt and other relatively nonunionized parts of the country, European employers have no place to hide. Indeed, Thomson notes that the union-free environment that still prevails in many parts of the United States has attracted some European employers to locate here.

Thomson sees at least three weaknesses in the U.S. system of industrial relations:

1. The lack of a coherent philosophy within the labor movement.

2. The apparent complacency about questions of union structure and level of organization.

3. The loss of political power and credibility of unions within American society, with the result that few issues of social significance are channeled through the industrial relations system.

Thomson concludes that one's judgment of how well the U.S. system of industrial relations is performing depends on what a society expects of the system: a limited but stable institution or a social change agent that challenges the existing order.

An Overall Assessment

An assessment of U.S. industrial relations cannot be limited to unionization and collective bargaining. While, in our view, a strong labor movement is essential to a democratic industrial society, employees' economic well-being can also be advanced in nonunion settings and through government legislation.

Thus the viability of the U.S. system of industrial relations in its present form depends on the existence of a labor movement strong enough to represent its members effectively and to present a credible threat to employers who prefer to operate nonunion; the availability of a nonunion option for those employees who do not wish to be organized and employers who are willing to pay the price of matching or exceeding unionized work conditions in order to remain nonunion; and a government that regulates collective bargaining behavior and is also sufficiently responsive to provide those elemental employee needs which are not provided by collective bargaining or unilateral employer action.

In order to operate effectively, this kind of system demands a balance of these three forces which cannot be defined in any precise way. One cannot say, ex ante, when the level of unionization would be too low to represent a credible threat to employers or too high to remove the nonunion option for employees and employers, which is an inherent aspect of the U.S. system. Nor can one say with certainty when government has failed to provide the necessary legislative framework for free collective bargaining or to guarantee fundamental employee rights and needs that have not been provided through collective bargaining or by employers alone. However, given the adversary relationship inherent in our industrial relations system and the responsiveness of a democratic society to public opinion, one can be certain that, at any given time, contending forces will be trying to change the existing balance, whatever that might be. Unions will be trying to organize a larger proportion of the labor force and to exact higher wages and better working conditions from employers. Employers will resist union organization and collective bargaining demands and will be making demands of their own. And unions, employers, and other interest groups will be trying to influence the political process to change the rules governing labor-management relations in their favor and to extend or retract government intervention in the employment relationship.

The net effect of these forces operating under varying economic, social, and political circumstances will result in an industrial relations system which will at different times consist of a different balance among the three actors: unions, employers, and government. Historically, over the past 50 years, we have seen a strong drift toward increasing and strengthening unionization in the 1930s and 1940s, a reaction against perceived union excesses resulting in restrictions on unions in 1947 and again in 1959, and a decline in unionization starting in the mid-1950s and continuing through the 1970s. This has been accompanied (and to some extent caused) by growing employer resistance and hostility to unions, and an increased involvement of government in the substantive aspects of the employment relationship.

None of these changes, in our view, has been of sufficient magnitude to threaten the viability of the U.S. system of industrial relations. Unions, despite the declining trend in labor force representation, remain strong enough to represent a credible threat to employers; the nonunion option for both employees and employers, while certainly stronger than at any time during the past two decades, is not so attractive as to swamp unionization efforts or to dull employer incentives to maintain union-like wages and benefits for their nonunion employees; and government has not intervened in the employment relationship to such an extent as to diminish significantly the role of unions and collective bargaining. Indeed, as this is written, we are entering into at least a four-year period of government withdrawal from a vast array of economic areas, including those regulating the employment relationship.

What then can we say about the future of the U.S. system of industrial relations? Will it remain viable in the 1980s and beyond to the end of this century, or are there indications that changes are occurring which will alter the balance among unions, employers, and government so as to result in a fundamental change in the system?

It would certainly be premature to predict the demise of the existing U.S. system of industrial relations based on assessments outlined in the preceding chapters. On the other hand, one would have to be myopic to disregard some of the developments noted in those chapters. The decline in unionization over a period of some 25 years cannot continue much longer without weakening the labor movement to the extent that it will cease to be a credible threat to employers or a force to be reckoned with politically. The nonunion option can only remain a positive aspect in our industrial relations system as long as employers have reason to fear unionization. Without the threat of unionization, Foulkes's concern whether even the most progressive employers will continue their enlightened employment policies becomes very relevant. Finally, the withdrawal or significant diminution in the role of government from such areas as equal employment opportunity, occupational safety and health, minimum wage regulation, and other aspects of the employment relationship will contribute further to weakening the balance among the forces which we consider essential to the continued viability of the U.S. system of industrial relations.

Present trends, which are fairly predictable through the first half of the 1980s, do not augur well for the U.S. system of industrial relations. Whether or not they continue through the rest of the decade or even longer will depend on economic and political developments that are beyond the purview of this volume as well as the predictive capacities of the authors. However, these developments may well determine the nature and direction of the U.S. industrial relations system for some time in the future.